Y0-BRM-340

BIBLIOGRAPHIES IN AMERICAN MUSIC

Editor James R. Heintze
The American University

THE COLLEGE MUSIC SOCIETY

President Elliott S. Schwartz
Bowdoin College

PUBLICATIONS COMMITTEE

Chairman David Butler
Ohio State University

James R. Heintze
The American University
Editor, *Bibliographies in American Music*

Arthur Komar
University of Cincinnati
Editor, *College Music Symposium*

Michael J. Budds
University of Missouri—Columbia
Editor, *CMS Proceedings*

Robby D. Gunstream *ex officio*
College Music Society

WILLIAM MASON (1829-1908)

An Annotated Bibliography

and

Catalog of Works

Kenneth Graber

BIBLIOGRAPHIES IN AMERICAN MUSIC   NUMBER THIRTEEN
PUBLISHED FOR THE COLLEGE MUSIC SOCIETY
HARMONIE PARK PRESS   MICHIGAN   1989

Frontispiece:

WILLIAM MASON
Pen drawing by Childe Hassam, 1891
Courtesy of Music Library, Yale University

Copyright © 1989 by Kenneth Graber

Printed and bound in the United States of America
Published by
Harmonie Park Press
23630 Pinewood
Warren, Michigan 48091

Editor, J. Bunker Clark
Book design, Elaine J. Gorzelski
Typographer, Colleen Osborne

Library of Congress Cataloging-in-Publication Data

Graber, Kenneth, 1942-
    William Mason (1829-1908) : an annotated bibliography and catalog
of works / by Kenneth Graber.
        p.   cm. — (Bibliographies in American music ; no. 13)
    Includes index.
    ISBN 0-89990-046-1
    1. Mason, William, 1829-1908 — Bibliography.   I. Title.
II. Series.
ML134.M465G7   1989
016.78'092 — dc20   89-11107
                                                          CIP
                                                          MN

016.78092
G728w

to Ruth and Kristine

Contents

Contents

Preface

WILLIAM MASON'S LIFE AND WORK was multifaceted. Equipped with superior musical and intellectual gifts, a solid musical training, and unflagging industry, Mason pursued an active career as pianist, organist, composer, teacher, author of books, and contributor of newspaper and periodical articles. All of these aspects of Mason's life and work are represented in this bibliography and catalog of works. Entries are grouped under five major divisions: 1) Literature on William Mason, 2) Literary Writings by William Mason, 3) Selected Programs of Performances, 4) Catalog of Compositions and Editions, and 5) Sources.

The literature on William Mason is both extensive and diverse. Works cited in this study include histories of music, dictionaries, encyclopedias, biographies, newspaper and periodical articles, doctoral dissertations, general books on music and musicians, and some master's theses. This section of the bibliography and catalog of works is, however, selective. Many advertisements of Mason's recitals and publications and other references to Mason in books, newspapers, and periodicals judged to be trivial in nature have been omitted; however, some otherwise insignificant, brief items have been included if they offer useful dates or other little-known facts. A winnowing process was particularly necessary in dealing with the large body of literature on Mason and his system of piano technique that was written by William Smythe Babcock Mathews. Mathews had gained a firsthand exposure to Mason's concepts of piano technique at the 1870 normal school in South Bend, Indiana, where both men were members of the faculty—Mason heading the keyboard department and Mathews assisting as an organ and piano instructor. Their collaboration at the normal school marked the beginning of a long personal and professional association, and Mathews soon became one of Mason's most avid and articulate advocates. The volume and variety of material that Mathews published, much of it based on Mason's concepts, was probably unmatched by any other American writer on music during the latter part of the nineteenth century. The sheer number of Mathews's publications, coupled with the fact that his writing is sometimes characterized by wordiness and redundancy, has made it necessary to limit citations of his works to those items believed to be of greatest significance. More complete bibliographies of Mathews's writings can be found in the dissertations by Clarke (no. **65**) and Groves (no. **130**).

In a 1947 article in the *Musical Digest* (no. **222**), Daniel Gregory Mason, nephew of William Mason, describes his uncle as an "American musical trailblazer." Two aspects of Mason's work as a trailblazer are emphasized: 1) his role in the development and promotion of chamber music performances in America, and 2) his leadership in the evolution of piano playing in the United States. Mason's ideas on piano playing and piano pedagogy, perhaps his greatest legacy to later generations of musicians, are extensively documented in his own writings. These writings and other articles, letters, and memoirs published by Mason, together with their reviews, are listed in the second section of this bibliography and catalog of works. (Manuscript writings are cited under Sources, section 5 of this work.)

Programs of Mason's performances, with selected reviews, comprise the third part of this bibliography and catalog of works. In 1854, when Mason returned to the United States from his studies in Europe, it was his intention to take up the career of a touring piano virtuoso. A variety of factors led Mason to abandon these plans upon the completion of a successful recital tour of the United States in the fall and winter of 1854-55 (see no. **624**). But piano and organ performance continued to make up a significant part of his professional activities. In selecting programs for this study, an attempt was made to include a sampling representative of the major aspects of Mason's performing career: solo piano recitals, chamber music concerts, concerto appearances, lecture-recitals, and organ improvisations. Mason was a generous and unassuming man, willing to share his gifts as a performer for a wide variety of causes and in the humblest of circumstances. Many of his performances have not been included in this work, especially those of a more secondary nature. Thus, for example, neither Mason's participation in the 10 February 1859 benefit concert in New York for Little Ella, the child reader — the object being to provide for the education of Little Ella and to discourage her appearance in public — nor the performance of George F. Root's *The Flower Queen* by Grammar School No. 11, on 17th Street, at the Academy of Music in New York on 12 December 1856, is mentioned (Mason and George F. Bristow shepherded them through!).

The programs themselves are listed in chronological order and include the following information: location, date, nature of the concert or sponsoring organization, assisting artists (if any), works performed, and selected reviews and announcements of the performance. Only those works in which Mason himself performed are included. For example, in concerto appearances with an orchestra, only the concerto performed and other solo works that Mason sometimes played on these occasions are listed; other works performed on the program by the orchestra or other artists are not mentioned. Exceptions are Mason's Boston debut recital on 3 October 1854, a second Boston recital on 7 October 1854, the debut performance of the Mason-Thomas Quartette in New York on 27 November 1855, and an organ recital in Orange, New Jersey, on 4 June 1870, for which the entire programs are given (nos. **618, 620, 632,** and **676**).

The fourth section of this study consists of a catalog of Mason's compositions and works edited or arranged by him. Titles of published works are italicized; titles of manuscript works are in roman type. (This method of citing titles is used throughout the bibliography and catalog of works.) The catalog is classified by performing medium. Works with opus numbers are listed in the order assigned by Mason; all other original compositions are in alphabetical order unless otherwise noted. Editions and arrangements are alphabetically listed by the names of the original composers, except for works published in collected editions, in which cases the collective titles are used. The catalog contains all of Mason's works that are known to me, but the listing of vocal music, particularly the section on hymn tunes, is undoubtedly incomplete. Mason left no thematic catalog of his own, and bibliographic control in this area is still sporadic at best. For the most part, works must be ferreted out by scanning nineteenth-century collections of vocal music—page by page.

Although Mason was active both as an organist and as a pianist, nearly all of his keyboard compositions are for the piano. A few works for organ exist (see nos. **713** and **855**), but Mason seems to have used this instrument primarily as a vehicle for improvisation. Almost all of Mason's published compositions are now out of print; a handful have been included in several anthologies (see nos. **75, 119, 142, 167, 208,** and **214;** in addition, the forthcoming series of scores *Three Centuries of American Music* [Boston: G. K. Hall] is projected to have several compositions by Mason included in volumes edited by Sylvia Glickman and J. Bunker Clark), but a collected edition of his works is not available, nor is one anticipated. To assist the interested reader, library locations of Mason's holograph scores and original compositions published in sheet music form are given. Library locations for some of Mason's works are also contained in the books by John and Anna Gillespie (no. **120**) and Cameron McGraw (no. **211**).

A helpful, though incomplete, list of Mason's works is contained in the Pazdírek *Universal-Handbuch der Musikliteratur* (no. **443**). This reference, however, must be used with caution; several opus numbers are incorrectly ascribed, and a number of works without opus number attributed to Mason seem to be spurious. Mason name-sakes were, and are, common. Many of these erroneously attributed works were written by one such person, a professional musician, contemporary with Mason, known to have been active in England, including the cities of Southwell, Lincoln, and London. Further research on this matter, on editions of Mason's works issued by European publishing houses, and on other European aspects of Mason's life and career is being carried out by Peg Shauck for her forthcoming doctoral dissertation on Mason.

Some of the major repositories and collections of primary source material on William Mason are listed in the fifth section of this bibliography and catalog of works. The corpus of such material is quite large. The following items, in particular, are of special interest: 1) the William Mason Papers (no. **1017**), 2) the William Mason Collection of Autograph Letters (no. **1017**), 3) the William Mason Collection of Autographs of Musicians (no. **1016**), 4) an Anniversary Book (no. **1017**), 5) a Scrapbook Containing Programs and Clippings (no. **1017**), and 6) the collection of holograph compositions in the Library of Congress (no. **1018**). Mason himself apparently destroyed a significant amount of primary source material. In a letter to Henry L. Mason, dated 17 April 1890, Mason writes: "I have been feeling miserably with dyspepsia and indigestion for some weeks and in the midst of it all have been looking over *loads* and masses of old letters, books, music, pamphlets[,] etc.[,] etc.[,] the accumulation of many years, which it now becomes necessary to dispose of or destroy."[1] That some of the items were lost or destroyed (then, or later) is particularly to be regretted. It is

---

[1] Autograph letter with the Lowell Mason Papers at Yale University. Quoted by permission.

known, for example, that Mason kept a daily journal, now missing, while a student in Europe in 1849-54. The journal would surely have been of great interest, especially in regard to any light it might have shed concerning Mason's studies with Liszt, Alexander Dreyschock, and Ignaz Moscheles.

The main body of this work does not contain Mason's discography because it is disappointingly small and can be quickly reviewed here. Two recordings have been made: 1) *The Wind Demon and Other Mid-Nineteenth-Century Piano Works*, Recorded Anthology of American Music (New World Records, NW 257), Ivan Davis, piano, contains Mason's *Silver Spring*, op. 6, and *A Pastoral Novellette*, with notes by Robert Offergeld and Edward A. Berlin (see no. **367**); and 2) *Music in America: Pianoforte Music of the 19th Century* (Society for the Preservation of the American Musical Heritage, MIA 109), Arthur Loesser, piano, contains Mason's *Silver Spring*, op. 6, *Toujours* from *Trois Valses de salon*, op. 7, no. 2, *Lullaby*, op. 10, and *Monody*, op. 13, with notes by Arthur Loesser (see nos. **121** and **190**).

Many persons have contributed to the preparation of this book. I am particularly grateful for the help and encouragement of the following individuals: Eleanor Anes, Ruth Bleecker, Barton Cantrell, Rosemary L. Cullen, Helen Hart Mason Endicott and Elizabeth Anne Mason Ginnel, great-nieces of William Mason, Gloria Gavert, Eleanor M. Gehres, Graham and Cornelia Hunter, Richard Jackson, Cecilia Jessum, Elfrieda A. Kraege, Charles Lindahl, Kenneth A. Lohf, Charles Merwin, Kathleen J. Moretto, Larry Mowers, Peg Shauck for sharing information on some of the European aspects of Mason's works, and Wayne Shirley. To the reference librarians and staffs of the following libraries and societies, a special word of thanks for their assistance in locating sometimes obscure material: Albany Public Library, Boston Athenaeum, Boston Public Library, Broadcast Music Inc. Archives, Brown University Libraries, Buffalo and Erie County Public Library System (New York), Chicago Public Library, Cleveland Public Library, Columbia University Libraries, Connecticut State Library, Dayton and Montgomery County Public Library (Ohio), Denver Public Library, Free Library of Philadelphia, Free Public Library of the City of Orange (New Jersey), Hartford Public Library, Harvard University Libraries, Libraries of the University of Illinois at Urbana-Champaign, Library of Congress, Louisville Free Public Library, Medfield Historical Society (Massachusetts), Monmouth County Historical Association (New Jersey), New York Public Libraries, New York State Library, Newark Public Library, Newberry Library, Onondaga County Public Library System (New York), Public Library of Cincinnati and Hamilton County, Rochester Public Library, Saint Olaf College Library, Sibley Music Library (Eastman School of Music), Springfield City Library (Massachusetts), Troy Public Library (New York), University of Iowa Libraries, University of Maryland Libraries, University of Minnesota Libraries, Utica Public Library (New York), Western Reserve Historical Society (Ohio), Worcester Public Library (Massachusetts), and Yale University Libraries. Finally, I would like to express my appreciation for the many helpful suggestions given to me by James R. Heintze, editor of *Bibliographies in American Music*, and J. Bunker Clark, general editor for Harmonie Park Press.

KENNETH GRABER

St. Olaf College
Northfield, Minnesota
April 1988

Courtesy of Elizabeth Mason Ginnel

William Mason as a student in Europe, ca. 1850

Chronology of Mason's Life

1829. William Mason was born in Boston on January 24, the third of four sons born to Lowell Mason (1792-1872) and Abigail Gregory (1797-1889). The other children of this marriage were Daniel Gregory (1820-69), Lowell, Jr. (1823-85), and Henry (1831-90). The history of the Mason family in America dates back to 12 June 1630, when Robert Mason settled in the Massachusetts Bay Colony in Salem. Although earlier family members are known to have been enthusiastic amateur musicians, William's father, Lowell, was the family's first professional musician. His achievements in the fields of music education and church music are well known. William's siblings were also involved in music-related professions: Daniel Gregory and Lowell, Jr., in music publishing, and Henry (later, also Lowell, Jr.) in the manufacture of musical instruments (the Mason & Hamlin Company). Several of William's nephews also gained national prominence in music, particularly Daniel Gregory (1873-1953), who was an author, composer, and professor of music at Columbia University for over thirty years.

ca. 1836. Lowell Mason is said to have placed his son William, now age seven, on the bench of the organ at the Bowdoin Congregational Church in Boston to accompany the choir. William had demonstrated an unusual aptitude for music at an early age. Although his talent was not neglected, William seems to have received only modest encouragement and supervision (primarily from his mother) in his early musical training, probably due to his father's dream that he become a member of the clergy. (To this end, arrangements were later made for William to study with the Reverend T. T. Thayer in Newport, Rhode Island; but Mason was to follow other paths.)

ca. 1845. Mason began piano lessons with Henry Schmidt, his father's colleague at the Boston Academy of Music. Mason also did some composing, and his first published piano music, *Deux Romances sans paroles*, op. 1, appeared in 1845.

Soirée musicale

des

Julius Pisařowitz.

Freitag den 31. Jänner 1851 um 5 Uhr
im Saale zum Erzherzog Stephan.

Programm:

1. *Vocal-Quartett* (O lächle stets) von Cherubini, vorgetragen von den Herren Emminger, Meyer, Strakaty und Kunz.
2. *Fantasie sur le motifs de Bellini pour la Clarinette* par Seemann, vorgetragen vom Concertgeber.
3. *Gedicht von Julius Mosen*, in Musik gesetzt von A. W. Ambros, vorgetragen von Frau Botschon–Soukup.
4. *Rhapsodie zum Wintermärchen*, von Alex. Dreyschock, vorgetragen von Mr. Mason aus Boston, Schüler des H. Alex. Dreyschok.
5. *Adelaide de L. van Beethoven* variée pour la Clarinette, vorgetragen vom Concertgeber.
6. *Lied* (Komm) von G. Meyerbeer, vorgetragen von Frau Botschon–Soukup.
7. *Vocal-Quartett* (Das ist der Tag des Herrn) von C. Kreutzer, vorgetragen von den Herren Emminger, Meyer, Strakaty und Kunz.
8. *Grand Duo* für Pianoforte und Clarinette von C. M. Weber, vorgetragen von Mr. Mason und dem Concertgeber.

Frau Botschon–Soukup, die Herren Mason, Emminger, Meyer, Strakaty und Kunz haben ihre gefällige Mitwirkung bereitwilligst zugesagt.

Druck von Fr. Rohliček.

Courtesy of the New York Public Library at Lincoln Center; Astor, Lenox, and Tilden Foundations, Music Division

Program of 31 January 1851 concert in Prague

1846-48. Mason made his professional debut as a pianist on 7 March 1846 at a concert of the Boston Academy of Music, performing Herz's *Variations on the "Air" from Méhul's "Joseph,"* op. 20, with quintet accompaniment. A few months later he played the piano parts in a series of six chamber music concerts sponsored by the Harvard Musical Association. These concerts were followed by other Boston appearances, and soon Mason was playing in various other cities, venturing as far west as Cincinnati, Ohio. In addition to his work as a pianist, Mason continued to perform on the organ and compose. He also edited two collections of vocal music.

1849. On April 20, Mason set sail on the *Hermann* for Bremen, Germany. He remained in Europe for the next five years, studying, traveling, and occasionally performing. Mason began his formal studies in Leipzig in October. He took piano lessons from Ignaz Moscheles, lessons in harmony and counterpoint from Moritz Hauptmann, and lessons in orchestration from Ernst Friedrich Richter.

1850-51. Mason took up residence in Prague in August 1850 and began a nine-month period of intensive piano study with Alexander Dreyschock (three lessons a week). Mason also appeared in public as a pianist on several occasions: at the Saale zum Erzherzog Stephan on 31 January 1851 (see p. xvi), the Palace of the Countess of Nostitz on 23 March 1851, and the Saale des Sophien Insel on 3 May 1851. His performances were well received by both the critics and the public.

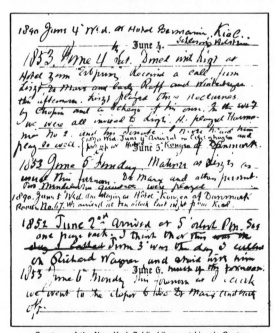

Courtesy of the New York Public Library at Lincoln Center; Astor, Lenox, and Tilden Foundations, Music Division

Entry from William Mason's Anniversary Book

1853-54. On 14 April 1853 Mason arrived in Weimar to begin lessons with Liszt. He remained there for more than a year. During most of this time only three other pianists were studying with Liszt: Karl Klindworth, Dionys Pruckner, and Joseph Joachim Raff. Klindworth and Pruckner joined Mason in performances of one of Bach's triple concertos at the Stadthaussaal on 13 December 1853 and 3 January 1854. Prior to Mason's arrival in Weimar, he had performed Weber's *Concertstück in F Minor*, op. 79, in London at the Harmonic Union Subscription Concert on 20 January 1853; Julius Benedict was the conductor.

1854. Mason left Europe in July to return to the United States, intent on continuing his career as a concert pianist. He played his debut recital in Boston on October 3, followed by a New York debut on October 12. A second recital was given in each of these cities, followed by a five-day concert tour of the New England area. Mason's recitals in the eastern cultural centers were very successful, and, encouraged by these efforts, he decided to embark on an extended concert tour that eventually took him as far west as Chicago. He played a total of twenty recitals in twelve different cities over a time span of about two months. It is significant that Mason performed without the assistance of singers or other instrumentalists. His tour was probably the first ever undertaken in the United States in which the programs consisted entirely of piano music. It was an achievement of which he was justifiably proud.

1855. After his return from his concert tour in late January, Mason came to a crossroads in his career. Although his concert tour had been a success, it had at the same time been disillusioning, for he quickly discovered that the public demanded frequent repetition of a few favorite pieces. Mason found this to be musically and intellectually stagnating, and he decided to forgo the life of a touring virtuoso, choosing instead to settle in one area to take up a career of performing, teaching, and composing. Although a native Bostonian, New York seemed to offer the most opportunities for professional advancement, and Mason, for the most part, made it the center of his activities for the remainder of his life, maintaining his principal place of residence either within New York City itself or in Orange, New Jersey.

Some of Mason's specific activities at this time are of particular interest. On April 21 he made his first appearance with the New York Philharmonic, performing Weber's *Concertstück in F Minor*, op. 79, under the baton of Carl Bergmann. (Later in the year, on December 22, he played the same work with Carl Zerrahn and the Boston Orchestra.) Mason also turned to another area of work which had interested him since childhood—the music of the church. On October 7 he began his tenure as organist at the Fifth Avenue Presbyterian Church in New York. In his work there, and in later positions at the New Jerusalem Church on 35th Street and the Valley Church in Orange, New Jersey, Mason gained some measure of celebrity for his elaborate, contrapuntal improvisations. Also at this time, Mason organized a chamber music ensemble (later to become known as the Mason-Thomas Quartette) which consisted of himself and a string quartet. The ensemble made its debut on November 27 at Dodworth's Hall in New York. Greeted by critical acclaim, Mason and his colleagues set up a series of concerts, which continued through 1868. Many works were given their first American performance by this group; the ensemble's American premiere of Brahms's *Trio in B Major*, op. 8, on their November 27 debut, was also its world premiere.

1856. Mason published several piano compositions: *Silver Spring*, op. 6; *Trois Valses de salon*, op. 7; *Trois Préludes*, op. 8; and *Étude de concert*, op. 9. Mason continued to compose at a moderate, steady rate throughout his career; his last published work, *Scherzo-Caprice*, op. 52, was issued in 1905, just three years before his death.

In June, a series of chamber music recitals—similar to that already established in New York—was begun by the Mason-Thomas Quartette at Miss Porter's School for Young Ladies in Farmington, Connecticut. These performances continued through 1870.

The Mason-Thomas Quartette
Left to right: George Matzka, Joseph Mosenthal, Frederic Bergner, Theodore Thomas, and William Mason

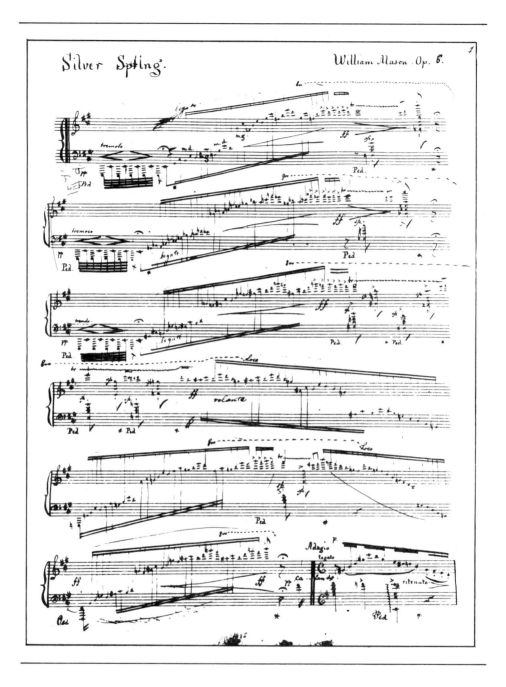

Courtesy of the Music Division, Library of Congress

Holograph score of *Silver Spring*, op. 6

1857. On March 12, William Mason and Mary Isabella Webb were married in the Swedenborgian Church on Bowdoin Street in Boston. Mary Isabella was the daughter of George James Webb, a longtime associate of Lowell Mason. Three children were born to this marriage: George Webb (1858-81), Marion Otis (1861-90), and Mary Wilhelmina (1863-1928).

1863. In August, Mason spent his summer vacation at Appledore House, a resort hotel on Appledore Island in the Isles of Shoals, off Portsmouth, New Hampshire, and thereby began a tradition of making this location his regular holiday retreat. Appledore House was owned by the family of the poet Celia Thaxter. Initially, Mason's vacations were taken up with fishing and general relaxation, but as the years passed by he began to participate in morning musical salons held in Celia Thaxter's cottage. Mason soon became the featured performer at these gatherings, playing for about 1½ hours every morning. Sunday mornings were devoted to the performance of Beethoven's sonatas.

Courtesy of the New York Public Library at Lincoln Center; Astor, Lenox, and Tilden Foundations, Music Division

William Mason and Theodore Thomas

1867. Mason's first pedagogical work was published: *A Method for the Piano-Forte*, coauthored by E. S. Hoadly. (Later, in 1871, Mason and Hoadly collaborated in the publication of another piano instruction book: *A System for Beginners in the Art of Playing upon the Piano-Forte*.) Mason also became involved in another educational project. He and Theodore Thomas founded a music conservatory at 129 Fifth Avenue in New York. Although the conservatory had a successful beginning, it proved to be a short-lived venture.

1868. A new Odell organ was installed in the Valley Church in Orange, New Jersey. Mason, who was the organist of the church at the time, had assisted in selecting the instrument and raising funds for its purchase.

1870. Mason had his first experience teaching in a normal music school. (The school was held in South Bend, Indiana.) Although the history of these schools dated back to the 1850s, Mason's participation in the normal school at South Bend marked the first time that instruction in piano and piano pedagogy was given on a significant scale. Following his work in South Bend, Mason taught in normal music schools held in several locations in the state of New York, including the following: Florida (1870), Binghamton (1871-73), and Watertown (1875-76). Other responsibilities were accepted. In the summer of 1870 Mason was elected president of the National Musical Congress. During this same year he was also named president of the Orange (New Jersey) Choral Union.

1872. Mason received an honorary doctorate from Yale University.

1878. Mason issued a piano instruction book titled *A System of Technical Exercises for the Piano-Forte*. William Smythe Babcock Mathews, whom Mason had met in Chicago in 1870, served as associate editor. Later, Mason and Mathews worked together in several other publications—notably, *A Primer of Music* and *A System of Fundamental Technics*.

1879-80. On 1 November 1879, Mason, his wife Mary, and two of his children (Marion and Mary Wilhelmina) left for Europe on the steamship *Donau*. Near the end of their stay, on 27 May 1880, tragedy struck: Mary, Mason's wife, died at the Hotel de Normandy in Paris.

1884. Mason was named a member of the board of piano examiners for the American College of Musicians, an organization of musicians which had been founded in July during the annual MTNA meeting in New York. Mason served in this capacity through 1892.

1885. In July, Mason read a paper on "Accentual Treatment of Exercises" at the national MTNA meeting in New York. Mason also presented a paper on "Touch" at the 1886 MTNA meeting in Boston and, in 1887, served on a MTNA committee that considered the question of "Notations and Terminology."

1887. Mason was named the first president of the American Vocal Music Association, organized for the purpose of raising the level of musical proficiency in the United States by the use of the tonic sol-fa system.

1890. On May 7, Mason embarked on another voyage to Europe on the steamer *Lahn*. One of the highlights of his journey was a visit with Grieg in the latter's home, Villa Troldhaugen, on July 1. Mason later recounted some aspects of this visit in his essay on Grieg published in *Century Magazine*.

1891. Mason's most famous pedagogical work was published (1891-92): *Touch and Technic*, op. 44. In December, Mason wrote a letter to *Musical Courier* in support of Paderewski, who was then in the early stages of his first recital tour of the United States. Mason's letter helped to pave the way for Paderewski's phenomenal success in this country.

1894. A four-week summer music school, organized by Theodore Presser, was held on the campus of the University of Pennsylvania in Philadelphia. One of the stated purposes of the school was to acquaint teachers with Mason's system of piano technique. Mason himself taught at the school for one week and gave two piano recitals.

Courtesy of the New York Public Library at Lincoln Center;
Astor, Lenox, and Tilden Foundations, Music Division
Photo by Gessford

William Mason, ca. 1899

1895. Mason was named a trustee of the American College of Musicians when it was granted a university charter by the state of New York.

1899. A celebration in honor of Mason's seventieth birthday was held in Steinway Hall in New York. Among the gifts that Mason received was a loving cup from his pupils and a new grand piano from the Steinways. Mason had occupied a teaching studio in Steinway Hall from about 1866. His friendship with the Steinways dated back to 1855.

1901. Mason's autobiography, *Memories of a Musical Life*, was published.

1908. After a brief illness, Mason died on July 14 at his home in New York on 1 West 81st Street. He had been actively engaged in teaching until early the previous winter and had occasionally gone to his studio in Steinway Hall until three weeks before his death. Mason was interred in the family burial plot at Rosedale Cemetery in Orange, New Jersey.

Abbreviations

AIKIN-MAIN-ALLEN/Imperial — AIKIN, Jesse B., Hubert P. MAIN, and Chester G. ALLEN, comps. *The Imperial Harmony: A Choice Collection of Sacred Music.* . . . New York: Biglow & Main, 1876.

ALLEN-SEWARD/Vineyard — ALLEN, Chester G., and Theodore F. SEWARD, eds. *The Vineyard of Song: Designed for Singing Schools, Institutes, Conventions, Day Schools, and Academies.* New York: Biglow & Main, 1874.

BRADBURY/Eclectic — BRADBURY, William B., ed. *The Eclectic Tune Book: A Selection of Standard Church Tunes.* . . . Philadelphia: Presbyterian Publication Committee, 1860.

BRADBURY/Jubilee — BRADBURY, William B., ed. *The Jubilee: An Extensive Collection of Church Music.* . . . New York: Mason Bros., 1857.

Also an 1858 enlarged edition by Mason Bros. (New York).

BRADBURY/Key-Note — BRADBURY, William B., ed. *The Key-Note: A Collection of Church and Singing School Music.* . . . New York: Mason Bros., 1863.

BRADBURY-ROOT/Shawm   BRADBURY, William B., and George F. ROOT, eds. *The Shawm: A Library of Church Music.* . . . Assisted by Thomas Hastings and T. B. Mason. New York: Mason Bros., 1853.

CTP   Collective Title Page.

CtY   Yale University, John Herrick Jackson Music Library, New Haven, Conn.

DLC   Library of Congress, Music Division.

IU   University of Illinois at Urbana-Champaign, Music Library. (Sources cited include works in the Joseffy Collection.)

MASON/American   MASON, Lowell, ed. *The American Tune Book.* . . . Boston: Oliver Ditson & Co., 1869.

MASON/Carmina   MASON, Lowell, ed. *Carmina Sacra; or, Boston Collection of Church Music.* . . . Boston: Oliver Ditson & Co., 1869.

MASON/Carmina Enlarged   MASON, Lowell, ed. *Carmina Sacra Enlarged: The American Tune Book.* . . . Boston: Oliver Ditson & Co., 1869.

      Contents the same as in Mason's *The American Tune Book.* See above.

MASON/Fireside   MASON, William, ed. *Fireside Harmony: A New Collection of Glees and Part Songs Arranged for Soprano, Alto, Tenor, and Base [sic] Voices.* Boston: Tappan, Whittemore & Mason, 1848 (no. **1006**).

MASON/Hallelujah   MASON, Lowell, ed. *The Hallelujah: A Book for the Service of Song in the House of the Lord.* . . . New York: Mason Bros., 1854.

MASON/Scrapbook   MASON, William. Scrapbook Containing Programs and Clippings (no. **1017**).

MASON/Singer

MASON, Lowell, ed. *Mason's Normal Singer: A Collection of Vocal Music for Singing Classes, Schools, and Social Circles.* . . . New York: Mason Bros., 1856.

MASON/Song-Garden (2)

MASON, Lowell, ed. *The Song-Garden: A Series of School Music Books* . . . , *Second Book.* Boston: Oliver Ditson & Co., 1864; New York: Charles H. Ditson & Co., 1864.

MASON/Song-Garden (3)

MASON, Lowell, ed. *The Song-Garden: A Series of School Music Books* . . . , *Third Book.* New York: Mason Bros., 1866.

MASON/Tune Book

MASON, Lowell, ed. *The People's Tune Book: A Class Book of Church Music.* . . . New York: Mason Bros., 1860.

MASON-BANCROFT/Glee

MASON, William, and Silas A. BANCROFT, comps. *The Social Glee Book: Being a Selection of Glees and Part Songs by Distinguished German Composers Never Before Published in This Country, Together with Original Pieces.* Boston: Wilkens, Carter & Co., 1847 (no. **1005**).

MASON-MASON/Asaph

MASON, Lowell, and William MASON, eds. *Asaph; or, the Choir Book: A Collection of Vocal Music, Sacred and Secular, for Choirs, Singing Schools, Musical Societies and Conventions, and Social and Religious Assemblies.* New York: Mason Bros., 1861 (no. **1009**).

MASON-MASON/Hymnist

MASON, Lowell, and William MASON, eds. *The Hymnist: A Collection of Sacred Music, Original and Selected.* 2 vols. Boston: Tappan, Whittemore & Mason, 1849 (no. **1007**).

MASON-PARK-PHELPS/
  New Sabbath

[MASON, Lowell, Edwards A. PARK, and Austin PHELPS], eds. *The New Sabbath Hymn and Tune Book.* . . . New York: Mason Bros., 1867.

MASON-PARK-PHELPS/ Sabbath Hymn	[MASON, Lowell, Edwards A. PARK, and Austin PHELPS], eds. *The Sabbath Hymn and Tune Book*. . . . New York: Mason Bros., 1859.
MASON-PARK-PHELPS/ Sabbath Tune	[MASON, Lowell, Edwards A. PARK, and Austin PHELPS], eds. *The Sabbath Tune Book*. . . . New York: Mason Bros., 1859.
MASON-WEBB/Cantica	MASON, Lowell, and George James WEBB, eds. *Cantica Laudis; or, the American Book of Church Music*. . . . New York: Mason & Law, 1850.
MASON-WEBB/Glee Hive	MASON, Lowell, and George James WEBB, eds. *The Glee Hive: A Collection of Glees and Part Songs*. . . . New York: Mason & Law, 1851.
MASON-WEBB/Glee Hive (rev.)	MASON, Lowell, and George James WEBB, eds. *The Glee Hive: A Collection of Glees and Part Songs*. Rev. and enlarged ed. New York: Mason Bros., 1853.
MASON-WEBB/Psalmist	MASON, Lowell, and George James WEBB, eds. *The National Psalmist*. . . . Boston: Tappan, Whittemore & Mason, 1848.
MASON-WEBB/Psaltery	MASON, Lowell, and George James WEBB, eds. *The Psaltery: A New Collection of Church Music*. . . . Boston: Wilkins, Carter & Co., 1845.
MASON-WEBB/Tune Book	MASON, Lowell, and George James WEBB, eds. *The Congregational Tune-Book*. . . . Boston: Tappan, Whittemore & Mason, 1848.
MB	Boston Public Library.
MH-Mu	Harvard University, Eda Kuhn Loeb Music Library, Cambridge, Mass.
MTNA	Music Teachers National Association.

NN	New York Public Library, Performing Arts Research Center, Lincoln Center.
NNC	Columbia University, New York City.
NRU-Mus	University of Rochester, Eastman School of Music, Sibley Music Library.
PARK-PHELPS-WAYLAND-MASON/Sabbath School	[PARK, Edwards A., Austin PHELPS, Francis WAYLAND, and Lowell MASON], eds. *The Sabbath School Hymn and Tune Book*. . . . New York: Mason Bros., 1860.
PP	Free Library of Philadelphia.
ROOT/Bell	ROOT, George F., ed. *The Sabbath Bell: A Collection of Music for Choirs, Musical Associations, Singing Schools, and the Home Circle*. . . . New York: Mason Bros., 1856.
ROOT/Choir	ROOT, George F., ed. *The Choir and Congregation*. . . . Cincinnati: John Church & Co., 1875.
ROOT/Diapason	ROOT, George F., ed. *The Diapason: A Collection of Church Music*. . . . New York: Mason Bros., 1860.
ROOT/Glee	ROOT, George F., ed. *The Festival Glee Book*. . . . New York: Mason Bros., 1857.
ROOT/New Choir	ROOT, George F., ed. *The New Choir and Congregation*. . . . Cincinnati: John Church & Co.; Chicago: Root & Sons Music Co., 1879.
ROOT/Singing Book	ROOT, George F., ed. *The Young Men's Singing Book*. . . . With the assistance of Lowell Mason. Boston: Oliver Ditson & Co., 1855.
ROOT/Vocalist	ROOT, George F., ed. *The Academy Vocalist; or, Vocal Music Arranged for the Use of Seminaries, High Schools, Singing Classes, etc*. . . . New York: F. J. Huntington; Mason & Law, 1852.

ROOT-SWEETSER/Collection	ROOT, George F., and Joseph E. SWEETSER, eds. *A Collection of Church Music.* . . . New York: John Wiley, 1849.
RPB	Brown University, John Hay Library, Harris Collection of American Poetry and Plays, Providence, R.I.
SEWARD/Glee	SEWARD, Theodore F., ed. *The Glee Circle.* . . . New York: Biglow & Main, 1879.
SEWARD/Temple Choir	SEWARD, Theodore F., ed. *The Temple Choir: A Collection of Sacred and Secular Music.* . . . Assisted by Lowell Mason and William B. Bradbury. New York: Mason Bros., 1867.
SEWARD-ALLEN/Coronation	SEWARD, Theodore F., and Chester G. ALLEN, eds. *The Coronation: A New Collection of Music for Choirs and Singing Schools.* Assisted by Lowell Mason. New York: Biglow & Main, 1872.
WEBB-MASON/Melodist	WEBB, George James, and William MASON, eds. *The Melodist: A Collection of Popular and Social Songs, Original or Selected, Harmonized and Arranged for Soprano, Alto, Tenor, and Base* [sic] *Voices.* New York: Mason & Law, 1850 (no. **1008**).
WEBB-MASON/Odeon	WEBB, George James, and Lowell MASON, eds. *The New Odeon: A Collection of Secular Melodies.* . . . New York: Mason Bros., 1855.

WILLIAM MASON (1829-1908)

An Annotated Bibliography

and

Catalog of Works

1

Literature on William Mason

1   "About Home Matters." *Boston Post*, 28 Sept 1854, p. [2], col. 3.

Reports that speculators attempted to purchase several hundred tickets for Mason's 3 October 1854 Boston debut recital (see no. **618**) prior to the announced opening date of ticket sales.

2   "About Normals." *Song Messenger: A Musical Monthly* 9/6 (June 1871): 90.

Announces plans for a six-week normal school to begin on July 6 in Binghamton, New York. Mason is listed as a piano instructor. For reports on this normal school, see nos. **71, 248, 253, 273, 358.**

3   "The A.C.M." *Music* 8 (Aug 1895): 418-19.

A summary of the activities at the first annual meeting of the trustees of the American College of Musicians held in New York City on 28 June 1895. Mason was one of ten trustees present.

See also nos. **14, 241.**

4   ADAMS, Oscar Fay. *A Dictionary of American Authors.* 5th ed., rev. and enlarged. Boston: Houghton Mifflin Co., 1904; reprint, Detroit: Gale Research Co., 1969. S.v. "Mason, William."

Mentions Mason's occupation and gives a short list of his writings.

5   "Advice and Caution." *Etude* 3/12 (Dec 1885): 273.

Two quotations by Mason are cited.

See also no. **372.**

6   ALDRICH, Richard. *Musical Discourse from the New York Times.* London: Oxford University Press, Humphrey Milford, 1928; reprint, Freeport, N.Y.: Books for Libraries Press, 1967.

Includes a summary of Mason's life and work; greatest emphasis is placed on his role in establishing the Mason-Thomas chamber music series in New York.

> Their [Mason, Theodore Thomas, and Carl Bergmann's] performance of Brahm's [*sic*] trio [in B major, op. 8], on November 27, 1855, at Dodworth's Hall, was its first performance in public anywhere. . . .

7   ALLEN, Chester G. "Editorial Correspondence." *New York Musical Gazette* 7/8 (Aug 1873): 120.

A letter telling of the normal school held in Binghamton, New York, in 1873. Mason was one of the instructors. At the end of the first week about seventy-five pupils had enrolled and more were "constantly arriving." Special arrangements had been made to provide good instruments for the piano students.

> The next day, after our arrival [July 4], we spent in superintending the moving and setting up of the pianos which had arrived from New-York. Before night we had ten of Steinway's splendid grands and uprights unpacked and set up; and so by working hard, we managed to have our machinery all fixed and ready to start promptly on Wednesday morning.

See also nos. **22, 151, 276, 361.**

8   ALLEN, Chester G. Letter to the editor, New York, 16 Aug 1875. *Song Messenger: A Musical Monthly* 13/9 (Sept 1875): 146.

Allen writes about the 1875 normal school held in Watertown, New York.

> We had also to regret that Dr. Mason was unable to remain during the last two weeks of the school, being obliged to return in time to prepare for the press his new work upon piano techniques [*A System of Technical Exercises*; see no. **575**]. He was able, however, to give us, in addition to his instructions to the piano class, five of his incomparable piano-forte recitals.

9   "An American Abroad." *Message Bird: A Literary and Musical Journal* 40 (15 Mar 1851): 661.

Mason is quoted as saying that Liszt would probably never visit America — a topic which aroused considerable interest in the American news media during this time. Also contains reviews of Mason's performance in Prague on 31 January 1851 (see no. **609**). This article was also published as "William Mason at Prague," *Choral Advocate and Singing-Class Journal* 1/11 (Apr 1851): 166-67.

10   "American College of Musicians." *Etude* 4/7 (July 1886): 159.

A report on the results of the exams administered to candidates applying for admission into the American College of Musicians. Mason served on the board of examiners for piano, a position he held from the inception of the American College of Musicians in 1884 through 1892. Identically titled articles giving similar reports of examinations (in which Mason participated) appeared in subsequent issues of the *Etude*: 5/8 (Aug 1887): 115; 7/9 (Sept 1889): 139; 8/5 (May 1890): 76; 8/9 (Sept 1890): 141.

See also nos. **11, 12, 13, 189.**

11   "American College of Musicians." *Musical Visitor* 20/8 (Aug 1891): 208.

Reports on a recent meeting of the American College of Musicians.

The annual meeting for the election of officers resulted in the selection of the following well-known musicians as examiners for the coming year: Piano—Wm. Mason, A. R. Parsons, Fanny Bloomfield-Zeisler, with Wm. H. Sherwood and Chas. H. Jarvis, alternates. . . .

See also nos. **10, 12, 13, 189.**

12   [American College of Musicians.] *Prospectus of the American College of Musicians: An Organization for the Encouragement of a High Standard of Musicianship.* N.p., 1886.

Copy held in Newberry Library, Chicago. A statement of the structure and objectives of the American College of Musicians. Mason is named as one of the members of the board of examiners for piano.

See also nos. **10, 11, 13, 189.**

13   "The American College of Musicians: How It Began—What It Has Done—Its New Era." *Musical Courier* 37/1 (4 July 1898): [59-61].

A summary of the early history of the American College of Musicians, including an account of some of the problems encountered in devising the format and content of the examinations.

. . . the newly elected board of examiners [included Mason] spent much time and effort in attempting to draw up a formula of examination. . . . Much difficulty was experienced owing to the novelty of the work and the impossibility of getting the board together, and so nothing was decided upon until the last week in June, 1885, when the entire board met in Dr. William Mason's studio. . . .

See also nos. **10, 11, 12, 189.**

14   "The American College of Musicians of the University of the State of New York." *Etude* 16/2 (Feb 1898): 57.

Announces plans and procedures recently adopted by the American College of Musicians. Mason continues to serve as a member of the board of trustees.

See also nos. **3, 241.**

15   *The American History and Encyclopedia of Music* (1908-10), ed. William Lines Hubbard, 12 vols. S.v. "Mason, William," in 2d of two vols. titled *Musical Biographies* by Janet M. Green.

Includes a biographical sketch, a partial list of works, and a summary of Mason's position in American music.

> William Mason is regarded as the first American piano virtuoso, a man of brilliant technical skill and . . . refinement of interpretation.

16   [American Institute of Applied Music.] Advertisement. *Etude* 19/6 (June 1901): 241.

Incorporated in 1900 by the regents of the University of the State of New York, the American Institute of Applied Music encompassed several divisions, including the Metropolitan College of Music, the Metropolitan Conservatory of Music, the American Institute of Normal Methods, and the Synthetic Piano School. Mason's name is on the roster of faculty and examiners. Similar advertisements listing Mason appear in subsequent issues of the *Etude* through 1906.

17   "The American Pianists, Gottschalk and Mason." *New York Musical Review and Gazette* 7/3 (9 Feb 1856): 38-39.

See no. **311.**

18   "American Pianists, VI: Dr. William Mason." *Musician* 2/4 (Apr 1879): 89.

Includes a full-page portrait as a "supplement" to the April issue. A brief review of Mason's career.

> His memory is prodigious, and at his present age his playing is that of a master. Only recently he played for two hours or more, one composition by Schumann after another, many of them having been untouched for years.

19   "American Vocal Music Association." *Musical Reform* 2/1 (Oct 1887): 2-3.

This article describes the origin of the American Vocal Music Association, organized for the purpose of raising the level of musical proficiency in America by the use of the tonic sol-fa system. Mason was named the first president of this association in 1887.

20   [ANGELL, Richard S.] *Catalogue of an Exhibition Illustrating the Life and Work of Edward MacDowell, 1861-1908, Professor of Music in Columbia University, 1896-1904, Together with the Addresses Delivered at the Opening Ceremony April 27, 1938.* N.p., n.d.

Copy held in Library of Congress. The MacDowell exhibit, mounted by Angell, included a number of items which reflected MacDowell's close friendship with Mason. Among them were eight autograph letters from MacDowell to Mason, an autograph transcript of Mason's first letter to MacDowell, and an autograph letter (now lost) from Mason to John W. Burgess, a professor at Columbia University, urging the appointment of MacDowell to the then newly created chair of music (see also nos. **50, 206, 1016**).

An address given by Daniel Gregory Mason at the opening of the exhibition, published in the catalog, also makes several references to the intertwining careers of William Mason and Edward MacDowell.

> . . . [MacDowell's] *Sonata Tragica* had been played by my uncle [William Mason] every day one summer at the Isles of Shoals, until people learned to like what was then thought by many ultra-modernistic. Perhaps partly in gratitude, the composer dedicated to the pianist another sonata, the Eroica, writing him: "I feared you might not like our Sonata, therefore you may judge how delighted to receive your letter I was. . . . That you can take the will for the deed in what may not appeal to you in it, and like the rest for its own sake, makes me feel the work has found something more than an indulgent god-father."

21   Anonymous. Anecdote about William Mason and Sebastian Bach Mills. *Song Messenger: A Musical Monthly* 9/12 (Dec 1871): 178.

An amusing account of Mason's conversation with a young lady who inquired whether Mills or Mason was the better teacher, not knowing the identity of the person she was addressing.

22   Anonymous. Report on the 1873 normal school in Binghamton, New York. *New York Musical Gazette* 7/9 (Sept 1873): 135.

Includes programs of eight recitals played by Mason and a description of his piano classes.

> Dr. Mason . . . gave four lectures each week before the class, in which the best methods of study and practice, the way to acquire technical skill, and to overcome certain difficulties, what constitutes style and expression, the characteristics of different composers and schools of music, and, in fact, all questions that pertain to success in piano playing were discussed, and illustrations given.

See also nos. **7, 151, 276, 361**.

23   Anonymous report. Clipping, identified only as taken from the *Kleine Musikzeitung* (Hamburg). In MASON/Scrapbook.

An account of Julius Schuberth's trip from New York to Bremen in company with three young Americans: Mason, Francis G. Hill, and one Mr. Gredly. A program of the concert given on board ship on 1 May 1849 is included. See nos. **25, 608**.

24   Anonymous report. *Dwight's Journal of Music* 2/23 (12 Mar 1853): 183.

Reports that Mason's performance in London on 7 February 1853 under the patronage of the Lord Mayor and Lady Mayoress was very successful. See no. **614**.

25   Anonymous report. *Musical Gazette* (Boston) 4/1 (1 June 1849): [5].

A trio of Americans leave for Europe:

> Wm. Mason, Francis G. Hill and Levi P. Homer, three young pianists of no small repute among the musical circles of Boston, sailed in the Steamship Herman [*sic*], for Breman [*sic*], April 20, to pursue their musical studies in Germany.

Homer may not have gone at this time. He is not mentioned as being a participant in the concert given on board ship on 1 May 1849. See nos. **23, 608**.

26   Anonymous report. *New York Musical Gazette* 1/10 (Aug 1867): 76.

Includes brief mention of a William Mason and Theodore Thomas educational venture.

> . . . William Mason & Theo. Thomas are about to establish a grand Conservatory of Music in this city [New York]. . . . Provision will be made for the best instruction in every branch of musical study.

See also nos. **27, 216, 351, 352, 353, 354**.

27   Anonymous report. *New York Musical Gazette* 1/12 (Oct 1867): 91.

An announcement that

> MR. S. B. MILLS is to be one of the professors in Mason & Thomas' new conservatoire.

See also nos. **26, 216, 351, 352, 353, 354**.

28   Anonymous report. *New York Times*, 15 Oct 1855, p. 4, col. 4.

An announcement of Mason's plans to organize an ensemble for the purpose of performing chamber music.

> A very desirable series of entertainments will commence shortly . . . when Mr. WILLIAM MASON . . . has started his *Matinées musicale*. . . . The programme will be composed of quartettes, trios and solos, all of which will be executed in the most perfect manner.

See no. **632**.

29   ANTRIM, Doron K. "A Musical Pioneer in America: Dr. William Mason." *Musical Observer* 27/12 (Dec 1928): 17-18.

      Pictures included. Contains an overview of Mason's career, emphasizing his work as a performer and teacher. Numerous quotations are made from Mason's *Memories of a Musical Life* (see no. **557**).

         I [Antrim] asked Thuel Burnham, who studied with Mason, what he considered Mason to be chiefly noted for in his teaching. "Tone," he said at once. "Mason had one of the most beautiful tones I have ever heard and he insisted on beautiful quality from his pupils. His thorough understanding of tone production enabled him to teach the subject intelligently."

      Also published by Antrim in a slightly revised and abridged form as ". . . Pioneer Piano Teacher in America," *Etude* 71/10 (Oct 1953): 26, 49, 64.

30   ANTRIM, Doron K. ". . . Pioneer Piano Teacher in America." *Etude* 71/10 (Oct 1953): 26, 49, 64.

      See previous item.

31   ANTRIM, Doron K. "Who Are the World's Greatest Piano Teachers?" *Etude* 71/2 (Feb 1953): 18, 20.

      Subtitled "How Would You Evaluate the Keyboard Technicians of the Past and Present? Here's a Striking Analysis Based on a Poll Conducted by Doron K. Antrim." Includes portrait. Antrim discusses the work of ten men: Muzio Clementi, John B. Cramer, Friedrich Wieck, Carl Czerny, Frédéric Chopin, Franz Liszt, Ludwig Deppe, Theodor Leschetizky, Tobias Matthay, and William Mason. Fannie Richards Pennypacker, in a letter to the editor, 72/1 (Jan 1954): 1, 3, in affirmation of the positive tone of Antrim's article regarding Mason's teaching, relates some of her experiences as a student of Mason.

32   ASHTON, Leonora Sill. "Technical Principles from the Classroom of Dr. William Mason." *Etude* 32/6 (June 1914): 420.

      A detailed, somewhat pedantic, set of instructions for teaching some of Mason's methods of piano touch.

33   *Baker's Biographical Dictionary of Musicians*, 7th ed. (1984). S.v. "Mason, William."

      Includes a biography, a partial list of compositions, and a one-item bibliography.

34   BERGENFELD, Nathan. "Piano Mastery: Profiles of Twentieth-Century Artist-Teachers." *Piano Quarterly* 75 (Spring 1971): 12-17.

The origin of Bergenfeld's article was his discovery of Harriette Brower's book *Piano Mastery* (see no. **49**). Material from Brower's book is used to create vignettes of nine artist-teachers: Teresa Carreño, Fannie Bloomfield Zeisler, Harold Bauer, Ignacy Jan Paderewski, Hans von Bülow, Edwin Hughes, Eleanor Spencer, William Mason, and Tobias Matthay. Mason's role as an exponent of the use of weight in playing is mentioned.

35   "The Binghamton Normal School." *New York Musical Gazette* 8/4 (Apr 1874): 248.

Announces that plans for the 1874 normal school in Binghamton, New York, have been dropped.

> The necessity which exists of holding the school at that season of the year which teachers usually devote to rest and recuperation is unfortunate.... Upon Dr. Mason and Mr. Webb, especially, both of whom have large classes in New York during nine or ten months of the year, the strain is excessive, and this Spring both gentlemen find the symptoms of overwork so serious that a vacation has become an imperative necessity. It is due to this fact principally that we are reluctantly compelled to give up holding a session of the school this summer.

36   *The Biographical Dictionary of America* . . . (1906), Rossiter Johnson, ed. in chief. S.v. "Mason, William."

Includes a concise biography (with portrait) and a short list of Mason's compositions and pedagogical works.

37   *Biographical Dictionary of Musicians: With a Bibliography of English Writings on Music.* London, 1886. S.v. "Mason, William," by James D. Brown.

Includes a thumbnail biographical sketch and a partial list of works.

38   "Biographies of American Musicians. Number Thirteen. William Mason." *Brainard's Musical World* 15/179 (Nov 1878): 169-70.

A five-column article. Includes Mason's biography (liberally sprinkled with anecdotes), a summary of his teaching methods, and a brief description of selected works. Among the anecdotes is a droll account of an incident involving Mason, Moscheles, and Liszt.

> On one occasion, when giving a lesson to a class, Moscheles was seated at the piano, illustrating a quiet position of the hands, and remarked that a friend of his in London used to require his pupils to play scales rapidly with a guinea piece on the back of their hands. "That's nothing," broke in Mason; I have a friend in New York who plays Chopin's Twelfth Study, in opus 10, *with a glass of water*

on his left hand!" "Dear me," said the good old Moscheles, "how very remarkable!" and never noticed the tongues suspiciously thrusting out one cheek of every boy in the class. . . . But Mason looked as innocent as Horace Greeley. (Some one told this story to Liszt a few years ago, and he said it didn't sound like Mason; for, in all the time he was with him—three years and a half—*he never heard him mention water*! . . .)

Excerpts from this story are also published as "William Mason as a Joker," *Score* 3/15 (Dec 1878): 271.

39   BONNER, Robert. "Congress of the American College of Musicians." *Etude* 11/6 (June 1893): 127.

Events scheduled for the meetings of the American College of Musicians in Chicago in 1893 are announced.

UNDER the auspices of the World's Fair Auxiliary, the American College of Musicians will hold a Congress in Chicago, Monday, July 3d. . . . Addresses are anticipated from . . . Past Chairman of the Pianoforte Examiners, Dr. William Mason, of New York, and others.

Apparently Mason was unable to carry out these plans. No evidence can be found indicating that he participated in, or even attended, the meetings. Also published with the same title, *Music Review* 2/9 (June 1893): 462.

40   BOWEN, Catherine Drinker. *"Free Artist": The Story of Anton and Nicholas Rubinstein.* New York: Random House, 1939.

Bowen makes several brief references to Mason's associations with Anton Rubinstein. In her description of Rubinstein's 1873 American concert tour, Bowen comments that

. . . [Mason] spent much time with Anton in New York, listening sympathetically to the bewildered questions of the Russian.

41   BOWMAN, Edward Morris. "The American College of Musicians: The Ally of the Competent Teacher." *Etude* 5/8 (Aug 1887): 109-10; 5/9 (Sept 1887): 121-22.

A paper read by Bowman at the 1887 MTNA meeting. Includes quotations from Mason's comments (made in a letter to Bowman?) about teaching legato touch.

A pure, *musically legato* touch must be the result of a naturally sensitive and musical ear; or, it may be developed by cultivating the habit of listening attentively while practicing. . . . A merely mechanically *legato* touch is no more to be desired than is mechanical poetry, and, in order to steer clear of this, the most careful attention should be given to *ear-cultivation* from the very outset.

42   BOWMAN, Edward Morris. "American Contributions to the Teaching of Piano-Playing: The Old and the New." *Musician* 17/12 (Dec 1912): 806-07.

Henri Bertini and Nathan Richardson are presented as representatives of the "old." Mason and A. K. Virgil are considered to be the standard-bearers of the "new." Mason's work receives a more detailed analysis than that of the others. Regarding Mason's *Touch and Technic*, op. 44, Bowman writes:

> . . . [Mason] sought continually to improve it. He was exacting to the last degree. His ideals continued to expand long after his physical strength began to wane. No effort, however great, was to him too costly a sacrifice to make in exchange for a nearer approach toward his ideal. . . . His sole reflection would naturally be expressed in the thought or the words "I wish that I could have done it better!"

43   BOWMAN, Edward Morris. "Dr. William Mason." *Pianist* 1/1 (Jan 1895): 5, 15.

Contains a concise biographical sketch and an assessment of Mason's contribution to the music profession. Bowman describes Mason's character as follows:

> Estimating him as a man, one has well said: "Dr. Mason is distinguished by his sterling integrity, his genuineness, his lack of pretension, his openness and candor, and his thoughtful consideration of others. He is quick to appreciate merit wherever found. . . . He is essentially and technically a *gentleman*, in the best sense of that abused word. . . ."

44   BOWMAN, Edward Morris. "A Glimpse into Dr. Mason's Studio." *Pianist* 1/2 (Feb 1895): 23-24.

Bowman gives a verbal description of Mason's studio in Steinway Hall. Includes a list of Mason's published compositions through op. 43.

45   BOWMAN, Edward Morris. "A Loving-Cup to Dr. Mason." *Etude* 17/3 (Mar 1899): 72.

An account of the party held in Steinway Hall on 24 January 1899 in celebration of Mason's seventieth birthday. Among the gifts Mason received was a loving cup from his pupils.

See also nos. **204, 432.**

46   BOWMAN, Edward Morris. "Reminiscences of Dr. William Mason." *Musical America* 11/2 (20 Nov 1909): 6, 35.

Pictures included. Bowman recalls some of the day-to-day experiences he shared with Mason as a fellow occupant of Steinway Hall.

It was the custom of every pianist coming to this country . . . to come
to . . . [Mason's] studio to pay his respects. . . . This studio has been
a veritable musical Mecca for great pianists and distinguished artists
in other branches of the musical profession. If its walls could speak,
they could repeat many an interesting conversation or reproduce
many a wonderful performance.

47   BOWMAN, Edward Morris. "With Dr. Mason in the Studio." *Etude* 26/9
       (Sept 1908): 559-60.

       Includes picture. After tracing the history of his own professional relation-
       ship with Mason, Bowman gives synopses of Mason's method of teaching,
       style of performance, technique of composition, and status as a teacher.
       Regarding Mason's teaching, Bowman comments:

           At school we were taught the "three R's." From William Mason
           we learned to set equal store on the three H's, namely:
               To understand with the Head. Intelligence.
               To feel with the Heart. Emotion.
               To express with the Hand. Execution.
           Dr. Mason's pedagogic system laid equal stress on each of these three.

       According to Bowman, a student in Mason's studio also learned that

           . . . [one should] practice according to the way the master preached,
           namely: SLOWLY, ACCURATELY, MUSICALLY.

48   BOYD, Patricia Williams. "Performers, Pedagogues, and Pertinent Method-
       ological Literature of the Pianoforte in Mid-Nineteenth Century United
       States, *ca.* 1830-1880: A Socio-Cultural Study." D.A. diss., Ball State
       University, 1975. 461 pp. UM 75-21458. *Dissertation Abstracts* 36/4
       (Oct 1975): 1885-86-A.

       Includes a short biography of Mason and an outline summary of the contents
       of his *Touch and Technic*, op. 44.

49   BROWER, Harriette. *Piano Mastery: Talks with Master Pianists and
       Teachers and an Account of a von Bülow Class; Hints on Interpretation
       by Two American Teachers (Dr. William Mason and William H.
       Sherwood) and a Summary by the Author.* New York: Frederick A.
       Stokes, 1915.

       Includes picture. Brower describes some of her lessons with Mason and para-
       phrases Mason's comments about general principles of piano performance
       as well as the interpretation of specific works—Schumann's *Sonata in F
       Minor*, op. 14, and Grieg's *Concerto in A Minor*, op. 16.

           . . . do not hurry in fugue playing, a universal fault. Bach needs
           a slower trill than modern music. Chords are not to be played with
           percussion but with pressure.

       See also no. 34.

50   BURGESS, John W. *Reminiscences of an American Scholar: The Beginning of Columbia University.* Foreword by Nicholas Murray Butler. New York: Columbia University Press, 1934; reprint, New York: AMS Press, 1966.

Burgess's book includes an account of the events leading to the appointment of Edward MacDowell to the newly endowed chair of music at Columbia University in 1896. Mason became actively involved in the selection process. His support for MacDowell was an important factor in the latter's appointment to the position.

See also nos. **20, 206.**

51   CALHOUN, William Lawrence. "Comparative Piano Methods." *Music* 18 (Oct 1900): 539-50.

The text of a paper read at a meeting of the Missouri State Teachers Association on 15 June 1900. Mason's work in piano pedagogy is mentioned briefly, with special note being made of his octave exercises.

> In the fourth book of his technics [*Touch and Technic*, op. 44], the one devoted to octave-playing, . . . [Mason] makes an important contribution to piano pedagogics, in that he is the first to define the function of the upper arm.

52   CAMPBELL, L. "What the Mason System Has Done for Me." *Etude* 16/10 (Oct 1898): 302.

A weakly written article in which Campbell credits Mason's system of technique for loosening up his playing, which had become stiff after studying in Germany.

53   "Cause and Effect in Pianoforte Touch: A Symposium." *Music* 6 (May 1894): 84-98.

This article grew out of a lecture given by J. B. Lang on "Cause and Effect in Piano Playing" in which he stated that because of the nature of the piano's action, no control of the hammers is possible other than to vary the degree of force with which they strike the strings, and that, consequently, all so-called tonal shading by means of touch is illusory. Reactions to Lang's ideas were solicited from a number of musicians by the editor of *Music*. Responses from Constantin Sternberg, Hans von Schiller, Carl Faelten, William H. Sherwood, Julia Caruthers, J. H. Hahn, Calvin B. Cady, August Hyllested, Arthur Foote, and H. A. Kelso, Jr., are published in this article. Later issues of *Music* included the views of other musicians, including Beveridge Webster (no. **449**), H. A. Kelso, Jr. (no. **181**), and William Mason. Mason's comments were made in a letter (*Music* 6 [June 1894]: 261-67), which included some points of disagreement with Lang's statements.

> . . . I am of the opinion that the tones of the Piano can be modified, both in quantity and quality, by means of different varieties of touch combined with the intelligent use of the pedals. Different degrees

of devitalization of the muscles deftly applied, and combined with simultaneous or syncopated use of the pedal, will undoubtedly cause a distinct crescendo in the tone after the finger-fall has taken place.

54   *Celebration of the Thirty-Fifth Anniversary of the Orange Valley Church of Orange, New Jersey . . . 1861-1896.* Newark, N.J.: L. J. Hardman, n.d.

A commemorative booklet. In the account of the planning of the anniversary celebration, it is noted that

> Many letters of invitation had been sent to clergymen and other friends at a distance, who sent messages of regret at not being able to be present. Among them . . . [was one] from Dr. William Mason, who had been invited to occupy his old seat at the organ on this occasion, but was detained by physical infirmity.

The booklet also tells of Mason's early involvement in the music program of the church.

> To Dr. William Mason also the church was indebted for his great care and skill in the choice and purchase of the organ, and for his gratuitous services as organist for more than ten years.

The new organ referred to above was installed in 1868. In addition to overseeing the purchase of the instrument, Mason was also involved in fund raising.

> . . . on March 12th of that year [1868], a concert was given in Library Hall [of Orange] by Mr. William Mason, assisted by Mr. Theodore Thomas and others, for the benefit of the organ fund . . . , which netted $500. The organ, which cost nearly $5,000, . . . was first used at a Sunday service August 1st, 1868, and from that time on until failing health made it necessary for him to go abroad, it was presided over by Dr. Mason, with a skill and delicacy of touch that made the Orange Valley Church famous far and wide.

See also no. **674.**

55   [*Century Magazine.*] Announcement of the imminent publication of Mason's "Memories of a Musical Life." *Etude* 18/6 (June 1900): 239.

> The managers of "The Century Magazine" take great pleasure in announcing that . . . the Reminiscences of Dr. William Mason . . . will be a feature of "The Century Magazine." "The Century" has printed many articles of great interest to musical people, — articles by Gounod, Grieg, Moszkowsky, and other well-known composers, but never in its history has it presented any papers that will give more delight to musical people than these reminiscences.

See also no. **557.**

56   *A Century of Service, 1860-1960: Historical Sketch of the Highland Avenue Congregational Church, Orange, New Jersey. Published on the Occasion of the 100th Anniversary Celebration, 1960.* N.p., n.d.

A commemorative booklet. The historical sketch includes an account of the music performed in the church during the early years of its existence.

His [Lowell Mason's] son, Dr. William Mason, was its first organist, and we read of his playing the harmonium for the congregational singing in the original church. [The cornerstone of the church was laid on 12 September 1859, and the edifice was completed and dedicated in January 1860.] He continued to be the organist when the new church was built. [The cornerstone was laid on 21 June 1867.]

57   "Chamber Music." *Music: A Review* 2/1 (8 Apr 1882): 4.

Includes a brief review of the history of chamber music performances in New York.

Years ago Mr. Thomas[,] William Mason and others gave several series of the best chamber music concerts that has ever been offered to the New York public, either before or since, but with the most disastrous financial results. . . .

58   CHAN, Anne Hui-Hua. "Beethoven in the United States to 1865." Ph.D. diss., University of North Carolina, 1976. 238 pp. UM 77-17308. *Dissertation Abstracts* 38/2 (Aug 1977): 536-A.

Chan discusses the importance of both the Mason-Thomas Quartette's chamber concerts and Mason's solo recitals in introducing Beethoven's works in America.

From his [Mason's] debut he strove for high standards, including in his programs more of serious piano music than the general trend for that period in America. It was Mason who first realized many of Beethoven's sonatas in sound for the first time before audiences outside of the three big eastern centers — New York, Boston, and Philadelphia.

59   CHASE, Gilbert. *America's Music: From the Pilgrims to the Present.* Rev. 3d ed., with a foreword by Richard Crawford and a discographical essay by William Brooks. Urbana: University of Illinois Press, 1987.

Chase includes several quotations from Mason's *Memories of a Musical Life.* He also comments briefly on the influence of the Mason family on nineteenth-century American musical life.

The reader is familiar with the name of Mason and what it stands for in America's music: the transition from the singing-school tradition of early New England to the "better music" movement of Lowell Mason and the aesthetic refinement of William Mason. Daniel Gregory was the nephew of William, and with him this New England dynasty reaches its culmination in an almost ecstatic surrender to the potent spell of the European Classic-Romantic tradition.

60   "The Children of Lowell Mason." *Song Messenger: A Musical Monthly* 10/9 (Sept 1872): 133.

Outlines the careers of Lowell Mason's four sons: Daniel Gregory, Lowell, Jr., William, and Henry.

> . . . William, the pianist, is carrying forward the work begun by his father, and diffusing among the American people . . . an appreciation for what is true and enduring in music.

61   "Church Music in New York." *Boston Daily Evening Transcript*, 7 Mar 1861, p. [1], cols. 1-2.

A summary (signed "AMATEUR") of the music programs of several New York churches, including the New Jerusalem Church on 35th Street, where Mason was then serving as organist.

> Mr. Wm. Mason . . . is one of our most talented organists. His merits as a pianist are well known and appreciated by all lovers of classical music; but it is not generally known that he also stands in the front ranks as a performer upon the organ. His playing belongs to the strict school of sacred music, and he ignores entirely the modern secular style, as inappropriate to the service of the church.

Mason's performances on the organ seem to have usually been done *ex tempore*. A review of such an improvisation by Mason when he was the organist at the Fifth Avenue Presbyterian Church in New York is cited:

> In nine cases out of ten, you know beforehand what is to come next in an organ voluntary, just as you know how nine out of ten newspaper stories are to end — or, if your ear is disappointed, it is because the organist knows not where to go nor what to do next. But Mason's themes were so fresh, his episodes so unexpected yet so pleasing, the forms adopted so varied — now a solo with answering chorus from the box celestore [*sic*], now the full rolling masses of tone from the grand organ, and at last a fugue moving onward with stately steps — that the ear was constantly and delightfully disappointed, the fancy continually excited, and the musical sense filled with enjoyment.

This article was also published as "Church Music in New York," *Dwight's Journal of Music* 19/1 (6 Apr 1861): 4.

62   "Church Opera." *New York Musical World: A Literary and Fine-Art Paper* 17/321 (23 May 1857): 322.

A review of the public exhibition of a new organ which had just been installed by Jardine and Son in the North Presbyterian Church on Ninth Avenue in New York. Mason performed two voluntaries, the first of which seemed to be out of step with the rest of the evening's entertainment.

> The services were introduced with (as it afterward seemed) rather mistaken solemnity by Mr. Wm. Mason, his voluntary being such as to inspire quite a churchly feeling. . . . This was soon corrected, however, by Mr. Lasar, the organist of the church, who followed Mr. Mason with an exhilarating dash of arias from the opera of *Il Trovatore*, which both served as a reproof to Mr. Mason and lightened our minds of any burden of seriousness left upon them by that injudicious gentleman.

Mason's second appearance—in the opinion of the reviewer—demonstrated a marked improvement in that

> . . . he seemed to have profited somewhat by Mr. Lasar's practical admonition, and before he got through varied ingeniously . . . that dear little song, "On the lake where drooped the willow."

63   CLAGHORN, Charles Eugene. *Biographical Dictionary of American Music.* West Nyack, N.Y.: Parker Publishing Co., 1973. S.v. "Mason, William."

A brief entry. Claghorn mentions some of the highlights of Mason's career.

64   CLARKE, Garry E. *Essays on American Music.* Contributions in American History, no. 62. Westport, Conn.: Greenwood Press, 1977.

Includes several quotations from Mason's writings in regard to Gottschalk's playing and compositions.

65   CLARKE, James Wesley. "Prof. W. S. B. Mathews (1837-1912): Self-Made Musician of the Gilded Age." Ph.D. diss., University of Minnesota, 1983. 323 pp. UM 83-18053. *Dissertation Abstracts* 44/4 (Oct 1983): 903-A.

A complementary work to the dissertation by Groves (see no. **130**). Clarke's study contains nine chapters: 1) "W. S. B. Mathews: A Biographical Sketch"; 2) "Mathews as Musical Missionary"; 3) "Mathews as Pedagogue"; 4) "Mathews as Advisor to the Profession"; 5) "Mathews as Writer"; 6) "Mathews as Editor"; 7) "Mathews and Music in the United States"; 8) "Mathews, Aesthetics, and Culture"; and 9) "To Light a Candle." The professional relationship of Mason and Mathews and the reciprocity of their work are discussed. The bibliography includes a list of Mathews's writings.

66   [COLLINS, William Francis.] "Dr. Wm. Mason." In his *Laurel Winners: Portraits and Silhouettes of American Composers*, 24-25. Cincinnati: John Church Co., 1898.

Includes a biographical sketch and a brief discussion of Mason's works.

67   "Concert Giving." *Boston Daily Evening Transcript*, 3 Oct 1854, p. [2], col. 1.

A sequel to "Overdoing the Matter" (see no. **369**).

68   "Concert Giving." *Dwight's Journal of Music* 6/1 (7 Oct 1854): 5.

A sequel to "Overdoing the Matter" (see no. **369**).

69   CONVERSE, Charles Crozat. "Reminiscences of Some Famous Musicians." *Etude* 30/10 (Oct 1912): 695-96.

Subtitled "Written Expressly for THE ETUDE by the Well-Known American Composer. . . ." Picture included. A short monograph outlining the careers of three musicians active in America during the nineteenth century: Louis Moreau Gottschalk, William Vincent Wallace, and William Mason. In regard to Mason, Converse states:

> He came back from his wonderful experiences with Moscheles, Hauptmann, Richter, Dreyschock and Liszt representing the forward movement in pianistic art in America. Like his father, Dr. Lowell Mason, he was very progressive, brilliant and tactful. His insight into educational problems at the keyboard was nothing short of remarkable. . . .

70   COOKE, James Francis. "Theodore Presser (1848-1925): A Centenary Biography, Part Six." *Etude* 66/12 (Dec 1948): 728, 781.

Includes picture. Cooke mentions Mason's professional relationship with Theodore Presser.

> In the same period [1890s] Mr. Presser published William Mason's "Touch and Technic" in four volumes. . . . "Touch and Technic," like . . . [William Smythe Babcock Mathews's] "Standard Graded Course," was a great success. These books, together with the mounting sales of all kinds of musical publications, brought Mr. Presser prosperity beyond his wildest dreams.

71   "Correspondence, Binghamton, New York, July 25th, 1871." *New York Musical Gazette* 5/8 (Aug 1871): 114-15.

An account (signed "HARLA") of the activities of the first three weeks of the normal school held in Binghamton. Includes the programs for three lecture-recitals given by Mason on July 15, 18, and 21.

> . . . [Mason's] recitals are accompanied by explanatory remarks, and are of inestimable practical value to the piano pupil.

See also nos. **2, 248, 253, 273, 358.**

72   "Correspondence . . . , New York, July 21st, 1854." *Boston Daily Evening Transcript*, 24 July 1854, p. [2], col. 2.

The letter (signed "X") includes brief mention of Mason's plans for returning to America from his European studies.

> I have learned, by private letters, that "our Boston boy," William Mason, was to sail from Liverpool on the 12th inst. in the Pacific. We may, therefore, expect to shake hands with him in a few days. He will not give any concerts before fall. He is now considered one of the best pianists in the world, and you Bostonians may well be proud of him.

Excerpts from the letter are also published as "Wm. Mason," *New York Musical Review and Choral Advocate* 5/16 (3 Aug 1854): 273.

73   CURRIER, T. P. "American Pioneers of Modern Piano Playing and Their
      Successors." *Musician* 17/12 (Dec 1912): 810-11; 18/1 (Jan 1913): 62-63.

      Currier analyzes the performance style of those pianists who he believes
      concertized sufficiently in this country to exert a significant influence on
      the art of piano playing in America. Besides Mason, some of the pianists
      mentioned are Gottschalk, William H. Sherwood, Rafael Joseffy, and
      Emil Liebling.

           William Mason's prolonged and intimate association with Liszt gave
           him opportunities which comparatively few others had to become
           familiar with the new technic which Liszt had evolved. His touch,
           passage playing, and pedalling were not only fine for those days,
           but revolutionary.

74   *Cyclopedia of Music and Musicians* (1888-90), ed. John Denison Champlin,
      Jr., critically ed. William Foster Apthorp. S.v. "Mason, William."

      A two-column entry. Includes a concise biography and a partial list of works.

75   DEGUIRE, William, ed. *The America Book for Piano.* . . . New York:
      Galaxy Music, 1975.

      Includes brief biographical notes about Mason as well as several of his
      compositions: *Lullaby*, op. 10; duos nos. 1 and 5 from *Teacher and Pupil*,
      op. 26; and *Home Sweet Home: A One-Finger Pedal Study* (see nos. **711,
      729-36, 769**).

76   "Departure of Mr. Lowell Mason for Europe." *Musical Review and Choral
      Advocate* 3/1 (1 Jan 1852): 10.

      Includes information on the activities of William Mason.

           One object of this journey is to visit his sons, Messrs. William and
           Henry Mason. The former, Mr. William Mason, it is known to
           most of our readers, has been for several years in Germany. . . . He
           gives the most brilliant promise for the future, and has already
           excited considerable attention in Prague and other cities where he
           has resided by his extraordinary musical attainments. . . . Mr.
           William Mason, it will be remembered, will hereafter be one of our
           stated correspondents.

77   DESPARD, Mabel H. *The Music of the United States, Its Sources and Its
      History: A Short Outline.* New York: J. H. H. Muirhead, 1936.

      Despard makes note of the work of both Lowell and William Mason in the
      development of music in America.

           Steadily, slowly, through the years of the young republic the seeds
           of American musicianship were sprouting, nourished by devoted

pioneers—teachers, publishers, [and] benefactors. . . . Lowell Mason's record [in this work] has been nobly supplemented by his son William, long Dean of American teachers of music. . . .

78   *Dictionary of American Biography* (1933). S.v. "Mason, William," by Frederick H. Martens.

     Includes a short biography, mention of a few works, a brief discussion of Mason's influence as a teacher, and a select bibliography.

79   *Dictionary of American Portraits: 4045 Pictures of Important Americans from Earliest Times to the Beginning of the Twentieth Century* (1967), ed. Hayward and Blanche Cirker, et al. S.v. "William Mason."

     Includes Mason's portrait, his dates of birth and death, and mention of his occupation.

80   *A Dictionary of North American Authors Deceased before 1950* (1951), comp. W. Stewart Wallace. S.v. 'Mason, William."

     Includes the places and dates of Mason's birth and death and a brief commentary on his work.

81   "A Disciple of Dr. William Mason." *Musical Courier* 51/25 (20 Dec 1905): 48.

     A brief sketch of Miss Martha Walther, Mason's pupil and, for many years, principal teaching assistant. Includes excerpts from two letters of recommendation written by Mason on Walther's behalf.

82   "Domestic Items." *Musical Times* 4/7 (20 Dec 1851): 109.

     Includes reports on the imminent departure of Lowell and Abigail Mason for Europe and on some of William Mason's activities in Leipzig.

         Lowell Mason and lady, of Boston, sail today in the Arctic, for Liverpool, on their way to Germany. . . . The object of the present visit to Europe is partly musical . . . and partly personal, being to visit two of his sons [William and Henry] who are at present residing in Germany. . . . We have learned that [William] . . . is to appear at the Gewandhaus concerts in Leipsic, this winter. . . .

     Plans for Mason's performance at the Gewandhaus must have been canceled. No documentation can be found that he performed at the Gewandhaus, or in any other public concert, in Leipzig.

83   "Dr. Mason and the Pressure Touch." *Music* 9 (Jan 1896): 322.

Cites an article from the *Toronto Week* which criticizes Mason's ideas on "pressure touch."

> . . . pressure touch has been lauded and praised to the skies, as if it were the beginning and end of everything pertaining to beauty of touch and tone. I do not think so. As a fundamental principle pressure touch is both mischievous, misleading and injurious. It destroys perfect naturalness and looseness of finger action, and abnormally develops the muscles of the wrist and lower arm.

Mason, in a letter dated 15 November 1895 (*Music* 9 [Jan 1896]: 323-24), responded to the contents of the *Toronto Week* article.

> I AM in such a rush that I have had no time to think about the extract from the "*Week*" which was enclosed. It seems impossible for me to make myself understood on the subject to which it has reference, and this is because some writers persist in emphasizing a part of the directions given in Touch and Technic out of all proportion. . . . If anything is insisted on all through the work it is the absolute essentiality of a constant and immediate relaxation of the muscles at the moment the blow is delivered. . . . Of course there must be some contraction or flaccidity and tameness would result, but the contraction, must be simultaneously accompanied by the "recover" in relaxation.

The *Toronto Week* article, with minor editorial changes, and Mason's letter were also published in "Dr. Mason and the Pressure Touch," *Etude* 14/4 (Apr 1896): 81.

84   "Dr. William Mason." *Brainard's Musical World* 29/347 (Nov 1892): 347.

Picture included. A summary of Mason's life through 1892; most of the high points of Mason's career as a student, performer, and teacher are mentioned.

85   "Dr. William Mason." *Musical Age* 25/1 (9 Feb 1899): 6.

A biographical sketch of the first seventy years of Mason's life.

> At a very early age Dr. Mason exhibited marked talent. . . . Dr. Lowell Mason had no desire that his son should follow the profession of music, nevertheless Master William persevered in self-study, and under his mother's supervision practiced daily, finally mastering the elementary principles of the art.

86   "Dr. William Mason." *Musician* 7/5 (May 1902): 150.

Simply a picture of Mason "from his latest photo."

87   "Dr. William Mason." *New York Musical Gazette* 7/10 (July 1873): 97-98.

Picture included. An informative biographical summary. Includes a one-column discussion of Mason's piano compositions.

It had been his father's desire that . . . [William] be educated for the ministry; but as in the case of the two elder brothers [Daniel Gregory and Lowell, Jr.], so here Providence pointed to a different field. . . .

88   "Dr. William Mason Dead at His Eightieth Year" (obituary). *Musical Age* 62/12 (18 July 1908): 278.

Picture included. Subtitled "Famous as the First Pianist to Give Concerts Alone in This Country—Was Intimate with Leading Musical Thought for Half a Century."

The funeral was held on July 16 and was attended by many of the most prominent musical people in the city.

89   "Dr. William Mason Dead" (obituary). *Music Trade Review* 47/3 (18 July 1908): 18-19.

Picture included. Subtitled "The Distinguished Musician and Teacher Reached His 80th Year and Was Teaching until Last Winter."

90   "Dr. William Mason Dead" (obituary). *New York Commercial*, 15 July 1908, p. 2, col. 6.

Subtitled "Well-Known Musician Had Written Many Works on Piano Instruction."

Death resulted from general debility incident to advanced age.

91   "Dr. William Mason Dead" (obituary). *Sun* (New York), 15 July 1908, p. 4, col. 2.

Dr. William Mason, the musician and pianist, died yesterday at his home. . . . Dr. Mason gave up active teaching early last winter, but had gone occasionally to his studio in Steinway Hall until three weeks ago. He was ill in bed but a few days.

92   "Dr. William Mason Dies" (obituary). *Musical America* 8/10 (18 July 1908): 5.

Picture included. Subheading reads "Career of America's Most Distinguished Pianist and Pedagog Ends During His Eightieth Year."

Dr. Mason gave up active teaching early last Winter, but had gone occasionally to his studio in Steinway Hall until three weeks ago.

93   "Dr. William Mason" (obituary). *Boston Daily Advertiser*, 16 July 1908, p. [8], col. 5.

A four-paragraph notice of Mason's death.

94 "Dr. William Mason" (obituary). *Musical Courier* 57/4 (22 July 1908): 24.

Picture included.

> Dr. William Mason, the well-known American pianist, teacher and composer, died at his home last Tuesday, in this city, 1 West Eighty-first street, after a short illness of several days, caused by an attack of heart disease and general debility.

95 "Dr. William Mason" (obituary). *New Music Review and Church Music Review* 7/82 (Sept 1908): 562.

Picture included.

> Dr. Mason's piano playing, in his prime, was an experience which no one sensitive to its rare charm could ever forget—an experience which is now irrecoverable, and which no words can describe. . . . His most far-reaching influence for the upbuilding of American music, however, was unquestionably exerted through his teaching. . . . For half a century Dr. Mason communicated to his pupils, men and women, professional and amateur, whatever they could individually grasp of his keen sense of tonal beauty as elicited by an incomparable touch, of his jealously accurate perception of rhythm, and of that characteristic conscientiousness and integrity of his nature which made a lesson with him almost as much a moral as an artistic experience.

96 "Dr. William Mason" (obituary). *New York American*, 16 July 1908, p. 2, col. 7.

A short notice of Mason's death.

97 "Dr. William Mason" (obituary). *Orange Advertiser*, 17 July 1908, p. [8], col. 3.

> Dr. William Mason, known as one of the foremost musicians, composers and teachers of America, died Tuesday at his home in the Hotel Beresford, New York. He was in his eightieth year and had been actively engaged in teaching until the past winter.

98 "Dr. William Mason, Pianist, Dies at 79" (obituary). *Boston Herald*, 15 July 1908, p. [3], col. 6.

Subheadings read: "Was First to Give Entire Concert Programme Alone—Born in Boston"; "Father Was Famous Dr. Lowell Mason"; "Spent the Greater Part of His Life as Resident of New York."

99 DUMM, Robert W. "Liszt's Piano Teaching: 1884-1886." *Journal of the American Liszt Society* 4 (Dec 1978): 23-36.

Although the main thrust of the article concerns Liszt's teaching methods from 1884-86 as reflected in August Göllerich's *Franz Liszts Klavierunterricht . . .* (Regensburg: Gustav Bosse Verlag, 1975), Dumm also gives an overview of Liszt's teaching style during the rest of his career. In his description of Liszt's teaching methods in the 1850s, Dumm includes extensive quotations from Mason's *Memories of a Musical Life.*

> Where to turn first [for information about Liszt's teaching in the 1850s]? One of the better places would be to William Mason, . . . who not only fulfilled his promise in Liszt's inner circle but continued for eminent years teaching in New York City those Americans who either did not get to Europe, or who returned to him for "finishing" after a brief stint there.

100   DWIGHT, John Sullivan. "The History of Music in Boston." In *The Memorial History of Boston, Including Suffolk County, Massachusetts, 1630-1880*, vol. 4, pp. 415-64. Ed. Justin Winsor. Boston: James R. Osgood & Co., 1880-81.

An interesting survey of Boston's musical life. Mason's participation in the series of chamber music concerts given by the Harvard Musical Association in 1846-47 is noted. Dwight also writes about two young Boston pianists who returned to their native city in 1854 following a period of study in Europe.

> In 1854 two of our own Boston aspirants brought home fruits of study from the Conservatorium of Leipsic. Mr. J. C. D. Parker was the first son of Harvard to forsake a dry profession (the Law) and follow the ruling passion of his life, devoting it professionally to the "higher law" of music. He at once became quietly but steadily active as pianist, organist, composer, teacher, and director of a vocal club. . . . The other young Bostonian who came back that year was the pianist William Mason (son of Dr. Lowell Mason), who after a few seasons settled in New York, where he ranks among the foremost teachers and pianists.

101   DWIGHT, John Sullivan. "Musical Review: The Prospects for the Season." *Harbinger* 3/19 (17 Oct 1846): 301.

Dwight eagerly anticipates the scheduled performances of chamber music:

> But nothing gives us so great pleasure as to be able to announce . . . the Harvard Musical Association . . . Chamber Concerts. The very quintessence of music will this be, . . . played by artists, and heard by the most select and appreciating audience to be found in Boston. In the course of these concerts, besides Mr. Lange and Mr. William Mason, pianists from New York are expected to take part, as Mr. Perabeau and Mr. Scharfenberg.

Mason ended up playing for all of the concerts.

102   EATON, Quaintance, ed. *Musical U.S.A.: How Music Developed in the Major American Cities.* . . . New York: Allen, Towne & Heath, 1949.

Includes a picture of the Mason-Thomas Quartette.

103   "Edward Morris Bowman" (obituary). *Musician* 18/10 (Oct 1913): 712.

His study with William Mason and his long and intimate association with that great teacher in after years, made him well-known as an exponent of Dr. Mason's system, and, after the death of the latter, as a representative of the method, although his individuality was too marked for him to be nothing more than a disciple.

104   EDWARDS, Arthur C., and W. Thomas MARROCCO. *Music in the United States.* The Brown Music Horizons Series. Dubuque, Iowa: Wm. C. Brown, 1968.

A short description of Mason's life and work is included.

His [Mason's] many compositions, mostly piano pieces, are in the typical Chopinesque style of rather free melodic figuration, regular rhythm and harmony but loosely knit forms. . . .

105   Elders' Minutes, Fifth Avenue Presbyterian Church, New York City.

The resignation of Mason as organist of the Fifth Avenue Presbyterian Church is documented in the Elders' Minutes of 5 May 1860:

Mr. William Mason resigned at the end of his term [evidently May 1].

Mason had begun his tenure as organist on 7 October 1855.

106   ELSON, Louis C. *The History of American Music.* Rev. to 1925 by Arthur Elson. History of American Art. New York: Macmillan Co., 1925; reprint, New York: B. Franklin, 1971.

Includes a picture of the Mason-Thomas chamber music ensemble and a portrait of Mason. A fairly complete biographical sketch is contained in the primary entry on Mason; additional brief references to him are scattered throughout the text.

It was very different with the American student abroad, in the middle of the nineteenth century, from what it is to-day. There was no great band of cisatlantic enthusiasts to be found in the conservatories at that time; J. C. D. Parker, the superficial Richardson . . . , and Mason were three of the earliest of the American Jasons. And it was different with Liszt, also, in 1853, from what it became in his later years. There was no cosmopolitan crowd of worshippers at the Weimar shrine, but in its place a small, highly appreciative artistic coterie. The young Mason became the companion and friend, as well as the pupil, of the great pianist.

107   ELSON, Louis C. "The Pioneers of American Music." *Etude* 32/3 (Mar 1914): 171-72; 32/5 (May 1914): 331-32.

Elson discusses Mason's work only superficially. His comments place greatest emphasis on the Mason-Thomas chamber music performances.

108   ESSEX [not otherwise identified]. Letter, Orange, N.J., 15 Dec 1869. *New York Musical Gazette* 4/3 (Jan 1870): 18.

Mason's teaching is mentioned.

> There is another Orange citizen whose residence among us is of immense practical benefit. That is William Mason . . . who, as he has for a number of years devoted one day in the week to teaching here, has done wonders for us in educating the popular taste.

109   "The Etude Gallery of Musical Celebrities." *Etude* 27/9 (Sept 1909): 591-92.

Subtitled "A Group of Famous American Composers." Includes a picture and biographical sketch of William Mason.

110   "The Exhibition of the Manuscript Society." *Pianist* 1/11 (Nov 1895): 206-07.

A description of the manuscripts exhibited by the New York Manuscript Society in connection with the opening of their new clubrooms at 17 East 22d Street.

> The most important and valuable single item contributed to the display is, without doubt, the autograph album of Dr. William Mason, loaned by his daughter. This is a veritable treasure-house of musical reminiscences, containing, as it does, the friendly testimonials, for the most part in connection with musical themes or extracts, of many of the most celebrated musicians of this century.

The collection of autographs referred to is probably that now housed at Columbia University.

See also nos. **411, 1016.**

111   FIELD, Carl. "A Word for American Composers." *Musical Courier* 44/10 (5 Mar 1902): 29.

A brief article of limited value in which Field examines the status of American composers and teachers. Mason's role in promoting the work of American musicians is acknowledged.

> DR. WILLIAM MASON'S recent work, entitled "Memories of a Musical Life," is attracting the attention of the best music critics and musicians, and will do more to place the work of American teachers and composers on a just and acknowledged plane of excellence than anything that has happened to them in a long time, both in this country and in Europe.

112   FIELDS, Annie. *Authors and Friends.* Boston and New York: Houghton Mifflin Co., 1896.

Includes comments about Mason's relationship with Celia Thaxter, the author.

> Later in life came Mr. William Mason, who was the chief minister to her joy in music, her enlightener, her consoler, to the end.

113   FILLMORE, John Comfort. "Dr. William Mason." *Etude* 7/11 (Nov 1889): 169.

Picture included. A three-column biography, including an account of Mason's childhood, study in Europe, friendship with Liszt, and work in the United States as a teacher, composer, and performer. The article—unsigned, in a slightly abridged form, with a more recent photo and an editor's note telling of Mason's death—was also published as "Life of Dr. William Mason, 1829-1908" (obituary), *Etude* 26/9 (Sept 1908): 555.

114   FINCK, Henry T. "William Mason: A Model Teacher." *Etude* 26/9 (Sept 1908): 557-58.

Under larger heading entitled "Tributes to Dr. Mason. . . ." Picture included. A potpourri of Mason's philosophies and methods of teaching.

> He held pronounced views as to the importance of providing good instruments for beginners. An expert pianist, he said, can get a fairly good tone out of almost any piano, but young folks ought to have their ear for beauty cultivated by having mellow tones at their command from the beginning.

115   FISHER, William Arms. *One Hundred and Fifty Years of Music Publishing in the United States.* . . . Boston: Oliver Ditson Co., 1933; reprint, St. Clair Shores, Mich.: Scholarly Press, 1977.

An expanded and revised edition of Fisher's *Notes on Music in Old Boston* (Boston: Oliver Ditson Co., 1918). Fisher mentions Mason's performance at a concert of the Boston Academy of Music on 7 March 1846, "his first appearance as a pianist" (see no. **587**).

116   "Foreign Musical News." *Musical World and New York Musical Times* 5/11 (12 Mar 1853): 164.

Includes a report, probably somewhat exaggerated, of Mason's popularity in the aristocratic circles of London during his brief residence there in 1853.

> WM. MASON is fast winning a reputation in London. . . . We learn that he is much sought after privately by the aristocrati *diletanti* [sic] of that aristocratic Capital, who make all sorts of musical parties for his benefit, and who have, in short, taken him under their especial care and guardianship.

117   GATES, W. F., comp. *Musical Mosaics: A Collection of Six Hundred Selections from Musical Literature, Ancient and Modern, Including Extracts from Many Later Critical and Aesthetical Writings.* Philadelphia: Theodore Presser, 1889.

See nos. **489, 577.**

118   GERIG, Reginald R. *Famous Pianists & Their Technique.* 3d ed. Washington: Robert B. Luce, 1978.

Gerig gives a lucid presentation and analysis of the main principles of Mason's system of piano technique. Includes musical examples and quotations from Mason's writings.

119   GILLESPIE, John, ed. *Nineteenth-Century American Piano Music.* New York: Dover Publications, 1978.

Gillespie gives a brief biographical sketch of Mason (includes a picture) in the Introduction (p. xiii). Mason's *Silver Spring*, op. 6, and *Novelette*, op. 31, no. 2, are in the collection of music (see nos. **703, 741-42**).

120   GILLESPIE, John, and Anna GILLESPIE. *A Bibliography of Nineteenth-Century American Piano Music: With Location Sources and Composer Biography-Index.* Music Reference Collection, no. 2. Westport, Conn.: Greenwood Press, 1984.

Includes a short biography of Mason and a list (with library locations) of more than forty of his piano works.

121   GOLDMAN, Richard Franko. "Those Forgotten American Composers." *Hi Fi/Stereo Review* 20/2 (Feb 1968): 114-15.

Goldman summarizes the history of the series of recordings (*Music in America: Pianoforte Music of the 19th Century*) issued by the Society for the Preservation of the American Musical Heritage. The recordings of Mason's compositions (see Preface) are not discussed.

122   "Gone to Europe." Unidentified clipping in MASON/Scrapbook.

A brief statement that

> William Mason, the pianist and composer, who surprised and gratified our citizens some months since by his exquisite skill as a performer, started on the 22d of this month [April 1849] for Europe.

The date is incorrect. Mason left on April 20.

123   GOODMAN, Alfred. *Die amerikanischen Schüler Franz Liszts.* Veröffentlichungen zur Musikforschung, Band 1. Wilhelmshaven: Heinrichshofen's Verlag, 1972.

     After some introductory comments about American music and Liszt's international standing and method of teaching, Goodman discusses the work of the following American students of Liszt: William Mason, Amy Fay, Otis Bardwell Boise, Silas Gamaliel Pratt, Carl Valentine Lachmund, Arthur Bird, Albert Morris Bagby, Richard Burmeister, Edward MacDowell, and Alexander Siloti. Goodman traces Mason's career in music and association with Liszt, primarily through quotations from Mason's own "Memories of a Musical Life" as it appeared in the *Century Magazine* (see no. **557**). Goodman also does comparative analyses of Mason's *Improvisation*, op. 51, and *Capriccio fantastico*, op. 50, with Liszt's "12 Étuden," nos. 2 and 4.

124   GOTTSCHALK, Louis Moreau. *Notes of a Pianist.* Ed. Jeanne Behrend, with a prelude, a postlude, and explanatory notes. New York: Alfred A. Knopf, 1964; reprint, New York: Da Capo Press, 1979.

     Gottschalk mentions seeing Mason by chance in the train while traveling to Providence, Rhode Island. Behrend discusses Mason's career as a touring virtuoso in her "prelude" to the book.

125   GRABER, A. T. "Concerning the Piano Champion." *Musical Courier* 26/18 (3 May 1893): 17.

     A response to Haas's "A Champion for the Piano" (see no. **131**).

126   GRABER, Kenneth G. "The Life and Works of William Mason (1829-1908)." Ph.D. diss., University of Iowa, 1976. 374 pp. UM 76-26286. *Dissertation Abstracts* 37/5 (Nov 1976): 2480-A.

     The main body of the dissertation contains four chapters. Chapter 1 consists of a biographical sketch. Chapter 2 deals with Mason's work as a composer. Chapter 3 is concerned with Mason's career as a performer. Chapter 4 is devoted to Mason's contribution to piano pedagogy. The thesis has six appendices: programs for the entire series of Mason-Thomas New York chamber music concerts, an annotated catalog of Mason's keyboard works, a catalog of Mason's vocal works, a list of works edited by Mason, a bibliography of manuscript letters and musical autographs, and copies of eight piano works representative of Mason's total output.

127   "Great Pianists at the Keyboard. . . ." *Etude* 30/5 (May 1912): 323.

     A series of photos showing the posture and hand position of well-known pianists at the keyboard. A picture of Mason is included with the caption "Dr. William Mason, America's Foremost Piano Pedagog."

128   GREENHOF, Rose W.   "Pithy Sayings by Dr. Mason."   *Etude* 26/9 (Sept 1908): 558.

Under larger heading entitled "Tributes to Dr. Mason. . . ."   Picture included. Greenhof relates some of her personal reminiscences of Mason's favorite teaching illustrations.

> His teaching was in principles which always involved more than the mere work on hand, and his constant aim was to make his pupils self-reliant.   He used to say, often, "You don't want to take music lessons all your life.   I want to make you independent as soon as possible."

129   *Grove's Dictionary of Music and Musicians*, 3d ed., American Supplement (1928).   S.v. "Mason, William."

Picture included.   A one-paragraph entry consisting of a brief biography and an incomplete catalog of Mason's works.

130   GROVES, Robert W.   "The Life and Works of W. S. B. Mathews (1837-1912)."   Ph.D. diss., University of Iowa, 1981.   287 pp.   UM 81-28397. *Dissertation Abstracts* 42/7 (Jan 1982): 2923-A.

A well-written, informative study.   Groves states that

> The purpose of this study is two-fold: (1) to present a comprehensive survey of Mathews's life, including basic biographical information as well as a thorough view of his career as a writer and teacher . . . ; (2) to examine closely Mathews's pedagogical concepts. . . . This latter objective is accomplished by studying his teaching in light of the following five subjects of concern: (1) technique and his use of Mason's system of exercises; (2) experimental methods for acquiring technical proficiency; (3) phrasing and interpretation; (4) ear training and memorization; and (5) pedaling.

See also no. **65**.

131   HAAS, Henry Hubert.   "A Champion for the Piano."   *Musical Courier* 26/15 (12 Apr 1893): 9-11.

A long, caustic attack on Mason and William Smythe Babcock Mathews. Haas's censure is wide-ranging.   Mason's opposition to the use of the wrist as a hinge for up-and-down motions of the hand, his use of the two-finger exercise, and the rhythmic notation of exercises published in some of Mason's books on technique are all subjected to a withering barrage of criticism.   The comments below are typical.

> . . . Mason's "Touch and Technique" is, like all American compositions, good or bad, "eo ipso," largely patronized and used by American piano teachers. . . .   It is likewise being widely propagated by the untiring efforts and ceaseless advertisements of the "Etude," of Philadelphia, published by the publisher of Mason's "Touch and Technique."

Haas intensifies his attack:

> With a keen eye to this chance, the publisher . . . advertises his publications in his journal; indeed it almost seems as if Mr. Matthews [*sic*] were on the editing staff solely for that very purpose, for — like the advertisements of some patented quack medicine, beginning with some far fetched, sensational and attractive object in order to trap people into reading them, and ending by recommending the use of the medicine — so, no matter what Mr. Matthews writes . . . , the refrain invariably is: "Use Mason's 'Touch and Technic,'" the greatest work of its kind extant, compiled by the "Grace of God."

Haas summarizes his feelings:

> Will you believe it if I assure you that after a most conscientious examination into the [*sic*] Mason's "Touch and Technic" I find absolutely nothing new or novel in it. . . .

Mathews, in an article titled "In Re 'Piano Champion,'" *Musical Courier* 26/16 (19 Apr 1893): 24, gives a point-by-point response, albeit in very diplomatic language, to the charges raised by Haas.

> In so far as regards the clearness, justice and thoroughly modern discussion which Dr. Mason makes of touch, it is too late to find fault. Every person who is able to judge what he sees and hears from first-class artists like Paderewski and Joseffy knows that the supposed elementary touches of such works as Plaidy's technics make but a very small part of what they use. Dr. Mason's book, so far as I know, is the first which has undertaken to describe these, illustrate them, classify them and explain the principles upon which they rest.

Mathews concludes:

> . . . permit me to extend to the correspondent [Haas] a sentiment of distinguished regret that my poor efforts in writing have not gained his approval.

Haas, unrepentant, in an article titled "The 'Champion' or 'Correspondent' Responds," *Musical Courier* 26/18 (3 May 1893): 20, reacts to Mathews's comments. Mathews's closing sentence (see above) offers a ready target.

> Do not, gentle sir, depreciate your own talents and extraordinary writing and talking powers by extending a gentle apology, as you did; you can never tire us, you are too amusing; it must be that the fault lies not so much in the "reiteration" of the subject, but with the subject itself.

In another, later article by Haas entitled "A Champion for the Piano," *Musical Courier* 26/20 (17 May 1893): 22, he shows signs of retreating — if only slightly — from his earlier position regarding Mason's work.

> IT seems I have been much misunderstood in my criticism on Mason's "Touch and Technic." . . . I never denied to his method certain merits, some few things that are good and true; on the contrary; but I did say, and repeat it here, that it contains nothing absolutely novel. What appears to be novel is of very questionable value . . . and should be rejected as faulty. Mason bases his method

principally on suggestions of Liszt. But Liszt was not a normal pianist, and therefore not a great instructor or pedagogue.

Other articles (supportive of Mason) appeared in the *Musical Courier* relating to this controversy, including those of A. T. Graber and Katherine P. Kelly (see nos. **125, 180**).

132   HAAS, Henry Hubert. "A Champion for the Piano." *Musical Courier* 26/20 (17 May 1893): 22.

See no. **131**.

133   HAAS, Henry Hubert. "The 'Champion' or 'Correspondent' Responds." *Musical Courier* 26/18 (3 May 1893): 20.

See no. **131**.

134   "Half Hours with the Best Composers." *Musical Courier* 29/17 (24 Oct 1894): 7.

Announces the publication plans of the J. B. Millet Company for the series "Half Hours with the Best Composers."

> Concerning the American music contained in the work Theodore Thomas writes in his introduction as follows: "The plan of this work I consider a very valuable one, both in influencing the taste and in bringing the average music lover in touch with the best compositions. That you include thirty original American compositions in the work is a very important feature. It is an endorsement of our national talent. . . .

Mason is listed as one of the composers who wrote a musical composition expressly for this publication (see nos. **458, 771**).

135   HAMILTON, Clarence G. "American Piano Music and Composers of Piano Music." *Musician* 17/12 (Dec 1912): 814-15.

Picture included. Hamilton gives brief summaries of the piano music of William Mason, Edward MacDowell, Louis Moreau Gottschalk, Ethelbert Nevin, Arthur Foote, William H. Sherwood, Sebastian Bach Mills, and Richard Hoffman. No detailed information is given.

136   HAMM, Charles. *Music in the New World*. New York: W. W. Norton & Co., 1983.

Hamm comments on the importance of the series of chamber music concerts presented by the Mason-Thomas Quartette (includes picture). Other aspects of Mason's life are also briefly chronicled; in discussing Mason's study in Europe, Hamm notes that it

... established a pattern of travel and study subsequently followed by almost all successful American performers, teachers, and composers of the second half of the nineteenth century.

137   *A Handbook of American Music and Musicians* (1886), ed. F. O. Jones. S.v. "Mason, William."

A four-column entry. Contains a good biographical sketch, a brief discussion of style, mention of pedagogical works, and a list of piano compositions through op. 43.

138   HART, James D. *The Oxford Companion to American Literature.* 3d ed., rev. and enlarged. New York: Oxford University Press, 1956. S.v. "Mason, Lowell."

The entry for Lowell Mason includes a separate paragraph on William Mason (a biographical sketch and mention of his writings and compositions). The paragraph on William Mason is also contained in the first and second editions, but is deleted in the fourth and subsequent editions.

139   HASKINS, Lyde Todd. "How Dr. Mason Taught Piano." *Musical Courier* 58/6 (10 Feb 1909): 26.

A series of anecdotes about Mason's teaching methods and procedures.

Dr. Mason employed four assistants (ladies), each of whom is a finished artist and expert teacher. . . . It was rarely that he accepted pupils for personal lessons, of an hour's duration, until he or she had received a few lessons from an assistant. . . .

140   [HENDERSON, William J.] "Live Musical Topics." *New York Times*, 6 Dec 1891, p. 12, col. 7.

See no. **482.**

141   *Herringshaw's Encyclopedia of American Biography of the Nineteenth Century* . . . (1904), ed. and comp. under the supervision of Thomas William Herringshaw. S.v. "Mason, William."

A one-paragraph entry. Includes mention of the Mason-Thomas soirées and Mason's piano compositions and books on piano technique.

142   HINSON, Maurice, comp. and ed. *Piano Music in Nineteenth Century America.* 2 vols. Chapel Hill, N.C.: Hinshaw Music, 1975.

Includes a summary of Mason's life. The collection of music contains Mason's *Dance Antique*, op. 38 (see no. **751**).

143   HITCHCOCK, H. Wiley. *Music in the United States: A Historical Introduction*. 3d ed. Prentice Hall History of Music Series. Englewood Cliffs, N.J.: Prentice Hall, 1988.

Includes musical example. Hitchcock briefly reviews the major aspects of Mason's career.

> His [Mason's] main role, like that of his father, was more that of tastemaker and teacher than composer; he was also a most competent performer.

144   HOFFMAN, Carl. "The Devitalized Wrist." *Etude* 12/4 (Apr 1894): 7.

Hoffman suggests some modifications for Mason's two-finger exercise which, in his view, would decrease the tendency toward rigidity in the wrist and arm which he believed was inherent in the exercise. Hoffman claims that his revisions are based on techniques developed by Riemann.

145   *Hofmeister's Handbuch der Musikliteratur*. 19 vols. to date. Leipzig: F. Hofmeister, 1844-.

Includes reference to Mason's *Amitié pour amitié*, op. 4 (see no. **701**).

146   HOLMES, Georgiana Cranmer. "An Hour with Dr. William Mason." *Musician* 13/10 (Oct 1908): 446.

A short article in which Holmes reflects on a lesson that she had with Mason on the teaching of piano technique.

147   "Honor to American Artists Abroad: William Mason & Moreau Gottschalk." *Musical World and New York Musical Times* 3/24 (16 Aug 1852): 416.

Chronicles recent successes of Gottschalk and Mason in Europe. A letter—published in a "southern paper"—from Gottschalk to his mother telling of a recent recital in Madrid is cited. Reviews of Mason's performance in Frankfurt on 20 June 1852 are also included (see no. **612**). Mason's effectiveness as an organist is also noted.

> Young Mason, though pleasing us as a pianoforte player, at that period [before he left for Europe in 1849], pleased us still more as an organist—for he evinced talents in embryo, for *extemporaneous playing*, of a very unusual stamp. His skilful and ingenius [*sic*] treatment of *themes*, in his church voluntaries, convinced us, at once, of that better than mechanical proficiency—musical *productiveness*: a gift far more valuable than any mere mechanical facility.

148   HORN, David. *The Literature of American Music in Books and Folk Music Collections: A Fully Annotated Bibliography*. Metuchen, N.J.: Scarecrow Press, 1977. *Supplement 1*, with Richard Jackson. Metuchen, N.J.: Scarecrow Press, 1988.

Mentions Mason's *Memories of a Musical Life*.

149 HORTON, Charles Allison. "Serious Art and Concert Music for Piano in America in the 100 Years from Alexander Reinagle to Edward MacDowell." Ph.D. diss., University of North Carolina, 1965. 225 pp. UM 67-999. *Dissertation Abstracts* 27/10 (Apr 1967): 3481-A.

> The purpose of this dissertation is to show the types of art and concert compositions that were written and/or performed in America during the period from about 1780 to 1880, and to determine who the composers were who dominated American music during the nineteenth century. . . . Whenever composers have been mentioned in one or more reliable sources, and when a listing of their piano compositions could be compiled from various sources, all of these compositions which have not been lost have been examined. . . .

Two of Mason's opuses are analyzed by Horton: *Trois Préludes*, op. 8, nos. 1-3, and *Monody*, op. 13.

150 "How Many Music Lessons a Week and at What Age to Begin." *Etude* 10/3 (Mar 1892): 53.

Cites Mason as stating that

> A lesson every day is desirable, and the child should practice under the supervision of the teacher as far as possible, and not be permitted to practice alone, and this is necessary in order to avoid mistakes and errors of every or any kind.

151 "How May Music-Teachers Qualify Themselves for Their Work?" *New York Musical Gazette* 7/3 (Mar 1873): 38.

Announces plans for the 1873 normal school in Binghamton, New York.

> The plan of the Normal Music-School was this. At some time during the summer months . . . to bring together a number of the very best . . . teachers and organize a school to be held for a few weeks . . . for the benefit of teachers of music and others. . . .

See also nos. **7, 22, 276, 361.**

152 HOWARD, John Tasker. *Our American Music: A Comprehensive History from 1620 to the Present.* 4th ed. New York: Thomas Y. Crowell Co., 1965.

Includes an extended, sympathetic description of the life and work of Mason.

> His [Mason's] place as a musical missionary, as a champion of the highest standards, and as the foremost piano teacher of his day, seems permanently assured. . . . He had a life full of many fine things; advantages of his youth that he was able to use; years of activity; and full recognition, by friends and the public, of all he had accomplished.

Howard's discussion of Mason is also contained in a truncated form in his *A Short History of Music in America*, coauthored by George Kent Bellows (see next item).

153   HOWARD, John Tasker, and George Kent BELLOWS. *A Short History of Music in America.* New York: Thomas Y. Crowell Co., 1957; reprint, New York: Apollo Editions, 1967.

See also the previous item.

154   HOWE, Granville L., and William Smythe Babcock MATHEWS, eds. *A Hundred Years of Music in America: An Account of Musical Effort in America during the Past Century . . . Together with Historical and Biographical Sketches of Important Personalities.* Chicago, 1889; reprint, New York: AMS Press, 1970.

Picture included. References to Mason, including a four-page biographical sketch, are scattered throughout the book.

155   HUGHES, Rupert. *American Composers: A Study of the Music of this Country, and of Its Future, with Biographies of the Leading Composers of the Present Time.* Rev. ed., with additional chapters by Arthur Elson. Boston: Page Co., 1914; reprint, New York: AMS Press, 1973.

Includes a three-paragraph discussion of Mason's life and work.

> His success in concerts abroad and here gave prestige to his philosophy of technic, and his books on method have taken the very highest rank.

156   HUNEKER, James Gibbons. "American Piano Composers." *Etude* 5/6 (June 1887): 83; 5/7 (July 1887): 93-94; 5/10 (Oct 1887): 136-37.

Huneker is lavish in his praise of Mason's compositions.

> They mirror perfectly his own pianism, and are sparklingly crisp, and full of a dewy freshness. . . . The various dance forms Dr. Mason particularly excels in. His mazurkas, valses, gavottes and figures are all excellent and the form always perfect. In point of fact, that is what first attracts the attention, both in the composer and the performer, his absolute mastery of the outline, so to speak, and his admirable use of technical resources.

The segment of Huneker's article dealing with Mason is also published (unsigned) as "Dr. William Mason," *Musical Reform* 2/2 (Nov 1887): 22.

157   [HUNEKER, James Gibbons.] "Old Fogy's Comments." *Etude* 23/3 (Mar 1905): 107.

A discussion of the importance and relationship of tone and technique in piano performance. Huneker recalls Mason's playing as follows:

> I am sure those who had the pleasure of listening to William Mason will recall the exquisite purity of his tone, the limpidity of his scales, the neat finish of his phrasing. Old style, I hear you say! Yes, old and ever new, because approaching more nearly perfection than the

splashing, floundering, fly-by-night, hysterical, smash-the-ivories school of these latter days. Music, not noise—that's what we are after in piano playing, the *higher* piano playing.

158   [HUNEKER, James Gibbons.] "Raconteur." *Musical Courier* 33/19 (4 Nov 1896): 20-21.

Huneker recounts a recent visit with Mason, during which Mason played some of his own compositions and MacDowell's second piano sonata.

I admired the solid, musical performance, the clean arpeggio and scale work, and complimented him upon the possession of a fifth finger that was most eloquent. . . . Mr. Mason has tamed his hands, which are soft, pliable, with the tips, the tract of tactile sensibility, immensely developed.

Huneker concludes:

It is for me an interesting and edifying spectacle to meet a man like Dr. Mason, who is as enthusiastic in the practice of his art [at age sixty-seven] as if he were a youth.

159   [HUNEKER, James Gibbons.] "Raconteur." *Musical Courier* 38/10 (8 Mar 1899): 30-32.

Picture included. Huneker comments on Mason's vitality at the age of seventy and pays tribute to his past musical achievements.

This country owes much to Dr. Mason. His musical piano playing, at a period when empty virtuoso glitter was the fashion, was like the still small voice of great art. . . . He has loved the best in music all his life long, and his receptive faculties, at a time when most men moodily nurse memories of the past, is remarkable. . . . He is one of the memorable figures of Steinway Hall, and in the evening of a richly endowed and well-ordered career Mr. Mason enjoys with dignity the honors which are justly his.

160   [HUNEKER, James Gibbons.] "Raconteur." *Musical Courier* 41/23 (5 Dec 1900): 37-39.

Huneker, in lamenting the prejudices with which some critics judge piano performances, writes:

Why is it that we can't enjoy a pianist for his or her particular methods of expression independent of bygone or preconceived standards? Why can't we all be as catholic as Dr. William Mason, for example, who entertained at his home three artists and enjoyed them all within one week—Gabrilowitsch, Dohnányi and Harold Bauer?

161   HUNEKER, James Gibbons. "Some Pianists in America." *Etude* 5/12 (Dec 1887): 167; 6/1 (Jan 1888): 1-2.

Mason is discussed only briefly.

> Dr. William Mason has not appeared in public for some years, devoting all his energies to teaching. His mellow touch and suave style are well known and the musical quality of his playing ever fresh and charming.

162   HUNEKER, James Gibbons. *Steeplejack*. 2 vols. New York: Charles Scribner's Sons, 1921.

Huneker's autobiography. Reminiscing about the musical delights of New York around 1885, Huneker writes:

> I breathed an atmosphere ozone-charged. The idols of my youth were to be seen perambulating Irving Place, Union Square, Fourteenth Street.

After mentioning William Steinway and Theodore Thomas, Huneker continues:

> William Mason would alight from the little blue horse-car, which ran across Seventeenth Street, at Union Square. He lived in Orange, N.J., and always stopped at Brubacher's, where he met S. B. Mills, before beginning his lessons at Steinway Hall. A polished pianist, delightful raconteur, Mr. Mason could discourse by the hour about Franz Liszt, with whom he had studied.

163   HUXFORD, John Calvitt. "John Knowles Paine: His Life and Works." Ph.D. diss., Florida State University, 1968. 261 pp. UM 69-13271. *Dissertation Abstracts* 30/2 (Aug 1969): 752-A.

Includes a short discussion of the use of the Isles of Shoals as a vacation spot by both Mason and Paine.

164   "Individualities." *Music: A Review* 1/3 (21 Jan 1882): 13.

Reports that Mason was temporarily forced to discontinue teaching because of rheumatism. An earlier announcement in the "Individualities" columns of *Music: A Review* (1/2 [14 Jan 1882]: 9) indicated that Mason was suffering severely from rheumatism.

165   *The International Cyclopedia of Music and Musicians*, 11th ed. (1985), Oscar Thompson, ed. in chief, 11th edition ed. Bruce Bohle. S.v. "Mason, William."

Includes a biography and a brief list of works.

166   JABLONSKI, Edward. *The Encyclopedia of American Music*. New York: Doubleday & Co., 1981. S.v. "Mason, William."

Includes a biographical sketch and a brief discussion of Mason's compositional style.

167 JACKSON, Richard, ed. *Democratic Souvenirs: An Historical Anthology of 19th-Century American Music.* Foreword by Virgil Thomson. The Americana Collection Music Series, no. 3. New York: C. F. Peters Corp., 1988.

Includes Mason's *Silver Spring*, op. 6. Jackson's comments in the Introduction and his biographical sketches of the composers represented in the anthology are very informative. The biographical notes on William Mason include a portrait of Mason at age 18 (as found in his *Memories of a Musical Life*) and a photo of Lowell Mason's house on the family estate in Orange, N.J., known as Silver Spring.

168 JAMES, Richard Lee. "A Survey of Teacher Training Programs in Music from the Early Musical Convention to the Introduction of Four-Year Degree Curricula." Ed.D. diss., University of Maryland, 1968. 307 pp. UM 70-23295. *Dissertation Abstracts* 31/6 (Dec 1970): 2958-A.

Includes a good overview of the origin and development of the normal musical institutes. William Mason's participation as a piano instructor in the institutes held in South Bend, Indiana (1870); Florida, New York (1870); and Binghamton, New York (1871-72) is mentioned.

169 JERVIS, Perlee V. "Dr. Mason's Personality." *Etude* 26/9 (Sept 1908): 558.

Under larger heading entitled "Tributes to Dr. Mason. . . ." Picture included. Jervis eulogizes the personal characteristics of his former teacher. Special attention is drawn to Mason's generosity, progressiveness, and professionalism.

> He was always up-to-date, nay, ahead of date; he knew all the great pianists, attended their recitals . . . and was ever on the lookout for better ways of doing things.

170 JERVIS, Perlee V. "The Main Essentials of Dr. William Mason's Principles of Pianoforte Instruction." *Etude* 31/11 (Nov 1913): 773-74.

Pictures included. Article subtitled "By His Well-Known Pupil and Exponent. . . ." Jervis describes how he uses Mason's methods in his own teaching. Little new or useful information is given.

> In the last analysis, Dr. Mason's method is based upon two principles which were first enunciated by him, and used in his teaching fifty years or more ago. These principles were, on the muscular side that of "devitalization," on the mental side that of the development of velocity through the grouping of a series of tones as a unit.

171 JONES, A. S. "Dr. William Mason: An Honored Career in Music in America" (obituary). *Boston Evening Transcript*, 18 July 1908, pt. 3, p. 8, col. 5.

Article subtitled "His Service to His Countrymen in Elevating Musical Taste—He Assisted Greatly in the Introduction of the Works of Schumann and Brahms into America — His Ability as a Pianist and Organist — The Man's Charming Personality." A good summary of Mason's life and career.

> William Mason, although he possessed considerable facility at an early age, did little serious work until seventeen or eighteen years old. At this time his father suggested that he learn Bach's Fugue in F-sharp major and offered him a grand piano if he did so. This task William soon accomplished. It is said that the only other musician in America who could play this piece without his notes, was Stephen Henry Cutler [*sic*], then organist of Trinity Church.

This obituary was also published (unsigned) as "The Life and Work of Dr. Wm. Mason," *New-Church Messenger* 95/6 (5 Aug 1908): 91-92.

172   JONES, F. O. "Eminent American Musicians: William Mason, Mus. D." *Folio Art* (Boston) 25/4 (Apr 1884): 152-53.

Picture included. Contains a biographical sketch, an analysis of Mason's musical style (no examples), and mention of his piano methods. In his description of Mason's boyhood, Jones states:

> Mr. Mason inherited considerable timidity of character, which for years prevented the full development of his powers. Even his friends feared that he would not accomplish much in life, and it was not thought possible that he could make a teacher, but his remarkable success in this very capacity shows how groundless were all fears.

Much of Jones's material seems to be based on an earlier (anonymous) article: "Dr. William Mason," *New York Musical Gazette* 7/10 (July 1873): 97-98 (see no. **87**).

173   "Journalistic Comment on Dr. Mason's Death." *Etude* 26/9 (Sept 1908): 555.

Cites an obituary from the *Sun* (New York). See no. **465**.

174   KAMMERER, Rafael. "The American Pianist." *Musical America* 80/3 (Feb 1960): 26-28, 168, 170.

Article subtitled "Has He Been a Stepchild among Performing Artists? A Survey from Gottschalk to the Present Points Out that It Took a Century to Give Him the Status He Deserves." Pictures included. This long, informative article includes discussions of the careers of a wide variety of American pianists, from the well-known — such as Gottschalk and Mason — to the little-known — such as Michael Zadora and Ethel Newcomb.

> Even though Gottschalk could . . . "play the birds off the trees and the heart out of your breast," as the eminent American soprano Clara Louise Kellogg wrote in her "Memoirs," Mason, in his less spectacular way, exerted a far more powerful influence for good in the musical life of this country.

175   KAMMERER, Rafael. "Piano Methods." *Musical America* 78/3 (Feb 1958): 29, 166, 168-69.

Article subtitled "Infallible Systems for Becoming Virtuosos Have Been Proclaimed by Each Generation." The purpose of Kammerer's article is clearly stated in the introductory paragraphs.

> In the light of our recent reappraisal of current educational methods in general, a backward glance — even a hasty one as this must of necessity be — at some of the piano methods in use in the past can be a pleasant and profitable diversion. And one that can be, we might add, not a little disquieting. Progress, we find, . . . has been in an oblique rather than a straight line. To be sure, the child learning to play the piano today lives in a paradise, but on closer examination this proves to be a fool's paradise. The "pill" of learning has now been sugar-coated to the point of almost no returns.

Kammerer begins his survey with C. P. E. Bach and continues through the early twentieth century. Mason's work is evaluated as follows:

> Mason's works, now unduly neglected, are among the finest of their kind; nothing has come along since then to surpass them.

176   KAUFMAN, Charles H. *Music in New Jersey, 1655-1860: A Study of Musical Activity and Musicians in New Jersey from Its First Settlement to the Civil War.* Rutherford, N.J.: Fairleigh Dickinson University Press, 1981.

Originally a dissertation under the same title (UM 74-29999; *Dissertation Abstracts* 35/7 [Jan 1975]: 4588-89-A). Kaufman mentions two recitals given by Mason in Newark (see nos. **637, 638**).

> Pianist William Mason (1829-1908), son of Lowell Mason and a leading performer and teacher in his own right, gave two concerts in Newark. . . . In both of them he was assisted by the Newark pianist John Nelson Pattison, who studied with Mason and later pursued his own career as a concert pianist and composer. . . .

177   KAUFMANN, Helen L. *From Jehovah to Jazz: Music in America from Psalmody to the Present Day.* New York: Dodd, Mead & Co., 1937; reprints, Freeport, N.Y.: Books for Libraries Press, 1968; Port Washington, N.Y.: Kennikat Press, 1969.

Includes a brief discussion of the origins of the Mason-Thomas Quartette.

178   KECK, George Russell. "Pre-1875 American Imprint Sheet Music in the Ernst C. Krohn Special Collections, Gaylord Music Library, Washington University, St. Louis, Missouri: A Catalog and Descriptive Study." Ph.D. diss., University of Iowa, 1982. 973 pp. UM 82-22245. *Dissertation Abstracts* 43/4 (Oct 1982): 967-A.

The collection includes some

> . . . works by several American composers of the cultivated tradition, musicians and composers trained in the fine arts music traditions of Europe. Among these are compositions by William Mason. . . .

The works by Mason are *Silver Spring*, op. 6; *Danse rustique à la gigue*, op. 16; "Charming Little Valley," "Life Let Us Cherish," and "Baby Bye, Here's a Fly," from *Teacher and Pupil*, op. 26, nos. 2, 4, and 6; and *Valse-Impromptu*, op. 28.

179   KEHLER, George. *The Piano in Concert*. 2 vols. Metuchen, N.J.: Scarecrow Press, 1982.

A list of pianists and the programs they played. Information given for most of the pianists includes a biographical sketch, a chronological list of programs played, and citations of sources. Eight of Mason's performances are mentioned.

180   KELLY, Katherine P. "Going for Mr. Haas." *Musical Courier* 26/17 (26 Apr 1893): 16.

A response to Haas's "A Champion for the Piano" (see no. 131).

181   KELSO, Hugh A., Jr. "Cause and Effect in Piano Playing." *Music* 6 (Aug 1894): 439-43.

A sequel to "Cause and Effect in Pianoforte Touch: A Symposium" (see no. 53).

182   KELSO, Hugh A., Jr. "A Reply to Dr. Wm. Mason's Article 'A New Chapter of Touch.'" *Music* 10 (Aug 1896): 422-24.

A response to Mason's "A New Chapter of Touch" (see no. 559).

183   KLEIN, Mary Justina, Sister. "The Contribution of Daniel Gregory Mason to American Music." Ph.D. diss., Catholic University of America, 1957.

Includes a short biography of William Mason, a genealogy of the Mason family, and a brief account of Daniel Gregory's close relationship with William Mason (his uncle) in the fall and winter of 1895-96, when both were living in the Washington Square area of New York City.

184   KRAEGE, Elfrieda A. "The Masons and the Beechers: Their Crusade for Congregational Singing in America." *Tracker* 25/1 (Autumn 1980): 101-08.

The main body of this article deals with Lowell and Timothy Mason, Lyman and Henry Ward Beecher, James Waddel Alexander, and Thomas Hastings. William Mason is mentioned for his work as organist in the Fifth Avenue Presbyterian Church in New York City and the Valley Church in Orange, New Jersey. Includes a stoplist of the organ Mason played in the Fifth Avenue Presbyterian Church.

43

185   KRAEGE, Elfrieda A. "William Mason as an Organist." *Tracker* 25/4 (Summer 1981): 11-17.

An informative article. Kraege traces the history of William Mason's involvement with the organ, beginning at age seven, when his father placed him on the bench at the organ of the Bowdoin Congregational Church in Boston to accompany the choir. The most detailed information is given on Mason's work at the Fifth Avenue Presbyterian Church in New York City and the Valley Church in Orange, New Jersey. Includes a short biography, reviews of Mason's organ playing, recital programs, and organ stoplists.

> William Mason seems not to be typical of certain organists of his period, who would yield to popular tastes in such ways as imitating thunderstorms and battles on the organ. He had developed a love for the great European composers, and used his arts to stimulate an interest in such music among his hearers. . . . It is of course noted that his improvisations must have been significant, because of their being constantly mentioned by knowledgeable critics.

186   KREHBIEL, Henry Edward. "Music in America." In *Famous Composers and Their Works*, vol. 4, pp. 933-60. Ed. John Knowles Paine, Theodore Thomas, and Karl Klauser. Boston, J. B. Millet Co., 1891.

Includes brief mention of Mason's work as a teacher, a performer, and a composer. Krehbiel's statement that "the last of his [Mason's] published pieces appeared in 1882" is incorrect. Mason continued composing and publishing piano music through 1905.

187   KREHBIEL, Henry Edward. *The Philharmonic Society of New York: A Memorial.* . . . New York and London: Novello, Ewer & Co., 1892. Reprint in *Early Histories of the New York Philharmonic.* New York: Da Capo Press, 1979.

Programs of the concerts played by the New York Philharmonic from 1842-92, including those in which Mason appeared, are listed.

188   KREHBIEL, Henry Edward. *Review of the New York Musical Season 1885-1886 [—] 1888-1890: Containing Programmes of Noteworthy Occurrences, with Numerous Criticisms.* 5 vols. New York: Novello, Ewer & Co., 1886-90.

Krehbiel lists performances of Mason's *Scherzo*, op. 41, by William Sherwood in Chickering Hall on 23 January 1886 and 19 November 1887.

189   KREHBIEL, Henry Edward. "The Work of the American College of Musicians." *Etude* 6/9 (Sept 1888): 139.

Krehbiel reports on the examinations being held in New York City. Mason was on the board of examiners in the piano division.

See also nos. **10, 11, 12, 13.**

190   KRUEGER, Karl. *The Musical Heritage of the United States: The Unknown Portion*. New York: Society for the Preservation of the American Musical Heritage, 1973.

Includes the record jacket notes written by Arthur Loesser for *Music in America: Pianoforte Music of the 19th Century*, MIA-109, which contains recordings of Mason's opuses 6; 7, no. 2; 10; and 13. See Preface.

191   LAHEE, Henry Charles. *Annals of Music in America: A Chronological Record of Significant Musical Events from 1640 to the Present Day*. . . . Boston: Marshall Jones Co., 1922; reprints, New York: AMS Press, 1969; Freeport, N.Y.: Books for Libraries Press, 1970.

Lahee's chronology includes Mason's dates of birth and death and his appearance with the Boston Philharmonic on 8 March 1862 (see no. **654**).

192   LAHEE, Henry Charles. *Famous Pianists of To-day and Yesterday*. Boston: L. C. Page, 1900.

Includes a short biography of Mason and an account of his appointment as a trustee of the $10,000 endowment fund set up by Paderewski for a triennial competition for the best American orchestral, concerto, and chamber music works (see nos. **370, 382**). In his discussion of Paderewski's career, Lahee uses extensive quotations from Mason's periodical article "Paderewski: A Critical Study" (see no. **566**).

193   LAIGHTON, Oscar. *Ninety Years at the Isles of Shoals*. Boston: Beacon Press, 1930.

A history of the Laighton family's involvement in operating a resort hotel in the Isles of Shoals. The close relationship William Mason developed with members of the Laighton family, particularly Celia Thaxter, is mentioned.

194   LANDON, Charles W. *Landon's Piano-Forte Method: Easily Graded for Beginners; Containing Melodious and Pleasing Exercises, Etudes and Pieces for the Acquirement of Taste and a Love for Music and for the Rapid Development of the Technical Ability Necessary to Perform with an Effective Expression*. Philadelphia: Theodore Presser, 1893.

Landon was an articulate advocate for Mason's system of technique, particularly during the time when he was associated with the *Etude*. In this method for beginners, Mason's influence on Landon is very evident.

195   LANDON, Charles W. "Studio Experiences." *Etude* 11/4 (Apr 1893): 86.

Landon tells of his experiences in teaching Mason's system of octave technique. The end result is an insignificant expansion of Mason's own instructions in the fourth volume of his *Touch and Technic*, op. 44.

196   LAWRENCE, Vera Brodsky. *Strong on Music: The New York Musical Scene in the Days of George Templeton Strong, 1836-1875.* Vol. 1: *Resonances, 1836-1850.* New York: Oxford University Press, 1988.

Contains two incidental references to Mason. Vol. 2: *Reverberations, 1850-1861* is forthcoming and will contain extensive information about William Mason.

197   LEONARD, Florence. "William Mason—An American Master." *Etude* 57/3 (Mar 1939): 157-58, 210.

Article subtitled "High Lights in the World's Famous Piano Methods." Picture included. A synopsis of Mason's two-finger exercise and his theories of finger, hand, and arm touches. Includes many direct quotations from Mason's books on technique.

> The general principles of his teaching, broadly stated, are examples of the change of viewpoint which was characteristic of this period. *How* to practice and to use the hand becomes as important as *what* to practice and *what finger* to use.

198   LEVY, Alan Howard. *Musical Nationalism: American Composers' Search for Identity.* Contributions in American Studies, no. 66. Westport, Conn.: Greenwood Press, 1983.

Levy briefly mentions Mason as one of the American composers working around 1865-1900 who was strongly influenced by the European, especially the Germanic, tradition.

199   "Liszt." *Choral Advocate and Singing-Class Journal* 1/2 (July 1850): 23.

Tells of Julius Schuberth's presentation of Mason's manuscript "Les Perles de rosée . . ." to Liszt, with Mason's request that Liszt accept his dedication of the piece to him (see nos. **349, 699**).

200   "Liszt and Dr. Mason's Eyeglasses." *Etude* 31/11 (Nov 1913): 774.

A paraphrase of the anecdote concerning Liszt's objection to Mason's eyeglasses which appears in the latter's *Memories of a Musical Life,* 106-07.

201   LISZT, Franz. *Letters.* . . . Collected and ed. Ida Maria Lipsius [La Mara], trans. Constance Bach. 2 vols. New York: Charles Scribner's Sons, 1894; reprints, New York: Haskell House Publishers, 1968; New York: Greenwood Press, 1969; St. Clair Shores, Mich.: Scholarly Press, 1972.

Includes three letters from Liszt to Mason: Weimar, 14 December 1854; Rome, 8 July 1867; and Rome, 26 May 1869. Holographs of these letters are with the William Mason Collection of Autographs of Musicians (see no. **1016**).

202 "Local Matters." *Orange Journal*, 8 Aug 1868, p. [2], cols. 3-4.

Includes an announcement of the installation of a new organ in the Valley Church in Orange, New Jersey.

The new organ placed last week in the Valley Church is a very fine instrument. On Saturday afternoon last we were permitted to listen to an exhibition of its capacities and powers under the accomplished hands of the organist of the church, Mr. William Mason, and greatly enjoyed the delicacy, elasticity, sweetness and power of tone displayed.

203 LOESSER, Arthur. *Men, Women, and Pianos: A Social History.* New York: Simon & Schuster, 1954.

Loesser makes several passing references to Mason, often to point out that Mason's choice of repertoire for his performances was based on a higher standard than that of most other pianists performing in the United States at that time.

204 "A Loving Cup to Dr. Wm. Mason." *Musical Courier* 38/4 (25 Jan 1899): 36.

Announces the celebration of Mason's seventieth birthday.

Just as this paper goes to press the pupils and admirers of Dr. Wm. Mason are engaged in the delightful task of presenting to him a loving cup on the occasion of his seventieth birthday. . . .

See also nos. **45, 432.**

205 LOWENS, Irving. "Liszt and America." *Journal of the American Liszt Society* 4 (Dec 1978): 4-10.

Lowens assesses the extent of Liszt's effect on nineteenth-century American musical life in four areas: mention of him in the press, publication of his music, performance of his music, and evidence of his influence on American piano pedagogy. Mason's role in introducing Liszt's music to the American public is noted.

Documented performances of Liszt's music in America before 1854 were . . . rare; indeed, after a diligent search I have been unable to turn up a single one. The first pianist to play Liszt in public was William Mason. . . .

Mason actually had performed Liszt's music in public as early as 1848; see no. **602.**

206 LOWENS, Margery Morgan. "The New York Years of Edward MacDowell." Ph.D. diss., University of Michigan, 1971. 437 pp. UM 71-23812. *Dissertation Abstracts* 32/3 (Sept 1971): 1553-A.

The purpose of this study is to present a detailed account of the life of Edward Alexander MacDowell (1861-1908), American composer, pianist, and teacher, from the time he moved from Boston to New York in the autumn of 1896 until his death there in January of 1908. This account attempts to treat all aspects of his professional life and many of his personal life during that twelve-year period.

Lowens's dissertation contains a detailed description of the events leading to MacDowell's appointment to the Columbia University faculty in 1896, a process in which Mason played a key role (see also nos. **20, 50**). Mason also supported MacDowell in other ways; Lowens writes that

> Between 1898 and 1901, MacDowell continued to receive requests from publishers for articles and inquiries from writers planning articles about him and his music. Upon the suggestion of William Mason in 1899, the Century Company requested an article on Anton Rubinstein. . . .

207   LYLE, Wilson. *A Dictionary of Pianists.* New York: Schirmer Books, 1984. S.v. "Mason, William."

A brief biographical sketch; includes a list of Mason's pupils.

208   McCLENNY, Anne, and Maurice HINSON, eds. *Duets of Early American Music.* Melville, N.Y.: Belwin-Mills Publishing Co., 1971.

Includes a short biographical note about Mason as well as the first and seventh duos from his *Teacher and Pupil*, op. 26 (see nos. **729-36**).

209   McCUSKER, Honor. *Fifty Years of Music in Boston: Based on Hitherto Unpublished Letters in the Boston Public Library.* Boston: Trustees of the Public Library, 1938.

Mason's role in the establishment of a pattern whereby nineteenth-century American musicians went to Europe to study is mentioned.

> Probably the first Boston students to work in Germany were Dr. Lowell Mason's son William, who sailed in 1849 to study with Moscheles and later Liszt, and James Parker. . . . Soon there were multitudes of their countrymen in Germany, for at the time it was impossible to get a thorough musical education at any one place in America.

210   McDONALD, Gail Faber. "The Piano Music of Daniel Gregory Mason: A Performance-Tape and Study of His Original Works for Piano Solo and Two Pianos." D.M.A. diss., University of Maryland, 1977. 43 pp. UM 77-28746. *Dissertation Abstracts* 38/7 (Jan 1978): 3795-A.

Includes a brief biography of Daniel Gregory Mason, an analysis of his musical style, and commentary on each of his piano pieces. McDonald discusses some of the interaction between Daniel Gregory Mason and his uncle William Mason, particularly during the time when both lived in the Washington Square area in New York.

211   McGRAW, Cameron. *Piano Duet Repertoire: Music Originally Written for One Piano, Four Hands.* Bloomington: Indiana University Press, 1981.

Following a two-sentence account of Mason's life, McGraw lists two duets: *Badinage*, op. 27, and *Teacher and Pupil*, op. 26. A brief description and library location is given for each work.

212   McKNIGHT, Mark Curtis. "Music Criticism in the New York Times and the New York Tribune, 1851-1876." Ph.D. diss., Louisiana State University and Agricultural and Mechanical College, 1980. 434 pp. UM 81-03641. *Dissertation Abstracts* 41/8 (Feb 1981): 3315-A.

Includes extensive comments regarding the history of the Mason-Thomas Quartette and the reviews of their performances as found in the *New York Times* and the *New York Tribune*. Some mention is also made of Mason's solo recitals and concerto performances with orchestras.

213   MANN, Charles H. "William Mason." *New-Church Messenger* 95/5 (29 July 1908): 74-75.

Charles Mann was the minister of the New Church (Swedenborgian) in Orange, New Jersey, during some of the time that Mason lived in that city. In this article Mann reminisces about some of his experiences with Mason, who was an active participant in the work of the New Church.

> After the death of his father and brother [Lowell, Jr.], Mr. Mason became a regular attendant upon our services, identifying himself fully with the New-Church society, and accepting office in it. [Mason joined the New Church in Orange on 20 October 1867.] He even volunteered to take the position of "assistant organist," which meant that he would play voluntaries for us whenever he could conveniently, but that he should have no responsibility in reference to it.

Mason's voluntaries were usually improvised, and Mann describes several specific performances, noting that

> His improvisations were never a wandering about in the realm of musical harmony, like a kind of aimless sauntering, ready either to continue indefinitely, or to stop at any moment. Rather Mr. Mason's improvisations were organic units. They had distinct themes, with beginnings, middle points, and ends.

214   MARROCCO, W. Thomas, and Harold GLEASON, eds. *Music in America: An Anthology from the Landing of the Pilgrims to the Close of the Civil War, 1620-1865.* New York: W. W. Norton & Co., 1964.

Includes Mason's *Lullaby*, op. 10, and a brief summary of his life and work (see no. **711**).

215   "Mason & Hoadly's Method for the Pianoforte." *New York Musical Gazette* 2/3 (Jan 1868): 19.

Announces that the work has already gone through five printings. Brief testimonials for the method by Julius Eichberg, Eugene Thayer, George James Webb, and John K. Paine are cited (see also no. **583**).

216   "Mason & Thomas' Conservatory of Music." *New York Musical Gazette* 1/11 (Sept 1867): 84.

Announces the curriculum and operating procedures of Mason and Thomas's music conservatory.

> The course embraces elementary instruction, formation of the voice, and its proper use in solo and chorus singing, instruction upon the piano-forte, organ, violin, harp, and all orchestral instruments, the study of harmony, counterpoint, and composition — in fact, it takes in the whole range of musical instruction from the simplest principles up to the highest capabilities of the art. . . . We believe there is nothing to compare with it, either in this country or in Europe. The European Conservatories are intended almost exclusively for those who are already well advanced in musical knowledge or skill. That of Mason & Thomas, while it provides the most thorough instruction in the higher branches, so that there will be no longer a necessity for students to go to Europe for the purpose of *finishing* their education (as it is unwisely termed), also affords an opportunity for the general cultivation of the many who do not wish to make an exhaustive study of music. . . .

See also nos. **26, 27, 351, 352, 353, 354.**

217   "Mason Autographs Seen at Columbia: Collection Made by Celebrated Piano Teacher Is Now on Exhibition." *Musical America* 53/18 (25 Nov 1933): 12.

Announces the exhibition of Mason's musical autographs at Columbia University's Avery Hall through the first of December. Some of the autographs in the collection are described, and a summary of the history of the Mason family is given (see also no. **1016**).

218   MASON, Daniel Gregory, ed. in chief. *The Art of Music: A Comprehensive Library of Information for Music Lovers and Musicians.* 14 vols. New York: National Society of Music, 1915. Vol. 4: *Music in America*, ed. Arthur Farwell and W. Dermot Darby.

Several references to Mason are scattered in the text. Mason's compositions are described as follows:

> They are all in the smaller mold, and, while they are rather stereotyped and conventional in their lines, they have found a place in the pianistic répertoire. . . .

219   MASON, Daniel Gregory. "Dr. William Mason." *Musician* 8/12 (Dec 1903): 421-22.

Pictures included. Daniel Gregory, William Mason's nephew, summarizes Mason's principal achievements as a musician.

> His career has been one that does credit to himself and to his profession. Steadily avoiding all commercialism, all compromise with unworthy standards, all facile and adventitious success, he has reached his high position by right of natural talent, unflagging industry, and the conscientious exercise of his unusual intellectual gifts.

220   MASON, Daniel Gregory. "Memories of William Mason and His Friends." *Etude* 54/9 (Sept 1936): 543-44.

Picture included. A miscellany of Daniel Gregory's memories of his uncle. From the fall of 1895 to the spring of 1896 Daniel Gregory lived in the Benedick in New York, across from William Mason's apartment in Washington Square, which enabled him to

> . . . meet on informal terms the stream of musicians, American and European, who frequented . . . [his] uncle's apartment. . . .

Visits—which sometimes included performances—by Paderewski, MacDowell, Dohnányi, and Gabrilowitsch are described. The playing of his own uncle made a deep impression on Daniel Gregory.

> His [William Mason's] rich and at the same time discriminating sensuous feeling voiced itself in the most exquisite piano touch I have ever heard.

Some of William Mason's eccentricities are also gently revealed.

> . . . he had never formed the habit of turning such humor as he had upon himself; and he would make without a tremor such remarks as "I shall never bear a grudge against any man—it might be a bad thing for me in the end." Cordially and genuinely interested as he was in younger musicians, they were obliged to adjust themselves to him, and were wise not to expect much adjusting from his end.

The entire contents of this article was also published by Daniel Gregory Mason in his book *Music in My Time and Other Reminiscences* (New York: Macmillan Co., 1938); see the next item.

221   MASON, Daniel Gregory. *Music in My Time and Other Reminiscences.*
       New York: Macmillan Co., 1938; reprints, Westport, Conn.: Greenwood
       Press, 1970; Freeport, N.Y.: Books for Libraries Press, 1970.

       Picture included. Daniel Gregory Mason's memoirs. The fourth chapter,
       entitled "William Mason and His Circle," contains Daniel Gregory's reminis-
       cences about his uncle, both personal and professional. About half of the
       material in this chapter had been published earlier as "Memories of William
       Mason and His Friends," *Etude* 54/9 (Sept 1936): 543-44 (see no. **220**).

222   MASON, Daniel Gregory. "Musical Trail Blazers . . . ; The Masons: Cultural
       Pioneers." *Musical Digest*, Dec 1946, pp. 10-12; Jan 1947, pp. 22-24, 29.

       Pictures included. A two-part article, the first dealing with Lowell Mason
       and the second with his son William. The section on William traces some
       of the major landmarks of his career: study in Europe, formulation of a
       theory regarding the use of the arm in piano playing, and work as a solo
       recitalist and as a member of the Mason-Thomas chamber music ensemble.
       Also includes a separate, one-column biographical sketch.

           As an American musical trail-blazer, William Mason had a two-
           fold importance. He did a great deal toward introducing chamber
           music to American audiences, and as a teacher was largely respon-
           sible for the development of piano playing in the United States.
           William Mason was the first American teacher to evolve a method
           of acquiring touch, the outstanding feature of his work being that
           he discovered by empirical methods certain principles of muscular
           control that have recently been evolved by scientists after years
           of research.

223   MASON, Daniel Gregory. "Perspective in Piano Playing." *Musical Digest*,
       July 1947, pp. 12-13.

       Daniel Gregory Mason laments what he perceives to be a growing trend
       among pianists to emphasize speed and power at the expense of poetry and
       sensitivity.

           If Touch and Technic, as named in the title of Dr. William Mason's
           manual of piano-playing, are indeed, as he thought, vital to the
           player in that order rather than the reverse, one will find oneself
           gradually shifting attention from the latter, more external element
           to the prior, subtler and deeper one. Progressively, one will realize
           that through adjustments of touch pressures and time durations
           alone is clarity of phrasing to be attained, through which alone,
           in turn, music reaches the mind, and through that the heart.

224   MASON, Lowell. *Musical Letters from Abroad. . . .* Boston, 1853; reprint
       of 1854 ed. (New York) with a new introduction by Elwyn A. Wienandt,
       New York: Da Capo Press, 1967.

A collection of letters written by Lowell Mason during his second trip to Europe in 1851-53. Most of the letters are concerned with public music performances — church services, concert halls, music festivals, and famous virtuoso performers. Because William Mason accompanied his father during most of the latter's travels in continental Europe, he presumably was present at many of the events described in the letters. Little direct information about William is contained in the letters. When Lowell Mason does write about his son, it is in a matter-of-fact tone, as in the following account of William's performance in Frankfurt on 20 June 1852 (see no. **612**):

> JUST before leaving Frankfort, we had an opportunity of attending a *matinée*, or very select morning concert, in the saloon of the Mozart House. Such morning concerts are quite common in the larger German cities. An individual, having the means to do it, employs at his own expense an orchestra, or more probably a quartet, or quintet, makes out his own programme, and invites his friends to spend a couple of hours in listening to fine music. . . . Strangers are sometimes invited to play in these concerts; and on the present occasion two pianoforte pieces, *"Amitie pour amitie,"* composed by the performer, and Doneyschock's [*sic*] *Rhapsodie in C Minor*, were played by Mr. William Mason. . . .

225   MASON, William Lyman, ed. *A Record of the Descendants of Robert Mason, of Roxbury, Mass.* . . . Milwaukee: Burdick, Armitage & Allen, 1891.

A record of the "American phase" of the Mason family, which began with the immigration of Robert Mason (ca. 1590-1667) from England to America in 1630. The genealogy is carried through ten generations. (William Mason was a member of the eighth generation of descendants.) Most of the entries include dates of birth and death, principal place of residence, and occupation.

226   "Mason's Pianoforte Technics." *Musician* 10/2 (Feb 1905): 78.

Picture included. Reports that work on Mason's *A System of Fundamental Technics* is nearing completion and that it will soon be published (see no. **574**).

227   [MATHEWS, William Smythe Babcock.] Advertisement for his *Standard Graded Course of Studies*. In *Etude* 16/8 (Aug 1898): 221.

This work is

> . . . supplemented with complete directions for the application of Mason's "System of Touch and Technic," for the production of a modern style of playing.

228   [MATHEWS, William Smythe Babcock.] Advertisement for his *Twenty Lessons to a Beginner*. In *Etude* 9/1 (Jan 1891): 19.

States that the "lessons" are

> . . . built upon the following three principles: (1) The supremacy
> of the ear or inner musical sense; (2) developing control of the
> fingers according to Mason's System of Technic; (3) reading music
> by thinking and conceiving its effect in advance of hearing it from
> the instrument.

229 MATHEWS, William Smythe Babcock. "American Composers of the Front
Rank." *Music* 2 (Sept 1892): 491-503.

Picture included. Mathews's "front rank" includes William Mason, Louis
Moreau Gottschalk, Edward MacDowell, Dudley Buck, Arthur Foote, and
George W. Chadwick. General analyses of compositional styles are given.
An excerpt from a letter by Mason is also cited (see no. **534**).

> Dr. Mason has not been a rapid composer. Scarcely more than one
> or two pieces a year proceed from his pen. Nevertheless, his works,
> when bound together, make two quite stout volumes. . . . They
> are all so unlike. Mason is not a composer who repeats himself.

230 MATHEWS, William Smythe Babcock. "Antoine Rubinstein." *Music* 7
(Feb 1895): 384-89.

Includes a description of the rehearsal Mason, Sebastian Bach Mills, and
Rubinstein had in preparation for their performance of Bach's *Triple
Concerto in D Minor*, BWV 1063 (see no. **681**).

> . . . foreseeing differences regarding the mordents, [Mason] took
> under his arm the clavier book of Emanuel Bach. . . . When the
> passage occurred containing the first, the three artists played them
> each in a different way. Then Mason called a halt and proposed
> that all play them in the same manner, and in order to settle doubt
> as to which *was* the manner, he produced his book. Whereupon
> Rubinstein said, "What is that?" and cast a glance over the examples,
> but went on immediately "This is how I play them," and the other
> two had to follow his way. . . .

A more complete, firsthand account of this incident is given in Mason's
Memories of a Musical Life, 230-32. The book brought to the rehearsal
was not by C. P. E. Bach; it was, in Mason's words, "an old book by Friedrich
Wilhelm Marpurg, published in Berlin in 1765" (probably Marpurg's
Anleitung zum Clavierspielen . . . , 2d rev. ed.).

231 MATHEWS, William Smythe Babcock. "An Appreciation." *Etude* 26/9
(Sept 1908): 557.

Under larger heading entitled "Tributes to Dr. Mason. . . ." Picture included.
Mathews outlines Mason's lifework as a performer and teacher.

> Some day he will be recognized as an epoch-marking authority in
> piano technic; because he tried to teach something besides keyboard

fluency, beginning where technic properly ought to begin, namely in "tone-production" — because tone-production is the source of expression in piano playing.

232   MATHEWS, William Smythe Babcock. "Concerning Elementary Pianoforte Instruction." *Dwight's Journal of Music* 35/13 (2 Oct 1875): 99-101.

In discussing the importance of developing good practice habits, Mathews writes:

> Mason says, in his queer way, that he hardly knows which most completely ruin their chance of becoming good players; those who make mistakes and correct them, or those who make mistakes and never correct them.

Mason's comments on practice techniques are also published by Mathews in "Letters to Teachers," *Etude* 9/1 (Jan 1891): 13.

233   MATHEWS, William Smythe Babcock. "Concerning Touch in Piano-Playing." *Dwight's Journal of Music* 37/17 (24 Nov 1877): 132-33.

Mathews explains some of the types of touch taught in the Mason system of technique. The so-called clinging pressure touch and two-finger exercise are described in detail; the "light legato" and "mild staccato" touches are given only cursory notice.

234   MATHEWS, William Smythe Babcock. "Developing Musical Feeling." *Etude* 14/2 (Feb 1896): 30.

See no. **255.**

235   MATHEWS, William Smythe Babcock. "Dr. Mason on the Arm in Playing." *Etude* 22/11 (Nov 1904): 447.

Article subtitled "What Does the Arm Actually Do in Good Playing?" The point of departure for Mathews's article is a letter he received from Mason containing some of Mason's most recent theories on the use of the arm and shoulder in piano playing. After paraphrasing portions of Mason's letter, Mathews continues with a long analysis of his own. Mason's letter, as paraphrased by Mathews, reads in part as follows:

> The scapular or shoulder muscles exercise an important influence in the production of a full, musical and sonorous tone. They are situated about the shoulder blades or upper back, and their action may be readily perceived through a sudden shrug of the shoulders. If they are trained to an extreme elasticity and freedom of movement, all hardness and harshness of tone will through their action disappear.

236   MATHEWS, William Smythe Babcock. "Dr. William Mason: A Visit and a Tribute." *Musical Standard* 7/11 (July 1907): 13-14.

Pictures included. Mathews writes about Mason's religious beliefs, his personal and professional relationship with Theodore Thomas, his support of young musicians trying to establish their careers, and his experiences in Weimar when he was studying with Liszt. This article, with a brief preface announcing Mason's death, was also published as "Dr. William Mason, 1829-1908, a Tribute," *Musical Standard* 8/11 (July 1908): 7-9.

> Mason was a fine player . . . , and he had also confidence in good music. It was this which brought out Theodore Thomas. I fully believe that but for his association with William Mason, the late Theodore Thomas would never have risen to the great and commanding position he occupied when he died.

237   MATHEWS, William Smythe Babcock. "Dr. William Mason, 1829-1908, a Tribute." *Musical Standard* 8/11 (July 1908): 7-9.

See the previous item.

238   MATHEWS, William Smythe Babcock. "Editorial Bric-a-Brac." *Music* 6 (Aug 1894): 444-61.

Includes a report on the four-week summer music school organized in 1894 by Theodore Presser in Philadelphia, one of the purposes of the school being to acquaint teachers with Mason's system of technique. Mason himself taught at the school for one week. Mathews's report centers on Mason's lectures, recitals, and piano compositions — some of which he performed at the school.

> The first week was made distinguished by the presence of Dr. William Mason. His talks to the class, and his playing of his own and other compositions endeared him to them as to all his hearers, so that when he departed many felt as if more than half the school had gone — which from a qualitative point of view was far within bounds.

See also nos. **378, 379, 380, 381, 428, 429.**

239   MATHEWS, William Smythe Babcock. "Editorial Bric-a-Brac." *Music* 8 (June 1895): 184-95.

Includes a comparison of Mason with Gottschalk.

> The names of Mason and Gottschalk used to be in everybody's mouth together. . . . As pianist Gottschalk was greatest always in his own works. . . . He represented a certain vein of originality; but as interpreter of works of others he did not so much distinguish himself, though very likely he played them well.

Mathews describes Mason as

> . . . the minister of the most advanced and the highest and most musical of German piano and chamber music. . . . I consider it very curious that two masters born the same year in America should have come to represent such opposite but equally honorable tendencies.

240   MATHEWS, William Smythe Babcock. "Editorial Bric-a-Brac." *Music* 8 (Oct 1895): 607-20.

Includes an account of Mason's summer vacations at the Isles of Shoals.

Dr. William Mason has spent his vacation at the Isle of Shoals, off Portsmouth, N.H., for about twenty-five years, except a single year, when he was in Europe. . . . One of his self-imposed regular duties is to play every morning to any body who cares to come and listen. He has a very nice small Mason & Hamlin grand. . . . At half past ten Dr. Mason begins to play. The room is generally filled before he begins.

241   MATHEWS, William Smythe Babcock. "Editorial Bric-a-Brac." *Music* 10 (May 1896): 71-86.

Contains a report of the work of the board of trustees of the American College of Musicians, of which Mason was a member.

The executive committee of the board of trustees has been in session every week during the winter. Trustees Superintendent William Bell Wait, Dr. William Mason, Samuel Prowse Warren, Edward Morris Bowman and Albert Ross Parsons being regularly in attendance. . . .

See also nos. **3, 14.**

242   MATHEWS, William Smythe Babcock. "Editorial Bric-a-Brac." *Music* 10 (July 1896): 304-14.

Includes a summary of the chronological development of Mason's theories on piano technique. Mason, in a different section of this article, is also quoted as having a very high regard for MacDowell's compositions.

243   MATHEWS, William Smythe Babcock. "Editorial Bric-a-Brac." *Music* 10 (Aug 1896): 397-409.

Includes Mathews's observations on the gradual acceptance of Mason's system of technique in the United States.

. . . it pleases me very much to see more and more evidence that the Mason system is being adapted by schools in all parts of the country.

See also no. **559.**

244   MATHEWS, William Smythe Babcock. "Editorial Bric-a-Brac." *Music* 12 (Oct 1897): 712-24.

Includes a comparison of the three "schools" of technique which Mathews believed were being most widely used by American teachers at that time: the so-called German method, which advocated a quiet hand and stationary arm; the Virgil system; and the Mason system. Mathews's opposition to the so-called German school is stated very bluntly.

The first one, naturally, is the old German idea of the quiet hand, stationary arm and the hammer finger, the point of the finger having little or no sensitiveness. This type of elementary training prevails almost uniformly in Germany and in all German educated teachers in this country, excepting the very small number who are able to play the piano.

245　　MATHEWS, William Smythe Babcock. "Editorial Bric-a-Brac." *Music* 15 (Mar 1899): 553-67.

Includes reminiscences of a recent visit Mathews had with Mason. Mathews comments on Mason's most recent compositions, his unique performance style, and his student and teaching assistant Martha Walther.

> The playing was what I was especially interested in. Mason's lovely touch still remains his peculiar possession, being the expression of a soul loyal, pure, true and strong.

246　　MATHEWS, William Smythe Babcock. "Editorial Bric-a-Brac." *Music* 19 (Dec 1900): 145-69.

Mathews states that Mason, on the whole, was not favorably impressed with Brahms's compositions. Mathews may have been mistaken. Daniel Gregory Mason notes that his uncle, especially in his later life, grew increasingly devoted to the music of Brahms, particularly to the intermezzi and capriccios (see Daniel Gregory Mason, no. **220**). Also includes a sketch of Martha Walther, Mason's pupil.

> Despite Brahms having developed new technical demands upon the pianoforte, . . . [Mason] thinks him of little account where the piano is concerned and that his works as a whole will go down to posterity mainly by reason of the structural mastership which they display.

247　　MATHEWS, William Smythe Babcock. "Editorial Correspondence." *Musical Independent* 3/33 (July 1871): 102-04.

An interesting travelogue of a trip to the eastern United States, which included visits with the William Mason and Lowell Mason families in Orange, New Jersey.

> On Sunday I attended church at the Congregationalist church, where Mr. Wm. Mason plays the organ. . . . The organist always improvises. His playing is remarkably ecclesiastical in tone, and the voluntaries are not only correct in form, but often very interesting in a contrapuntal point of view, Mr. Mason having a rare facility in getting up canons and fugues on small provocation.

248　　MATHEWS, William Smythe Babcock. "Editorial Correspondence." *Musical Independent* 3/34 (Aug 1871): 118-19.

Contains a description of the 1871 normal school in Binghamton, New York. The programs of three recitals performed by Mason up to the time the letter was written are included.

> The piano department is in charge of Mr. William Mason, and his time is all taken and crowded. Indeed, it has been necessary to classify the instruction in some cases, leaving the writer to give the lessons in technique, while Mr. Mason confined himself to phrasing and style.

Mathews also mentions the performance of some of Mason's vocal music.

> The first public concert was . . . a very good programme. Among the vocal selections were some very pretty glees by Mr. Mason, one of which (a "shuttle song") is very charming, indeed, and would, I think, make a pretty recreation for the cabinet organ.

See also nos. **2, 71, 253, 273, 358.**

249 [MATHEWS, William Smythe Babcock.] "An Evening with American Composers." *Music* 13 (Jan 1898): 351-59.

Under larger heading entitled "Musical Clubs." Gottschalk and Mason are the primary subjects of this article (unsigned, but almost certainly written by Mathews). The same format is used for both composers: a biographical sketch, a brief analysis of style, and a description of representative works.

Also published by Mathews as "Gottschalk and Mason," chapter 6 (pp. 214-27) of his *The Masters and Their Music* (see no. **254**).

250 MATHEWS, William Smythe Babcock. "For Piano Teachers." *New York Musical Gazette* 6/3 (Mar 1872): 45.

Announces plans for the 1872 normal school in Binghamton, New York. Mason was scheduled to perform two recitals a week and teach a piano pedagogy class, meeting five days a week, in collaboration with Mathews.

See also nos. **277, 298, 299, 356, 357.**

251 MATHEWS, William Smythe Babcock. "Franz Liszt: Pianist, Composer, and Master." *Music* 4 (May 1893): 53-72.

A rambling article. In one of Mathews's digressions, he relates the story of Mason's introduction to the music of Schumann in Leipzig in 1849. Also includes a brief account of Mason's study with Liszt and a facsimile of a letter from Liszt to Mason dated 2 March 1877.

> Almost immediately upon his arrival at Leipsic he [Mason] heard a symphony of Schumann. It was like opening a new world to him. . . . The next day he hurried to the music store of Breitkopf & Haertel and bought the score and orchestral parts of the Symphony No. 1, in B flat major and had it sent to Boston as a present to the "Musical Fund Orchestra" of that city.

252 MATHEWS, William Smythe Babcock. "German Influence upon American Music as Noted in the Work of Dudley Buck, J. K. Paine, William Mason, J. C. D. Parker, and Stephen A. Emery." *Musician* 15/3 (Mar 1910): 160, 208.

Picture included. A brief article, in light of the scope of the topic. No specific examples of German influence on Mason's compositions are given. Mathews does describe the process by which Mason composed his *Silver Spring*, op. 6.

> . . . when Haberbier came to Weimar and played his original interlocking and cadenza passages, all the boys thought that piano playing would follow this new direction. . . . Mason experimented until he found a good chord to work such an accompaniment figure as he had in mind, and the key which would afford the largest number of inviting possibilities, which he decided to be A. Then when he had composed the accompaniment he wrote in the melody, *à la chorale.* . . .

Mathews also relates this story—with embellishments—in "An Evening with American Composers" (see no. 249) and "Gottschalk and Mason" (see no. 254).

253 MATHEWS, William Smythe Babcock. "Gossip." *Musical Independent* 3/34 (Aug 1871): 122-23.

Unsigned, but listed under editorials in the index. Includes the program of the fourth recital played by Mason at the 1871 normal school in Binghamton, New York.

> The programmes of the piano recitals played by Mr. Mason at Binghamton were arranged with reference to their educational value. Every one contained a sonata by Beethoven, something by Schumann, several pieces by Chopin, followed by some of the works of more recent composers.

See also nos. 2, 71, 248, 273, 358.

254 MATHEWS, William Smythe Babcock. "Gottschalk and Mason." Chap. 6 in his *The Masters and Their Music: A Series of Illustrative Programs, with Biographical, Esthetical, and Critical Annotations; Designed as an Introduction to Music as Literature for the Use of Clubs, Classes, and Private Study.* Philadelphia: Theodore Presser, 1898; reprint, New York: AMS Press, 1971.

Includes biographical overviews and discussions of the compositional styles of both men.

> The works of both these composers have a distinct and pronounced pedagogic value, but in wholly different directions. . . . While the Gottschalk pieces improve the style of melody and the sparkle of the playing, the Mason pieces conduce to system and regularity in study and to a serious and careful treatment of the left-hand part as

well as the right, and they have in them some of that quality which belongs to nearly all the works of Bach, when undertaken by students: they promote seriousness and musical feeling.

Also published by Mathews as "An Evening with American Composers" (see no. 249).

255   MATHEWS, William Smythe Babcock. "How to Develop Musical Feeling in Piano Pupils." *Musical Record* 408 (Jan 1896): 3.

Includes Mathews's description of Mason's use of ensemble literature in his teaching, especially eight-hand arrangements for two pianos.

> Dr. William Mason for many years conducted reading-classes of this kind [two piano — eight hand], reading at sight all the orchestral *répertoire*. He conducted with a baton, and nobody stopped, there being some one to turn the leaves.

Excerpts from this article were also published by Mathews as "Developing Musical Feeling," *Etude* 14/2 (Feb 1896): 30.

See also the following item.

256   MATHEWS, William Smythe Babcock. "How to Play Easily at Sight." *New York Musical Gazette* 7/5 (May 1873): 67-68.

Mathews advocates the use of one of Mason's methods of teaching sight reading — the playing of ensemble music.

> Mr. William Mason has "reading classes," in which four pupils play through at sight eight-hand arrangements of symphonies, etc.

See also the previous item.

257   MATHEWS, William Smythe Babcock. "How to Use the Mason System." *Etude* 16/11 (Nov 1898): 322-23.

Mathews indicates which of the exercises in the fourth volume of Mason's *Touch and Technic*, op. 44, he believes to be of greatest value. He also lists the order in which he believes the exercises should be practiced. Unless one has a copy of Mason's work to consult, the article is difficult to comprehend; even if read in conjunction with Mason's work, the article is of limited value.

258   MATHEWS, William Smythe Babcock. "In Re 'Piano Champion.'" *Musical Courier* 26/16 (19 Apr 1893): 24.

A response to Haas's "A Champion for the Piano" (see no. 131).

259   MATHEWS, William Smythe Babcock. "Lessons from Memorable Piano Recitals." *Etude* 28/12 (Dec 1910): 797-98; 29/1 (Jan 1911): 23.

Mathews met Mason and heard him play for the first time in the summer of 1870, when Mason stopped briefly in Chicago on his way to South Bend, Indiana, to teach in George F. Root's normal school.

> During that summer and the next five or six I heard Mason in some twenty or thirty recitals in every one of which there was at least one thing, and sometimes several things, beautifully done. Although Mason was terribly nervous before an audience, when he forgot himself, as he did in playing a program for musical purposes, he often played splendidly.

260   MATHEWS, William Smythe Babcock. "Letters to Teachers." *Etude* 8/4 (Apr 1890): 56-57.

> Dr. Mason has often said that if a young man cannot play the piano with four hours a day practice, he could not with forty.

261   MATHEWS, William Smythe Babcock. "Letters to Teachers." *Etude* 9/1 (Jan 1891): 13.

See no. **232**.

262   MATHEWS, William Smythe Babcock. "Letters to Teachers." *Etude* 14/5 (May 1896): 104.

> If you wish to study in New York with Dr. Mason or Mr. Joseffy, your lessons will cost at least three dollars and a half for half hours.

263   MATHEWS, William Smythe Babcock. "Letters to Teachers." *Etude* 16/5 (May 1898): 138.

Includes a summary of the events — as recalled by Mathews — which led to the collaboration by Mason and E. S. Hoadly in the publication of *A Method for the Piano-Forte* (see no. **583**).

> Some time in 1866 Mr. E. S. Hoadley [*sic*] . . . prepared very carefully an instruction book, but when it was completed he found it impossible to get a publisher. He went to the firm of Mason Brothers . . . and submitted the manuscript. The modifications from existing books were so marked that Mason Brothers were rather afraid to undertake it; so they sent him over to their brother, Dr. William Mason, to examine the work. His report being favorable, the firm of Mason Brothers replied that if William Mason would put in his accent exercises they would publish the book as a method by Mason and Hoadley, all the work in the first part having been done by Mr. Hoadley with the exceptions, perhaps, of a few slight modifications which Dr. Mason made after the manuscript had been completed.

264   MATHEWS, William Smythe Babcock. "Liszt as Pianist and Piano-Composer." *Etude* 20/5 (May 1902): 170-71.

Mathews assesses Mason's role in promoting Liszt's piano music in the United States.

> In 1855, when Dr. Mason returned from Weimar, he had no more than at the outside a half-dozen concert-pieces by Liszt in his repertory. He used to play the "Lucia," the "Rigoletto" occasionally, and the "Second Hungarian Rhapsody," having been the first to play it in this country.

265   MATHEWS, William Smythe Babcock. "Lowell Mason and the Higher Art of Music in America." *Music* 9 (Feb 1896): 378-88; 9 (Apr 1896): 575-91.

Article subtitled "Prepared after Original Research for Mr. Wilber M. Derthick, and Published Here by His Permission, for the Musical Literary Clubs." Mathews's description of Lowell Mason's work as the precentor at the Valley Church in Orange, New Jersey, includes some comments on William Mason's organ playing.

> During the last years of Dr. Mason's life he still continued to officiate as precentor in the little valley church at Orange. The organist was William Mason. There was no choir; the venerable Dr. Mason, in his black skull cap, stood before the pulpit and led the congregational singing. Everybody sung, minister and all the people. The organ was played in the same spirit, so that repeatedly the trustees at their annual meetings voted that the organ was an important help in the religious impressiveness of the services.

266   MATHEWS, William Smythe Babcock. "Mason's Practice Methods — II." *Musician* 11/3 (Mar 1906): 146.

Mathews limits his comments to several of Mason's exercise forms: velocity studies, arpeggios based on diminished seventh chords, and scales in canonic motion.

> Among the . . . illusions I formerly cherished with regard to Mason's system, was that of supposing a general chorus of admiration would be awakened at his original idea of applying the canon principle to scale work. . . .

267   MATHEWS, William Smythe Babcock. "Mason's Principle of Velocity and Arm Touches." *Etude* 10/6 (June 1892): 118.

Mathews's comments on velocity are a regurgitation of information already published as early as 1867 in Mason and Hoadly's *A Method for the Piano-Forte*. In his description of the arm touches, Mathews stresses that the entire arm must be flexible.

268   MATHEWS, William Smythe Babcock. "Mason's Two-Finger Exercise and the Doctrine of Touch." *Music* 8 (Oct 1895): 626-28.

Under larger heading entitled "The Practical Teacher." Mathews presents the main features of Mason's two-finger exercise and gives practical suggestions for teaching it to students.

> In some talk that I had lately with Dr. Mason, another question was raised. . . . It is as to what touches ought to be taught to the beginner first; and what ones might well be left until a later time. I found Dr. Mason rather disposed to take the suggestion of his assistants, Miss Madeline Buck and Mrs. Gregory Murray, to defer the arm touches until a later time. . . .

269   MATHEWS, William Smythe Babcock. "Mason's Two-Finger Exercises, and Piano Touch." *Music* 4 (Sept 1893): 508-13.

A long article in which Mathews gives painstaking instructions for the proper performance of those exercises in Mason's *Touch and Technic*, op. 44, which he found to be most frequently misunderstood.

270   [MATHEWS, William Smythe Babcock.] "Measure." *Song Messenger: A Musical Monthly* 10/2 (Feb 1872): 21-22.

A short explanation of the meaning of "measure" in music.

> Mr. Wm. Mason makes it out "the space between two bars," a most illogical conclusion to which he has been driven by the difficulty of reconciling the peculiar rhythms of Schumann's music with the Dr.'s idea that measure is the unit of rhythm. To us it is plain that the beat, or pulse, is the unit of rhythm.

Mason, in an article in the *Song Messenger: A Musical Monthly* (10/4 [Apr 1872]: 55), charges Mathews with misrepresenting his ideas on "measure."

> I do not like to be recorded as defining a "measure" to be "the space between two bars," as such a statement is not in accordance with my ideas. . . . My idea of the word measure as applied to music is simply that it means "portion of time." During the performance of a piece of music time passes; the time is divided into portions; the portions of time are measures. . . . I cannot see that the manner of marking off, or dividing the time, whether by beats or otherwise, affects the measure as a fact, however it may vary its kind or genus. My eye fell on the following lines of Swift today, which I annex as *apropos*:
>
> > "— —Naturalists observe a flea / Has smaller fleas that on him prey; / And these have smaller still to bite 'em, / And so proceed *ad infinitum*."
>
> A flea is always a flea — a beat is always a beat — and a measure always a — measure.

271   MATHEWS, William Smythe Babcock. "Mental Action and Piano-Playing."
       New York Musical Gazette 7/4 (Apr 1873): 52.

       Mathews presents the argument that all piano instruction rests on the
       following three points:

> First, rendering all the muscular motions so habitual and easy that
> they can be performed by local nervous action without distinct acts
> of volition. Second, the formation of orderly habits of analyzing a
> new piece so that the mind can in the easiest and quickest way arrive
> at a comprehension of its contents. Third, the cultivation of the
> musical susceptibilities to the highest point, in order to give every
> player as many points of contact with the world of music as possible.

       Examples of the application of these principles in Mason's system of
       technique are given and discussed.

272   MATHEWS, William Smythe Babcock. "Mental Action in Piano Playing."
       Dwight's Journal of Music 33/7 (12 July 1873): 50-51.

       Mathews argues that good piano playing is directly related to good mental
       habits. Mason's system of technique is presented as being especially helpful
       in fostering mental concentration.

> I think it has been too generally overlooked that . . . the chief
> difficulties of piano playing are mental and not muscular. When
> a passage is once comprehended so that the player can attend
> exclusively to performing the actions, a fairly trained hand will soon
> learn to do it successfully.

273   MATHEWS, William Smythe Babcock. "Monthly Summary of Musical
       Doings." *Musical Independent* 3/35 (Sept 1871): 137-38.

       Unsigned, but listed under editorials in the index. Includes a correspondent's
       report from Binghamton, New York, containing the programs of Mason's
       final two lecture-recitals (his fourth and fifth) at the normal school. Some
       of the explanatory remarks made by Mason at his recitals are paraphrased
       in the report.

       See also nos. **2, 71, 248, 253, 358.**

274   MATHEWS, William Smythe Babcock. "Music Extension Society." *Music*
       2 (July 1892): 318-22.

       A bulletin (unsigned, but listed under Mathews in the index) announcing the
       formation of the Music Extension Society for the purpose of systematizing
       piano instruction on a national level. Mason is named as an officer of the
       society.

> A Temporary organization has been effected, as follows: President,
> Dr. William Mason; 1st. Vice President, Mr. E. M. Bowman;
> Secretary and Treasurer, W. S. B. Mathews; Directors, William
> Mason, E. M. Bowman. . . .

275   MATHEWS, William Smythe Babcock. "Music in the Columbian Fair."
       Music 1 (Nov 1891): 39-53; 1 (Dec 1891): 165-73.

A long, enthusiastic report about the musical prospects for the Columbian
Exposition in Chicago. A music advisory committee had been appointed
to help plan the exposition. Mathews's article includes a list of its members:

> PARTIAL LIST OF THE ADVISORY COUNCIL OF THE WORLD'S
> CONGRESS AUXILIARY ON A MUSICAL CONGRESS. Mr.
> William Mason, Mus. Doc., 29 Washington square, New York. . . .

276   MATHEWS, William Smythe Babcock [Der Freyschütz, pseud.]. "Musical
       Correspondence, Binghamton, N.Y." *Dwight's Journal of Music* 33/12
       (20 Sept 1873): 95-96.

An account of the 1873 normal school in Binghamton, New York. Includes
the programs of the eight piano recitals which Mason played.

> The piano recitals were held Wednesday afternoon at 4.15, and
> Saturday morning at 9, and were attended by an audience of about
> a hundred and twenty-five. The programmes were arranged from
> an educational stand-point, and each piece was introduced with a
> few words of explanation, in which Mr. Mason was generally very
> happy, saying just enough.

See also nos. **7, 22, 151, 361.**

277   MATHEWS, William Smythe Babcock. "The 'Normal' Music School."
       Dwight's Journal of Music 32/12 (7 Sept 1872): 302-03.

The article begins with a history of the development of the normal music
school.

> The growth of pianoforte instruction in the "Normal" has been
> chiefly remarkable within four years, and dates more particularly
> from Mr. William Mason's engagement in Mr. Root's "Normal"
> at South Bend, Ind., in 1870.

Mathews continues with a description of the 1872 normal school in
Binghamton, New York. His report includes a résumé of the daily schedule
of classes and the programs of the first four lecture-recitals which Mason
played.

See also nos. **250, 298, 299, 356, 357.**

278   MATHEWS, William Smythe Babcock. "An Old Programme Book: The
       Mason and Thomas Concerts." *Music* 2 (May 1892): 51-60.

Picture of the Mason-Thomas chamber music ensemble is included. This
article (signed "Westerner," but listed under Mathews's name in the index)
includes a brief history of the group's origin, a summary of the kind of
repertory they performed, and quotations from performance reviews. Some
of Mason's work as a solo recitalist is also mentioned. Information used by

Mathews in writing this article was apparently taken from scrapbooks of programs and newspaper clippings which Mason had compiled. The scrapbooks were probably those now in the holdings of the New York Public Library (see no. **1017**).

279   MATHEWS, William Smythe Babcock. *Pronouncing Dictionary and Condensed Encyclopedia of Musical Terms, Instruments, Composers, and Important Works; Designed to Accompany "How to Understand Music."* Chicago: Donnelley, Gassette & Lloyd, 1880; reprint, New York: T. MacCoun, 1884; subsequent printings by Theodore Presser (Philadelphia). S.v. "Mason, William."

A concise description of Mason's life and work.

280   MATHEWS, William Smythe Babcock. "The Rationale of Mason's 'Technics.'" *Musician* 11/1 (Jan 1906): 31.

This article consists of three parts: 1) an analysis of the unique traits of the Mason system, 2) a summary of the teaching methods of Mason's "chief competitor"—Leschetizky, and 3) a brief history of the gradual evolution of Mason's theories of technique. In regard to Mason's theory of pedaling, Mathews writes:

> It is curious that even as late as about 1892 Mason thought it would be impossible to teach the pedal in a book of technique. He said that if a player was musical, he would "get on to it"; if he was not musical, he never would, nor could it be taught to him. I called his attention to the fact that in forty years of teaching he had taught about every pupil he had had the same things concerning the pedal. . . . This he saw, and so managed to invent two or three innocent little exercises, which, following after the scale exercise proposed by some French pedal master, gave a clue to the whole thing.

281   MATHEWS, William Smythe Babcock. "The Secret of Rapid Progress." *Etude* 10/2 (Feb 1892): 31.

A summary of the underlying principles of Mason's system of technique.

> Mason's system of pianoforte technics consists of two radical elements: (1) A combination of certain types of exercises; and (2) An extraordinary range of touch and speed in the daily practice, in other words, a *Method of Practice.*

282   MATHEWS, William Smythe Babcock. "Something About Grading Pieces." *Musical Independent* 3/36 (Oct 1871): 151-52.

Unsigned, but listed under editorials in the index. Announces that Mason and Mathews had compiled a "list of favorite teaching pieces," selected and classified according to character and difficulty. The list extended through seven grades and consisted of about 150 works.

There are a few copies of this list left, which may be had by sending twenty-five cents to the editor [Mathews], or to Mr. William Mason, at Orange, New Jersey.

No copy of this publication has been found.

283 MATHEWS, William Smythe Babcock, ed. *Standard Graded Course of Studies for the Pianoforte in Ten Grades: Consisting of Standard Etudes and Studies . . . Carefully Edited and Annotated and Supplemented with Complete Directions for the Application of Mason's System of Technics in Each Grade. . . .* 10 pts. in 1 vol. Philadelphia: Theodore Presser, 1892.

Instructions prefacing each of the ten parts of the book include suggestions for the application of Mason's system of technique for that particular grade level. Mason's *Toccatina*, op. 46, no. 1, is one of the repertory pieces included in grade nine.

See also no. **227**.

284 MATHEWS, William Smythe Babcock. *Studies in Phrasing: Selected from the Works of the Best Classic and Romantic Masters, Principally with Reference to Forming a Good Cantabile Delivery. . . .* 3 vols. Philadelphia: Theodore Presser, 1889-90.

Vol. 1 was published (1890) as *First Lessons in Phrasing and Musical Interpretation*; vol. 2 was first published in 1883 by Mathews as *Studies in Phrasing, Memorizing, and Interpretation . . .* ; a rev. ed. of vol. 2 was published by Theodore Presser in 1892.

Mathews makes scattered references to Mason's *Touch and Technic*, op. 44, and the work as a whole is clearly influenced by Mason's theories.

285 MATHEWS, William Smythe Babcock. "The Teachers' Forum." *Musician* 15/2 (Feb 1910): 134-35.

Includes a chronological list of Mason's books on piano technique and a description of Mathews's role in the preparation of several of the works. During the time *Touch and Technic*, op. 44, was being written, Mathews writes that Mason was

> . . . just then greatly taken with the idea of condensing. He sent me one time four cabinet photographs of his hand on the fifteen chords of his changes, and declared that that was all the instruction anybody needed to master that part of the idea.

286 MATHEWS, William Smythe Babcock. "The Teachers' Forum." *Musician* 15/4 (Apr 1910): 278-79.

Includes comments on Mason's interpretation of the slur.

The late Dr. Mason always maintained that according to the understanding of Liszt, Raff, and Klindworth, and the rest at Weimar, the slur meant only and singly a legato under it; and that it conveyed no suggestion or implication of shortening its final note.

287   MATHEWS, William Smythe Babcock. "The Teachers' Forum." *Musician* 15/9 (Sept 1910): 630.

Includes a discussion of the memorization process in which Mathews relates one of Mason's rules for memorizing.

> . . . you will find Dr. Mason's rule useful; which was, to begin a difficult passage or division of a concert work at the end, and play one measure, two measures, three measures, and so on until you had backed up to the beginning. The net result of this cute device is that the farther in you get the better you know the way, having practiced it more. . . .

288   MATHEWS, William Smythe Babcock. *Teacher's Manual of Mason's Pianoforte Technics: A Guide to the Practical Application of the Mason Exercises for Modifying Touch and Developing Superior Technic in Every Direction; Together with a Discussion of the Principles upon Which Mason's System Rests.* . . . Chicago: Music Magazine Publishing Co., 1901.

A set of explanations for the use of Mason's *Touch and Technic*, op. 44. In the course of his discussion, Mathews, as might be expected, interjects some of his own ideas on technique and tone production. No musical examples are given, but references to corresponding segments in Mason's work are carefully noted. Because of this format, Mathews's *Teacher's Manual* cannot be effectively used without a copy of Mason's work in hand.

289   MATHEWS, William Smythe Babcock. *Twenty Lessons to a Beginner in Piano Playing: Involving Ear Training, Technic According to Mason's System, and Writing Music before Reading It; the Whole Affording a Rapid and Thorough Development of Musical Qualities of Playing.* Philadelphia: Theodore Presser, 1889.

A rather brief beginning piano method written by Mathews to teach students the basic elements of note reading and technique in combination with the rudiments of ear training. The system of technique and the accompanying exercises are closely patterned on Mason's theories.

See also no. 228.

290   MATHEWS, William Smythe Babcock. "Wanted: The True Art of Piano Practice." *Music* 1 (Dec 1891): 128-41.

A long, discursive article in which Mathews explains many of Mason's technical exercises and the rationale for using them. Includes an excerpt from a letter written by Mason (see no. **532**).

291   MATHEWS, William Smythe Babcock. "William Mason, Mus. Doc." In his *The Great in Music: A Systematic Course of Study in the Music of Classical and Modern Composers . . .* , vol. 1, pp. 66-75. Chicago: Music Magazine Publishing Co., 1900-02; reprint, Chicago: Clayton F. Summy, 1910.

Picture (pen drawing by Childe Hassam) included. Contains a series of essays or "educational programs" on well-known musicians originally written for the use of a network of student clubs—called the Music Students' Club Extension—founded by Mathews in 1899. The essays were compiled into two volumes and published as *The Great in Music*, each volume containing programs designed to cover one year of work. The essay on Mason begins with a biography, blemished by occasional inaccuracies. This is followed by descriptions—usually containing an analysis of style—of nine of Mason's piano works: opuses 6; 7, no. 2; 13; 16; 24; 32; 42; and 51.

> Mason was . . . the first American player of Schumann, having for this kind of work very rare qualities, in his full, mellow and musical touch, his sensitive pedaling and his enthusiastic musical nature—not to mention a very capable hand.

292   MATHEWS, William Smythe Babcock. "William Mason, Pianist and Composer." Chap. 16 in his *Music, Its Ideals and Methods: A Collection of Essays for Young Teachers, Amateurs, and Students.* Philadelphia: Theodore Presser, 1897; reprint, New York: AMS Press, 1972.

This essay is divided into three parts: a review of Mason's career as a performer, an analysis of his compositional style, and an explanation of the principles underlying his theories on piano technique.

> The prevailing quality of Mason's playing is musical. Necessarily, he does not care for display. He never plays for any other purpose than for the expression of musical ideas.

293   MATHEWS, William Smythe Babcock. "William Mason: Teacher, Musician, Composer, Man—An Outline." *Musician* 13/9 (Sept 1908): 389-93, 422.

Pictures included. An interesting retrospect on Mason's life and career. Although marred as a source of factual biographical data by inaccuracies, the article is still a valuable one, especially for the information it contains about Mason's personal relationships with family members and friends.

> There was in him a most curious conflict, unconscious I think, between the Mason business capacity, which is great, and the altruistic and money-disregarding spirit of the true artist. I remember that I once said to him that I thought Liszt had made a great

discovery in giving lessons without taking pay. To which Mason pointedly dissented. He said that it would have been better all around if Liszt had affixed a price to his lessons and made himself responsible for them. For himself, he did not believe in giving lessons for nothing.

294   MATHEWS, William Smythe Babcock. "Wm. Mason's Piano Technics." *Dwight's Journal of Music* 31/25 (9 Mar 1872): 195-97.

Outlines Mason's theories on developing finger technique.

Nearly two years ago I had the opportunity of observing the method in which Mr. Mason himself applied . . . [his] system. . . . By degrees . . . I discovered that the great distinguishing trait of his system of exercises was . . . in the peculiar combination of arpeggio and scale practice, together with his own modification of Liszt's two-finger exercise; and that this combination was based on a practical experience of the benefit therefrom derived, as well as from a philosophical analysis of the various groups of muscles employed in piano-playing.

295   MATTOON, Edmund S. "Piano Technic." *Etude* 1/3 (Dec 1883): 25-26.

Includes a strong endorsement of Mason's system of technique.

. . . Mr. William Mason and his collaborateur in the same field, Mr. W. S. B. Mathews, of Chicago, have had considerable to say about the "flexor" and "extensor" muscles of the hand, devising certain exercises, bringing into direct use these particular muscles. This is a *common sense* idea, and I advise the zealous seeker after musical truth to gather up what they have written on the subject, as what these gentlemen do not know of the anatomy of the Technic is not well worth knowing. . . .

296   "The Mills' Silver Wedding." *Musical Courier* 8/9 (27 Feb 1884): 134.

A report on the celebration held in honor of Mr. and Mrs. Sebastian Bach Mills's silver wedding anniversary.

It may be of interest to state that the witnesses to Mr. and Mrs. S. B. Mill's [sic] marriage twenty-five years ago were Messrs. Charles Fradel and William Mason.

297   MINOR, Andrew C. "Piano Concerts in New York City, 1849-1865." M.Mus. thesis, University of Michigan, 1947.

Data compiled by Minor indicate that Mason performed in eighty-seven concerts in the city of New York during the time period of 1854 to 1865. In his analysis of Mason's performances, Minor comments that

From his debut William Mason strove to perform good music, and he included in his programs more good music than any other pianist of the period. . . . He introduced many new compositions of Chopin and Schumann to New York and probably gave the first performance there of Beethoven's Op. 101 and 111 Sonatas, and Schubert's Sonata in C minor, Op. Post.

298   "Monthly Musical Record." *Song Messenger: A Musical Monthly* 10/8 (Aug 1872): 119-20.

Contains a report from Binghamton, New York, which gives the programs of the first four piano recitals Mason played at the normal school.

See also nos. **250, 277, 299, 356, 357.**

299   "Monthly Musical Record." *Song Messenger: A Musical Monthly* 10/9 (Sept 1872): 135.

Includes a correspondent's report from Binghamton, New York, which gives the program of Mason's sixth piano recital performed at the normal school.

See also nos. **250, 277, 298, 356, 357.**

300   "Moonlight and Music." *Orange Chronicle*, 19 Mar 1870, p. [3], col. 2.

A review of the concert given in Orange, New Jersey, on 16 March 1870 for the purpose of raising money to purchase a set of chimes for the Valley Church. Mason's role as an accompanist is noted:

> . . . Mr. Mason . . . performed the accompaniment with scrupulous regard to the dramatic demands of the composition.

See also nos. **446, 447.**

301   MOORE, John W. *A Dictionary of Musical Information: Containing Also a Vocabulary of Musical Terms and a List of Modern Musical Works Published in the United States from 1640 to 1875.* Boston: O. Ditson, 1876; reprints, New York: B. Franklin, 1971; New York: AMS Press, 1977. S.v. "Mason, William."

A brief, two-sentence entry.

302   "Mr. William Mason." *Daily Evening Traveller* (Boston), 16 Apr 1850, p. 2, col. 1.

Reports that Mason had moved from Leipzig to Dresden to continue his musical studies.

> At a *soirée*, given by Carl Mayer, the distinguished pianist of that city, which was attended by the celebrated musical characters of

the day, Mr. Mason acquitted himself on the piano in a manner which called forth the warmest applause from all present. They were rather surprised that the Yankees could boast of a pianist of such fine talent.

303 "Mr. William Mason." *Dwight's Journal of Music* 2/23 (12 Mar 1853): 183.

Reports Mason's successful appearance in London in a concert given under the patronage of the Lord Mayor (see no. **614**).

304 "Mr. William Mason." *Message Bird: A Literary and Musical Journal* 34 (16 Dec 1850): 562.

A one-paragraph report of Mason's activities in Europe.

MR. WILLIAM MASON . . . is now in Germany pursuing the study of music under Dreyschock, and is, we learn, to appear with this eminent pianist at some of the Vienna winter concerts. Mr. Mason (who is now but twenty-one years old) has already spent nearly two years abroad, availing himself of the instructions of Hauptman [*sic*], Moschelles [*sic*] and others. . . .

305 "Mr. William Mason." *Musical Review and Choral Advocate* 4/3 (Mar 1853): 43.

A short article which tells of Mason's successful appearances in London at a concert of the Harmonic Union and a concert given under the patronage of the Lord Mayer (see nos. **613, 614**). Excerpts from reviews of the Harmonic Union concert are included.

. . . [Mason] has made his appearance before a London public. It could scarcely be called a débût, for, as we learn from private advices, he merely consented to take the place of a young lady whom indisposition prevented from playing. So short was the notice, that there was no time for preparation on the part of the orchestra, and Mr. Mason was obliged to select a piece with which they were familiar, Weber's *"Concert Stück."*

306 "M.T.N.A." *Etude* 4/7 (July 1886): 160-61.

A report on the activities of the 1886 MTNA convention.

The Piano section was intensely interesting. The essay of Dr. Mason, of New York, on "Touch," of course being looked for eagerly, as naturally what the foremost teacher of this country would have to say on the subject of subjects to piano players, would certainly be of lasting value and importance. Nor was any one disappointed.

See also nos. **376, 577**.

307   "Music in America." *Boston Daily Globe*, 16 July 1908, p. 6, col. 2.

> A reflection — prompted by William Mason's death — on the role musicians from Massachusetts played in the development of music in America.

> > Dr. William Mason said once, in describing his father's work, that Lowell Mason made Boston a self-developing musical city, while New York received its musical culture from abroad. This distinction it may be added, existed almost from the beginning, the first promoters of popular music having been Massachusetts men.

308   "Music Teachers' Institute." *Rochester Daily Democrat*, 22 Sept 1848, p. [2], col. 3.

> A brief report on the commencement of a music teachers' institute in Rochester, New York, led by Lowell Mason, George James Webb, and A. N. Johnson. Mention is made that one of the staff members was

> > ... Mr. WM. MASON, one of the best pianists in the country.

> See also nos. **309**, **603**.

309   "Music Teacher's Institute." *Rochester Daily Democrat*, 23 Sept 1848, p. [2], col. 3; 24 Sept 1848, p. [2], col. 5; 27 Sept 1848, p. [2], col. 4; 28 Sept 1848, p. [2], col. 3.

> An account (September 23d segment, signed "GENESEE") of an eight-day music institute for teachers — led by Lowell Mason, George James Webb, and A. N. Johnson — held in September 1848 in Rochester, New York. William Mason, in addition to serving as one of the accompanists (piano and organ) for the institute, appeared as a piano soloist on six different occasions, performing unidentified pieces by Thalberg and von Meyer, a waltz of his own composition, arrangements of "The Last Rose of Summer" and "My Lodging Is on the Cold Ground," and improvisations on "National Airs" (see no. **603**). At the close of the institute, its members passed a resolution stating that

> > ... Mr. WILLIAM MASON has established himself in our estimation, both as a Pianist and Organist, of a very high order; that our congratulations be presented to this young gentleman for his eminent success, and that he receive assurance of our sincere wishes that his professional course may add honor to the name, and be long useful and happy.

> This report was also cited in the *Musical Gazette* (Boston) as "Sixth Annual Meeting of the Musical Institute," 3/20 (23 Oct 1848): 153-55.

> See also the previous item.

310   "Musical." *Orange Chronicle*, 18 June 1870, p. [2], col. 1.

> Includes commentary on the activities of the Orange, New Jersey, Choral Union.

The society has changed officers within a few weeks. Mr. Wm. Mason is now the president. Confidence is reposed in this gentleman's ability to direct the work of the Union into safe channels.

311   "Musical and Dramatic." *New York Evening Express*, 30 Jan 1856, p. [1], col. 4.

Includes a long critique of the performance styles of Mason and Gottschalk.

> Between these artists there can be little comparison. . . . They diverge at right angles. . . . It is only in the matter of mechanical execution that they can be in any respect weighed against each other. In this respect we give "the palm" to Gottschalk, yet, nevertheless, our preference to Mason. . . . He [Gottschalk] is cleaner in his rendering than Mr. Mason, and leaves him no apparent approach in the execution of a certain attenuated gossamer fingering, as well as the expression of a quaint filmy music. . . . Mr. Mason, however, together with a most splendid and spirited executive grasp of the piano, unites great ductility and comprehensiveness of hand. . . . Where the test should be as to the higher class of music, devoid of mannerism, or the accessories of a delicate or fanciful finnical [*sic*] skill, the style and the actual execution of Mr. Mason has all the preference. Gottschalk is the jeweler, Mason the Gothic architect. It is a comparison of the art of Cellini to that of Angelo.

Excerpts also published as "The American Pianists, Gottschalk and Mason," *New York Musical Review and Gazette* 7/3 (9 Feb 1856): 38-39.

The above critique on Mason and Gottschalk and other recently published reviews of Ole Bull and Gustav Satter are cited by John Sullivan Dwight, in an article titled "Superlatives," *Dwight's Journal of Music* 9/2 (12 Apr 1856): 14, as examples of journalistic excesses. With regard to Mason and Gottschalk, Dwight writes:

> . . . "Gottschalk is the jeweller, Mason the Gothic architect. It is a comparison of the art of Cellini to that of Angelo." Rather a tall comparison that! – to say nothing of the originality of the connection indicated between Michael Angelo and Gothic architecture!

Mason and Gottschalk, as far as can be determined, never made a formal reply to Dwight's comments. But Satter, in a remarkably blunt and witty letter to J. S. Dwight (*New York Musical World* 14/264 [19 Apr 1856]: 189-90), gives a long and forceful response to his charges. Although Satter devotes most of his letter to his own defense, several references are made to Mason and Gottschalk, including the following:

> Gottschalk enjoyed a great reputation, long before J. S. Dwight thought of enjoying the editorship of a paper, and William Mason will be a fine and thoroughbred artist, despite all the Dwights in the world. . . . Gottschalk and Mason do at all events infinitely better in their way than J. S. Dwight in his, for they are *modest*, at least in a certain degree. They do not attempt to do anything beyond their sphere, and their success is sure; I wish I could say the same of J. S. Dwight.

Dwight responded to Satter's letter in an article titled "A New Composition by Satter," *Dwight's Journal of Music* 9/4 (26 Apr 1856): 29-31. He notes that his "Superlatives" article was not meant to be a personal attack on the artists mentioned, but merely a commentary on the tendency of journalists to turn reviews into extravagant eulogies. Satter's letter is reprinted in its entirety. As to the contents of the letter, Dwight dismisses it as an

... incoherent mess of boyish rage and nonsense.

312   "Musical Chit-Chat." *Dwight's Journal of Music* 8/4 (27 Oct 1855): 28-30.

Two of the news items pertain to Mason: an announcement of the formation of the Mason-Bergmann chamber music ensemble, and a brief reference to the music program at the Fifth Avenue Presbyterian Church in New York, where Mason was organist.

Congregational singing has been introduced at Rev. Dr. Alexander's church, Fifth Avenue, New York. One of Jardine's organs is placed behind the pulpit, and is played by WILLIAM MASON.

313   "Musical Chit-Chat." *Dwight's Journal of Music* 8/6 (10 Nov 1855): 47.

Includes an announcement that the Mason-Bergmann chamber music concerts will begin on 27 November 1854. The other members of the ensemble are named, and a summary of the group's goals is given.

The later quartets of Beethoven, (so rarely heard—*never* in this country,) the works of Schumann, Schubert, Frank, Volckmann [*sic*], Brahms, Rubinstein, and Berwald, will form the leading features of the programmes. The model followed is the celebrated matinées of LISZT at Weimar.

See no. **632.**

314   "Musical Chit-Chat." *Dwight's Journal of Music* 12/22 (27 Feb 1858): 382.

Reports the demise of the American Music Association. Mason was a charter member of this group.

The American Music Association, established some three years ago in New York, for the encouragement of American composers, has disbanded. It is but a fortnight since it gave a concert, highly praised in the *Tribune*. . . .

315   "The Musical Congress." *Boston Daily Advertiser*, 21 June 1871, p. 1, cols. 6-7.

A report on the third annual convention of the National Musical Congress in Boston.

The secretary, Dr. Eben Tourjée, read a letter from the president of the association, Mr. William Mason of New York, regretting his inability to attend, owing to the illness of his father, the venerable Lowell Mason.

Mason was elected as one of the vice-presidents for the following year. Also published as "The Musical Congress," *Dwight's Journal of Music* 31/7 (1 July 1871): 52-53, 56; 31/8 (15 July 1871): 64.

See also nos. **342, 343**.

316   "Musical Correspondence, New York, Dec. 10." *Dwight's Journal of Music* 18/11 (15 Dec 1860): 302.

The writer (identified as "TROVATOR") tells of the pleasures — some musical and some not — of the Mason-Thomas chamber music concerts.

> Dodsworth's [*sic*] room is never crowded to them, and I don't see how they pay. But the audience, though small, is always a splendid one to look at, and you know that staring at people is one of the great delights of going out to public places. There are more strongly individualized "characters" at one of there [*sic*] soirées than in any other assemblage of the same size I have ever joined.

317   "Musical Correspondence, New York, Dec. 16." *Dwight's Journal of Music* 10/12 (20 Dec 1856): 93-94.

The reporter (identified as "TROVATOR") gives a brief summary of the purpose and method of operation of the newly formed American Music Association. Mason was an active member of this group.

> . . . though intended as an *American* society, and as such presenting special claims to public regard, it is by no means proscriptive in its regulations. *Any* resident composer has a right to present his works for public presentation by the Society, on the payment of a fee of $5.00, and the society already enjoys unusual facilities for a proper presentation of such works.

318   "Musical Correspondence, New York, Dec. 24." *Dwight's Journal of Music* 18/13 (29 Dec 1860): 318.

Includes an account (signed "-t-") of Carl Bergmann's defection from the Mason-Thomas chamber music group.

> MASON & THOMAS' Soirées have met with a very annoying interruption. Mr. BERGMANN, infected probably by the spirit of a portion of his adopted country, has quarreled with the rest of the Quartet, and followed the example of "our little sister Caroline." As he is a rather more important element in the Union to which he belonged, than the above-named young lady in hers, the delightful concerts in which he took a part, have come to a sudden stop. The general sympathy is with the deserted, however, and everyone hopes that they will find some one to show that Mr. Bergmann's place *can* be filled.

319   "Musical Correspondence, New York, Dec. 26." *Dwight's Journal of Music* 8/13 (29 Dec 1855): 100-01.

Dwight's correspondent (identified as "MILAMO") briefly mentions the new organ installed at the Fifth Avenue Presbyterian Church in New York.

> A very fine organ has recently been erected by Mr. GEORGE JARDINE of this city (Mr. WILLIAM MASON presides at it) for Dr. ALEXANDER'S Presbyterian church. It is a powerful, rich and varied toned instrument. . . .

320   "Musical Correspondence, [New York,] March 1." *Dwight's Journal of Music* 28/26 (13 Mar 1869): 416.

The correspondent's letter (signed "F") includes a report on the disbanding of the Mason-Thomas chamber music ensemble.

> As I had surmised, the Mason and Thomas Chamber Music Soirées have been given up for the present, and perhaps for all time. Although musically successful and enjoyable, they have been failures pecuniarily, and therefore they have been discontinued. It is a shame and a disgrace to our city that this step was found to be necessary. While we are thankful to these five gentlemen . . . for past favors, we cannot expect that they will continue their entertainments at a pecuniary sacrifice.

321   "Musical Correspondence, New York, May 30." *Dwight's Journal of Music* 9/10 (7 June 1856): 76-77.

A report (signed "J. P.") on the organ recital held in May 1856 in the Fifth Avenue Presbyterian Church of New York to exhibit the newly installed Jardine organ. William Mason, George Washbourne Morgan, and "Edw'd" Jardine were the performers. The recital program and organ specifications are included.

> . . . while listening to the finished and classical style of Mr. WM. MASON, who is (fortunately for the Messrs. JARDINE) the organist of the church, the brilliant playing of Mr. G. W. MORGAN, and the profound knowledge of the almost inexhaustible resources of the instrument displayed by Mr. EDW'D JARDINE in his performance, the hearer could not but feel the truth that, "Peace hath its victories no less than war," and this was indeed a triumph of science and art.

See also nos. **329, 368.**

322   "Musical Correspondence, New York, Oct. 31." *Dwight's Journal of Music* 8/5 (3 Nov 1855): 36.

The correspondent (identified as "-t-") laments the lack of public enthusiasm for Mason and Bergmann's proposed series of chamber music.

> . . . the matinée plan of Messrs. MASON and BERGMANN meets with so little encouragement that there is small hope of its being carried out.

Mason and Bergmann, however, did begin their series of concerts on 27 November 1855 as planned (see no. **632**).

323   "The Musical Courier on Tonic Sol-Fa." *Musical Reform* 2/1 (Oct 1887): 6.

States that Mason was a member of a committee organized by the MTNA to consider the question of "notations and terminology."

324   "Musical Gossip." *Musical Gazette* (New York) 2 (18 Nov 1854): 9.

Reports Mason's impending 1854-55 concert tour (see no. **624**).

WILLIAM MASON is this week in our city preparing for his Western and Southern concert tour. . . .

A running commentary on the progress of Mason's tour is given in the "Musical Gossip" columns of subsequent issues of the *Musical Gazette*. In particular, see the following: no. 3 (25 Nov 1854): 17; no. 5 (9 Dec 1854): 33; no. 6 (16 Dec 1854): 41; no. 7 (23 Dec 1854): 49; no. 9 (6 Jan 1855): 65.

325   "Musical Gossip." *Musical Gazette* (New York) 12 (27 Jan 1855): 89.

Includes an evaluation of Mason's recently completed western concert tour (see no. **624**).

Mr. WM. MASON has returned to New-York, from his Western concert-tour. During his absence, he has given twenty concerts, without assistance, and everywhere has achieved the greatest success. The critics are almost unanimous in his praise, and his second concerts in any place have always been more fully attended than the first. This experiment, the first of the kind made in America, has proved that a true artist can make a piano-forte concert most interesting. At least Mr. Mason has done this.

Also published in "Musical Gossip," *New York Musical Review and Choral Advocate* 6/3 (1 Feb 1855): 42.

326   "Musical Gossip." *Musical Gazette* (New York) 20 (24 Mar 1855): 153.

Explains the circumstances surrounding Mason's invitation to play at Theodor Eisfeld's soirée (see no. **625**).

We regret to learn that Mr. Eisfeld is still so unwell as to be unable to leave his room. . . . Mr. WILLIAM MASON'S services have been secured for this occasion. . . .

Also published (with minor revisions) as "Musical Gossip," *New York Musical Review and Choral Advocate* 6/7 (29 Mar 1855): 104-05.

327   "Musical Gossip." *New York Musical Review and Gazette* 6/18 (25 Aug 1855): 281-84.

Includes brief mention of Mason's activities.

Mr. WILLIAM MASON is rusticating in the neighborhood of this city, engaged principally in composing. We have learned nothing as to his concert intentions. . . .

328   "Musical Gossip." *New York Musical Review and Gazette* 6/22 (20 Oct 1855): 349-50.

Includes an announcement of the formation of the Mason-Bergmann chamber music ensemble in New York. Mention is also made of Mason's work as the organist at the Fifth Avenue Presbyterian Church.

> An example of what congregational singing should be, may now be heard at the Presbyterian church in Fifth avenue, corner of Nineteenth street. . . . Supported by the organ, (Mr. William Mason is organist,) and guided by the voice of Dr. [Lowell] Mason (who stands fronting the congregation) only at the commencement of the verses, the people all join in the song, and the effect is grand.

329   "Musical Gossip." *New York Musical Review and Gazette* 7/11 (31 May 1856): 161-62.

Briefly mentions a recital held in May 1856 to exhibit the new Jardine organ recently installed in the Fifth Avenue Presbyterian Church in New York.

> The . . . instrument was well displayed . . . by Messrs. Morgan, Jardine, and Wm. Mason. Mr. Mason, the organist of the church, played twice, extemporizing on each occasion in a thorough musical manner.

See also nos. **321, 368.**

330   "Musical Gossip." *New York Musical Review and Gazette* 8/6 (21 Mar 1857): 81-82.

An announcement of Mason's wedding.

> Married, in Boston, at the New-Jerusalem Church, on Thursday, the 12th inst., by the Rev. T. Worcester, Mr. William Mason, the pianist, to Miss Maria Isabella, daughter of George J. Webb, Esq., the well-known composer, of Boston.

331   "Musical Intelligence." *Dwight's Journal of Music* 5/8 (27 May 1854): 63.

Makes mention of Mason's plans for his return to the United States from his studies in Europe.

> Mason proposes to return to this country in July or August, in company with a distinguished violinist, Herr LAUB, with whom he will give concerts, making his *début* in his native Boston.

Mason had become acquainted with Ferdinand Laub in Weimar. Either Mason, Laub, or both must have had a change of heart, for Laub did not come to the United States with Mason.

332   "Musical Intelligence, Boston." *New York Musical Review and Choral Advocate* 5/18 (31 Aug 1854): 306-07.

Includes a description of Bostonians' interest in Mason following his return from Europe in 1854.

> The return and expected public professional appearance of WM. MASON, is exciting much talk and interest among musical people here, and not only among musicians, but among all classes. Some few of our leading amateurs have accidentally heard him play (he seldom or never, I believe, gives any one an opportunity to hear him play, if he can avoid it) and they tell wonderful stories of his touch, his power, his exquisite taste, his execution, his genius, etc., etc. In short, they are driving us less favored mortals who have not heard him, nearly frantic with their portrayals of his entrancing powers.

The article continues with a brief description of Mason's organ playing.

333   "Musical Intelligence, Boston, Sept. 11." *New York Musical Review and Choral Advocate* 5/19 (14 Sept 1854): 323.

Includes a description of Mason's hermitic behavior in the few weeks prior to his Boston debut recital on 3 October 1854 (see no. **618**).

> "When is WILLIAM MASON to give his first concert?" is a frequent question, but I have not the means of supplying any information. . . . I am told that Mr. Mason is in the country, a few miles from Boston, practicing on one of Chickering's Grands.

334   "Musical Intelligence, Foreign." *Musical Review and Choral Advocate* 4/4 (Apr 1853): 59.

A report on Mason's success in London following his performance at Exeter Hall on 20 January 1853 (see no. **613**).

> MR. WILLIAM MASON, though we believe he has not appeared publicly since our last, is creating quite a sensation in the aristocratic circles of the English metropolis.

335   "Musical Intelligence, William Mason." *Dwight's Journal of Music* 5/24 (16 Sept 1854): 190-91.

A very favorable assessment of Mason's piano playing, evidently written after the reviewer (J.S. Dwight?) had heard Mason perform in some unidentified setting prior to his matinée in Boston on 22 September 1854 (see no. **617**).

> He is not merely a brilliant virtuoso, but a fine musician, familiar with the whole musical repertory of his instrument. . . . He also knows how to improvise, in a manner at once scholar-like and interesting, upon given themes, and to vary and embellish popular melodies, so as to win uncultivated ears without offending those severely loyal to high Art.

Also published as "Wm. Mason," *Boston Daily Evening Transcript*, 18 Sept 1854, p. [1], col. 5.

336   "Musical Items." *Etude* 14/7 (July 1896): 149.

    Includes a report that

> DR. WILLIAM MASON has purchased of Preble Tucker, for
> $29,500, the four-story brick dwelling, with lot 21 x 103.3, No. 14
> West Sixteenth Street, New York.

337   *Die Musik in Geschichte und Gegenwart* (1949-68). S.v. "Mason, Lowell,"
       by Irving Lowens.

    Includes a paragraph on William Mason. Lowens describes Mason's study in
    Europe, his work in promoting chamber music, and his success as a teacher.

338   MUSSULMAN, Joseph A. *Music in the Cultured Generation: A Social
       History of Music in America, 1870-1900.* Evanston: Northwestern
       University Press, 1971.

    Mussulman cites several of Mason's literary writings.

339   "My Teacher Fifty-five Years Ago: As Told by a Pupil of Mason's."
       Keyboard 1/2 (Apr 1939): 9.

    Subheading reads "This Article Was Written Almost Word for Word from
    an Interview with a Most Remarkable and Lovely Lady of Eighty-five, Who
    Had Been a Pupil of William Mason. . . ." A rather nostalgic retrospect
    in which some of Mason's personal characteristics and methods of teaching
    are described. Includes a letter written by Mason to the author (see no. **556**).

> . . . [Mason] studied constantly, and was an omnivorous reader.
> Nearly everything interested him — science, literature, painting,
> travel. His background was vast, his mind alive and vital, and his
> students were encouraged to draw from them as much as they could
> assimilate. He talked a great deal during the lesson, feeding the
> mind as well as training the fingers.

340   *National Cyclopedia of American Biography.* S.v. "Mason, William," vol.
       7 (1897): 423.

    Includes a picture, a short biography, a brief description of Mason's musical
    style, and a partial list of his works.

341   "The 'National Musical Congress.'" *Dwight's Journal of Music* 30/13 (10
       Sept 1870): 309-10.

    See no. **343**.

342   "The National Musical Congress." *New York Musical Gazette* 4/11 (Sept
       1870): 81-82.

Contains an account of the second annual convention of the National Musical Congress. Mention is made of Mason's election as president of the organization for the ensuing year.

See also nos. **315, 343.**

343   "National Musical Congress." *New York Tribune*, 2 Sept 1870, p. 8, cols. 2-3.

Reports the proceedings of the second annual convention of the National Musical Congress. Mason performed in a recital held on the first day of the meetings (see no. **678**). Also published as "The 'National Musical Congress,'" *Dwight's Journal of Music* 30/13 (10 Sept 1870): 309-10.

See also nos. **315, 342.**

344   NELSON, Lilian A. "What Dr. Mason's Methods Have Done for Me." *Music* 18 (Oct 1900): 597-98.

A saccharine testimonial for Mason's method books.

345   "A New Composition by Satter." *Dwight's Journal of Music* 9/4 (26 Apr 1856): 29-31.

A sequel to "Musical and Dramatic" (see no. **311**).

346   "The New Etude Gallery of Musical Celebrities." *Etude* 47/4 (Apr 1929): 279-80.

Includes Mason's portrait, a brief biography, and mention of some of his works.

347   *The New Grove Dictionary of American Music* (1986). S.v. "Chamber Music," by Leonard Burkat (with Gilbert Ross); "Mason," by Harry Eskew, W. Thomas Marrocco, Mark Jacobs, William E. Boswell, and Boris Schwarz; "New York," by Irving Kolodin, Francis D. Perkins, Susan Thiemann Sommer, John Shepard, Sara Velez, Nina Davis-Millis, John Rockwell, Edward A. Berlin, J. Bradford Robinson; "Thomas, Theodore (Christian Friedrich)," by Ezra Schabas.

The "Chamber Music" article includes a photo of the Mason-Thomas Quartette.

In the entry under "Mason," various members of the Mason family of musicians are mentioned. The segment on William Mason (written by William E. Boswell) includes a biographical sketch, a select list of works, and a five-item bibliography.

348   *The New Grove Dictionary of Music and Musicians* (1980). S.v. "Mason," by Harry Eskew, W. Thomas Marrocco, Mark Jacobs, William E. Boswell, and Boris Schwarz; "New York," by Irving Kolodin, Francis D. Perkins, and Susan Thiemann Sommer.

The articles provide similar, but slightly less detailed, information to that found in the corresponding entries in *The New Grove Dictionary of American Music* (see previous item).

349   "New Musical Publications." *Saroni's Musical Times* 1/36 (1 June 1850): 421.

Includes a review of Mason's *Les Perles de rosée*, [op. 2], and a brief anecdote about Liszt (see no. **699**). The anecdote about Liszt is also published in "Liszt," *Choral Advocate and Singing-Class Journal* 1/2 (July 1850): 23 (see no. **199**).

350   "A New Philharmonic Society." *Dwight's Journal of Music* 5/3 (22 Apr 1854): 23.

Announces George Frederick Bristow's intention to form "The *American* Philharmonic Society" (upon its actual organization the group was named the American Music Association). Mason was an active member of this organization.

> . . . measures are on foot in New York for the establishment of "The *American* Philharmonic Society," which is to be "free from all *cliques*, and whose aim will be to promote and cultivate the Divine Art, regardless of any *national* prejudices;"—that is, to give the fairest chance to all American composers.

351   "New York." *New York Musical Gazette* 1/12 (Oct 1867): 93.

Announces the opening of Mason and Thomas's music conservatory.

> The Mason & Thomas Conservatory was opened Sept. 16th, at 129 Fifth Avenue. The beginning was an excellent one.

See also nos. **26, 27, 216, 352, 353, 354.**

352   "New York." *New York Musical Gazette* 2/2 (Dec 1867): 12.

Includes a brief reference to Mason and Thomas's music conservatory.

> Wm. Mason and Theo. Thomas's Conservatory of Music has been successful beyond anticipation, and their house at 129 Fifth avenue is thronged with a most desirable class of pupils.

See also nos. **26, 27, 216, 351, 353, 354.**

353   "New York." *New York Musical Gazette* 2/12 (Oct 1868): 93.

Announces the beginning of the second year of classes at Mason and Thomas's music conservatory.

> Mason and Thomas' Conservatory of Music, No. 129 Fifth Avenue, is beginning its second season well.

See also nos. **26, 27, 216, 351, 352, 354.**

354 "New York." *New York Musical Gazette* 5/6 (June 1871): 84.

One of the news items tells of the successes and disappointments of Theodore Thomas. Among the latter was the conservatory of music he had begun with Mason.

> There is no one whose success affords us such sincere pleasure as does that of Mr. Thomas. . . . There are few who know anything of the discouragements of his earlier experiences. . . . We remember well a time several years ago when he seemed to come as near to a state of despondency as his hopeful nature is capable of. . . . It was acknowledged that . . . his symphony concerts were far in advance of those of the Philharmonic society. Yet the latter were "the fashion," and enjoyed the lion's share of public patronage. It was a dark time for him. The Conservatory of music which he had started in connection with Mr. William Mason, was a comparative failure. The conception was a fine one, but the public were not ready for it.

See also nos. **26, 27, 216, 351, 352, 353.**

355 "New York — Season of 1866-7 — ." *New York Musical Gazette* 1/1 (Nov 1866): 5.

Includes an announcement of the plans to hold a series of chamber music concerts which would feature the use of the cabinet organ. Mason was scheduled to be one of the performers.

> Mr. THOMAS will . . . superintend the Musical Recreations at Messrs. MASON and HAMLIN's Cabinet Organ Warerooms, which were so successful and popular last year. The introduction of Cabinet Organs in chamber concerts has proved a very interesting feature, and makes accessible and intelligible much music which has hitherto required the orchestra. During the summer, Mr. THOMAS and others have arranged many selections for the Cabinet Organ, pianoforte, violin, and violincello [*sic*], and these will be rendered by Messrs. BERGNER, WM. MASON, THOMAS, and S. P. WARREN. These recreations will be given on Tuesday afternoons, and will commence during the month of November.

Also includes a report on the 20 October 1866 concert by the Thomas Orchestra in which Mason played Beethoven's *Concerto in G Major*, op. 58 (see no. **670**).

356 "The Normal." *New York Musical Gazette* 6/8 (Aug 1872): 113-14.

A summary of the activities of the first few days of the 1872 normal school in Binghamton, New York. While Mason was teaching at the school he learned that he had been awarded an honorary doctorate from Yale University. The article includes a quotation from the *Binghamton Republican* describing the reaction of the students and faculty at the normal school to the news of Mason's honorary degree.

Mr. Mason had no intimation of the honor that awaited him, and only received the announcement yesterday morning—of course to his complete surprise. The fact coming to the knowledge of some members of the school, it was resolved to visit his room at once, and offer him the hearty congratulations of the class. Accordingly, they adjourned in a body to the room in which he was engaged in teaching and quietly took their seats, paying no attention to the look of astonishment with which he regarded the intrusion. Mr. Seward then made a short address . . . presenting the congratulations of the class. . . . Mr. Mason responded very happily, and the interview was concluded with a general hand-shaking. . . .

See also nos. **250, 277, 298, 299, 357.**

357   "The Normal for 1872." *New York Musical Gazette* 6/2 (Feb 1872): 18.

An announcement of the 1872 normal school in Binghamton, New York. Special attention is drawn to the fact that Mason was to be one of the teachers.

See also nos. **250, 277, 298, 299, 356.**

358   "Normal Music School." *New York Musical Gazette* 5/4 (Apr 1871): 51.

An announcement of the 1871 normal school in Binghamton, New York.

Mr. William Mason will again be at the head of the piano-forte department. . . .

See also nos. **2, 71, 248, 253, 273.**

359   [Normal Music School, Watertown, N.Y.] *Normal Music School for 1876, Sixth Annual Session, (Previously Held in Binghamton, N.Y., This Year in Watertown) from July 12 to Aug. 9.* In volume 1 of the William Smythe Babcock Mathews Scrapbooks, Newberry Library, Chicago.

A prospectus. Includes an outline of the daily course of study and a list of the instructors. In addition to performing two or more recitals a week, Mason is also scheduled to teach a "Piano Teachers' Class," described as consisting of

. . . Instructions and Lecture[s] upon Technique, Phrasing, Musical Expression and [the] Best Methods of Teaching (three lessons each week). . . .

Mason's recitals and teachers' class are heralded as offering

. . . advantages for critical study, and an opportunity to learn how to *listen* as well as how to *play*, which cannot be found elsewhere at any price, even in our largest cities.

Quote by courtesy of the Newberry Library, Chicago.

360   "Normal Musical Institute." *Song Messenger* 8/4, double issue (Apr 1870): 2-5.

This special "double issue" is devoted primarily to announcements pertaining to the normal school scheduled to open on July 6 in South Bend, Indiana. In addition to the regular course of study offered at the school, prospective students are advised that

> Members of the Institute wishing *private lessons* in addition to the Institute course can obtain them of *MR. [CARLO] BASSINI* and *MR. MASON* at *Three Dollars* a lesson of half an hour. . . .

Perhaps in anticipation of a negative reaction to the amount of the fee, it is noted that

> . . . these gentlemen are *fully occupied* in New York City at *Five Dollars* for eac. [*sic*] lesson of forty-five minutes, and therefore . . . they will be teaching in the Institute *below* their *regular price*.

See also nos. **402, 404.**

361   "Normal Notes." *New York Musical Gazette* 7/12 (Dec 1873): 183.

Includes mention of Mason and George James Webb's weekly work schedule.

> Four days of the week they teach in the city, and on the other two days give lessons at their homes, in Orange, N.J. One unpleasant feature of their work is the constant necessity of refusing to take more pupils on account of their hours being all engaged. We need not add that it is a duty which few teachers in New York are called upon to perform this winter.

See also nos. **7, 22, 151, 276.**

362   NORMAN, John Love. "A Historical Study of the Changes in Attitudes toward the Teaching of Piano Technique from 1800 to the Present Time." Ph.D. diss., Michigan State University, 1969. 184 pp. UM 69-05924. *Dissertation Abstracts* 29/10 (Apr 1969): 3633-34-A.

Mason's emphasis on the use of the triceps and scapular muscles in piano playing is noted.

363   "Notes and Gossip." *Musical Visitor* 23/10 (Oct 1894): 262-63.

Includes a report on Mason's recent ill health.

> Dr. William Mason has been seriously ill since his return to New York from his summer home at the Isle of Shoals. We are glad to learn that a dangerous operation that was at one time considered unavoidable has been rendered unnecessary by a change for the better.

364   "Notes from the Normal." *New York Musical Gazette* 4/10 (Aug 1870): 76.

A report on the normal school in progress at Florida, New York.

> Mr. William Mason has filled us all with a new enthusiasm for the piano-forte. Most of us feel that we never before had any sort of an idea of the instrument, but his playing, wonderful as it is, does not astonish us so much as his teaching.

A second report on this normal school appeared under the same heading in the next issue of the *New York Musical Gazette* (4/11 [Sept 1870]: 84).

365   "Obituary Notes." *New York Times*, 15 July 1908, p. 5, col. 5.

Includes a brief notice of Mason's death.

> Dr. WILLIAM MASON, 79 years old, for fifty years a teacher of music in this city and a composer of note, died yesterday. . . .

366   ODELL, George C. D. *Annals of the New York Stage.* 15 vols. New York: Columbia University Press, 1927-49; reprint, New York: AMS Press, 1970.

Contains many entries of performances by William Mason.

367   OFFERGELD, Robert. "Gottschalk & Company: The Music of Democratic Sociability." Record jacket notes (with additions by Edward A. Berlin) for *The Wind Demon and Other Mid-Nineteenth-Century Piano Music*, New World Records, NW 257 (1976).

See Preface.

368   OGASAPIAN, John. *Organ Building in New York City: 1700-1900.* Braintree, Mass.: Organ Literature Foundation, 1977.

Originally a dissertation under the same title (UM 77-11412; *Dissertation Abstracts* 37/12 [June 1977]: 7397-A). Ogasapian describes the Jardine organ installed in the Fifth Avenue Presbyterian Church in New York in the summer of 1855. William Mason was the organist of the church at the time. Includes the program for the 25 May 1856 public "exhibition" of the organ in which Mason played two improvisations (see also nos. **321, 329**).

369   "Overdoing the Matter." *Dwight's Journal of Music* 5/26 (30 Sept 1854): 206.

Dwight lashes out against the heavy-handedness of press agents, including Mason's:

> The newspaper practice of trumpeting and puffing musical artists on the eve of their début, has become so rife, that many have actually come to believe that the success of an artist is a thing to be created less by himself than by his man of business or advertising agent. . . . And straightway the indefatigable, unabashable, Barnum-bewitched agent opens a ten days' siege of daily and thrice daily visits upon all luckless editors. . . . Now a true artist does not need such help. . . . Our young pianist [Mason] will surely make his own mark; by no means can he do more; and we are quite sure that it will be a deep one.

A different viewpoint appears in the *Boston Daily Evening Transcript* in an article titled "Concert Giving," 3 Oct 1854, p. [2], col. 1.

> Genius and virtuosity are indispensable to great and permanent success, but of themselves they are not sufficient. The *administrative* element must be supplied, else genius and virtuosity may starve, as they *have* starved before now. . . . Mr. Mason is particularly fortunate in having for his manager a warm personal friend [probably Oliver Dyer], who possesses all the managerial requisites. . . . Being an editor of experience himself, he knows how to regulate his intercourse with the profession — when to call, what to say, how to say it, and when to bow an adieu. . . . This, taken in connection with Mr. Mason's surpassing artistic accomplishments, will account for the unparalleled success attendant upon the concerts now about to come off.

Dwight was not one to retreat under fire, and in an article titled "Concert Giving," *Dwight's Journal of Music* 6/1 (7 Oct 1854): 5, he responded to the comments made in the *Boston Daily Evening Transcript*.

> Under this head our neighbor of the *Transcript* has an article, evidently designed to offset our brief and unfinished remarks of last week. . . . Now, with all due respect for business management, . . . we still think that the newspaper heralding . . . was greatly overdone. . . . However scrupulously and unimportuningly the business man or agent may have acted in the case in question, who could read the newspaper rhapsodies the morning after our young friend's private *matinée* [22 September 1854] without suspecting that one mind dictated or prompted all those utterances, in many instances not native to the source from which they seemed to emanate? that one breath, as it were, blew all those trumpets? that the glowing criticisms, (hearty as they were and to a very great extent just too) were, to say the least, written under pretty persevering pressure? . . . The legitimate ends of editorship and criticism . . . are necessarily jeopardized by too much outward pressure. . . . We still maintain, therefore, that a concert agent's business should be confined to *business*. . . . And we totally dissent from the practice that seems to be coming into vogue in concert-giving, and which the *Transcript* favors, of bringing manager as well as artist out upon the stage.

370   PADEREWSKI, Ignacy Jan. Letter to William Steinway, 21 Apr 1896. Published in "Editorial Bric-a-Brac." *Music* 10 (May 1896): 71-86.

In his letter Paderewski announces his desire to establish a triennial competition with prizes of $500, $300, and $200 for the best American orchestral, concerto, and chamber music works.

> To this purpose I send you herewith $10,000, asking you to accept, together with Col. H. L. Higginson of Boston and Dr. William Mason of New York, the trusteeship of this sum.

See also nos. **192, 382.**

371 PAIGE, Paul Eric. "Musical Organizations in Boston: 1830-1850." Ph.D. diss., Boston University, 1967. 486 pp. UM 67-13308. *Dissertation Abstracts* 28/5 (Nov 1967): 1838-39-A.

An examination of the development of musical organizations in Boston during the years 1830 to 1850, including an analysis of their aims, activities, and performances. Appearances by Mason with the Musical Education Society, the Boston Academy of Music, the Boston Philharmonic Society, the Boston Musical Fund Society, and the Harvard Musical Association are noted and described. A brief biography of Mason is included in an appendix.

372 PALMER, Horatio Richmond. *Palmer's Piano Primer: A Systematic and Clear Explanation of the Fundamental Principles of Piano-Forte Playing.* . . . New York: H. R. Palmer, 1885.

The subject matter is arranged in the form of questions and answers, interspersed with quotations from well-known musicians, including William Mason. Two of the Mason quotations, including the one below on lifting the fingers, are cited in "Advice and Caution," *Etude* 3/2 (Dec 1885): 273.

I wish something could be said to call attention to the evil results of lifting the fingers too high in pianoforte practice. Many persons fail to acquire a good touch simply because they fall into this habit.

See also no. **526**.

373 PAYNE, Albert [A. Ehrlich]. *Celebrated Pianists of the Past and Present.* . . . Enlarged American ed. Philadelphia: Theodore Presser, 1894.

Picture included. A two-page biographical sketch which outlines the major events of Mason's life.

As a pianist he is still one of the greatest, in quality as well as technic, in memory prodigious, recalling, as he can, pieces not played for years, and yet giving them a finished performance.

374 PEMBERTON, Carol Ann. *Lowell Mason: His Life and Work.* Studies in Musicology, no. 86. Ann Arbor: UMI Research Press, 1985.

Originally a dissertation under the same title (UM 71-28272; *Dissertation Abstracts* 32/5 [Nov 1971]: 2732-A). The first full-length biography of Lowell Mason. Comments about William Mason are interspersed throughout the text, apparently based, for the most part, on data obtained from the Lowell Mason Papers at Yale University.

375 PENNYPACKER, Fannie Richards. Letter to the editor, n.p., n.d. *Etude* 72/1 (Jan 1954): 1, 3.

See no. **31**.

376   "Personal Mention." *Musical Items* 3/11 (Oct 1886): 4-6.

Includes a report on Mason's presentation of a paper on "Touch" at the 1886 MTNA meeting. Several quotations are given from the paper and mention is made of Mason's own beautiful touch and many years of teaching experience.

See also nos. **306, 577.**

377   PHELPS, Roger Paul. "The History and Practice of Chamber Music in the United States from Earliest Times up to 1875." 2 vols. Ph.D. diss., University of Iowa, 1951. 991 pp.

Includes a good, accurate account of the performances by the Mason-Thomas chamber music ensemble in New York from 1855 to 1868.

378   [Philadelphia Summer Music School.] Advertisement. *Etude* 12/6 (June 1894): 142.

A full-page advertisement for the four-week summer music school to be held in Philadelphia on the campus of the University of Pennsylvania. The school's faculty, course of study, and registration procedures are all listed. Organized by Theodore Presser, the objectives of the school, as stated in the advertisement, were

> . . . to furnish the best facilities for Musical Culture. Not alone for teachers, but also for students in every stage of advancement. Unusual advantages will be given to those desiring the best method of imparting Dr. Wm. Mason's System of Technic as set forth in "Touch and Technic."

See also nos. **238, 379, 380, 381, 428, 429.**

379   "Philadelphia Summer Music School." *Etude* 12/4 (Apr 1894): 75-76.

Announces that arrangements for the summer music school have been nearly completed.

> The chief feature . . . will be "Mason's Touch and Technic."

See also nos. **238, 378, 380, 381, 428, 429.**

380   "Philadelphia Summer Music School." *Etude* 12/6 (June 1894): 124.

Provides some last-minute information about the summer music school concerning such matters as rental of pianos and guest recitalists.

See also nos. **238, 378, 379, 381, 428, 429.**

381   "The Philadelphia Summer Music School." *Etude* 12/8 (Aug 1894): 169.

A report on the activities of the recently completed summer music school.

Dr. Mason, to the great delight of all, gave two piano recitals. This feature was a surprise, and of it many remarked, that they were more than repaid for all the expense incurred in the enjoyment and instruction gained in listening to his wonderful technic, and especially in the ideal tone-quality, touch and soulful expression of his playing. . . . His playing was a revelation on the possibilities of emotional power in the pianoforte.

See also nos. **238, 378, 379, 380, 428, 429.**

382   PHILLIPS, Charles. *Paderewski: The Story of a Modern Immortal.* Introduction by Edward Mandell House. New York: Macmillan Co., 1934; reprint, New York: Da Capo Press, 1978.

Contains an account of Paderewski's donation of ten thousand dollars for the establishment of a triennial competition for the best American orchestral, chamber, and solo concerto works. Paderewski's letter to William Steinway of 21 April 1896, announcing the gift and naming Mason as one of the trustees of the fund, is cited. Paderewski writes:

I do not intend to thank the American people for all they have done for me, because my gratitude to your noble nation is, and will be, beyond expression. But I desire to extend a friendly hand toward my American brother musicians. . . . To this purpose I send you herewith $10,000. . . .

A list of some of the subsequent winners of the award is given by Phillips.
See also nos. **192, 370.**

383   "Piano Playing in America." *Musical Courier* 37/1 (4 July 1898): [81-83].

Pictures included. A review of some of the pianists who performed in America, beginning with Henry C. Timm in 1835 and ending with the pianists in vogue at the time the article was written. A brief description is given of the careers of the more important pianists; secondary pianists are mentioned only by name. The author's evaluation of Mason reads, in part, as follows:

As a pianist he has a supple technic, a sonorous, singing tone, and has a style of his own. He was one of the pioneers of music in this country, introducing Schumann, Brahms and Chopin.

384   "Prize Piano Method." *Etude* 3/8 (Aug 1885): 163.

Announces a competition sponsored by the *Etude* for the best beginning piano method. William Mason, Edward Morris Bowman, and Albert R. Parsons are named as judges of the competition.

385   "Publisher's Notes." *Etude* 8/12 (Dec 1890): 191.

Announces the imminent publication of a reed organ method written by Charles W. Landon. Landon's method is declared to be unique for the emphasis it places on teaching "reed organ touch." More specifically:

> Mason's "Touch and Technic" is applied to the development of a fine reed organ touch. The Wrist Touch is especially taught and practically applied, and its almost constant use in reed organ music pointed out and put in daily practice.

No copy of Landon's work has been located.

386   "Publisher's Notes." *Etude* 9/7 (July 1891): 135.

Announces that Mason is in the process of preparing the manuscript of *Touch and Technic*, op. 44.

> . . . [It] is to be an entirely new work, a work embodying his own experience of more than thirty years and that of a multitude of his best scholars who are now teachers, which has been gathered by an extensive correspondence as well as by many personal interviews.

387   "Publisher's Notes." *Etude* 11/3 (Mar 1893): 66.

Reports that advance subscription sales of *Landon's Piano-Forte Method* have been excellent. Landon's book is described as being

> . . . up to the times. The system advocated in "Touch and Technic" of Dr. Mason, is the basis of the work.

See no. **194**.

388   "Publisher's Notes." *Etude* 13/12 (Dec 1895): 275.

Includes an announcement that the publisher of the *Etude* was compiling a list of the names of teachers who were competent to give instruction in Mason's system of technique.

> Almost daily we receive word from teachers of music who are desirous of perfecting themselves in this method and request the name of some teacher near their home from whom they can receive the necessary instruction.

In subsequent issues of the *Etude* from January through November 1896, over one hundred teachers' names were published serially in the columns of "Publisher's Notes." The names were also cataloged according to geographic location and filed in the offices of the *Etude* as a permanent reference source. A second list with more than two hundred additional names was compiled and published by the *Etude* in 1898-99.

389   QUIGG, J. Travis. "The Lounger in Europe." *American Musician* 18/9 (30 Aug 1890): 17-18.

Quigg and Mason, who were both traveling in Europe in the summer of 1890, happened to meet at the Hotel Victoria in Wiesbaden. Quigg's column contains a long account of Mason's travel experiences, including his visits with Edvard Grieg and Heinrich Ehrlich.

> He [Mason] had been suffering for some time before with nervous dyspepsia, and had been reduced by that and overwork to a condition bordering on nervous prostration. By the advice of his doctor he concluded to give up worrying over the progress of his pupils and devote himself to his health for five or six months. He had been doing this for just three months when I met him, and I could see the improvement in his appearance, from the last time I saw him on Union Square in April last. His face was fuller, his eyes clearer, and in his cheeks there was the rosy color of good health.

390   "1829 — The Real Wm. Mason — 1908." *Etude* 32/11 (Nov 1914): 785-86.

Under larger heading entitled "The Etude Master Study Page." Pictures included. A fine summary of Mason's life and career.

391   RICE, Edwin T. "Thomas and Central Park Garden." *Musical Quarterly* 26/2 (Apr 1940): 143-52.

Includes a summary of Thomas's professional relationship with Mason.

392   RICHARDS, Marie Juliette, Sister. "The Role of William Mason in American Music Education." M.A. thesis, Catholic University of America, 1959. 58 pp.

Richards's thesis contains four chapters: 1) "Introduction," 2) "Historical Aspects of His Life," 3) "Contributions to Music Education," and 4) "Conclusion." The means by which Richards evaluates Mason's contribution to music education (in the third chapter) are an examination of his methods of teaching and an analysis of the structure of several of his compositions for piano. The final chapter is a summary statement assessing Mason's importance to pianists and students of music education.

393   RICHARDSON, Nathan. Letter to John Sullivan Dwight, Leipzig, 28 Apr 1853. Published in "Our Correspondence from Germany." *Dwight's Journal of Music* 3/7 (21 May 1853): 54-55.

Richardson's letter contains a brief reference to Mason.

> I also met Mr. William Mason, the American pianist, of Boston. He has now gone to Weimar, where he intends to remain several months, in company with the great Liszt.

394   RICHARDSON, Nathan. Letter to John Sullivan Dwight, London, 20 May 1853. Published as "American Students of Music in Europe." *Dwight's Journal of Music* 3/10 (11 June 1853): 78-79.

Richardson's letter includes a report on Mason's activities as a student in Weimar.

> Mr. WILLIAM MASON is in Weimar, under the instruction of LISZT. He is located in a very pleasant part of the city, under every possible advantage. . . . He is soon to play before the Grand Duke of Weimar and I fear not that he will give perfect satisfaction.

No record has been found of this performance.

395   RICHARDSON, Nathan. Letter to the editor of the *Boston Daily Journal*. Published in "William Mason." *Boston Daily Journal*, 25 Sept 1854, p. [1], col. 6.

A very long letter in which Richardson summarizes Mason's experiences in Europe and reviews his performance style. Richardson's comments are very flattering and, written just prior to Mason's Boston debut recital on 3 October 1854 (see no. **618**), probably contributed substantially to the excitement which surrounded Mason at that time.

> In Prague, Mr. Mason's wonderful talent for improvisation, which had so astonished "the old folks at home," was for the first time exhibited in Europe. A party of musicians, including Mr. M., attended a performance of the opera of *Joseph*, by MEHUL. . . . After the opera, the party attended a *soiree* at the rooms of Mr. Brandeis, the celebrated Bohemian portrait painter. In the course of the evening, Mr. Mason sat down to the pianoforte and played from memory a great portion of the opera, producing the original harmonies, and imitating . . . the entire orchestral performance. . . . This is a talent which few possess, and its exhibition on that occasion made an impression on Mr. M's Bohemian friends which will not soon be effaced.

Richardson's letter is also cited in "William Mason," *Musical World and Times* 10/5 (7 Oct 1854): 67-68; "William Mason in Europe," *New York Musical Review and Choral Advocate* 5/21 (12 Oct 1854): 354-55.

396   RICHARDSON, Nathan. *Richardson's New Method for the Pianoforte* . . . (Boston, 1859). Revised by William Smythe Babcock Mathews, with an appendix containing a synopsis of the famous pianoforte technics of William Mason, Mus. Doc. Boston: Oliver Ditson, 1894.

The Appendix includes the main forms of Mason's two-finger exercises, arpeggios on the diminished seventh chord, and accentuation patterns applied to technical exercises.

Review of no. **396**:

"Reviews and Notices: Richardson's New Method for Pianoforte. . . ." *Music* 7 (Dec 1894): 199-200.

> A generally favorable review.

> > All the matter in the original edition is here included, and a considerable number of new amusements are added, as well as important appendices,

and a newly written system of the Elements of Music. . . . The addition of the Mason principles of accentuation and the two-finger exercises will undoubtedly please many.

397   RICKER, Herbert. "William Mason: A Compact Summary of His Contribution to American Teaching." *Keyboard* 1/2 (Apr 1939): 8.

Picture included. As the title implies, Ricker's article is a résumé of Mason's teaching methods.

> Mason's advice upon the most effective way of practicing a composition is . . . worth considering. The student was first advised to study the composition carefully, at the same time forming an ideal of the correct rendition. He suggested that the pupil use his inner ear to idealize the phrase, and after playing it that he listen again to see if the effect measured up to the ideal.

398   *Riemann Musik Lexikon*, 12th ed. (1961). S.v. "Mason."

Various members of the Mason family of musicians are discussed. The entry on William Mason includes a brief summary of his life and career.

399   RITTER, Frédéric Louis. *Music in America.* New ed., with additions. New York: Charles Scribner's Sons, 1890; reprints, New York: Johnson Reprint Co., 1970; New York: B. Franklin, 1972.

Somewhat surprisingly, Mason is given only brief mention in this history of American music. Ritter comments about Mason's performances with the Harvard Musical Association, the New York Philharmonic Society, and the Mason-Thomas Quartette, but gives only cursory biographical information.

400   RIVERS, Travis Suttle. *"The Etude* Magazine: A Mirror of the Genteel Tradition in American Music." Ph.D. diss., University of Iowa, 1974. 334 pp. UM 75-13811. *Dissertation Abstracts* 35/12 (June 1975): 7950-A.

A study of the so-called genteel tradition in American music—belief in optimistic idealism, the continuity of Western culture, the permanence of established standards of taste, and the value of beauty in human life—as reflected in the *Etude* magazine. In tracing the early history of the magazine and its publisher, Theodore Presser, Rivers comments that

> In . . . [1889] Presser bought the rights to one of the first important pedagogical works for the piano by an American [Mason's *Touch and Technic*, op. 44]. It was the success of this work that firmly established Presser as a publisher of "educational music."

Mason, of course, also benefited from this relationship. The columns of the *Etude* were consistently used to promote, both directly and indirectly, Mason's compositions and works on piano technique.

401   ROGERS, Delmer Dalzell. "Nineteenth Century Music in New York City as Reflected in the Career of George Frederick Bristow." Ph.D. diss., University of Michigan, 1967. 216 pp. UM 67-15684. *Dissertation Abstracts* 28/7 (Jan 1968): 2718-19-A.

Rogers discusses the formation of the American Music Association, a group with which Mason was associated throughout its short existence. Mason's participation as a pianist in some of the concerts given by Bristow is also mentioned.

402   ROOT, George F. "About 'Normal.'" *Song Messenger of the Northwest* 8/8 (Aug 1870): 115.

A report on the 1870 normal school in South Bend, Indiana. Mason taught piano lessons and an advanced harmony class. He also played piano recitals, one of which Root describes as follows:

> A Steck, full grand, on a platform prepared for the purpose in a large, fine hall, so arranged that the largest number can see the keyboard, and Mr. Mason alternately explaining the characteristics of Beethoven, Schumann, Chopin, Liszt, and other composers, and bringing out with classic care the true meanings of their compositions, intellectual and emotional.

See also nos. **360, 404.**

403   ROOT, George F. "Mr. Geo. F. Root to His Friends, Greeting." *Song Messenger of the Northwest* 4/9 (Dec 1866): 137-38.

Root relates his vacation experiences at the Isles of Shoals.

> There were Mr. Geo. Jas. Webb and family, Mr. Wm. Mason and family, Messrs. Lowell Mason, jr., and Henry Mason, of the firms of Mason Brothers, and Mason & Hamlin. . . . I cannot stop to tell about the fishing, but will only say that it was droll to see the fingers that perhaps touch the piano better than any others in our country, tugging away at a twenty pound cod.

404   ROOT, George F. *The Story of a Musical Life: An Autobiography.* Cincinnati: John Church Co., 1891; reprints, New York: Da Capo Press, 1970; New York: AMS Press, 1973.

Includes a detailed description of the series of events which led to the performance of Mason's *Serenade* at a New York Philharmonic concert on 5 March 1853 by a vocal quartet which had been organized and trained by Root. The book also contains Root's comments about Mason's work in the normal music school held in South Bend, Indiana, in 1870 (see also nos. **360, 402**).

405   RUSSELL, Charles Edward. *The American Orchestra and Theodore Thomas.* New York: Doubleday, Page & Co., 1927; reprint, Westport, Conn.: Greenwood Press, 1971.

Although the book deals mainly with Thomas's work as a conductor, it also includes a description of the close personal and professional relationship between Mason and Thomas.

406 RUSSELL, Theodore Caskey. "Theodore Thomas: His Role in the Development of Musical Culture in the United States, 1835-1905." Ph.D. diss., University of Minnesota, 1969. 233 pp. UM 70-5642. *Dissertation Abstracts* 31/5 (Nov 1970): 2425-A.

> This study of the nineteenth century American conductor, Theodore Thomas, presents 1) an organized account of his life, his personality, and his achievements; 2) a perspective on his career through an investigation of the conditions under which he worked, the major factors influencing his work, and the activities of his musical contemporaries; and 3) an assessment of his contributions to the present state of musical culture in the United States.

Among the early influences on Thomas examined by Russell are his career as an orchestra violinist and chamber music player in association with William Mason.

407 RUTLEDGE, Lyman V. *The Isles of Shoals in Lore and Legend.* Barre, Mass.: Barre Publishers, 1965.

Includes a chapter on Celia Thaxter's "parlor" in her cottage where she organized literary discussions and musical performances. William Mason frequently participated in these gatherings when he was a guest on the island.

> If by chance William Mason was in Celia's parlor back of the wistaria vines, the Preludes of Chopin would mingle with the choir of birds, over the garden.

408 SABLOSKY, Irving. *American Music.* The Chicago History of American Civilization. Chicago: University of Chicago Press, 1969.

Sablosky gives a short overview of Mason's life; greatest emphasis is given to Mason's work in the field of chamber music.

> Mason and [Theodore] Thomas shared high standards and a sense of mission. By standing on the street and passing out handbills to advertise their [chamber music] concerts, they gradually won an audience in New York City and up the coast. . . . The thirteen-year career of the Mason-Thomas Quartette established a standard of chamber music performance and program-making where scarcely any had existed.

409 SAERCHINGER, César. "Musical Landmarks in New York." *Musical Quarterly* 6/1 (Jan 1920): 69-90; 6/2 (Apr 1920): 227-56.

An interesting history of New York's concert halls and the musicians who performed in them. Mason's career as a performer, particularly his work in chamber music, is briefly chronicled.

> Gifted as virtuoso, as well as pedagogue, having studied in Leipzig and Prague, hobnobbed with Liszt at Weimar and played before courts, [Mason] . . . was a real cosmopolitan, a man of the world as well as a solid artist, a musician of fine taste and broad sympathy, an all-round man such as New York, as the artistic gateway of America, needed at this juncture.

410   SAGUL, Edith A. "Development of Chamber Music Performance in the United States. . . ." Ed.D. diss., Columbia University, 1952. 215 pp.

Sagul mentions the Mason-Thomas Quartette in her discussion of the development of chamber music performances in New York City.

411   SALTER, Sumner. "Early Encouragements to American Composers." *Musical Quarterly* 18/1 (Jan 1932): 76-105.

Salter outlines the activities of several organizations, notably the MTNA and the Manuscript Society of New York, which supported American composers in the nineteenth century. One of the items concerning the Manuscript Society is of particular interest. When the society moved to a new location on 17 East 22d Street in November 1895, they sponsored an exhibition of autograph manuscripts of music, letters of composers, facsimiles, prints, and souvenirs of musical interest.

> The representation of the classical composers included specimens . . . loaned by members or friends of the society, including . . . William Mason. . . .

Much to the embarrassment of the Manuscript Society, the items exhibited were later lost.

See also nos. **110, 1016.**

412   SALTER, Sumner. "Gottschalk — Brahms — Mackenzie." *Pianist and Organist* 3/6 (June 1897): 155.

As the title suggests, this article includes three different subjects: Gottschalk, Brahms, and Alexander C. Mackenzie. Only the sections on Gottschalk and Brahms involve Mason. The segment on Brahms is an account of Mason's often repeated story of Brahms's first meeting with Liszt. The section on Gottschalk reports that Mason was in the process of preparing an edition of Gottschalk's "Last Hope" for publication by Theodore Presser. Regarding Gottschalk's performance of Beethoven, Mason is quoted as saying:

> He [Gottschalk] is said to have been a great Beethoven player and to have played all the sonatas by heart, but nothing was further from the truth. As a matter of fact he disliked Beethoven and played only one sonata, the "Pathetique," and of that cared only for the andante.

413   SATTER, Gustav. "An Open Letter to J. S. Dwight." *New York Musical World* 14/264 (19 Apr 1856): 189-90.

A sequel to "Musical and Dramatic" (see no. **311**).

414   SCHMIDT, John C. *The Life and Works of John Knowles Paine*. Studies in Musicology, no. 34. Ann Arbor: UMI Research Press, 1980.

Originally a dissertation under the same title (UM 79-25522; *Dissertation Abstracts* 40/5 [Nov 1979]: 2347-A). Schmidt mentions Paine's summer vacations at the Isles of Shoals, a resort area also frequented by Mason. Descriptions of the Isles of Shoals given in Mason's *Memories of a Musical Life* are cited. Schmidt describes some of the guests of the islands as follows:

> Appledore House, since its opening in 1848, had become a small summer intellectual and artistic gathering place, attracting literary notables such as James Russell Lowell (1819-91), Henry David Thoreau (1817-62), and John Greenleaf Whittier (1807-92), and artists such as William Morris Hunt (1824-79) and Childe Hassam (1859-1935). Many of the Harvard faculty spent their summers there. . . . Paine was not the only musician to enjoy Shoals. William Mason, the famed pianist, had been visiting Appledore regularly since 1863.

415   SCHONBERG, Harold C. *The Great Pianists*. New York: Simon & Schuster, 1963.

Includes a one-paragraph description of Mason's life and work as well as several citations of Mason's critical analyses of the playing of some of his contemporaries.

> When he came home in 1854 it was with a set of ideals and accomplishments that no American musician could match. He promptly started introducing Beethoven, Chopin and Schumann to his bemused audiences, followed Liszt's lead in giving recitals without assisting artists, and concentrated primarily on the best music. In that, during the 1850s, he was unique in America and, with the exception of von Bülow and Clara Schumann, in Europe, too.

416   SCHWAB, Arnold T. *James Gibbons Huneker: Critic of the Seven Arts*. Stanford, Calif.: Stanford University Press, 1963.

A comprehensive biography. Schwab briefly mentions Huneker's assertion — made in a letter to W. D. Moffat on 12 February 1901 — that he had written the article on Paderewski signed by William Mason and published in the *Century Magazine* in March 1892. Huneker's claim of authorship seems to be an exaggeration. Both the content of the essay, some of which was taken from an earlier article written by Mason and published in the *Musical Courier*, and the style of writing point to Mason as being the author; however, in a footnote to the essay Mason does acknowledge Huneker's assistance in "the preparation of this paper at a time when the writer was seriously indisposed."

See also no. **566**.

417   SHERWOOD, William H. "Dr. Mason's Genius as a Teacher." *Etude* 26/9 (Sept 1908): 557.

Under larger heading entitled "Tributes to Dr. Mason. . . ." Picture included. A short, retrospective article in which Sherwood reflects on the pedagogical ideas and performance style he associated with Mason.

> Dr. Mason had the idea that the intellectual training of a piano player should be begun and carried on alongside of the technical and musical, in the very first stages or *formative period* of a student's career.

418   [SHIMER, Carrie E.] Advertisement for her *Preparatory "Touch and Technic," Introductory to Dr. Wm. Mason's System.* In *Etude* 14/1 (Jan 1896): 17.

An announcement that Shimer's book (see next item), which was meant to serve as an introduction to Mason's *Touch and Technic*, op. 44, was in press.

> The work was written under the supervision of Dr. Mason, whose endorsement goes on the title page. . . .

419   SHIMER, Carrie E. *Preparatory "Touch and Technic," Introductory to Dr. Wm. Mason's System for Artistic Piano-Forte Playing . . . ; Presenting in a Concise Form the Fundamental Principles and a Series of Exercises Which Lead Directly to and Prepare for "Touch and Technic."* Philadelphia: Theodore Presser, 1896.

Review of no. **419:**

MATHEWS, William Smythe Babcock. "Reviews and Notices: Preparatory Touch and Technic. . . ." *Music* 10 (Sept 1896): 523-24.

A negative review.

> In this little work of thirty-six pages Miss Shimer undertakes to present a simplification of the Mason system. . . . It is the opinion of the writer, however, that the original work offers certain advantages which this one fails of. First, there are here no diagrams of positions of hands; then the directions are little if any better than the original.

See also the previous item.

420   SILVER, Ednah C. *Sketches of the New Church in America on a Background of Civic and Social Life. . . .* Boston: Massachusetts New Church Union, 1920.

Includes a brief biography of Mason and a partial account of his work as an organist in New Churches (Swedenborgian) in both New York City and Orange, New Jersey.

421   "Sixth Annual Meeting of the Musical Institute." *Musical Gazette* (Boston) 3/20 (23 Oct 1848): 153-55.

See no. **309.**

422   SKINNER, O. R. "Dr. William Mason." *Etude* 11/5 (May 1893): 104.

The article begins with a succinct biographical sketch of Mason. This is followed by a lengthy statement in which Skinner explains why he discarded other systems of piano technique and adopted Mason's.

This is an age of improvement; why should there not be radical improvements in technical methods? Why should not America, which has produced so many inventive geniuses in the world of science, give us a mind which should be capable of selecting from all systems the best, and, leaving out the dross, give us the pure gold—an epoch-making work, which shall contain the essence of modern technic? It seems to me that Mason has satisfactorily done this.

423   "Some Interesting Incidents in the Career of the Late Dr. William Mason." *Musical America* 8/11 (25 July 1908): 13.

Subtitled "In His 'Memories of a Musical Life' He Told of His Associations with the Great Contemporary Masters of Europe—His Visits to Liszt and Wagner—His Impressions of Schumann—How Paderewski Was Discouraged in His Attempt to Compose a Fantaisie on 'Yankee Doodle'—A Chance Meeting with Meyerbeer." Consists of quotations taken from Mason's *Memories of a Musical Life* interspersed with editorial comments.

424   SPANGLER, Harry S. "A History of Pianoforte Methods." Ph.D. diss., University of North Dakota, 1951. 242 pp.

Spangler cites Mason as a major contributor to piano instruction in the United States. Some of the unique features of Mason's teaching are noted.

425   STEINBERG, Arne. "Franz Liszt's Approach to Piano Playing." D.M.A. diss., University of Maryland, 1971. 263 pp. UM 71-25283. *Dissertation Abstracts* 32/4 (Oct 1971): 2124-A.

One of the methods used by Steinberg to determine Liszt's approach to piano playing was to examine various aspects of Liszt's students' work: their editions, their published "methods," and accounts of their teaching. Mason was one of twenty-four musicians selected for this purpose. Steinberg gives a synopsis of Mason's relationship with Liszt, his style of performance, and the fundamentals of his system of technique. Citations from Mason's writings are scattered throughout the dissertation.

Even critics who were antagonistic to Mason admitted his technical mastery, and for this reason his extensive writings on technique are of great value, especially since they were strongly influenced by Liszt. As a pianist, Mason was noted for his "pearly touch" in passagework, a characteristic often mentioned in connection with [the] playing of all of Liszt's better students.

426   STEINWAY, William. Letter to Theodore Presser, New York, 23 Dec 1895. Published on the cover of *Etude* 14/1 (Jan 1896).

Steinway, having recently read the endorsement of Mason's piano method by Paderewski (see no. **578**), writes about the occasions when two other famous musicians — Rubinstein and Liszt — made favorable comments about Mason to members of the Steinway family. Also published as "William Steinway to William Mason," *Music* 11 (Feb 1897): 468-69.

427   "Studio of William Mason, Steinway Hall, New York." *Musician* 4/11 (Nov 1899): 416.

Simply a picture of Mason's studio "as it appeared on the Anniversary of his Seventieth Birthday."

428   "Summer Music School." *Etude* 13/4 (Apr 1895): 80.

An announcement that the Theodore Presser Company would not be sponsoring a summer music school in Philadelphia as they had the previous year.

> Our reason for not continuing the work this summer is because we have not the strength. . . . We were in hopes that the work could be carried on, on the scale that was laid down last summer, but it seems that there is no one to assume the responsibility.

See also nos. **238, 378, 379, 380, 381, 429.**

429   "A Summer School in Prospect." *Etude* 12/3 (Mar 1894): 53.

An announcement of the general objectives set up for the 1894 summer music school in Philadelphia.

> It is to meet the demand for higher culture that we are moved to announce a summer school in Philadelphia for teachers of music, and others. The proper understanding of "Touch and Technic" by Dr. Wm. Mason requires the living example. We are deluged with letters from all parts of the country, inquiring where "Touch and Technic" may be learned. We purpose to afford every advantage to teachers in the way of gaining a knowledge of piano technic based on "Touch and Technic."

See also nos. **238, 378, 379, 380, 381, 428.**

430   "Superlatives." *Dwight's Journal of Music* 9/2 (12 Apr 1856): 14.

A sequel to "Musical and Dramatic" (see no. **311**).

431   SWAYNE, Egbert. "Dr. William Mason in His Studio." *Music* 11 (Nov 1896): 84-86.

Unsigned, but Swayne is named as the author in the index. Swayne may have been a pseudonym for William Smythe Babcock Mathews. Pictures included. A three-page description of the arrangement of Mason's studio in Steinway Hall.

His [Mason's] place at Steinway hall has been occupied ever since the hall was built, and aside from William Steinway himself or Mr. Nahum Stetson, the comfort of no person about the house is more regarded.

432   SWAYNE, Egbert. "William Mason's Seventieth Birthday." *Music* 15 (Mar 1899): 516-24.

Picture included. Swayne (William Smythe Babcock Mathews?) begins his article with a sketchy biography of Mason, laced with personal anecdotes and a history of Mason's relationship with the Steinways. The second part of the article quotes a description of the birthday celebration at Steinway Hall as reported in the *Musical Age*. Among the gifts Mason received was a grand piano from the Steinways.

See also nos. **45, 204.**

433   "Systematic Accentuation Applied to Technical Training in Playing the Piano-Forte." *New York Musical Gazette* 1/12 (Oct 1867): 92-93.

A discussion of the accentuation exercises recently published in Mason and Hoadly's *A Method for the Piano-Forte.* Some of the benefits said to be gained by the use of the accentuation system are explained, including: 1) an awakened interest in exercises, 2) increased finger strength, 3) improved voicing, 4) greater rhythmic stability, and 5) improved concentration.

434   "Teachers' Class of the Boston Academy of Music." *Musical Gazette* (Boston) 3/16 (28 Aug 1848): 121-23.

A report on the meetings of the musical institute for teachers held in Boston from the eighth through the eighteenth of August. William Mason was one of the accompanists (piano and organ) for the institute. He also performed solo works on at least two occasions: an improvised voluntary on the organ during one of the afternoon sessions, and an unidentified piece on the piano for the closing concert on August 18.

435   "The Teachers of Music: Eighth Annual Meeting of the Music Teacher's National Association." *Etude* 2/7 (July 1884): 114-15.

A summary of the events of the 1884 MTNA meeting, which included the formation of the American College of Musicians.

The spare time of the last meeting was . . . nearly all taken up in forming THE AMERICAN COLLEGE OF MUSICIANS. . . . There were some half-dozen meetings in all before the plan of organization was consumated [*sic*]. The final thereof was the election of a board of examiners who will formulate a system of examinations. . . . The following are the names: *Pianoforte.* — William H. Sherwood, Boston; Dr. Louis Maas, Boston; Dr. William Mason, New York.

436 "Testimonial Dinner to Theodore Thomas." *Musical Courier* 22/17 (29 Apr 1891): 416-20.

A detailed account of the testimonial dinner held for Theodore Thomas in New York in April 1891 prior to his departure for Chicago. Thomas's remarks at the dinner, transcribed in this article, included frequent references to Mason.

> When I speak of the music of thirty or forty years ago, my friend on my left, Mr. William Mason ("Bravo!" and cheers), makes the best suggestion to me—that is, his presence itself.

437 THAXTER, Celia. *Letters*. . . . Ed. A.[nnie] F.[ields] and R.[ose] L.[amb]. Boston and New York: Houghton, Mifflin & Co., 1895.

Several of Thaxter's letters mention Mason's performances in the "parlor recitals" held in her cottage. In a letter to Rose Lamb of 29 July 1888, she writes:

> Yesterday morning Mr. Mason played, like one inspired, for two hours.

438 THAXTER, Rosamund. *Sandpiper: The Life & Letters of Celia Thaxter and Her Home on the Isles of Shoals; Her Family, Friends, & Favorite Poems*. Rev. ed. Francestown, N.H.: Marshall Jones Co., 1963.

Includes a group photograph of William Mason, Ross Turner, Appleton Brown, John Knowles Paine, and William Winchel vacationing at the Isles of Shoals.

439 THOMAS, Rose Fay. *Memoirs of Theodore Thomas*. New York: Moffat, Yard & Co., 1911; reprint, Freeport, N.Y.: Books for Libraries Press, 1971.

Mrs. Thomas makes several references to the positive influence Mason had upon her husband's life and career.

> The year 1855 was an important one for Thomas, for it brought him under one of the best influences of his life, both in music and friendship. It was in this year that William Mason, a refined, sincere, and highly-educated musician, organized a quartette of string players, to give a series of chamber concerts in New York, and invited Thomas to be its first violin. A man of his caliber naturally selected for his musical associates men who were not only fine musicians, but who were also refined and sincere in character.

440 THOMAS, Theodore. *A Musical Autobiography*. Ed. George P. Upton. 2 vols. Chicago: A. C. McClurg, 1905; reprint (2 vols. in 1, pp. 35-356 of vol. 2 deleted), with a new introduction by Leon Stein, New York: Da Capo Press, 1964.

Pictures included. Programs of the Mason-Thomas chamber music concerts in New York are contained in the second volume (deleted in the reprint edition). The autobiography itself is terse, and Thomas's descriptions of his contemporaries, including Mason, are generally limited to brief sketches.

> William Mason, as sincere in art as in his daily life, had a genuine musical nature. He showed talent at an early age, and was sent to Europe, where he had exceptional opportunities for study, and favorable surroundings. After his return, he appeared as a virtuoso.... Mr. Mason afterwards turned his attention to teaching, and we all know how successful and influential his work has been.

441 "Tributes to Dr. Mason." *Musical Age* 62/13 (25 July 1908): 289.

Makes note of the various accolades given to Mason following his death. Includes quotations from an article in the New York *Sun* (see no. **465**) and remarks made by Nahum Stetson of Steinway & Sons.

442 Trustees' Minutes, Fifth Avenue Presbyterian Church, New York.

Contain several entries about Mason's employment as the church organist. The minutes for 13 April 1858 state:

> It was amended that an offer of $500 per annum be tendered to Mr. William Mason to remain as organist. As his performances are so entirely satisfactory to this Board and the congregation generally, this Board is in favor of paying him $100 per annum more than they would pay to any other man.

443 *Universal-Handbuch der Musikliteratur aller Zeiten und Völker . . .* [Pazdírek] (1904-10). S.v. "Mason, William."

Contains a long list of works, including many of Mason's compositions with opus numbers. (Some of the opus numbers listed are incorrect.) Numerous other works without opus numbers are also mentioned, many of which seem to be spurious. See Preface.

444 U.S. Library of Congress. *Report of the Librarian of Congress . . . for the Fiscal Year Ending June 30, 1912.* Washington, D.C.: Government Printing Office, 1912.

Reports that Rudolph E. Schirmer, head of the publishing firm of G. Schirmer, had given selected original manuscripts from the firm's archives to the Library of Congress. One of the manuscripts transferred was that of Mason's *Scherzo-Caprice*, op. 52 (see no. **765**).

445 U.S. Library of Congress. *Report of the Librarian of Congress for the Fiscal Year Ending June 30, 1930.* Washington, D.C.: Government Printing Office, 1930.

Includes a report of the library's acquisition of over thirty holograph manuscripts by Mason.

> From Howard van Sinderen, Esq., Tuxedo Park, N.Y., [the library received] a collection of over 30 holograph compositions for the piano by the late Dr. William Mason (1829-1908), the donor's father-in-law. These manuscripts date from the early fifties, when Mason studied under Moscheles and Liszt in Germany, to an "Ecossaise" written on June 8, 1903, as a contribution to a "Souvenir magazine" sold at the Orange Memorial Hospital Fair.

446   "The Valley Chimes." *Orange Chronicle*, 18 June 1870, p. [3], col. 4.

Reports on the arrival of a new set of chimes for the Valley Church in Orange, New Jersey, — a project to which Mason had contributed by performing in a benefit concert given to raise money for their purchase.

> The chime numbers ten bells, the largest of which weighs 2,500 pounds and the smallest 350.

See also nos. **300, 447.**

447   "Valley Church Concert." *Orange Chronicle*, 12 Mar 1870, p. [3], col. 3.

Announces a benefit concert to be given in Orange, New Jersey, for the purpose of raising money for the purchase of chimes for the Valley Church. Mason participated as an organ soloist and accompanist.

> The object to which the proceeds of this concert are to be applied, is one that commends itself to the whole community. A pleasant chime of bells can be enjoyed by every one. . . .

For a review of this concert, see no. **300.** See also no. **446.**

448   "A Vital Moment in American Music." *Etude* 32/11 (Nov 1914): 773.

A brief statement that

> In 1901, Dr. William Mason proclaimed: "The time has gone by when it was necessary for students to go abroad to complete a musical education."

449   WEBSTER, Beveridge. "Piano Touch, Again." *Music* 6 (July 1894): 317-22.

A sequel to "Cause and Effect in Pianoforte Touch: A Symposium" (see no. **53**).

450   "Weimar, Germany." *New York Musical Review and Choral Advocate* 5/11 (25 May 1854): 188-89.

A long letter (signed "N. R." — Nathan Richardson?), much of which deals with Mason's life as a student in Weimar.

I called at Mr. Mason's rooms for the purpose of being favored
with a specimen of his performance. My wishes were gratified. He
commenced with an original fantasia, and afterward played some of
the most difficult compositions of Liszt; also, part of Mendelssohn's
concerto in G minor, and some other saloon pieces, in a manner
that was very striking and effective. . . .

451   "What Sometimes Happens to Concert-Givers." *Musical Gazette* (New York)
16 (24 Feb 1855): 124-25.

A series of anecdotes about Mason's recently completed western recital tour
(see no. **624**).

His [Mason's] concerts were always closed by a series of "improvisations on themes handed in by the audience;" each auditor sending
in the name of any piece he or she wished to hear improvised
upon. . . . *Jordan is a hard road to travel*, and *Old Hundred* seemed
to be the greatest favorites with every audience; and requests were
often sent in that "Mr. Mason would play *Old Hundred* with one
hand, and *Jordan* with the other, at the same time;" which requests
he sometimes complied with. . . .

Also published as "What Sometimes Happens to Concert-Givers," *New York
Musical Review and Choral Advocate* 6/5 (1 Mar 1855): 76.

452   WHISTLER, Harvey Samuel, Jr. "The Life and Work of Theodore Thomas."
Ph.D. diss., Ohio State University, 1942. 1007 pp.

A massive study, including a thorough account of the Mason-Thomas
chamber music concerts. Appendix no. 5 contains a copy of an undated
prospectus announcing the "Wm. Mason & Theo Thomas' Conservatory
of Music."

453   *Who Was Who in America: A Companion Volume to Who's Who in America*
(1942-). S.v. "Mason, William," vol. 2, p. 786.

Gives a brief outline of Mason's life and lists his major publications.

454   *Who's Who in America: A Biographical Dictionary of Living Men and
Women of the United States, 1899-1900* (1899), ed. John W. Leonard.
S.v. "Mason, William."

Includes a short biography, a brief list of Mason's published works, and
his current office and residence addresses. Entries for William Mason are
also contained in the 1901-02, 1903-05, 1906-07, and 1908-09 editions of
Who's Who.

455   WIER, Albert E., ed. *The Days of Joachim and Hellmesberger: Forty
Compositions by Composers of All Nationalities in the Period from 1821
to 1834*. New York: Harcourt, Brace & Co., 1936.

Includes an arrangement for violin and piano (entitled *Lyric Poem*) of Mason's *Amitié pour amitié: Morceau de salon*, op. 4 (see no. **701**). A brief summary of Mason's student years in Europe, his work with the Mason-Thomas Quartette, and his style of composition is given with the violin score (p. 40).

456   WIER, Albert E. *The Piano: Its History, Makers, Players and Music.* London: Longmans, Green & Co., 1940.

Wier includes a short biography of Mason in his "Dictionary of Pianists."

457   "William Mason." *Daily Evening Traveller* (Boston), 23 Sept 1854, p. [1], cols. 3-4.

This article consists of three parts: a review of Mason's private recital given in Boston on 22 September 1854 (see no. **617**), a biography of the first twenty-five years of Mason's life, and a copy of a letter written by Mason on 14 September 1854 in which he explained some of his ideas on composition and piano performance (see no. **520**). In the biographical sketch it is stated that

> His [Mason's] memory and powers of imitation have always been great. When but a mere child he would catch airs from street organs, and play them on the pianoforte at home, with all the parts just as they were played on the organ.

The biographical portion of this article was also published as "William Mason," *Dwight's Journal of Music* 5/26 (30 Sept 1854): 203-04; "William Mason," *New York Musical Review and Choral Advocate* 5/20 (28 Sept 1854): 337. Mason's letter was also published as "Letter from William Mason," *Dwight's Journal of Music* 6/1 (7 Oct 1854): 2-3; "William Mason: His Ideas on Musical Composition and Piano-forte Playing," *Musical Gazette* (New York) 1 (11 Nov 1854): 6-7.

458   "William Mason." In *Half Hours with the Best Composers*, pt. 25, pp. 1251-58. Ed. Karl Klauser, with an introduction by Theodore Thomas. Boston: J. B. Millet Co., 1894-95.

Contains a biographical sketch and Mason's piano composition *A Pastoral Novellette* (see no. **771**). A facsimile of the first fourteen measures of the holograph score of *A Pastoral Novellette* is also included.

See also no. **134**.

459   "William Mason." *Musical Courier* 8/4 (23 Jan 1884): 51.

The front cover of this issue has a portrait of Mason with the caption "Dr. William Mason." A good biographical sketch.

> During the last thirty years he [Mason] has followed very closely his vocation as a teacher of the pianoforte, and many of his pupils have attained eminence in the musical world, some of them being artists of the front rank.

460   "William Mason." *New York Musical Review and Choral Advocate* 5/11 (25 May 1854): 185.

A report on Mason's plans to return to the United States from Europe to begin his professional career.

> RECENT letters from WILLIAM MASON . . . announce his intention of returning to America, for the purpose of making his *début* in August or September next. Though solicited to give concerts in Europe, he has steadily refused, and has only appeared publicly so far as to play a single piece on a few important occasions, when he has uniformly met the most flattering receptions. Unlike many American artists, he has chosen his native city as the scene of his *début*. . . .

461   "William Mason." *Outlook* 69/14 (7 Dec 1901): 899.

A full-page photo taken for the *Outlook* by Gertrude Kasebier. A brief caption announces the recent publication of Mason's *Memories of a Musical Life*.

462   "William Mason as a Joker." *Score* 3/15 (Dec 1878): 271.

See no. **38.**

463   "William Mason at Prague." *Choral Advocate and Singing-Class Journal* 1/11 (Apr 1851): 166-67.

See no. **9.**

464   "William Mason Dead at 80" (obituary). *New York Herald*, 16 July 1908, p. 7, col. 1.

> William Mason, well known as a pianist and teacher, died of heart disease Tuesday at his home, at No. 1 West Eighty-first street.

465   "William Mason, Musician" (obituary). *Sun* (New York), 18 July 1908, p. 4, cols. 2-3.

> . . . his playing was characterized by finish, a sensitive delicacy, a sweetness of tone and touch, a poetic style; above all, he was what most pianists are not, he was thoroughly musical. No one who ever heard him play in old Steinway Hall the Mozart concertos for pianoforte and orchestra under the conductorship of THEODORE THOMAS will forget the plangent charm, the pearliness of scale and passage work, or the intimate, mellow interpretation.

Also published in "Journalistic Comment on Dr. Mason's Death," *Etude* 26/9 (Sept 1908): 555.

466 "William Mason" (obituary). *New York Tribune*, 15 July 1908, p. 7, col. 4.

Picture included.

> William Mason, the pianist, died yesterday at his home, No. 1 West 81st street, in his eightieth year. Death was due to heart disease and the excessive heat.

467 "William Mason" (obituary). *Outlook* 89/13 (25 July 1908): 637-38.

> No other American had more intimate relations with the great men of music in his day than William Mason. His death last week, in his eightieth year, severs one of the few strands that have connected this day with one of the golden eras in music.

468 "William Mason's Concert." *Boston Daily Evening Transcript*, 23 Sept 1854, p. [4], col. 2.

> This article is divided into two sections. The first part is an announcement of Mason's recital in Boston on 3 October 1854 (see no. **618**). The second part consists of a highly complimentary review (signed "E. A. S.") of Mason's piano performance skills.

> > . . . all who attend the concert announced by Mr. Mason will, we are satisfied, be convinced that in the most important qualities of pianoforte concert playing, we have never had a performer here, who could carry away the victory from him.

> Also published in an elongated form as "William Mason's Concerts," *Dwight's Journal of Music* 5/25 (23 Sept 1854): 198.

469 "William Mason's Concert." *Dwight's Journal of Music* 5/26 (30 Sept 1854): 204-05.

> This article consists of two parts: a review of Mason's Boston matinée on 22 September 1854 and an announcement of Mason's program selections — with explanatory notes — for his recital on October 3 (see nos. **617, 618**). Dwight hints at the expectations held by Bostonians for Mason's recital on the third of October.

> > Verily a piano-forte concert, in a large hall [Tremont Temple], and on the Lind and Sontag scale of audiences, is a new thing under the sun; a new thing too is a pianist of such high claims, whom we can call our own; and one new thing explains the other.

470 "William Mason's Concerts." *Dwight's Journal of Music* 5/25 (23 Sept 1854): 198.

See no. **468**.

471   "William Mason's Reminiscences of Theodore Thomas." *Inter Ocean*, 15 Jan 1905, pt. [5] (*Inter Ocean Magazine*), p. [2], cols. 1-7.

The transcript of an interview of Mason by an anonymous reporter in which Mason reminisces about his friendship and work with Theodore Thomas. In some introductory comments, the reporter refers to a picture of Thomas which hung in Mason's house on West 16th Street.

> It shows an assertive, spirited, masterful young man looking out from the frame as if already impatient to take in the world the place he intended to occupy. Although the picture was taken many years ago, Mr. Mason received it only in 1902. So says the inscription in Theodore Thomas' handwriting, reading: "Zu meinem einzigen lieben freund, 1855-1902."

472   "Wm. Mason." *Boston Daily Evening Transcript*, 18 Sept 1854, p. [1], col. 5.

See no. **335**.

473   "Wm. Mason." *New York Musical Review and Choral Advocate* 5/16 (3 Aug 1854): 273.

See no. **72**.

474   "Wm. Mason's Concert Tour." *Musical Gazette* (New York) 2 (18 Nov 1854): 16.

An advertisement for Mason's concert tour in the fall and winter of 1854-55 (see no. **624**). A partial itinerary, information regarding ticket sales, and a description of the general character of the repertory to be performed are announced.

> The Programmes will comprise compositions by the best writers for the piano-forte; including selections from the works of HANDEL, BEETHOVEN, MENDELSSOHN, CHOPIN, LISZT, STEPHEN HELLER, and others; also, Popular Arrangements of National Airs, and IMPROVISATIONS on familiar melodies.

This advertisement continued to run in the next three issues of the *Musical Gazette*. It was also published as "Wm. Mason's Concert Tour," *New York Musical Review and Choral Advocate* 5/24 (23 Nov 1854): 405.

475   WOLFF, Konrad. "Liszt's Approach to Piano Technique." *Journal of the American Liszt Society* 4 (Dec 1978): 45-51.

Wolff cites Mason's *Touch and Technic*, op. 44, as one of the resources which are available for reconstructing details of Liszt's attitude toward piano technique.

> Mason makes it clear where Liszt ends and his own contribution begins; he was also intelligent and educated enough to express

technical ideas unambiguously, which was not an easy thing to do at that time in the absence of any other such books. Without Mason I am convinced that there would not have been a Breithaupt; and even Ortmann still owes the clarity of his style surely in part to Mason.

476 "Worcester's Improvement in the Pianoforte." *New York Times*, 21 July 1862, p. 5, cols. 3-4.

Mentions Mason's endorsement of the improvements made by the company.

The cast-iron plate is in these divided into two nearly equal portions — one of which is affixed to the case in the common way, while the second is coupled with it at the base [sic] end, and held in position by the string tension exerted in an opposite direction. The modification is termed "Hinging the Plate." The improvement is so marked and substantial that it needs not the many indorsements [sic] received at the hands of Messrs. GOTTSCHALK, MASON, . . . and other esteemed *artistes*, to satisfy even incipient amateurs of its value.

477 Yale University. *Divinity School Exercises at the Opening of "The Lowell Mason Library of Music" in the Yale Divinity School, May 11th, 1875.* N.p., n.d.

Copy held in Beinecke Rare Book and Manuscript Library, Yale University. A pamphlet issued to record the ceremonies held at the opening of the Lowell Mason Library of Music. This collection of materials, consisting of Lowell Mason's personal music library, had been donated to Yale in 1873. William Mason was an active participant in the dedicatory exercises.

The audience then listened, for an hour, with great delight, to selections of music from ancient and modern masters, as prefaced in each instance by a few words of introduction and criticism, and rendered on the piano by William Mason, Mus. Doc.

478 YOUNG, Percy Marshall. *Biographical Dictionary of Composers: With Classified List of Music for Performance and Study.* New York: Thomas Y. Crowell Co., 1954.

Includes a short entry on William Mason.

He [Mason] was principally concerned with pianoforte and chamber music. In these respects he was a great pioneer.

2

Literary Writings by William Mason

Mason as Sole Author

WRITINGS BY MASON IN MANUSCRIPT ARE CITED UNDER SOURCES, SECTION 5 OF THE BIBLIOGRAPHY.

SEE ALSO NOS. **41, 49, 81, 150, 235, 372, 412, 471.**

479 MASON, William. "Accentual Treatment of Exercises as Applied to Piano-Forte Exercises." *Ninth Annual Meeting of the Music Teachers' National Association . . . Official Report* (1885), 86-91.

Mason's essay, read at the MTNA meeting held in New York City in July 1885, was reprinted in the following publications: *Accentual Treatment of Exercises as Applied to Pianoforte Practice . . .* (New York: Edward Schuberth & Co., 1885); "Accentual Treatment of Exercises as Applied to Pianoforte Practice," *Musical Items* 2/9 (Aug 1885): 1-4; "Accentual Treatment of Exercises as Applied to Piano-Forte Exercises," *Etude* 3/10 (Oct 1885): 218; 3/11 (Nov 1885): 243.

> If exercises are properly practiced without any accent, there will quickly be manifested an obvious increase in physical power and skill, but if accent is simultaneously applied, a habit of close attention to inflections and musical punctuation will also be cultivated, and this, combined with emphasis [defined by Mason as transferred or displaced accent], will contribute in an important degree to the attainment of musical expression.

A transcript of the discussion held by members of the MTNA following Mason's presentation of his paper is printed in the *Ninth Annual Meeting of the Music Teachers' National Association . . . Official Report* (1885), 91-95. The discussion transcript was also published as "Accentual Treatment of Exercises as Applied to Piano-Forte Exercises . . . : Discussion," *Etude* 4/1 (Jan 1886): 9-10.

480 MASON, William. "Alexander Dreyschock and His Octaves." *Music* 19 (Dec 1900): 191-93.

An excerpt from Mason's *Memories of a Musical Life* (see no. **557**).

481   MASON, William. "Anecdote of Henselt." *Music* 8 (July 1895): 327-28.

Mason relates Dreyschock's account of the effect nervousness had on the piano playing of Henselt—at least on the one occasion referred to by Dreyschock.

> Such was his nervousness and constraint in the presence of a listener that the playing was entirely different from that which he had done while unconscious of a hearer. Not only was the phrasing less finished and the conception less intense, but the very tone itself had lost its round, full and satisfying quality. This was the effect of constriction due to nervousness.

482   MASON, William. ". . . Beethoven Playing." *Musical Courier* 23/23 (2 Dec 1891): 642.

Although the title of the article refers to Beethoven, Mason's primary reason for writing this article was to express support for Paderewski's playing, especially his playing of Beethoven, which had come under criticism. After commenting at some length that Beethoven's compositions are not "klaviermässig," Mason writes:

> Moscheles has always been an acknowledged authority as to Beethoven, and he told me once during a lesson that he considered Liszt an ideal, or perhaps his words were a "great" Beethoven player. . . . But even Liszt, who possessed in such an unexampled degree all of the faculties which in the aggregate make up the equipment of a perfect and even phenomenal player, had his limitations in certain directions and details. His touch was not so musically emotional as it might have been, and other pianists, notably Henselt, Chopin, Tausig, Rubinstein and now Paderewski and some others excel him in the art of producing beautiful and varied tone colors, together with sympathetic and singing quality of tone.

Addressing himself to the nature of Paderewski's playing, Mason writes:

> It seems to me that in this matter of touch Paderewski is as near perfection, or perhaps more so than any pianist I ever heard, while in other respects he stands more nearly on a plane with Liszt than any other virtuoso since Tausig. His conception of Beethoven combines the emotional with the intellectual in admirable poise and proportion; thus he plays with a big, warm heart as well as with a clear, calm and discriminative head, hence a thoroughly satisfactory result.

Also published with minor revisions as ". . . Beethoven Playing," *Music* 5 (Feb 1894): 434-38. Excerpts (interspersed with favorable editorial comments) are also published as "Paderewski and Beethoven," *Evening Post* (New York), 3 Dec 1891, p. 11, cols. 3-4. Mason later expanded this article into an essay on Paderewski for the *Century Magazine* (see no. **566**).

Mason's comments on Beethoven and Paderewski caught the attention of William J. Henderson, who, in an article in the *New York Times* titled "Live Musical Topics" (6 Dec 1891, p. 12, col. 7), gently disagreed with some of Mason's statements.

Dr. Mason's assertion that Beethoven's piano compositions are not "klaviermässig" . . . is too sweeping. Some, indeed a goodly number, of them are not, but the majority of them are. . . . No doubt Dr. Mason had the redoubtable Opus 106 and Opus 111 in mind when he wrote his letter. . . .

Turning to the issue of Paderewski, Henderson states:

. . . it appears that there was once a pianist who could play Beethoven, and he was the greatest pianist that ever lived [Liszt]. It seems, therefore, that those critics who have denied that Paderewski is the greatest, and have pointed out as one evidence of his failure to reach the top his inability to handle the music of Beethoven adequately, are not so far out of the way, after all.

Mason, warming up to the issue, responded to Henderson's comments and restated his own position in an article titled " . . . on Paderewski and Beethoven," *Evening Post* (New York), 11 Dec 1891, p. 6, col. 1.

Mr. Henderson, while courteous in his criticism in the *Times* of last Sunday, does not recognize the force of my argument, and takes a mistaken position, as it seems to me, and one which cannot be logically maintained. My object in writing to the *Musical Courier* was to give an opinion strongly in favor of Paderewski as a thoroughly satisfactory Beethoven player, and to call attention to the fact, patent to every pianist, that Beethoven was not an idiomatic writer for the pianoforte.

Mason's response to Henderson was also published as "Dr. Mason and the 'Evening Post,'" *Musical Courier* 23/26 (23 Dec 1891): 768-69.

Some final afterthoughts on the Paderewski controversy were given by Mason in an article titled "Musical Gossip," *Evening Post* (New York), 19 Dec 1891, pt. 2, p. 8, col. 2.

. . . there was an important omission in my *Musical Courier* letter. I ought to have added that, notwithstanding the favorable opinion of Moscheles and other prominent musicians regarding Liszt's Beethoven playing, many of the critics of those days — 1849 — especially the younger ones, were of contrary mind, and earnestly and positively asserted that Liszt was no Beethoven player. At that time as well as at the present there were two parties of very positive opinions. It seems therefore that the ideal Beethoven player is yet to come, if he is possible.

483   MASON, William. "Chopin Playing." *Musical Courier* 18/20 (15 May 1889): 398.

A three-paragraph letter in which Mason relates three anecdotes dating from his student life in Germany which are relevant to Chopin performance practice: Moscheles's comments on Chopin's compositional style made to Mason during a private lesson, Dreyschock's account of Thalberg shouting at the top of his voice following a concert given by Chopin, and Liszt's story about the delight expressed by Chopin following a student's string-breaking performance of one of Chopin's polonaises. The latter two incidents have been widely cited. The Moscheles lesson is described by Mason as follows:

Chopin died on October 17, 1849, and I remember well when the news of his death was first received in Leipsic, where I was at that time studying the piano under Moscheles. The playing of Chopin was then fresh before the public, and during one of my lessons Moscheles very naturally referred to and commented on it. He said that Chopin, judging from the distinguishing features of his compositions and from his characteristically delicate and tender style of playing, seemed to have a decided fancy for and desire to imitate the soft and weird breathings of the aeolian harp. . . . Moscheles furthermore cautioned his pupils against a too close imitation of Chopin as leading away from a habit of breadth and solidity and tending toward effeminacy of style.

Also published as " . . . Chopin and Chopin-Playing," *Music* 4 (June 1893): 207-08.

484   [MASON, William.] "Corrections in Touch and Technic. Part II. Scales." *Etude* 9/12 (Dec 1891): 226.

See no. **578**.

485   MASON, William. "Danger in Unduly Magnifying the Importance of Technic." *Musician* 7/3 (Mar 1902): 77.

A short article in which Mason elaborates on the comments he had previously made in his *Memories of a Musical Life* concerning Liszt's attitude toward piano technique.

He [Liszt] is quoted as having said that there were three essentials to piano playing[:] "First, technic; second, technic; third, technic." It is true that Liszt did have a wonderful technic, but in his case a technic implied something more than a wonderful power of prestidigitation, or facility in the manipulation of an instrument. It implied qualities of mind and heart—which are essential to an all-round musical development—and the ability to give them adequate expression.

486   MASON, William. Definition of measure. In "Personal." *Song Messenger: A Musical Monthly* 10/4 (Apr 1872): 55.

A sequel to Mathews's "Measure" (see no. **270**).

487   MASON, William. "Edvard Grieg." *Century Magazine* n.s. 25/5 (Mar 1894): 701-04.

Mason's admiration for Grieg is clearly reflected in this essay. It includes a biography, a discussion of style (with musical examples), and an assessment of Grieg's contribution to nineteenth-century music. Frequent comparisons are made between the compositional techniques of Grieg and Chopin. Mason closes with an account of his visit to Grieg's home on 1 July 1890.

Grieg's revolt against German classicism was the healthy instinct of a man who has a message to deliver, and seeks for it the most natural means of expression. His esteem for the highest and best in German music was none the less, and he would doubtless be among the first to acknowledge how much he has profited by its influence; but his imagination and feeling were imbued with the legends, the traditions, the folk songs, and poetry of the peasant, and the scenery of Norway. He has expressed and translated these into music, and thus has directed the attention of the outside world to his native land, and brought its distinguishing characteristics more clearly into view.

Mason's essay (with more pictures relating to Grieg added) was also published as "Edvard Hagerup Grieg," *Century Library of Music*, ed. Ignacy Jan Paderewski, Fanny Morris Smith, and Bernard Boekelman, 20 vols. (New York: Century Co., 1900-02), 5:151-58; "Edvard Hagerup Grieg," *The International Library of Music . . .* , 8 vols. (New York: University Society, 1934), vol. 1: *The History of Music . . .* , 253-59. (The 1948 four-volume edition of *The International Library of Music . . .* [New York, University Society] also contains this article in vol. 1, pp. 253-59.) Excerpts from Mason's essay were also published as "The Art of Grieg," *Masters in Music* 1/5 (May 1903): 197-204; "Edvard Grieg," *Etude* 12/4 (Apr 1894): 90.

488   MASON, William. Endorsement of Evelyn Ashton [Fletcher] Copp's *Fletcher Music Method: Simplex and Kindergarten* (n.p., 1901). In *Etude* 20/6 (June 1902): 235.

Mason praises the method for

> . . . its tendency to immediately arrest attention, to arouse interest and thus to promote a habit of mental concentration on the part of young children.

489   MASON, William. Endorsement of W. F. Gates's *Musical Mosaics: A Collection of Six Hundred Selections from Musical Literature . . .* (Philadelphia: Theodore Presser, 1889). In "Testimonials." *Etude* 7/12 (Dec 1889): 186.

> The editor has reaped his mosaics from a rich and wide field, and has manifested excellent judgment in their selection.

Mason is one of the authors quoted in Gates's book (see no. **577**).

490   MASON, William. Endorsement of Mary Gregory Murray as a lecturer on his piano method, as outlined in *Touch and Technic*, op. 44. In *Etude* 13/1 (Jan 1895): 25.

During the course of his endorsement of Murray, Mason mentions his own deteriorating health.

119

491   MASON, William. Endorsement of the National College of Teachers. In "National College of Teachers." *Etude* 2/4 (Apr 1884): 58.

> My whole heart is with you in your present work, looking toward good and wholesome teaching and honest and competent teachers. Any work which I can do, from time to time, to forward the cause will be most heartily and cordially contributed.

492   MASON, William. Endorsement of normal music schools. In "Musical Normals." *Kunkel's Musical Review* 7/1 (Jan 1884): 5-6.

> So much however is certain, that from a teacher who has the ability of imparting knowledge, one may learn more in an hour than can be learned in a year from a teacher who has not the ability. As an instance of the faculty of imparting knowledge pressed by some highly-favored men, the writer looks back to a conversation it was his privilege to enjoy with Richard Wagner in Zurich, Switzerland, in the year 1852, and he often wonders to the present day that so much information could have been crowded into the short space of an hour and ideas expressed in such a way as to have proved of such enduring and permanent value.

Excerpts from Mason's endorsement are also published in "The Teacher's Column," *Etude* 2/3 (Mar 1884): 49.

493   MASON, William. Endorsement of Carl A. Preyer's *Twenty Progressive Octave Studies for the Pianoforte*, op. 30, 2 vols. (Boston: Oliver Ditson, 1902). In *Etude* 21/4 (Apr 1903): 126.

> It seems to me that they are especially well adapted to the accomplishment of the purpose for which they are intended, lying well under the hand, and being musically melodious, thus interesting the pupil, and promoting the acquiring of a free, elastic and easy wrist movement.

494   MASON, William. Endorsement of E. M. Sefton's *The Teachers' Help and Students' Guide in First Lessons on the Piano or Organ* (Cedar Rapids, Iowa: E. M. Sefton, 1889). In *Etude* 8/5 (May 1890): 79.

> The various exercises are arranged in a systematic way, tending toward orderly and rapid development.

495   MASON, William. Endorsement of the technicon. In *Etude* 5/10 (Oct 1887): 148.

A very short, and less than enthusiastic, endorsement.

> I regard the Technicon as very helpful to piano players.

See also no. **524**.

496   MASON, William. Endorsement of the tonic sol-fa system. In Theodore
        F. Seward's *A Revolution in Music-Teaching: A Treatise on the Tonic
        Sol-Fa System*, 16-17. N.p., 1888.

        Copy held in New York Public Library.

> MY first impressions of the Tonic Sol-fa system were unfavor-
> able. . . . Having recently given the subject a more thorough
> investigation and also seen its practical application to difficult vocal
> music, I must confess that my opinion is entirely changed. I see
> that the notation simplifies the reading of chromatic passages, and
> what is of still greater importance, that it advises the reader of every
> passing modulation.

        See also no. **528**.

497   MASON, William. "The Fingers, Wrist, and Arm." *Etude* 14/8 (Aug
        1896): 185.

        Mason explains some of the methods he uses to teach the correct use of the
        fingers, wrist, and arm to beginning piano students.

498   [MASON, William.] "The Following Is a Complete List of Mr. Mason's
        Compositions." *Etude* 7/11 (Nov 1889): 170.

        Includes opuses 1-43, several duets without opus numbers, and Mason's piano
        methods published through 1889.

499   MASON, William. "How to Secure a Good Tone." *Music* 7 (Mar 1895):
        529-31.

        See no. **577**.

500   MASON, William. Letter, n.p., n.d. Excerpt published in "Euterpe Concert,
        Leipzig." *Choral Advocate and Singing-Class Journal* 1/2 (July 1850):
        20-21.

        Subheading reads "Extract of a Letter from a Young American, a Musical
        Student, in Germany." Mason describes a recent Euterpe concert he attended
        and comments about the quality of musical performance in Germany.

> It is true that there are many more professional musicians here, and
> that amongst the people in general the average of those who can
> understand classical music is greater than perhaps in any other
> country; but I think that the Germans in America are apt to talk a
> little too loudly, and to overrate a little. For instance, I have fre-
> quently been told by good German musicians in America that I should
> find "a far different state of things when I arrived in Germany; that
> certain performances that are frequently heard in our concerts,
> and which are denounced as humbugs by the appreciating part of
> the audience, would never be allowed or listened to there. . . ." Yet
> I must confess, that since my arrival in Germany, I have listened to

several pretty decided "humbugs," to my great astonishment; and stranger still, some of these "humbugs" have been loudly applauded. . . .

501 MASON, William. Letter, Dresden, 22 June 1850. Published as "Music in Germany." *Daily Evening Traveller* (Boston), 15 July 1850, p. [2], col. 2.

Mason writes about recent musical events in Leipzig.

> Robert Schumann everybody knows; he is almost looked upon as Mendelssohn's successor. His new opera, called *Genoveva*, is soon to be brought out at Leipzig. This is the first opera he has composed, and there is a deal of anxiety to hear it. The music is undoubtedly very fine; but I do not think it is light and melodical enough for popular taste even here.

502 MASON, William. Letter, Dresden, July 1850. Published as "Painting and Music in Germany." *Daily Evening Traveller* (Boston), 6 Aug 1850, p. 2, col. 3.

Mason describes the exhibits of a Dresden art gallery, the celebration of mass in a Catholic church, an organ recital by Johann Schneider, and congregational singing in Protestant churches.

> John Schneider, the organist, played in private, before the Austrian minister the other day. I managed to get into the church. . . . He played several fugues by Bach, and indeed he played no other music than Bach's. It was perhaps the best organ playing that I have yet heard, though it did not quite equal my previous anticipations; *perhaps I had expected too much.*

Also published as "Painting and Music in Germany," *Choral Advocate and Singing-Class Journal* 1/4 (Sept 1850): 57.

503 MASON, William. Letter, Dresden, 28 July 1850. Excerpt published in ". . . Letter from Mr. Wm. Mason. . . ." *Saroni's Musical Times* 1/48 (24 Aug 1850): 568-69.

Mason writes about two concerts performed in Dresden on the twenty-fifth and twenty-sixth of July in commemoration of the hundredth anniversary of Bach's death. Mason attended the first concert in company with Johann Schneider and Moritz Hauptmann.

> It was really interesting to watch the countenances and to catch the remarks of these two distinguished musicians [Schneider and Hauptmann] during the performance. Schneider is full of Bach's music, and he was often calling my attention to some particular or distinguishing point in the compositions. When the two *Gavotten* were played he caught hold of my arm saying: *"Come, we must dance!"* and jumping up from his chair he executed two or three manoeuvres to the great delight of Mr. Hauptmann, and myself, and also other people in the garden who knew him by reputation.

504   [MASON, William.] Letter, n.p., n.d. Published as "From Germany—Berlin." *Choral Advocate and Singing-Class Journal* 1/3 (Aug 1850): 36.

The writer is identified only as "M," but the contents of the letter point to Mason as the probable author. The letter contains an account of a variety of musical events Mason attended in Berlin.

505   MASON, William. Letter, Vienna, 9 Aug 1850. Published in "Notes from the Journal of an American Musical Student in Germany." *Message Bird: A Literary and Musical Journal* 32 (15 Nov 1850): 525-26.

Although dated August 9, the letter records Mason's activities through the fourteenth of August. Mason comments on a variety of topics, including the piano playing of Rudolf Willmers.

> . . . Wilmers [*sic*] sat down to a Piano and played for nearly two hours without cessation. He is really a splendid Pianist, but, I think, more of a *natural* or *born Pianist*, so to speak, than a *mechanical* or *made* performer. . . . In his own compositions he produces tremendous effect. His touch is exceedingly crisp and brilliant, and with his left hand he grasps such handfulls of notes that one would think there were two performers on the instrument.

506   MASON, William. Letter, n.p., n.d. Published in "Music in Prague." Unidentified clipping in MASON/Scrapbook.

This letter, probably dating from 1851, includes comments about several concerts Mason attended in Prague. Among the performers Mason heard was one Fr. Smulan, a pianist. Mason's reaction to Smulan's playing was unfavorable.

> I must say, I have never heard such poor Piano Forte playing in public before, either in America or Europe. His piece, which was Thalberg's Somnambula [*sic*], (which you will remember I have played many times in public and at home, and of course, know thoroughly by memory,) was nothing but *confusion throughout*, and yet, strange to say, *he was very loudly applauded*!

507   MASON, William. Letter, n.p., n.d. Excerpt published in "Editor's Table." *Choral Advocate and Singing-Class Journal* 1/10 (Mar 1851): 155.

Mason refutes the rumor that Liszt was planning to visit America.

> LISZT, in all probability, will never go to America; *at least he told me so.*

508   MASON, William. Letter, Prague, 21 Mar 1851. Published as "Quartette Concerts—Haydn—Mozart—Mendelssohn—Beethoven—Prague Conservatoire." *Saroni's Musical Times* 3/4 (19 Apr 1851): 42-43.

Includes an account of two "quartette concerts" which Mason heard in Prague in which compositions by Haydn, Veith, Mozart, Mendelssohn, Beethoven, and Gade were performed.

> Mozart's Quintett is a gem indeed. Oh! how *fresh*, *frolicsome* and *playful* is this charming composition. After hearing such music, one must be very misanthropic and destitue [*sic*] of a soul for music, if he is not made *perfectly happy* for the time being.

509   MASON, William. Letter, Prague, 3 Apr 1851. Published as "Matinée Musicale." *Saroni's Musical Times* 3/5 (26 Apr 1851): 52-53.

Contains Mason's impressions of a concert given in Prague at the palace of the Countess of Nostitz on 23 March 1851 under the patronage of Countess Schlik. Mason himself was one of the performers.

> The Countess Schlik, then invited me to play, and I performed two pieces on the Piano Forte. The first an Impromptu of my own in A^b major [*Amitié pour amitié*, op. 4?], and the second "La Coupe," an Impromptu composed by Alex. Dreyschock. I felt grateful for the favor with which the performance of an American was received by a select musical party in Germany. And here it may be proper to say, that every where in Germany thus far, in Hamburg, Leipzig, Dresden and Prague I have received the kindest attentions.

See also no. **610**.

510   MASON, William. Letter, n.p., n.d. Published as "From Germany." *Choral Advocate and Singing-Class Journal* 1/12 (May 1851): 182-83.

Contains Mason's reactions to two concerts that he attended. Among the works performed was Beethoven's *Quartet in A Minor*, op. 132.

> The Quartett by Beethoven . . . is one of those Quartetts which nobody can understand, and yet they do not like to lay it aside, but continue to perform it from time to time, in hopes, I suppose, that after a while somebody will be able to appreciate it. The Andante is very strange, consisting of the harshest suspensions, syncopations, &c., any thing but pleasant to my ears. I saw Moscheles the day after the concert, and in speaking to him of this Quartett, I told him that I could not at all understand the Andante. "Neither can I," was all the remark he made.

511   MASON, William. Letter, Prague, 26 Apr 1851. Published as "From Prague." *Choral Advocate and Singing-Class Journal* 2/1 (June 1851): 7.

Mason writes about services held in Prague's Catholic churches and Jewish synagogues and a performance of Ferdinand Hiller's oratorio *The Destruction of Jerusalem*.

> I think you must have a copy of this oratorio, for it has been some time published. If so, you have found it a truly scientific and tasteful work for the *eye*; and I can assure you that when heard it

loses none of its interest. There are, as you will know, musical compositions which appear well on paper, but disappoint us when heard; not so with this oratorio, which, like all good music, must be heard to be appreciated.

Also published as "From Prague," *Saroni's Musical Times* 3/10 (31 May 1851): 103.

512   MASON, William. Letter, Berlin, 2 Dec 1851. Published as "Correspondence: Concert at Berlin—Dome Choir—Mr. Von Heeringen and His New System." *Musical Times* 4/9 (3 Jan 1852): 140.

Contains Mason's comments about a concert given in Berlin which featured a performance of Beethoven's ninth symphony and the efforts of Ernst von Heeringen to introduce a new system of musical notation.

> Mr. Von Heeringen thinks there is no question but that he shall revolutionize the world with his new system, and that he is just now on the eve of success. He says he has showed his system to Dr. Marx, who expresses himself greatly pleased with it, as have also Meyerbeer and many other of the principal musicians here. . . .

513   MASON, William. Letter, Berlin, 30 Dec 1851. Published as "The Concert Season—A Programme from Beethoven—Fraulein Ebeling—Her Death—Some Account of Her, &c." *Musical Times* 4/12 (24 Jan 1852): 188-89.

The major portion of this two-column letter deals with one Miss Ebeling, a Swedish singer, who died suddenly at the age of twenty-three.

514   MASON, William. Letter, Frankfurt, 24 Oct 1852. Excerpt published as "German Items." *Musical World and New York Musical Times* 4/12 (20 Nov 1852): 180-81.

Contains an account of a concert Mason attended in Frankfurt which included performances of works by Mendelssohn and Beethoven.

> By the way I have a little anecdote to relate of Professor [Anton] Schindler. . . . I noticed that he left the Hall directly after Mendelssohn's concerto was played and did not return. . . . After the concert was finished we went to a café to supper, and found the Professor there. . . . Pretty soon the first violinist came in; addressing him, the Professor said, "Well, Mr. — —, in what key did you play Beethoven's A Symphony this evening?" This question was asked in such a way as to produce a general laugh throughout the room, and the *primo violino* was obliged to ask for an explanation. "Why," said Mr. Schindler, "last year I went to the same Hall to hear the same Symphony, it was crowded and hot as it was this evening, and the concert was very long. . . . The orchestra began, but what was my astonishment to hear them commence the A Symphony in B flat! thus giving to it quite a different character. Since then I always leave before the Symphony, if the weather is warm and the Hall crowded!"

515   MASON, William. Letter, Frankfurt, Oct 1852. Excerpt published as "German Items." *Musical World and New York Musical Times* 4/14 (4 Dec 1852): 212.

Mason comments about a variety of musical events in Frankfurt, including the recent departure of Rudolf Willmers for Stuttgart.

> Wilmers [*sic*] left here, a short time ago, for Stuttgart, having received an invitation to play at court. I was sorry to have him go, as I have become much attached to him. — He is an amiable man, and one of the few really good Pianists living. He has honored me by dedicating three pianoforte pieces to me, which are now being published by Schott & Co., of Mayence. . . .

516   MASON, William. Letter, Frankfurt, 2 Jan 1853. Excerpt published as "Extract of a Letter from Mr. William Mason." *Musical Review and Choral Advocate* 4/2 (Feb 1853): 27.

Mason describes four concerts given by the "Gebrüder Müller" string quartet.

> Their performance is perfection itself: it is as one man, one soul; and it seems impossible to find the slightest fault with them. The perfect subordination of each instrument to the general effect produces a unity that I cannot describe.

517   MASON, William. Letter, Weimar, 5 June 1853. Published as "Musical Advantages in Germany." *Musical Review and Choral Advocate* 4/9 (Sept 1853): 134.

Most of the letter consists of extracts taken from a journal Mason was keeping. The entries, dating from May 16 through June 6, describe Mason's activities in Weimar.

> I have now opportunities of seeing and hearing Liszt almost every day, and the more I see of him, the more I admire his immense genius and talent; he is undoubtedly the greatest musician with whom I have yet had intercourse, and I *know* that his future compositions will prove this.

518   MASON, William. Letter, Weimar, 14 Nov 1853. Published as "Musical Festival at Carlsruhe [*sic*]." Unidentified clipping in MASON/Scrapbook.

The music festival, directed by Liszt, was held in Karlsruhe in October 1853. Mason's letter includes his impressions of the festival's opening concert.

> Beethoven's Ninth closed the Concert, and was generally well played, particularly the first and second movements, (the latter of which was encored.) The third movement did not go off so well, though the chorus (about 200 singers) was magnificent. Where the march commences in B flat major, all were obliged to re-commence after playing six measures, on account of a mistake made by the bassoon. . . .

519   MASON, William. Letter, n.p., n.d. Excerpt published in "A Lesson by Liszt." *New York Musical Review and Choral Advocate* 5/14 (6 July 1854): 235.

A long letter in which Mason describes his life as a student of Liszt.

> One of the great advantages of a residence here, as students, is this: we are often brought into contact with the most celebrated musicians of Germany, and indeed of the world. There is some such one here almost all the time, and for these visitors, quartet and trio *matinées* or *soirées* are made very frequent; and these little parties are often, not so much to hear music, as to examine, or criticize or analyze it professionally. They are to music what the dissecting-room is to the young surgeon or physician. The students are always invited to attend these meetings.

520   MASON, William. Letter, Medfield (Mass.), 14 Sept 1854. Published in "William Mason." *Daily Evening Traveller* (Boston), 23 Sept 1854, p. [1], cols. 3-4.

Mason writes about some of his views on composition and the philosophy of performance.

> A person may observe, in his playing, every mark of expression, and execute a composition just right in every mechanical particular, and yet fail to give anything like a true or proper interpretation thereof, inasmuch as the *spirit*, the *soul* of the composition may be wanting. Mere talent may *understand* genius; but it seems to me that nothing short of genius itself can *interpret* genius, can reproduce its utterances so as to bring their meanings home to the souls of all.

Also published as "Letter from William Mason," *Dwight's Journal of Music* 6/1 (7 Oct 1854): 2-3; "William Mason: His Ideas on Musical Composition and Piano-forte Playing," *Musical Gazette* (New York) 1 (11 Nov 1854): 6-7.

See also no. **457.**

521   MASON, William. Letter, New York, 23 Dec 1865. Published in "Notices of Curriculum." *Song Messenger of the Northwest* 3/11 (Feb 1866): 176.

An endorsement of George F. Root's *The Musical Curriculum* (Chicago: Root & Cady, 1865).

> . . . it is made on the sensible idea that the study of music should be a pleasure from the beginning. . . .

522   MASON, William. Letter to Messrs. J. H. and C. S. Odell, New York, 8 Feb 1869. Published in an undated Odell church organ brochure: J. H. and C. S. Odell; Church Organs; Manufacturers of Improved Pipe Organs of All Sizes; 407 and 409 West 42nd St. near Ninth Avenue.

Mason expresses his satisfaction with the newly installed Odell organ at the Valley Church in Orange, New Jersey.

> It gives me great pleasure to be able to say that the organ built by you for the Orange Valley Church gives thorough satisfaction. I regard it as a very fine instrument in all respects. Your open Diapason deserves especial mention as it is very powerful without being harsh, and the tones are uniformly smooth without undue softness; this is universally acknowledged as being the most important stop in an organ, as it forms a solid and satisfactory groundwork for all the other stops.

523   MASON, William. Letter to William Smythe Babcock Mathews, Orange, N.J., 27 Oct 1884. Published in Mathews's *How to Understand Music* . . . , vol. 2, pp. 117-18. 5th ed. Philadelphia: Theodore Presser, 1900-01; reprint, New York: AMS Press, 1971.

Written in response to a questionnaire sent by Mathews to several well-known pianists regarding a list of what they believed to be the ten best books of piano studies. Mason summarizes his preferences as follows:

CLEMENTI – BACH – CHOPIN.

> These three, I should say, are indispensable to any one who aspires to an all comprehensive technique, ancient and modern. . . . As a rule, it seems to me that too much time is given to mere technics or finger gymnastics and exercises. These, of course, have their proper use, but they should be employed with great temperance and moderation. . . . A student who has good judgment will learn how to utilize for purposes of teaching all sorts of passages in the various compositions which they study, be these composers Beethoven, Schumann, or any other great composers.

524   MASON, William. Letter to the editor of the *Etude*, n.p., n.d. Excerpt published in *Etude* 3/2 (Feb 1885): 28.

Mason gives his opinion on the use of mechanical devices to develop piano technique.

> This matter comes up periodically every few years, and there is something to be said in favor of as well as against it. Mr. Brotherhood has in a lengthy communication given me some ideas of his Technicon. I replied to him that "if given in very small doses" and judiciously administered, I should not object to merely mechanical gymnastics, but my own experience favors the maxim, *never* to practice without *listening*, and *never* to play pieces or *even mere finger exercises* without carefully observing both *heart* and *feeling* (or *expression*) as well as *head* and reason, or, in other words, never to *divorce* the *intellectual* from the *emotional* element.

See also nos. **495, 539, 576.**

525   MASON, William. Letter, Orange, N.J., 16 Jan 1885. Published in *Etude* 3/2 (Feb 1885): 29.

An endorsement of the *Etude* magazine.

> I THINK THE ETUDE a very useful and interesting paper. It aims to be fair and just in its treatment and investigation of the merits of the various methods of piano-forte teaching and practice. . . .

Also published in "Testimonials," *Etude* 9/12 (Dec 1891): 237.

526   MASON, William. Letter to Horatio Richmond Palmer, Orange, N.J., 6 May 1885. Published in Palmer's . . . *Piano Primer* . . . , 4. New York: H. R. Palmer, 1885.

An endorsement of Palmer's primer.

> Although small in size it is comprehensive, and contains the pith of the subject matter of which it treats, expressed in clear and concise language.

527   MASON, William. Letter to the editor of the *Etude*, Orange, N.J., 21 June 1886. Published in *Etude* 4/7 (July 1886): 177.

A brief, one-paragraph letter.

> In an article in your June number, entitled "What Method do You Use," [*Etude* 4/6 (June 1886): 137] occurs the following statement: "Another gentleman, well known in the profession of the country, would have us understand that through a careful use of his system of accents all things can be accomplished in piano playing." It is hardly credible that any teacher of experience could make such a claim as this, for it is unreasonable, even to absurdity. . . . Accents, in their proper place and degree, serve a very useful purpose; but they constitute only one of many equally necessary features, which in the aggregate and in combination produce the completed and satisfactory result.

528   MASON, William. Letter to Henry Edward Krehbiel, Orange, N.J., 24 Nov 1887. Published in "Tonic Sol-Fa." *Musical Courier* 15/22 (30 Nov 1887): 356.

A letter sent by Mason expressing his regret that he was not able to attend a reception held in New York City for John Spencer Curwen, president of the Tonic Sol-Fa College in London, who was visiting America to advocate the use of the tonic sol-fa system.

> . . . an impression still prevails that the tonic sol-fa system is only an excellent primary method, adapted solely for the kindergarten and the lower grades of schools. It seems to me that the opportunity offered by the reception tendered Mr. Curwen should be made available, as far as possible, for the purpose of correcting this

misapprehension, so that the musical profession may be led to realize that the tonic sol-fa notation, by emphasizing the relationship of tones in key—which is the basis of the art of music—furnishes as valuable an aid in advanced as in elementary study.

Typographical errors in the letter are corrected in the next issue of the *Musical Courier* (15/23 [7 Dec 1887]: 373). The letter is also published in "Mr. Curwen's Tour," *Musical Reform* 2/1 (Jan 1888): 4-6, 11.

See also no. **496**.

529   MASON, William. Letter, Orange, N.J., 30 May 1889. Published as "Brahms' First Visit to Liszt." *Music* 10 (July 1896): 326-27.

Mason gives an account (later amplified in his *Memories of a Musical Life*) of Brahms's first meeting with Liszt in Weimar in June 1853.

See also no. **552**.

530   MASON, William. Letter to the editors of the *Musical Courier*, Orange, N.J., 21 Mar 1890. Published in the *Musical Courier* 20/13 (26 Mar 1890): 274.

Mason commends the editors of the *Musical Courier* for their recent publication on Wagner entitled "Wagner and Now," 20/12 (19 Mar 1890): 250-51.

Permit a musician who was acquainted with and had experience in Weimar among the original Wagnerites, some forty years ago, to congratulate you. . . . It was hard enough to make even the musical part of the German public accept Wagner at the time referred to, and later on they went over to the opposite extreme, which, although natural enough, was almost as bad. But your article seems to present the truth and gives Wagner the grand credit which rightfully belongs to him, without at the same time disparaging the greatness of other composers.

531   MASON, William. Letter to Charles W. Landon, Orange, N.J., 24 Apr 1890. Published in "Where to Study Music." *Etude* 8/7 (July 1890): 103.

Mason declines an invitation made by Charles Landon, editor of the *Etude*, to write an article on the merits of studying music in Germany. Mason does, however, express some of his thoughts on this matter in his letter.

When one goes so many miles away from home into a strange country with a foreign language, and meets many others who have gone abroad under like circumstances and with a common object in view, there is a certain spirit of emulation aroused and a "desire to show the natives what we can do when we get home." But after the most of us get home we settle down into a uniform humdrum of daily routine, and those who have not been abroad succeed about as well as those who have. Nevertheless, it must be conceded that the experience of foreign travel, or travel in our native country, broadens our view of things in general, and adds substantially to our experience. I am inclined to think, while not disparaging the eminent ability of the teachers one meets abroad, that, nevertheless, we have just as good teachers at home, who moreover better understand, and are, therefore, better adapted to develop and guide, the American temperament and organization.

532   MASON, William. Letter, n.p., n.d. Excerpt published in William Smythe Babcock Mathews's "Wanted: The True Art of Piano Practice." *Music* 1 (Dec 1891): 128-41.

Mason responds to critics who object to his piano method because arpeggios are taught without an explanation of the harmonic function of the chords.

> In learning the piano the attention must be fixed upon the fingers and hand in gaining correct position and methods of use, because the pupil is learning *to play*. In learning to pronounce distinctly, pronunciation is the primary thought. The harmonies have not relation primarily to *playing*, but to *music*. Let a beginner play these various arpeggios, having learned to form them by change of finger, and the harmonies become quickly familiar to the ear, and the resolution of each chord comes, as it were, unconsciously and unawares.

Excerpts from this letter are also published in Mathews's "Letters to Teachers," *Etude* 9/12 (Dec 1891): 232.

533   MASON, William. Letter to S. Brainard's Sons Co., New York, 10 Mar 1892. Published in *Brainard's Musical World* 29/340 (Apr 1892): 108.

An endorsement of Emil Liebling's edition of Stephen Heller's *Piano Studies*, published by S. Brainard's Sons Co. (It has not been possible to obtain complete bibliographical information of this work.)

> Your very attractive edition of this extremely useful work is decidedly the best I have ever seen.

Also published in *Music* 2 (July 1892): vi.

534   MASON, William. Letter, n.p., n.d. Excerpt published in William Smythe Babcock Mathews's "American Composers of the Front Rank." *Music* 2 (Sept 1892): 491-503.

The letter includes Mason's assessment of American composers.

> Krehbiel wrote me some time since. . . . I replied that up to date America had produced no composer of originality, but that if MacDowell grew up in the way he is at present trending we should have a composer of the first rank.

535   MASON, William. Letter to Edgar Kelly, New York, 8 Oct 1892. Published in "Edgar Kelly's 'Puritania' Music." *Music* 3 (Jan 1893): 323-31.

Mason expresses his pleasure with a recent performance of Kelly's opera *Puritania*.

> I heartily congratulate you on your complete musical and artistic success. The music is delightful, fresh and original throughout, and the instrumentation is fully up to it, exhibiting, as it does, such varieties and beauties of tone color, and all of those together are natural, free from constraint, and spontaneous, giving almost the idea of an improvisation.

536   MASON, William. Letter, n.p., 15 Apr 1893. Published in *Etude* 11/5 (May 1893): 112.

An endorsement of Wilson G. Smith's *Special Exercises in Scale Playing*. No copy of Smith's work has been located.

537   MASON, William. Letter, n.p., n.d. Excerpt published in "The Clinging Touch." *Etude* 12/2 (Feb 1894): 37.

A response to a question which had been raised by a correspondent of the *Etude* concerning an exercise in Mason's *Touch and Technic*, op. 44.

538   MASON, William. Letter, n.p., n.d. Excerpt published in "Letters to Teachers." *Music* 6 (June 1894): 261-67.

A sequel to "Cause and Effect in Pianoforte Touch: A Symposium" (see no. 53).

539   MASON, William. Letter to William Smythe Babcock Mathews, n.p., n.d. Excerpt published in Mathews's "Editorial Bric-a-Brac." *Music* 6 (July 1894): 366-76.

An endorsement of the Virgil Practice Clavier.

> It is a machine — an invaluable one — and helps one more than anything that I know of to obtain an accurate, even, well-balanced, and thoroughly developed technic — *so far as purely mechanical results are concerned*. There are emotional things; and there are mechanical things: — there is such a thing as an *emotional* legato and there is also one other thing of strictly different character, namely, a *mechanical* legato. The emotional legatos, as compared with the mechanical legatos, are extremely rare in the world — although legatos of either kind are not common by any means.

See also nos. **524, 576.**

540   MASON, William. Letter, n.p., n.d. Published in Adelaide K. Sutherland's *What Shall I Play? Preferences for Piano and Organ: A Guide to Choice Musical Compositions* . . . , 62. Chicago: Gladstone Publishing Co., 1895.

What Shall I Play? is a compilation of lists of pieces for the piano and organ which had been solicited from about one hundred teachers. Mason's "list" took the form of a letter.

> The proper selection of music for pupils is a matter that worries me more than any other single thing connected with pianoforte teaching. Furthermore, the whole thing is a matter of taste. There are many modern compositions which are liked by many people, but which I do not like, and *vice versa*. Therefore, I would not undertake to select for anybody. In my teaching I use almost exclusively Bach, Beethoven, Schumann, Chopin, Grieg, and other authors well known to you.

Mason's letter is also published in "Reviews," *Pianist* 1/6 (June 1895): 116.

541   MASON, William. Letter to the editor of the *New York Tribune*, New York, 2 June 1895. Published in "Musical Notes." *New York Tribune*, 16 June 1895, pt. 2, p. 14, col. 2.

Mason gives his assessment of Mme Anna Caroline de la Grange's singing.

> I am surprised to find in to-day's Tribune a statement to the effect that Madame de la Grange "introduced the tremolo here when she came forty years ago." I heard Madame de la Grange for the first time in Leipsic about the year 1851 or 1852. . . . I remember especially her pure, steady, unwavering and sostenuto tones, and this characteristic of her singing impressed me as being exceedingly rare and commendable. . . . The tremolo nuisance is altogether beyond endurance, and for Madame de la Grange to be accused of its introduction here appears to me to be exceedingly unjust.

Also published as "To the Tribune," *Musical Courier* 30/26 (19 June 1895): 24.

542   MASON, William. Letter, New York, 15 Nov 1895. Published in "Dr. Mason's Reply." *Music* 9 (Jan 1896): 323-24.

A response to "Dr. Mason and the Pressure Touch" (see no. **83**).

543   MASON, William. Letter to Sumner Salter, n.p., n.d. Published in "Queries." *Pianist* 2/1 (Jan 1896): 11-12.

Contains Mason's assessment of the Janko keyboard.

> I am not sufficiently familiar with the Janko keyboard to warrant a decided opinion as to its merits and destiny. The general arrangement of this keyboard makes possible certain effects, such as chords of widely dispersed harmony, etc., which are not attainable on the

old keyboard. . . . I judge, too, . . . that the old keyboard is characterized by certain effects which are peculiarly its own or idiomatic, so to speak. . . . If these conclusions are correct, it would seem that the Janko keyboard, as well as the old keyboard, hold certain positions to which they are fairly entitled, independently of each other, and consequently neither one of them will supercede or replace the other.

544   MASON, William. Letter to William L. Hawes, n.p., 13 June 1896. Excerpt published in Hawes's "Gottschalk's 'Last Hope.'" *Musician* 13/10 (Oct 1908): 440.

Mason comments on the publication history of Gottschalk's *Last Hope*, including the error made by the William Hall publishing company in titling Gottschalk's work "The Latest Hops" on a proof copy. Mason also describes this incident in his *Memories of a Musical Life*.

545   MASON, William. Letter to Hugh A. Kelso, Jr., n.p., n.d. Published in "Dr. William Mason to Mr. H. A. Kelso, Jr." *Music* 10 (Sept 1896): 521-22.

A sequel to Mason's "A New Chapter of Touch" (see no. **559**).

546   MASON, William. Letter to Sumner Salter, n.p., n.d. Published in Salter's "Hand Lifting—A Basic Principle in Octave-Playing." *Pianist and Organist* 2/10 (Oct 1896): 183-84; 2/11 (Nov 1896): 199-200.

Contains Mason's reaction to the theory of playing octaves with an up-and-down motion of the hand at the wrist.

I have never met with a concert player of first-class reputation who uses this stroke, and I have always regarded the wrist action which it involves as opposed to truly scientific mechanism—therefore, have never used it in my playing or teaching.

547   MASON, William. Letter to Gustav L. Becker, New York, 7 Feb 1897. Published in Becker's "Musical Progress of America during the Last Decade." *Etude* 32/11 (Nov 1914): 795-96; 33/1 (Jan 1915): 15-16.

Written in response to Becker's request for Mason's point of view on musical progress in America. To illustrate the progress which had been made, Mason contrasts the resistance to the music of Schumann, which he encountered in America when he began performing after his return from Europe in 1854, to the general acceptance of Schumann's music at the end of the nineteenth century.

. . . when I returned to America in the month of July, 1854, and began my concert playing, Schumann occupied a prominent place in my programmes. Many of the musicians, however, and especially the newspapers, criticized these compositions severely and were disposed to regard them as crazy and far-fetched. However, in the Mason-Thomas Matinées and Soirées we persistently continued to give Schumann's music and . . . public appreciation grew slowly but surely.

548   MASON, William. Letter, n.p., n.d. Published in "How to Make Music Studios Attractive." *Etude* 16/4 (Apr 1898): 117; 16/5 (May 1898): 148-49.

Picture included. Mason's reply to a questionnaire sent out by the *Etude* magazine to various piano teachers regarding the furnishing of a teaching studio.

> I WILL send you an excellent picture of my studio in Steinway Hall, and this will give you an idea of an arrangement which for years has proved satisfactory. . . .

549   MASON, William. Letter to William Smythe Babcock Mathews, n.p., n.d. Excerpt published in "Letter from Dr. Mason." *Music* 13 (Apr 1898): 781-83.

A long letter in which Mason lists the names of prominent musicians who had commended his system of piano technique. After mentioning Liszt's recommendation, Mason writes:

> Several of Tausig's pupils have frequently testified to me of his high estimate of the two-finger exercise and of his daily and constant use of it for years. Joseffy, in particular, has told me more than once (quoting his own words): "Whenever I went to Tausig for my lesson I found him practicing the two-finger exercise."

550   MASON, William. Letter to William Smythe Babcock Mathews, n.p., n.d. Excerpt published in "Answers to Correspondents." *Music* 16 (Oct 1899): 620-27.

Mason describes a letter that he had received from Sigismund de Seyfried, a piano teacher in Paris, praising his *Touch and Technic*, op. 44.

> His praise is so excessive that I almost feel ashamed to publish it. . . . But you will see that he has given the work a thorough trial in a practical way, both individually and with his pupils, and he finds the result "simply marvelous."

Mason also explains his system of fingering for playing arpeggios.

> One of my teachers, Alexander Dreyschock, directed me to use the same order of fingering throughout all triad arpeggios and broken chords, i.e., in the same way as those of C. I was inclined to rebel at first, as many of the positions seemed awkward and constrained,

but after . . . a little while I found that my hands were gaining in many ways not only in adapting themselves to the varied positions of the triads, but the metacarpal muscles by means of the stretching and limbering process which they were constantly undergoing, became stronger as well as more flexible and elastic and more responsive and obedient to the will.

551   MASON, William. Letter, n.p., n.d. Published in "Letter from Dr. Wm. Mason." *Music* 17 (Feb 1900): 428-29.

Mason tells of an evening he had recently spent in his home in the company of Leopold Godowsky and Mark Hambourg.

I am especially pleased with his [Godowsky's] very ingenious and thoroughly musical treatment of all of the Chopin Etudes, and his wonderful and transcendent technic in their performance takes away all appearance of difficulty and produces a supreme sense of quiet and repose. In order to their finished and artistic performance quite as much is demanded of the left hand as of the right, and the decided advance in the requirements of technic is almost, if not quite, epoch-making.

552   MASON, William. Letter to William Smythe Babcock Mathews, n.p., n.d. Published in "Short Letter from Dr. William Mason." *Music* 18 (Aug 1900): 396.

Mason relates the story of Brahms's first meeting with Liszt, at which Mason was present, as evidence that Liszt was initially unfavorably impressed with Brahms's compositions.

I have seen several accounts of this interview but none of them are in accordance with the facts, and this experience has always impressed me with the flimsy way in which history is constructed.

See also no. **529.**

553   MASON, William. Letter to the *Etude*, n.p., n.d. Published in "New Year's Greeting to 'The Etude.'" *Etude* 19/1 (Jan 1901): 7.

A one-sentence greeting.

554   MASON, William. Letter to "Pianoforte Students," n.p., n.d. Published in "Christmas Thoughts for Music Lovers." *Etude* 21/12 (Dec 1903): 466.

A one-paragraph statement stressing the fact that even beginning piano students should practice on good instruments.

Daily practice upon and close companionship with a pianoforte of mellow tone and delicately adjusted action, including also perfect responsive pedal arrangements, awakens, fosters, intensifies and facilitates the growth of musical perceptions and develops a *musical* touch which becomes automatic and involuntary, thus as it were, a second nature.

555 MASON, William. Letter, n.p., n.d. Excerpt published in Hawes's "Gottschalk's Views Regarding Beethoven's Sonatas." *Musician* 13/10 (Oct 1908): 440.

Includes excerpts of a letter from Mason to "a friend" of Hawes commenting both on Gottschalk's playing and his opinion of Beethoven's sonatas.

> I know how well he played Bach and the classics, and I have never heard his playing of Chopin's *Fantaisie* in F minor equaled. He told me, however, during one of our conversations, that he felt that Beethoven could not write for the pianoforte, or at least, that his pianoforte writing was not his strong point. . . .

556 MASON, William. Letter, n.p., n.d. Published in "My Teacher Fifty-five Years Ago: As Told by a Pupil of Mason's." *Keyboard* 1/2 (Apr 1939): 9.

Mason advocates the practice of introducing scales to the student quite early in the course of study.

See also no. 339.

557 MASON, William. *Memories of a Musical Life.* New York: Century Co., 1901; reprints, New York: AMS Press, 1970; New York: Da Capo Press, 1970.

An autobiography. Pictures and facsimiles of musical autographs included. The main body of the book is divided into four sections: "Early Days in New England," "Student Life Abroad," "At Work in America," and "Music in America Today." Much of the material is anecdotal. Of special interest are Mason's sketches of leading nineteenth-century musicians. A substantial segment of Mason's book had been published earlier in a series of periodical articles: "Memories of a Musical Life," *Century Magazine* n.s. 38/3 (July 1900): 438-49; 38/4 (Aug 1900): 569-74; 38/5 (Sept 1900): 763-76; 38/6 (Oct 1900): 848-64. Part of Mason's description of Alexander Dreyschock was also published as "Alexander Dreyschock and His Octaves," *Music* 19 (Dec 1900): 191-93.

See also no. 55.

Reviews of no. 557:

Anonymous review. *Nation* 73/1898 (14 Nov 1901): 383.

A favorable review.

> Dr. Mason got the benefit of . . . being able to study abroad from 1849 to 1854. During these years he met and got more or less intimately acquainted with many of the most distinguished composers and players of the time, and he has plenty of interesting things to tell about them, without ever becoming garrulous or pedantic.

APTHORP, William F. "Mr. Mason's Reminiscences." *Book Buyer* 23/4 (Nov 1901): 281-84.

Pictures included. A positive review.

Those were interesting times; and Mr. Mason reports on them, and upon many of the men who were chiefly engaged in making history in them, not garrulously, not at random, but nearly always telling some characteristic anecdote, giving added sharpness of contour to already partly known individualities, or else the correct version of some discussed happening. Being essentially of a true, unwarped nature himself, having large and eager sympathies, he sees clearly what he sees; he is not feazed by the embarrassment of hero-worship, but keeps a cool head and discerning eye.

"Books of the Week." *Outlook* 69/11 (16 Nov 1901): 742-50.

Mason's book is among those reviewed.

From his large store of . . . associations he has published these well-chosen reminiscences, which will interest every musician and music-lover; the volume, which is handsomely printed and illustrated, contains much that is instructive as well as readable.

[HUNEKER, James Gibbons.] "Raconteur." *Musical Courier* 44/10 (5 Mar 1902): 22-24.

Includes a very favorable review.

Dr. Mason discusses the playing of various pianists — Chopin, Thalberg, Liszt, Moscheles, Henselt, Dreyschock — with whom he studied — Carl Mayer and many others. Anecdotes in profusion are related of all these composers and players. The most interesting section of the book is, naturally enough, devoted to Liszt and Weimar.

MATHEWS, William Smythe Babcock. "Editorial Bric-a-Brac." *Music* 18 (Oct 1900): 551-67.

Includes an assessment of the first three segments of Mason's "Memories" as published in the *Century Magazine*. Perhaps more of a commentary than a review.

The "Musical Memories" of Dr. William Mason are nearing their close in the Century Magazine. . . . They give charming glimpses of the Liszt coterie at Weimar between 1850 and 1855, and corresponding side lights upon the Leipsic circles and those at Prague. The charming letters of Miss Amy Fay relate to an entirely different period in Liszt's life. . . .

"The Nestor of American Musicians: Dr. William Mason's Reminiscences." *Etude* 19/10 (Oct 1901): 351-52.

Pictures included. A favorable, prepublication review, much of it consisting of quotations taken from the advance sheets of Mason's book.

Dr. Mason's book, as may be expected, includes memories of the most famous names in modern music, — from his delicate picture of Moritz Hauptmann, on whose "stove, a regular old-fashioned German structure of porcelain nearly as high as the ceiling, there was always a row of apples in process of slow baking," to his unexpected addition to the Brahms ana, — every picture is graphic and delightful.

"Reviews and Notices: Memories of a Musical Life. . . ." *Music* 21 (Dec 1901): 85-92.

A favorable review.

> The Memories are not so voluminous as they would have been if undertaken earlier, when the writer was more active; but what they may have lost in volume by keeping (like raisins and figs dried in the sun) they perhaps have gained in sweetness.

558   MASON, William. "Miss Szumoska's [*sic*] Debut." *Pianist* 1/4 (Apr 1895): 77-78.

A review (prefaced by some introductory remarks by the editor) of Antoinette Szumowska's New York City debut recital.

> A charming pianist, whose freedom and spontaneity of style bears no trace of academic and conventional training; whose warm heart, clear head, and musical temperament are evidenced and interpreted by means of a sympathetic touch, and unimpeachable technique.

559   MASON, William. "A New Chapter of Touch." *Music* 10 (July 1896): 267-68.

An explanation of the use of the triceps muscle in piano playing. Mason makes the claim that the action of this muscle "is here explained in print for the *first* time in the world."

> This element [triceps muscle] is the one operative in all forms of up-arm touch, and generally in all cantabile passages where the tone is produced without preliminary raising of the fingers; also in all tones produced by a springing motion in direction away from the keys, the finger points having been in actual contact with the keys at the moment of beginning the touch.

Also published as "A New Chapter of Touch," *Pianist and Organist* 2/8 (Aug 1896): 147; "A New Chapter of Touch," *Etude* 14/9 (Sept 1896): 207.

Mason's statement that he was the first to describe the action of the triceps muscle created a minor controversy. Hugh A. Kelso, Jr., in an article titled "A Reply to Dr. Wm. Mason's Article 'A New Chapter of Touch,'" *Music* 10 (Aug 1896): 422-24, stated that he, not Mason, could lay claim to that distinction.

> If Mr. Mason will read my article entitled, "Psychological Technic" which was read before the Illinois Music Teachers Ass. in the spring of 1892 and published in MUSIC in the August issue of the same year he will find explained, from a psycho-physiological basis the exact reasons why and when the aforesaid muscles are brought into action in piano playing. . . .

At this point, William Smythe Babcock Mathews entered the discussion. In his column "Editorial Bric-a-Brac," *Music* 10 (Aug 1896): 397-409, Mathews revealed that Mason's statement concerning the originality of his article had been made inadvertently.

> It is proper to say that Dr. Mason in his habitual modesty, crossed ont [*sic*] in the proof of his article the words "for the first time in the world," but that the correction failed of being made. The present writer, therefore, and not Dr. Mason is responsible for the words.

Mason, in a letter to Kelso published in "Dr. William Mason to Mr. H. A. Kelso, Jr.," *Music* 10 (Sept 1896): 521-22, also responded to the latter's charges. Mason, somewhat characteristically, avoided a direct confrontation with Kelso and limited his comments to a summary of the chronological development of his ideas on the use of the arm in piano playing, citing Henry Schmidt, Leopold von Meyer, and Alexander Dreyschock as being particularly influential in the formulation of his theories.

> . . . I have found that I could more quickly than in any other way, bring about a state of complete relaxation of muscles from finger tip to shoulder by making my pupils understand, through personal experience, the action and feeling of the triceps muscle, which I regard as the emotional center. . . .

560   MASON, William. "Notes from the Journal of a Young American, a Musical Student in Germany." *Home Journal* 223 (18 May 1850): [3].

Includes Mason's comments on a wide variety of topics: performances by the pianist Mortier de Fontaine, services at the St. Thomas Church in Leipzig, the anniversary celebration of Goethe's birthday at St. Paul's Church in Leipzig, and a trip to Weimar, where Mason had his first meetings with Liszt.

> . . . I called . . . on Listz [*sic*] and was immediately invited up to his room. . . . Listz requested me to play, but I preferred not to do so at present as there were so many people there, and persons were continually coming and going. . . . He played me a piece by *Chopin* and one by *Rob. Schumann*; but I could not judge much from these. . . . I could not remain with him long, as the cars left for Leipzig. . . . He invited me to visit him again at Weimar sometime during the coming winter and spend a quiet week with him — said he would then play to me as much as I wished.

A clipping of this article in the MASON/Scrapbook has the following annotation (in Mason's handwriting): "The above was written in Hamburg and Leipzig about the 31st August 1849."

561   MASON, William. "Notes from the Journal of a Young American, a Musical Student in Germany." *Home Journal* 224 (25 May 1850): [2-3].

Includes an account of concerts that Mason attended in Leipzig and Weimar and his plans to study piano with Moscheles.

> I go to take my first lesson from Moscheles, this afternoon, and although my expectations are that I shall not be so much interested

in his style as in that of the modern pianists, yet, as I have placed myself under him, I intend most exactly to follow his directions. He is perfectly acquainted with the works of Beethoven, was personally acquainted with Beethoven himself, and knows the exact style in which he designed his works to be performed.

562   MASON, William. "Notes from the Journal of a Young American, a Musical Student in Germany." *Home Journal* 225 (1 June 1850): [2].

Mason writes about two Gewandhaus concerts he had recently attended in Leipzig and comments on musical criticism in European newspapers in comparison to that of American papers.

It is my opinion that if some of our American critics and newspaper writers were here, they would find as much fault with these concerts as they do with ours at home. But there seems to be this difference between the American and the German critics, that while the Americans go to a concert with a determination to find fault, the Germans go with the intention of being pleased, and with determination of finding *something good* in each piece that is presented.

563   MASON, William. "Notes from the Journal of a Young American, a Musical Student in Germany." *Home Journal* 226 (8 June 1850): [2].

Mason comments about a recent Gewandhaus concert, audience etiquette at a concert in a German beer garden, and Charles Mayer's professional opinion of Leopold von Meyer. Mason also evaluates Charles Mayer's piano playing.

C. Mayer is one of the most finished pianists in Germany, or in the world; he is a perfect artist; having not only great power over his instrument, but also a most perfect and finished touch. I have never heard the pianoforte more beautifully played than by him. Having been introduced to him in Hamburg, I have seen much of him; he has played hours to me in my room. I have also visited him in Dresden, . . . so that I can speak of his playing with some confidence. . . . He has not the tremendous power of Leopold de Meyer, and perhaps has not sufficient power for a large orchestra and concert-room; but the beauty and wonder of his playing is its peculiar delicacy and finish; he has especially an equality of touch . . . and this perfection is always to be observed in his playing; he never strikes a wrong key. . . .

564   MASON, William. "Notes from the Journal of a Young American, a Musical Student in Germany." *Home Journal* 228 (22 June 1850): [2].

Mason gives his impressions of a recital given by pupils at a conservatory (in Leipzig?) and comments about the piano playing of Leopold von Meyer and Dreyschock.

141

AMONG the many pretended pianists that have visited America, I can find only one that is regarded here as a really good player, and that is Leopold de Meyer. He is here considered as one of the greatest modern pianists; though he is not regarded as a good musician or composer. Charles Mayer . . . told me that, as far as piano-forte execution is concerned, there is not, perhaps, de Meyer's equal in Europe, unless Dreyschock be excepted. Dreyschock may carry the difficulties of execution quite as far, or even farther than de Meyer. These two now stand at the head of modern bravura players, and both have amazing execution with the left hand.

565   MASON, William. ". . . on Paderewski and Beethoven." *Evening Post* (New York), 11 Dec 1891, p. 6, col. 1.

A sequel to Mason's "Beethoven Playing" (see no. **482**).

566   MASON, William. "Paderewski: A Critical Study." *Century Magazine* n.s. 21/5 (Mar 1892): 721-24.

A major essay, based on an earlier article Mason had written on Paderewski for the *Musical Courier* (see no. **482**). Mason's analysis of Paderewski's playing is clear and discerning, and includes frequent references to the performance styles of other leading nineteenth-century pianists. As might be expected in an essay of this nature, much of Mason's own philosophy of performance is indirectly revealed.

> . . . Paderewski's original touch is full of melancholy pathos, without sentimental mawkishness, and without finical cynicism. . . . It possesses that subtle quality expressed in some measure by the German word *Sehnsucht*, and in English as "intensity of aspiration." This quality Chopin had, and Liszt frequently spoke of it. It is the undefinably poetic haze with which Paderewski invests and surrounds all that he plays which renders him so unique and impressive among modern pianists.

Mason's essay was also published as "Paderewski: A Critical Study," *The Century Library of Music*, ed. Ignacy Jan Paderewski, Fanny Morris Smith, and Bernard Boekelman, 20 vols. (New York: Century Co., 1900-02), 18:577-84; "Paderewski: A Critical Study," *The International Library of Music* . . . , 8 vols. (New York: University Society, 1934), vol. 3: *The Pianist's Guide* . . . , 13-20. (The 1948 four-volume edition of *The International Library of Music* . . . [University Society, New York] also contains this essay in vol. 3, pp. 13-20.) Excerpts from Mason's essay were published as "Dr. Mason upon Paderewski," *Music* 1 (Apr 1892): 592-94; "Great Pianists Compared," *Musical Visitor* 21/4 (Apr 1892): 96-97; Henry Charles Lahee's *Famous Pianists of To-day and Yesterday* (Boston: L. C. Page, 1900), 227-31; "Paderewski's Playing," *Etude* 10/5 (May 1892): 92.

See also no. **416**.

567   MASON, William. ". . . Piano Touch." *Musical Courier* 29/16 (17 Oct 1894): 8.

This article consists of two parts: Mason's remarks on touch (made in the form of a letter), followed by two paragraphs of editorial commentary. Mason presents the thesis that one of the most important aspects of piano touch is a true legato. Rubinstein is given as an example of a pianist who possessed such a legato, one which combined mechanical and poetical elements.

> It is never too early to begin to cultivate and persist in the practice of that peculiar manner of touch which leads to the development of beauty, color and singing quality of tone, as this is far more to be desired than mere mechanical technic and finger skill, and really, if it is only properly cultivated and persistently followed up, it brings with it and leads constantly to the acquirement of a technic which at the same time is musical and poetical, thus far above and beyond mere machine effects.

Mason's article (with the editorial commentary deleted) was also published as ". . . Rubinstein's Touch," *Music* 7 (Feb 1895): 390-92. Also published with minor revisions as ". . . Piano Touch," *Etude* 13/1 (Jan 1895): 13.

568   MASON, William. "Practical Application and Use of Accents in Piano-Forte Practice." *Etude* 4/6 (June 1886): 136-37.

A four-column article in which Mason explains how to devise exercises utilizing different accentuation patterns for application to specific musical passages. The seventh measure of the opening movement of Beethoven's *Sonata in E-flat Major*, op. 31, no. 3, is used to illustrate the process.

> This method is extremely simple, and if once understood, it is easily applied by the student to all sorts and kinds of passages, in any and every piece requiring finger dexterity and strength, and the student will thus be making his own exercises from day to day, and they will certainly prove to be the exercises best adapted to immediate necessities, as well as to the securing of permanent results.

569   MASON, William. "Questions." *New York Musical Gazette* 7/10 (July 1873): 102.

Mason answers several questions apparently sent in to the editor of the magazine by correspondents. His response to a query about the relationship of andante to andantino reads as follows:

> Andantino is the diminutive of andante, and as such properly signifies a "little" or "small" andante. The term — as now used, however, has reference to the movement of a piece of music, and on this point authorities disagree. It seems to us that its proper meaning is a little faster than andante, or between andante and allegretto.

570   [MASON, William.] "Questions and Answers." *Etude* 5/2 (Feb 1887): 28-29.

Several of the responses are identified (initialed "W. M.") as being written by Mason. (A number of typographical errors in Mason's answers are corrected on page 41 of the subsequent issue, March 1887.) Mason had been an anonymous contributor to this department of the *Etude* for some time. Page 19 of the February 1887 issue announces that Mason had "in the past answered some questions concerning piano technic." Interestingly enough, following this disclosure, Mason apparently discontinued writing for the "Questions and Answers" columns.

571   MASON, William. "Radical Types of Pianoforte Touch: A New Statement. . . ." *Music* 1 (Mar 1892): 413-27.

A summary of the major types of arm, hand, and finger touches as described in the advance sheets of a revised edition of the first volume of *Touch and Technic*, op. 44, which was then in preparation. Editorial comments by William Smythe Babcock Mathews are interspersed throughout the article.

> All touches partake more or less of the arm, the hand, and the finger. Whatever the shade or quality, all parts of the entire apparatus, from the shoulder to the points of the fingers, cooperate, and perform vitally essential functions. The only ground, therefore, upon which touches can be distinguished as finger, hand, or arm, is found in the preponderance of motion in one or the other of these parts of the apparatus.

Also published as "Radical Types of Pianoforte Touch: A New Statement . . . ," *Etude* 10/8 (Aug 1892): 153-54; 10/9 (Sept 1892): 173-74.

572   MASON, William. ". . . Sherwood." *Musical Courier* 8/8 (20 Feb 1884): 115.

A review of William Sherwood's *Suite*, op. 5, nos. 1, 3-5; *Mazurka*, op. 6, no. 1; *Romanza appassionata*, op. 8; *Scherzo Caprice*, op. 9; and *Gipsy Dance*.

> The "Scherzo Caprice" and "Romanza Appassionata" are somewhat more important, earnest and serious than the other pieces enumerated on the list, and both show thought and ability in the way of musical thematic development and elaboration. . . .

Also published as "New Pianoforte Compositions by Wm. H. Sherwood," *Musical Items* 1/3 (Feb 1884): 3.

573   MASON, William. "A Statement. . . ." *Etude* 11/1 (Jan 1893): 8.

Mason explains his use of a minor scale which combines the melodic form (ascending) and the harmonic form (descending).

> The usual and improperly called "melodic" form, having a major sixth in ascending, but both a minor seventh and sixth in descending, . . . is not a true scale. It never occurs in music but where a modulation is implied, since by introducing a minor seventh the minor scale gives up its leading tone and thereby its most appealing peculiarity.

574   MASON, William. *A System of Fundamental Technics for Modern Piano Playing: Containing Tone Production for Melody, Chords, Octaves, Pedal, Passage-Work, Together with a Complete Apparatus of Scale and Arpeggio Forms for Practice; with Methods of Treating the Same for Developing Concert Fluency, Brilliancy, and Elegance of Style.* New ed., greatly enlarged, rev. and improved, with new illustrations of all important hand positions by William Smythe Babcock Mathews. Boston: Oliver Ditson Co., 1905.

This work is in essence a substantially revised version of Mason's *A System of Technical Exercises* (see next item). The content of *A System of Fundamental Technics* strongly reflects the literary style of William Smythe Babcock Mathews. It seems probable that most of the writing was done by him, a likely supposition considering Mason's advanced age and declining health at this time. Nevertheless, Mason, at the very least, probably participated as a consultant during the preparation of this work and undoubtedly approved of its final content before publication.

The imprint of Mathews's writing style is also very strong in two other works he collaborated on with Mason: Mason's *A System of Technical Exercises* (see next item), in which Mathews is listed as associate editor, and *A Primer of Music* (see no. **586**), coauthored by Mason and Mathews. In both of these texts it seems probable that the explanatory materials—at least the final drafts—were written by Mathews.

575   MASON, William. *A System of Technical Exercises for the Piano-Forte: Including a New and Complete Treatment of Scale and Arpeggio Forms; A School of Touch; A New Method of Octave Practice; An Explanation of Mason's Method of the Rhythmic Treatment of Exercises, Together with a Plan of Daily Practice.* . . . William Smythe Babcock Mathews, assoc. ed. Boston: Oliver Ditson Co., 1878.

See also the commentary to Mason's *A System of Fundamental Technics*, no. **574**.

Reviews of no. **575**:

CADY, Calvin Brainerd. "Mason's Piano-Forte Technics." *Dwight's Journal of Music* 39/987 (15 Feb 1879): 28-29; 39/988 (1 Mar 1879): 35-36.

A long, generally favorable review with thoughtful analyses of the key aspects of the work.

Scores of technical works have been written, and exercises innumerable, but one looks in vain for the principles upon which these have been formed, or a hint as to the mental processes involved. *Are* there any principles? What relation does the mind sustain to this matter? Can new life be infused into the dry bones of technique? . . . [Mason's] work [is] based upon the physiology of mind and muscle, and their relations to one another, and is certainly a new departure in the right direction.

JOHNSON, J. C. "The Simplicity of Technique; Chapter VII: The Technique of the Instruction Books." *Etude* 4/10 (Oct 1886): 252-53.

In this book . . . we have . . . technical exercises . . . by themselves, filling a hundred large pages. Mr. Mason carries out his peculiar idea of *accents* throughout, and it is undoubtedly valuable and time saving.

"Mason's Pianoforte Technics." *Score* 4/17 (Feb 1879): 327.

Besides able treaties [*sic*] on "The Hand in Playing," "The Mind in Playing," on "Touch," on "Velocity," &c., the author has inserted about 500 most ingenious Technical Exercises, in which Scales, Arpeggios and other *material* of execution are played with many variations of accent and rhythm. These Rhythmical and accented exercises are the characteristic of the book. . . .

576   MASON, William. "To the Earnest Student and Player of the Piano." *American Musician* 17/2 (12 Apr 1890): 9.

An endorsement of the Virgil Practice Clavier.

I have always regarded mute keyboards with disfavor, since they neither respond to the attack nor afford accurate means of determining the quality of the work. The clavier, however, enables one to temporerily [*sic*] banish the stimulating influence of the pianoforte tones without suspending the means of defining the rhythm and verifying the touch.

A minor typographical error in the article is corrected in "An Error in Dr. William Mason's Article," *American Musician* 17/4 (26 Apr 1890): 7. Also published as "To the Earnest Student and Player of the Piano," *Musical Courier* 20/16 (16 Apr 1890): 349; "To the Earnest Student and Player of the Pianoforte," *Etude* 8/5 (May 1890): 77; "Wm. Mason to the Earnest Student and Player of the Pianoforte," *American Art Journal* 55/3 (3 May 1890): 41-42 (picture included). Excerpts from Mason's endorsement were also published intermittently in various periodicals in advertisements run for the Virgil Practice Clavier.

See also nos. **524, 539.**

577   MASON, William. "Touch." *Official Report of the Tenth Annual Meeting of the Music Teachers' National Association* . . . (1886), 64-71.

A paper read by Mason at the 1886 MTNA meeting held in Boston.

One of the earliest directions to the beginner is to invariably lift the fingers high before striking the keys. . . . This kind of practice is important and useful, and should receive its daily share of attention; but while this is done, another principle which relates to rapid motion should not be forgotten, but should receive equal attention in practice. . . . In order to produce a good effect with . . . scales, arpeggios, broken chords, or, indeed, of any series of tones following in rapid succession, it is necessary that the fingers should rise but a short distance above the keys, and the player must be able to produce a full tone of adequate and varying power without using the straight up-and-down, hammer-like stroke.

Also published as "Touch," *Etude* 4/12 (Dec 1886): 297-98, 316; *Touch, as Applied to Pianoforte Practice* . . . ([Orange, N.J.]: Press of the Orange Chronicle, 1886). Excerpts from the essay were published in the following: W. F. Gates's *Musical Mosaics: A Collection of Six Hundred Selections from Musical Literature* . . . (Philadelphia: Theodore Presser, 1889), 136-38; "Piano Touch," *Musical Reform* 1/3 (Dec 1886): 36. Excerpts from the essay with additional material interpolated were published as "How to Secure a Good Tone," in William Mason and William Smythe Babcock Mathews's *A Primer of Music* . . . (Cincinnati: John Church Co., 1894), 152-55; "How to Secure a Good Tone," *Music* 7 (Mar 1895): 529-31.

A transcript of the response made by S. Austen Pearce to Mason's presentation of his paper at the MTNA meeting is published in the *Official Report of the Tenth Annual Meeting of the Music Teachers' National Association* . . . (1886), 71-75.

See also nos. **306, 376.**

578   MASON, William. *Touch and Technic: For Artistic Piano Playing by Means of a New Combination of Exercise-Forms and Method of Practice, Conducting Rapidly to Equality of Finger Power, Facility, and Expressive Quality of Tone*, op. 44. 4 vols. in 1. Philadelphia: Theodore Presser, 1891-92.

Contents: vol. 1, Two-Finger Exercises (School of Touch); vol. 2, Complete School of Scales (School for Brilliant Passages); vol. 3, Complete School of Arpeggios (Passage School); vol. 4, School of Octaves and Bravoura.

Several minor corrections for vol. 2 are given in "Corrections in Touch and Technic. Part II. Scales," *Etude* 9/12 (Dec 1891): 226. A revised edition of the first volume was published in 1897 (Boston: Theodore Presser). See also no. **579.**

An interesting edition of this work was also published in England: *Touch and Technic: For Artistic Pianoforte Playing by Means of a New Combination of Exercise-Forms and Method of Practice, Conducing Rapidly to Equality of Finger Power, Facility, and Expressive Quality of Tone*, by Dr. William Mason (of New York), op. 44; ed., with numerous additions by Ridley Prentice (Associate of the Royal Academy of Music; Professor of the Piano-forte, Guildhall School of Music; Principal of the "Mason" School of Pianoforte-playing; Author of "The Musician," &c.) . . . (London: J. Curwen & Sons, [1894?]). At the head of the title page is written: "This Edition is published in England with the special sanction of Dr. Mason; who has considered, and approved of, many important alterations and additions. . . ." Copies of vols. 1 and 2 only have been located in the British Library; no copyright date is given, but the editor's preface is dated 1894.

Of all of Mason's writings, *Touch and Technic* contains the clearest and most concise exposition of his theories on piano technique. It is the central pillar of his system.

Reviews and testimonials for no. **578:**

FOOTE, Arthur. "Testimonials." *Etude* 9/11 (Nov 1891): 216.
    Refers to the third volume only.

In looking over the ". . . School of Arpeggio Playing," which you have just published, one is especially struck by seeing the great help it will be to pupils in showing them not only a way, but a first rate, practical and musical way of doing their work. . . .

JERVIS, Perlee V. "Mason's 'Touch and Technic.'" *Etude* 10/1 (Jan 1892): 13.

Perhaps more of a testimonial than a review. Jervis at one time was Mason's pupil. Not surprisingly, the tone of the article is very encomiastic.

JOSEFFY, Rafael. Letter to William Mason, n.p., 22 Mar 1893. Published in "Testimonials." *Etude* 11/6 (June 1893): 133.

I feel myself impelled to say to you to-day, after thorough investigation, that I regard your technical studies as a masterpiece which can claim an unapproachable position among the most important pedagogic works. . . . The last volume on octaves and chords seems to me very important; it contains much that is new and nothing that is superfluous, and is especially masterly in its combination and sequence of exercises.

Joseffy's letter was also published in "Publisher's Notes," *Etude* 20/10 (Oct 1902): 382-83.

MATHEWS, William Smythe Babcock. "Reviews and Notices: Touch and Technic, Vol. I, the Two Finger Exercises; Vol. IV, Octaves and Bravoura. . . ." *Music* 2 (Sept 1892): 530-32.

A very favorable review.

In certain quarters, lately, there has appeared a tendency to object to Dr. Mason's system, on the ground that it proceeds from the external, and regards the hand as an apparatus, ignoring the inner qualities of musical perception, which if they are right, the technic, these objectors tell us, will take care of itself. It is quite true that the four volumes do unite in regarding the playing parts of the human body as forming a mechanical apparatus, which plays as it is moved by the spirit within.

PADEREWSKI, Ignacy Jan. Letter to William Mason, Paris, 9 July 1894. MS with the William Mason Collection of Autograph Letters, New York Public Library; also published in *Etude* 12/9 (Sept 1894): 203.

The work is full of original and practical views. Your system for the development of Piano Technic, with all its rhythmical combinations, is of a most convincing simplicity.

PADEREWSKI, Ignacy Jan. Letter to William Mason, New York, 12 Nov 1895. Published in the original French and in English translation in "Paderewski *and* 'Touch and Technic.'" *Etude* 14/2 (Feb 1896): [24c].

. . . IT IS THE BEST PIANO METHOD WHICH I KNOW. . . .

Paderewski's letter is also published in English translation in the following: "Mr. Paderewski's Tribute to Dr. Mason's Touch and Technic," *Pianist* 1/12 (Dec 1895): 246; "Publisher's Notes," *Etude* 20/10 (Oct 1902): 382-83.

"Reviews and Notices: The Two-Finger Exercise. . . ." *Music* 13 (Nov 1897): 131-32.

A review of the first volume (1897 ed.).

> Among the novelties of this edition is the explanation of the tricep [sic] muscle and its office in piano touch. . . .

"Reviews and Notices: . . . Touch and Technic, Vol. II. . . ." *Music* 1 (Mar 1892): 518.

A short, favorable review.

"Reviews and Notices: Touch and Technic, Vol. III. . . ." *Music* 1 (Nov 1891): 88-89.

A positive review. Although unsigned, the review was probably written by William Smythe Babcock Mathews.

> . . . arpeggios are practiced with hands singly, in direct motion (i.e., where the hands play toward the strong fingers) and in reverse. . . . Then with both hands together. Later there are triad arpeggios, and the broken chords. Although the book is small, it contains an exhaustive school of arpeggios.

Also published in *Etude* 10/11 (Nov 1892): 211.

SALTER, Sumner. "Piano Notes." *Pianist and Organist* 3/11 (Nov 1897): 279-80.

Includes a review of the first volume (1897 ed.).

> Two prominent features in the new edition . . . are the accounts given: first, of the use of the *triceps* muscle, . . . which, while not claiming as a discovery, Dr. Mason is the first to emphasize the importance of; and second, of the history of the two-finger exercise. . . .

STERNBERG, Constantin. Letter to William Mason, Philadelphia, 11 Mar 1896. Published on the cover of *Etude* 14/6 (June 1896).

> Undoubtedly, among all the Piano methods that appeared within my life-time, your "Touch and Technic" is the first and only one embodying a new principle; it acts quick [sic], saving three-fourths of the time formerly needed to put a hand into shape and discipline, and is especially sympathetic to me, because of its direct bearing upon musical phrase-ology, having the germ of a phrase for its basis.

WEBER, Julius. "Modern Practical Pianoforte Technique." *Musician* 10/9 (Sept 1905): 361.

Includes a lukewarm review of Mason's piano method.

579   MASON, William. *Touch and Technic; or, the Technic of Artistic Touch by Means of Two-Finger Exercises; Conducing Rapidly to Equality of Finger Power and Expressive Quality of Tone.* Philadelphia: Theodore Presser, 1889.

This work was also published serially in the *Etude* 7/9 (Sept 1889): 135-38; 7/10 (Oct 1889): 155-58; 7/11 (Nov 1889): 174. It was later published by Theodore Presser as the first volume of Mason's *Touch and Technic: For Artistic Piano Playing*, op. 44 (see no. 578).

Reviews of no. **579**:

BOWMAN, Edward Morris. Letter to the publisher, n.p., n.d. *Etude* 7/10 (Oct 1889): 154.

Laudatory review.

Touch and Technic is a restatement of the use and value of the Two-finger Exercise . . . , and the whole subject is here presented in language and illustration so lucid, succinct, comprehensive, and, withal, so wonderfully concise . . . with a gravity and force which might well characterize the diction of a last will and testament. . . .

HUNT, G. W. "Mason's Touch and Technic." *Etude* 7/8 (Aug 1889): 114.

A prepublication announcement/review.

The only way to understand them [two-finger exercises] thoroughly is to study them with the author in person or some one of his private pupils; however, much may be gained by intelligent teachers from a careful study of the printed copy.

JOSEFFY, Rafael. Letter to William Mason, n.p., n.d. Published in "Testimonials." *Etude* 8/3 (Mar 1890): 34.

Many thanks for sending me your studies, "Touch and Technic." I am quite familiar with them. This affords me the opportunity to repeat what I have often said, that I consider your exercises extraordinary.

"Touch and Technic." *Musical Courier* 19/22 (27 Nov 1889): 446.

A very favorable review.

Pianists have found out that it is not necessary to wade through deserts of weary trash in order to acquire a good touch and technic. A few carefully chosen studies played in all keys and tempo will accomplish the desired results most expeditiously. These Mr. Mason has given. . . .

580   MASON, William. "The Two-Finger Exercise." *University Musical Encyclopedia.* Louis C. Elson, chief ed. 12 vols. New York: University Society, 1912-14. Vol. 8: *The Theory of Music and Piano Technique,* 218-23.

The article is subtitled "Rhythm in Technical Practice — Value of Accent — Control of Muscles — Elasticity, Rigidity, and Relaxation — Correct Attack." A summary of the origins and principal features of the two-finger exercise.

The normal condition of a pianist's hand in the act of playing is one of controlled elasticity, combined with relaxation at the completion of each motion; that is, the hand must not be flabby — it must be supple. In all correct attack three moments are clearly discernible: that of preparation — this should be deliberate; that of attack — this must be as swift as thought; that of recovery — this must be conscious.

Also published as "The Two-Finger Exercise," *The International Library of Music . . .* , 8 vols. (New York: University Society, 1934), vol. 3: *The Pianist's*

Guide . . ., 124-25. (The 1948 four-volume edition of *The International Library of Music . . .* [University Society, New York] also contains this essay in vol. 3, pp. 124-25.)

581   MASON, William. ". . . the Value of Touch." *Musical Courier*, cited in *Music* 11 (Dec 1896): 209-10.

Mason presents arguments against a statement which had appeared in the *Musical Courier* that "the worse a piano is, the worse it will sound the better the player is."

> While it is true, as the Scripture has it, that men do not "gather grapes of thorns or figs of thistles," there is nevertheless a way of getting a better or worse tone out of a piano — good, bad or indifferent — according to manner of touch and general treatment.

Mason summarizes his position by stating that a

> . . . skillful mechanic with a poor set of tools will turn out better work than a bungler with a good set. A good pianist on a poor piano is preferable to a poor pianist on a good one. . . .

582   MASON, William. "What Is Classical Music?" *Music* 7 (Mar 1895): 520.

A two-paragraph definition.

> MUSIC which through prolonged usage has proved its possession of those qualities which entitle it to be taken as a standard of excellence, and which has come to be acknowledged, first by competent judges, and subsequently by the public generally as representing the highest expression of musical taste and hence authorative [*sic*] as a model. Such music . . . is characterized by the union of the emotional and the intellectual in proper equipoise and through the possession of those qualities in their right adjustment, combination and relationship, it is delightful and instructive, — always fresh and incapable of growing old.

Also published as "What Is Classical Music?" *Etude* 13/4 (Apr 1895): 86.

Mason as Coauthor

583   MASON, William, and E. S. HOADLY. *A Method for the Piano-Forte.* Boston: Oliver Ditson & Co., 1867.

This method was also published in 1867 by Mason Brothers, New York. Both firms issued this work in separate editions with "American" or "European" fingering.

For an account of the circumstances under which the work was published, see no. **263**.

See also nos. **215, 433, 584.**

Reviews of no. **583**:

Anonymous review. *New York Musical Gazette* 1/11 (Sept 1867): 84-85.

> It is modern, original and complete. . . . The method teaches the art
> of fingering more fully than any previous work, introducing new modes
> of overcoming difficulties, elucidating principles by copious analyses,
> and thus enabling the learner to understand them easily. . . . It teaches
> the true mode of accompanying . . . and imparts sufficient instruction
> in harmony for those who wish to extemporize interludes and other
> short passages.

JOHNSON, J. C. "The Simplicity of Technique; Chapter VII: The Technique
of the Instruction Books." *Etude* 4/10 (Oct 1886): 252-53.

> . . . [It] contains a very common-sense system used by Mr. Hoadly,
> and masterly instructions in technique by Mr. Mason, and is enriched
> with many cuts showing the proper position of hands and fingers. . . .

MATHEWS, William Smythe Babcock. "Concerning Instruction Books for
the Piano." *Musical Independent* 1/14 (Dec 1869): 414-15.

> A very positive review (unsigned, but listed under editorials in the index).

> The early introduction of exercises in all the keys tends to make the
> pupils good readers, and prevents the superstitious horror of sharps
> and flats that torments so many players.

"New Books." *New York Musical Gazette* 2/1 (Nov 1867): 3.

> A laudatory review. Special attention is drawn to the helpful drawings
> and cuts, the gradual progression of the exercises, the good quality of the
> "recreations" (compositions), and the excellence of the typography.

> Incomparably the best work of the class ever issued in this country.

"New Books and Music." *New York Musical Gazette* 3/2 (Dec 1868): 12-13.

> A ringing review.

> One of its strong merits is the fullness and clearness of its explanations,
> which are intelligible to those who have had no previous advantages. . . .
> The methods pursued, exercises selected, and directions constantly given,
> are not the result of any untried theory, but from their exact adaptedness
> to the exigencies of actual teaching, prove that they could have come
> only from . . . experience.

584   MASON, William, and E. S. HOADLY. *A System for Beginners in the Art
of Playing upon the Piano-Forte.* Boston: Oliver Ditson & Co., 1871.

Review of no. **584**:

MATHEWS, William Smythe Babcock. "Mason & Hoadley's [*sic*] System for
Beginners in Piano Playing." *Musical Independent* 3/31 (May 1871): 70-71.

> A very favorable review (unsigned, but listed under editorials in the index).
> Principal features of Mason & Hoadly's earlier work, *A Method for the
> Piano-Forte* (see no. **583**), are also mentioned. The actual review is pre-
> faced by a history of the use of piano methods in the United States.

. . . it remains to say this: This "System for Beginners" is what we have long looked for in vain—an elementary book, easy enough to be interesting, progressive in its arrangement, and sufficiently thoughtful to command the respect of the best teacher. Every step is practicable; yet every step is forward; and the ultimate gaol [sic] is the *modern method of piano playing*, and not that of our grandfathers.

Also published, with the prefatory historical sketch deleted, as "Mason and Hoadley's [sic] System for Beginners in Piano Playing," *Dwight's Journal of Music* 31/5 (3 June 1871): 36-37.

585   [MASON, William, and William Smythe Babcock MATHEWS.] Combined advertisement for Mason's *Touch and Technic*, op. 44, and Mathews's *Standard Graded Course of Studies*. In *Etude* 26/9 (Sept 1908): 549.

Reports total combined sales of over one million copies.

586   MASON, William, and William Smythe Babcock MATHEWS. *A Primer of Music: Being the First Steps in Musicianship; for Students of the Piano-forte; the Keyboard, Touch, Musical Notation, Scales, Chords, Keys, Transposition, Rudiments of Musical Form and Musical Taste, Principles of Good Fingering, Embellishments, etc., Together with Standard Forms of All the Scales with Their Correct Fingering.* Cincinnati: John Church Co., 1894.

Written in the format of a catechism handbook, this work provides, as the title indicates, a general introduction to the piano and to keyboard musicianship. For the origin of the section on "How to Secure a Good Tone" (pp. 152-55), see no. **577**.

See also the commentary to Mason's *A System of Fundamental Technics*, no. **574**.

Review of no. **586**:

CADY, Calvin Brainerd. "Reviews: Books." *Music Review* 4/3 (Dec 1894): 97-98.

Cady endorses the book, but with some reservations.

If music concepts should come first [as stated by Mason and Mathews in the Preface, p. ii], why should the most fundamental element—rather the essential basis—of *music* concepts not appear for treatment till the ninth chapter? . . . And why should a whole system of mere fractions be presented—Chapter III, Notes, etc.—before the fundamental concepts of rhythm be brought out in the mind of the student?

Cady continues, but on a more positive note.

Its [the book's] real value lies in presenting . . . a systematic course of definitions of music ideas, symbols, and technique, together with much admirable advice and many helpful rules for practice. The definitions of many terms are not only made clear, but truly define the ideas for which the terms stand, and this is what makes the work of practical value.

3

Selected Programs of Performances

REVIEWS AND ANNOUNCEMENTS ARE CITED
IN CHRONOLOGICAL ORDER.

587   Boston, Odeon, 7 Mar 1846

Boston Academy of Music

Henri Herz, *Variations on the "Air" from Méhul's "Joseph,"* op. 20 (performed with quintet accompaniment)

This was probably Mason's first public appearance as a pianist. In his Anniversary Book, Mason comments that he may have played in Dedham, Massachusetts, previous to this concert, but no documentation of such a performance has been found.

Reviews/Announcements of no. **587**:

"The Academy Concert." *Boston Daily Advertiser*, 7 Mar 1846, p. [2], col. 3.

A brief announcement of the concert.

"Academy Concert." *Boston Daily Atlas*, 7 Mar 1846, p. [2], col. 4.

Announces the concert.

"The Academy Concert." *Daily Evening Transcript* (Boston), 7 Mar 1846, p. [2], col. 3.

Announces the concert.

"Concerts in Boston." *Musical Gazette* (Boston) 1/4 (16 Mar 1846): 30.

A favorable review.

DWIGHT, John Sullivan. "Musical Review." *Harbinger* 2/19 (18 Apr 1846): 298-99.

Mr. Mason has but lately made his very successful *debut* as a pianist at the concerts of the Boston Academy. His selection of music was not of the most profound, but suited to the reigning taste for labored brilliancy. This was perhaps a necessity of the occasion. The facile skill of the performer, as then exhibited, derives its chief worth from our knowledge of the fact that there was more behind; that the player also has some of Bach's fugues at his fingers' ends for those who call for them, and that he is at home among the sonatas of Mozart and Beethoven; that he makes the modern piano music his gymnastics and his pastime, but loves the classic masters better. . . .

588   Boston, Chickering's Music Room, 3 Nov 1846

Harvard Musical Association Chamber Concert

Joseph Mayseder, *Second Grand Trio*

Gustave Blessner, violin; E. Groenevelt, cello

Reviews of no. **588**:

"Concerts in Boston." *Musical Gazette* (Boston) 1/21 (9 Nov 1846): 166.

The Harvard Musical Association advertises a series of six chamber concerts, to be given at Mr. Chickering's piano forte warerooms, on every other Tuesday evening. The performers are, Mr. Wm. Mason, piano; Mr. Blessner, first violin; Messrs. Groenveldt [*sic*], Werner, and Meyer, second violin, viola, and violoncello. — The first concert took place on Tuesday evening, October 27.

The date of the opening concert is corrected from October 27 to November 3 in "Concerts in Boston," *Musical Gazette* (Boston) 1/22 (23 Nov 1846): 174.

DWIGHT, John Sullivan. "Musical Review: Chamber Concerts of the Harvard Musical Association." *Harbinger* 3/25 (28 Nov 1846): 394-95.

But we had every reason to be satisfied with the graceful, well-studied, and well-felt accompaniment of our young native artist, Mr. William Mason. . . .

589   Boston, Chickering's Music Room, 17 Nov 1846

Harvard Musical Association Chamber Concert

Carl Reissiger, *Trio*, op. 25

Gustave Blessner, violin; E. Groenevelt, cello

Review of no. **589**:

DWIGHT, John Sullivan. "Musical Review: Chamber Concerts of the Harvard Musical Association." *Harbinger* 3/25 (28 Nov 1846): 394-95.

The Trio by Reissiger . . . was a most delicious, uninterrupted, perfect dream of beauty; the glossy notes flowed out in copious streams from Chickering's grand piano, so that our mouth waters at the recollection, as at the taste of luscious grapes.

590   Boston, Chickering's Music Room, 1 Dec 1846

Harvard Musical Association Chamber Concert

Joseph Mayseder, *Trio*, op. 54

> Gustave Blessner, violin; E. Groenevelt, cello

> Review of no. **590:**

> DWIGHT, John Sullivan. "Musical Review: Harvard Musical Association."
> *Harbinger* 4/8 (30 Jan 1847): 124.
>> The performance is mentioned only in passing.

591   Boston, Chickering's Music Room, 15 Dec 1846

Harvard Musical Association Chamber Concert

Beethoven, *Trio in E-flat Major*, op. 38 (arrangement of the *Septet in E-flat Major*, op. 20)

> Review of no. **591:**

> DWIGHT, John Sullivan. "Musical Review: Harvard Musical Association."
> *Harbinger* 4/8 (30 Jan 1847): 124.
>> The Grand Trio of Beethoven, collated, so to speak, from his Septette, may be considered the central figure of the series. It was a great task for our young pianist, Mason, and the performance did him credit, though there was a certain flagging of strength, too evident to those who had heard the more practised master, Lange, in the same part.

592   Boston, Chickering's Music Room, 29 Dec 1846

Harvard Musical Association Chamber Concert

Joseph Mayseder, *Trio* (not otherwise identified)

> Gustave Blessner, violin; E. Groenevelt, cello

> Review of no. **592:**

> DWIGHT, John Sullivan. "Musical Review: Harvard Musical Association."
> *Harbinger* 4/8 (30 Jan 1847): 124.
>> Mason's performance is not mentioned.

593   Boston, Chickering's Music Room, 12 Jan 1847

Harvard Musical Association Chamber Concert

Carl Reissiger, *Trio*, op. 25

> Gustave Blessner, violin; E. Groenevelt, cello

> Review of no. **593:**

DWIGHT, John Sullivan. "Musical Review: Harvard Musical Association." *Harbinger* 4/8 (30 Jan 1847): 124.

> Mason's performance is not mentioned.

594   Boston, Melodeon, 6 Feb 1847

Boston Academy of Music

Henri Herz and Charles-Philippe Lafont, *Duo Concertant — with Variations on "C'est un Larme"*

William Keyzer, violin

Reviews/Announcements of no. **594**:

"Boston Academy of Music." *Daily Evening Transcript* (Boston), 5 Feb 1847, p. [2], col. 3.

> Announces the concert.

"Academy's Concert." *Boston Daily Atlas*, 6 Feb 1847, p. [2], col. 6.

> Announces the concert.

"Academy of Music." *Boston Post*, 9 Feb 1847, p. [1], cols. 6-7.

> Master Mason evidently had not studied his part, and lacked the depth of mind or executive talent such a performance needs.

"Concerts." *Musical Gazette* (Boston) 2/2 (15 Feb 1847): 14.

> Merely reports that the concert was given; not a review as such.

DWIGHT, John Sullivan. "Musical Review: Boston Academy of Music." *Harbinger* 4/12 (27 Feb 1847): 186-87.

> Mr. Mason played with spirit, precision, and apparent ease, although with a lame arm.

595   Boston, Melodeon, 27 Feb 1847

Boston Academy of Music

Leopold von Meyer, *March triomphale d'Isly*

Reviews/Announcements of no. **595**:

"The Academy's Concert." *Daily Evening Transcript* (Boston), 27 Feb 1847, p. [2], col. 4.

> Announces the concert.

DWIGHT, John Sullivan. "Musical Review: Music in Boston." *Harbinger* 4/16 (27 Mar 1847): 251-52.

> We arrived late and thereby lost . . . what we most regretted, the performance by Mr. William Mason of a couple of De Meyer's pieces on the piano forte.

596   Boston, Tremont Temple, 6 Mar 1847

Boston Philharmonic Society

Henri Herz, *Variations — di bravura — for Piano Forte and Orchestra on the March from "Guillaume Tell,"* op. 57

Reviews/Announcements of no. **596**:

"Boston Philharmonic Society." *Boston Daily Atlas*, 6 Mar 1847, p. [2], col. 4.

A brief announcement of the concert.

"The Philharmonic Festival." *Daily Evening Transcript* (Boston), 6 Mar 1847, p. [2], col. 3.

Announces the concert.

Anonymous review. *Boston Post*, 8 Mar 1847, p. [2], col. 6.

A favorable review.

"Concerts." *Musical Gazette* (Boston) 2/4 (15 Mar 1847): 30.

Merely reports that the concert was given; not a review as such.

DWIGHT, John Sullivan. "Musical Review: Music in Boston." *Harbinger* 4/16 (27 Mar 1847): 251-52.

Mr. William Mason performed a fantasia of Herz . . . with great clearness, freedom and elegance of execution, though not with the infallible precision which usually marks his playing. On being called out he gave De Meyer's version of the celebrated horn quartette in *Semiramide*, in a style of less imperial mastery of course than that peculiar to Leopold himself, but nevertheless which did good justice to the piece, extremely difficult as it must be.

"Philharmonic Concert." Unidentified clipping in MASON/Scrapbook.

A positive review.

597   Boston, Melodeon, 17 Mar 1847

Recital of A. L. de Ribas

Leopold von Meyer, specific titles not identified

Reviews/Announcements of no. **597**:

"Music." *Boston Daily Atlas*, 17 Mar 1847, p. [2], col. 6.

Announces the concert.

"Signor Ribas's Concert." *Daily Evening Transcript* (Boston), 17 Mar 1847, p. [2], col. 3.

A brief announcement of the recital.

Anonymous review. *Boston Post*, 19 Mar 1847, p. [2], col. 4.

Mr. Ribas's concert had not a large audience, the multitude of entertainment diverting attention from concerts, unless announced by some blazing star.

598   Boston, Tremont Temple, 24 and 26 Aug 1847

Boston Academy of Music Teachers' Institute

Leopold von Meyer, unidentified fantasy (August 24)

Henri Herz, unidentified concerto (August 26)

Reviews of no. **598**:

"Boston Academy of Music's Teachers' Institute." *Musical Gazette* (Boston) 2/16 (30 Aug 1847): 121-22; 2/17 (13 Sept 1847): 129-31.

Merely reports that the concerts were given; not a review as such.

DWIGHT, John Sullivan. "Musical Review: Teachers' Convention in Boston." *Harbinger* 5/13 (4 Sept 1847): 203-05.

A general review of the activities of the convention. Includes comments about Mason's work as an accompanist, an activity he carried out in addition to his solo performances.

The evenings were given to public concerts. . . . The great choir of about six hundred filled both of the broad side galleries . . . ; a smaller sub-choir . . . occupied the seats in front of the organ, at which Mr. [George] Webb presided. In front of all were also two pianos, at which Mr. [Silas] Bancroft and the younger Mason accompanied.

599   Cincinnati, Melodeon, 2 Nov 1847

Madame Ablamowicz Concert

Leopold von Meyer, *Fantasie on "Semiramis"*

Mason, "Grand Fantasie and Variations on National Airs"

Review of no. **599**:

"The Last Concert of Madame Ablamowicz. . . ." Unidentified clipping in MASON/Scrapbook.

Much as we admire his *execution* in . . . the Variations on Hail Columbia and Yankee Doodle, we must admire the *beauty* of his "Last Rose of Summer" more [apparently played by Mason as an encore]. Beautiful as is the music of the piece as it stands written, he added to its melody till the Rose of Summer seemed like a parterre of all lovely flowers.

600   Boston, Tremont Temple, 25 Dec 1847

Musical Fund Society

Sigismond Thalberg, *Fantasia on Themes from "La Sonnambula"* (probably Thalberg's *Grand Caprice on Bellini's "Sonnambula,"* op. 46)

Reviews/Announcements of no. **600**:

"The Boston Musical Fund Society." *Boston Daily Atlas*, 24 Dec 1847, p. [2], col. 3.

A four-paragraph announcement of the concert.

DWIGHT, John Sullivan. "Art Review: . . . Music in Boston." *Harbinger* 6/9 (1 Jan 1848): 70-71.

> Mr. William Mason's solo . . . was given with great freedom and expression, only wanting somewhat in force. It was enthusiastically and deservedly encored. . . .

"Concerts." *Musical Gazette* (Boston) 2/25 (3 Jan 1848): 196-97.

> The members of the orchestra in Boston have formed an association, called the Boston Musical Fund Society, for the purpose of giving instrumental concerts. . . . On Saturday, Dec. 25, they gave their second public performance. Among the solo performers on this occasion, was Mr. Wm. Mason, his last appearance before his departure for Europe.

601   Boston, Melodeon, 29 Apr 1848

Joseph Gear Complimentary Concert

Sigismond Thalberg, *Fantasia on Themes from "La Sonnambula"* (probably Thalberg's *Grand Caprice on Bellini's "Sonnambula,"* op. 46)

Announcement of no. **601**:

"Gear's Concert." *Daily Evening Transcript* (Boston), 28 Apr 1848, p. [2], col. 2.

A brief announcement of the recital.

602   Cincinnati, Melodeon, 16 Sept 1848

Joint recital with August Kreissman, tenor

Leopold von Meyer, *Fantasie on "Semiramis"*

Sigismond Thalberg, *Fantasia on Themes from "La Sonnambula"* (probably Thalberg's *Grand Caprice on Bellini's "Sonnambula,"* op. 46)

Liszt, *Fantasia on "Lucia di Lammermoor"* (probably Liszt's *Réminiscences de "Lucia di Lammermoor"*)

Mason, "Grand Fantasie and Variations on National Airs"

Reviews/Announcements of no. **602**:

"William Mason." *Cincinnati Daily Enquirer*, 15 Sept 1848, p. 3, col. 2.

> WILLIAM MASON, has the pleasure of announcing that Mr. AUGUST KREISSMAN . . . will unite with him in giving a concert. . . . The programme will embrace some of the finest songs . . . and selections from the [works] . . . of Thalberg, Liszt, De Meyer, &c., for the piano.

"The Musical Season." *Daily Cincinnati Gazette*, 16 Sept 1848, p. [2], col. 3.

Includes an announcement of Mason's recital.

> Mr. MASON'S eminent abilities are well known to many of our citizens. . . . He is unquestionably, though yet a very young man, one of the few really great pianists that have ever visited Cincinnati. . . . It was he whom we spoke of having heard last season, execute two pieces at one time. . . .

"William Mason and August Kreissman." *Daily Cincinnati Gazette*, 19 Sept 1848, p. [2], col. 4.

> We were about to make some notice of the beautiful and wonderful performances of Mr. MASON on the piano, when we met with the following verses from the August number of *Frazer's Edinburgh Magazine*, on the similar performances of a kindred spirit, M. CHOPIN, which we substitute on account of their felicitous expression, and their singular applicability to the playing of Mr. Mason Saturday evening. . . .

"Musical." *Cincinnati Daily Enquirer*, 20 Sept 1848, p. [3], col. 1.

> Mr. Mason displays *prodigious* musical talents; he has already acquired extraordinary execution; in some of his pieces he appeared a perfect duplicate of De Meyer. . . . When he responded to the encore of Lucia Di Lammermor [sic], he gave the Last Rose of Summer with variations, with a touching pathos not easily described. A more delightful piece of music we have seldom listened to; such a perfect crescendo and diminuendo. . . .

The reviewer was also impressed by Mason's variations on "National Airs."

> Mr. M. manifested a great degree of genius, particularly in his fantasia on the national melodies. . . . He commenced with an introduction in a Fugue style, which, in our opinion, is the most difficult of Piano studies. He handled the melody with the dexterity of a juggler. . . . His happiest effort in this piece, was, uniting the two subjects . . . without any molestation of the laws of harmony. . . .

Anonymous review. Clipping identified only as "from the . . . [illegible]." In MASON/Scrapbook.

A positive assessment.

Anonymous review. Unidentified clipping in MASON/Scrapbook.

> . . . Mason's variations on "Yankee Doodle" and "Hail Columbia" . . . took the audience by storm. In this piece he gave us an example of a tune played with the left hand alone, and so well played that had we not seen it, we should never have suspected that both were not employed. Mr. Mason may fairly be considered as a *great* player. With a force, precision and correctness, rivalling that of De Meyer, he has a rapidity of fingering which can hardly be excelled by any one.

603   Rochester, N.Y., Sept 1848

Meetings of the Teachers' Institute

Sigismond Thalberg, specific titles not identified

Leopold von Meyer, specific titles not identified

Mason, arrangements of "The Last Rose of Summer" and "My Lodging Is on the Cold Ground"

Mason, "Grand Fantasie and Variations on National Airs"

Mason, "Waltz" (not otherwise identified)

> Review of no. 603:
>
> "Music Teacher's Institute." *Rochester Daily Democrat*, 23 Sept 1848, p. [2], col. 3; 24 Sept 1848, p. [2], col. 5; 27 Sept 1848, p. [2], col. 4; 28 Sept 1848, p. [2], col. 3.
>
> Mason's variations created the greatest excitement.
>
>> Fragments of the melody ["Yankee Doodle"] were constantly being heard, scattered from one end of the key-board to the other, attended with the most difficult forms of accompaniment either in Arpeggio, running passages, or trills, requiring, one might suppose, six or eight hands to execute, rather than two. To crown the whole he introduced "Hail Columbia," and finally united the two themes, giving the effect of two Bands. . . . It is really astonishing that so large a body of tone can be produced from a single Pianoforte, as it was our privilege to hear in this remarkable performance. . . . We understand this highly talented gentleman is yet only in his nineteenth year.
>
> Also cited in the *Musical Gazette* (Boston) as "Sixth Annual Meeting of the Musical Institute" 3/20 (23 Oct 1848): 153-55.
>
> See also nos. **308, 309.**

604 Waltham, Mass., Rumfordhall, 27 Dec 1848

Boston Amateur Glee Club

Leopold von Meyer, *Fantasie on "Semiramis"*

Mason, "Grande Valse de concert" (not otherwise identified)

Mason, "Grand Fantasie and Variations on National Airs"

605 Boston, Melodeon, 10 Feb 1849

Musical Fund Society

Mason, "La Goutte de rosée: Mélodie variée" (later published as *Les Perles de rosée: Mélodie variée*, [op. 2]?)

> Reviews/Announcements of no. **605:**
>
> "Boston Musical Fund." *Boston Daily Atlas*, 10 Feb 1849, p. [2], col. 4.
> Announces the concert.
>
> "Musical Fund Society." *Daily Evening Transcript* (Boston), 10 Feb 1849, p. [2], col. 4.

Announces the recital.

> . . . Mr. W. Mason, the talented young pianist, will play one of his own compositions. . . .

"Fourth Musical Fund Concert." *Daily Chronotype* (Boston), 12 Feb 1849, p. [2], col. 1.

A favorable review.

"Fourth Musical Fund Concert." *Boston Post*, 13 Feb 1849, p. [2], col. 4.

> His performances are remarkable for an innate purity of style, brilliancy, finish and delicacy of execution. . . .

"The Musical Fund Concert." *Boston Daily Atlas*, 13 Feb 1849, p. [2], col. 2.

> He took Yankee Doodle and Hail Columbia [for an encore], and mingled them together in the strangest combinations, now marking them out distinctly, and now covering them up with changing chords. He carried them, apparently, through every key in the scale, major and minor. There was a beginning and an end to it, to be sure, and that was all that could be well fixed upon in the piece; but still it was a most ingenious piece of harmony, and exhibited great ability in the youthful composer. He is the first one who has united our two national airs in a like manner, playing them both at once.

"Musical Fund Society." *Daily Evening Transcript* (Boston), 13 Feb 1849, p. 2, col. 3.

> Mr. Mason possesses extraordinary talents, and has it in his power to become a great artist. . . .

"Musical Fund Society's Concert." *Boston Daily Journal*, 13 Feb 1849, p. [2], col. 5.

A positive review.

606   Boston, Melodeon, 10 Mar 1849

Musical Fund Society

Leopold von Meyer, *Fantasie on "Semiramis"*

Reviews of no. **606**:

"The Boston Musical Fund Society." *Boston Post*, 12 Mar 1849, p. [2], col. 3.

> . . . Mr. William Mason, in a Fantasie by De Meyer, on the piano, was loudly encored, and responding to the call, his delightful execution of the "Last Rose of Summer" was rapturously received.

"The Musical Fund Concert." *Boston Daily Atlas*, 15 Mar 1849, p. [2], col. 2.

> Mason's performance is not mentioned.

"Last Concert of the Musical Fund." Unidentified clipping in MASON/ Scrapbook.

> . . . a more spirited and elegant exhibition of pianoforte playing is seldom heard. . . .

607   Cambridge, Mass., City Hall, 15 Mar 1849

Cambridge Musical Association

Mason, "Grand Fantasie [and Variations on National Airs?]"

608   Atlantic Ocean, Mail Steamer *Hermann*, 1 May 1849

Grand vocal and instrumental concert

Unidentified, *Grand Polonaise for Four Hands*

> Julius Schuberth, second pianist

Unidentified, *Grand Air from "Lucia"* (transcribed for violin and piano)

> Julius Schuberth, violin

Leopold von Meyer, *Marcia d'Italy*

Unidentified, *Ave Maria for Violin and Piano*

> Julius Schuberth, violin

Mason, "Improvisation"

> For additional information regarding this concert, see no. **23**.

609   Prague, Saale zum Erzherzog Stephan, 31 Jan 1851

Soirée musicale des Julius Pisařowitz

Alexander Dreyschock, *Rhapsodie zum Wintermärchen*, op. 40

Weber, *Grand Duo Concertant*, op. 48

> Julius Pisařowitz, clarinet

> Reviews of no. **609**:

> "American Musicians Abroad." *Saroni's Musical Times* 2/24 (8 Mar 1851): 244.

>> Cites favorable reviews (in English translation) from the *Bohemia* (Prague) of 2 February 1851 and the *Prager Zeitung* [sic] of 2 February 1851. The latter states:

>>> Mr. Mason justifies the most exulting hopes. In the beautiful *"Winter Story"* by Dreyschock, which we have always heard played by the master himself with so much satisfaction, Mr. Mason showed evidently great power and brilliancy of execution, particularly in the octave passages in G minor, though on the other side he marked too little the light and shade. He succeeded still better in the duo by Weber. . . .

"An American Abroad." *Message Bird: A Literary and Musical Journal* 40 (15 Mar 1851): 661.

Cites reviews (in English translation) from the *Salon* and the *Deutsche Zeitung*—both published in Prague. The *Salon* comments:

> Mr. Mason . . . played . . . the *Rhapsody to the Winter Story* . . . with astonishing purity and precision. He conquered not only the external, but also the more inward and spiritual difficulties of the composition with rare calmness and ease, and gave us an interesting miniature of the very celebrated performance of his master [Dreyschock].

This article was also published as "William Mason at Prague," *Choral Advocate and Singing-Class Journal* 1/11 (Apr 1851): 166-67.

"Letter from Prague." *Message Bird: A Literary and Musical Journal* 40 (15 Mar 1851): 658.

Contains an account (signed "M. H.") of the Pisařowitz concert. Mason performed Dreyschock's *Rhapsodie*

> . . . with entire success. Mr. Dreyschock who was standing by my side remarked as he closed that he was perfectly satisfied with the performance, and this, considering the character of the critic was praise enough.

"Musikalisches: Soirée musicale des Hrn. J. Pisařowitz. . . ." Unidentified clipping in MASON/Scrapbook.

A favorable review. Excerpts from this review in English translation, cited as taken from the *Salon*, are published in "An American Abroad," *Message Bird: A Literary and Musical Journal* 40 (15 Mar 1851): 661. See above.

610   Prague, Palace of the Countess of Nostitz, 23 Mar 1851

Matinée musicale under the patronage of Countess Schlik

Mason, "Impromptu in A-flat" (later published as *Amitié pour amitié*, op. 4?)

Alexander Dreyschock, *La Coupe: Impromptu* (probably Dreyschock's *La Coupe: Chanson à boire*, op. 25)

For additional information regarding this concert, see no. **509**.

611   Prague, Saale des Sophien Insel, 3 May 1851

Concert under the patronage of Prince Rohan

Alexander Dreyschock, *Gruss an Wien*, op. 32

Review of no. **611**:

"Musikalisches: . . . des Privatvereins für Haus-Arme. . . ." Clipping identified only as from the *Salon* (Prague), 6 May 1851. In MASON/Scrapbook.

A short, favorable review.

612   Frankfurt, Salon des Hauses Mozart, 20 June 1852

Mason, *Amitié pour amitié: Morceau de salon*, op. 4

Alexander Dreyschock, *Rhapsodie in C Minor*

> Review of no. **612**:
>
> "Honor to American Artists Abroad: William Mason & Moreau Gottschalk."
> *Musical World and New York Musical Times* 3/24 (16 Aug 1852): 416.
>
> > Cites reviews (in English translation) from the *Frankfurter Anzeiger* and
> > the *Signal* (identified only as a "German musical journal"). The *Anzeiger*
> > is quoted as follows:
> >
> > > Two Saloon [*sic*] pieces for the pianoforte, played by the American
> > > pianist, Wm. Mason, were received with great and very general applause;
> > > viz.: *Amitié pour Amitié*, from the pen of the pianist, and a *Rhapsodie*
> > > by Dreyschock, (which name, by the bye, cloaks a great absurdity, as
> > > the piece opens in C minor and ends in G minor.) Yet this remark does
> > > not refer to our still youthful *virtuoso*, who played these difficult and
> > > chromatic compositions with the greatest correctness and finish.
>
> See also no. **224**.

613   London, Exeter Hall, 20 Jan 1853

Harmonic Union Subscription Concert — Julius Benedict

Weber, *Concertstück in F Minor*, op. 79

> For information regarding some of the circumstances surrounding Mason's
> performance, see nos. **305, 1014**.
>
> Reviews of no. **613**:
>
> "Harmonic Union." *Times* (London), 21 Jan 1853, p. 5, col. 6.
>
> > Happily Mr. Mason possesses talent; and, though very young, already
> > exhibits promise of excellence. He played the pianoforte part in Weber's
> > *Concert Stück* with a great deal of spirit. . . . It is in mechanism that Mr.
> > Mason is deficient. This deficiency makes him nervous and uncertain,
> > imparts unsteadiness to his accentuation, and robs his passages of
> > clearness. He has, nevertheless, a light and elastic touch, and evidently
> > understands his author.
>
> "Music: Harmonic Union." Clipping identified only as from the *Daily News*,
> 21 Jan 1853. In MASON/Scrapbook.
>
> > . . . Mr. William Mason . . . made his first appearance in this country.
> > He has studied, we anderstand [*sic*], in Germany, and is an accomplished
> > performer. He played Weber's well-known Concert Stück with great
> > judgment, expression and brilliancy.
>
> "Harmonic Union." *Musical Times and Singing-Class Circular* 5/105 (1 Feb
> 1853): 140.
>
> > A young pianist, Mr. W. Mason, created a favourable impression in the
> > neatness of his performance of Weber's *Concert Stück*.

"Musical Intelligence, England." *Dwight's Journal of Music* 2/20 (19 Feb 1853): 159.

> Cites reviews from the following London newspapers: *Daily News* (see above), *Times* (see above), *Chronicle*, and *Athenaeum*.

"The Harmonic Union." Clipping identified only as from the *Globe*. In MASON/Scrapbook.

> Mr. William Mason, a sparkling pianist from New York, and Her [sic] Nabich, a German, who extracts wonderful notes from the trombone, made their first appearance in London, and were received with general appoobation [sic].

614 London, Angel Hotel Assembly Rooms, 7 Feb 1853

Plummer and Mitchell Concert under the patronage of the Lord Mayor and Lady Mayoress

Rudolf Willmers, *Sehnsucht am Meere*

Leopold von Meyer, *Nocturne*

Alexander Dreyschock, *Saltarello*

> For additional information regarding this concert, see nos. **24, 303, 305.**

615 Weimar, Stadthaussaal, 13 Dec 1853

Vier Quartett-Soiréen

J. S. Bach, one of the triple concertos

> Karl Klindworth and Dionys Pruckner, second and third pianists

616 Weimar, Stadthaussaal, 3 Jan 1854

Vier Quartett-Soiréen

J. S. Bach, one of the triple concertos

> Karl Klindworth and Dionys Pruckner, second and third pianists

617 Boston, Chickering's Warerooms, 22 Sept 1854

Matinée musicale for invited guests

> Mason's program selections were apparently chosen *ex tempore*. Reviews indicate that he performed works by Liszt, Weber, Beethoven, Handel, Chopin, Kontski, Willmers, and himself.

> Reviews of no. **617:**

> "The Debut of William Mason." *Boston Daily Journal*, 23 Sept 1854, p. [1], col. 3.

Among the more prominent features of Mr. Mason's playing, the perfect ease with which he accomplishes the greatest difficulties must strike every one. There is no swaying of the body, or swinging of the arms, or undulations of the head; in fact, there is an entire absence of all that clap-trap with which charlatans seek to impress the public with a sense of their powers.

"Musical." *Boston Daily Evening Transcript*, 23 Sept 1854, p. [2], col. 2.

It was our privilege, yesterday afternoon, to be present at the entertainment which Mr. William Mason gave at the Messrs. Chickering's Rooms, in consequence of the general desire which had been expressed, that he should afford his friends and those interested an opportunity of judging of his proficiency, unbiased by the accessories of the concert room.

"William Mason." *Daily Evening Traveller* (Boston), 23 Sept 1854, p. [1], cols. 3-4.

The audience was too high-bred to be very demonstrative; but as the player's fingers flew over the keys, flashing out dazzling ribbons of sound, and seeming to fill the room with the voices of a whole wood full of nightingales, an involuntary murmer [sic] of delight would run through the audience, often culminating, at some exhibition of surpassing skill, in a burst of hearty applause.

"William Mason, the Pianist." *Boston Post*, 23 Sept 1854, p. [2], col. 1.

Some of those who had not previously listened to his [Mason's] performances, but had heard the encomiums which his playing has elicited since his arrival on our shores, were in a very exacting mood; but as his performances were admirable in every respect, a hearty recognition of such undeniable and varied merit could not be withheld.

"William Mason's Concert." *Dwight's Journal of Music* 5/26 (30 Sept 1854): 204-05.

All felt that here was truly a complete pianist, and felt it with peculiar pride and pleasure, that he was a Boston boy. It was one of the little feasts to be remembered.

618 Boston, Tremont Temple, 3 Oct 1854

Mason's debut recital, assisted by Eduard and Friedrich Mollenhauer

[Mollenhauer], *Grand Fantasie: Duo for Two Violins*

  Eduard and Friedrich Mollenhauer

Liszt, *Rhapsody on Hungarian Airs* (not further identified)

[Heinrich Wilhelm?] Ernst, identified only as "Solo"

  Eduard Mollenhauer

Chopin, *Impromptu in A-flat Major*, op. 29

Heller, *Saltarello*

Beethoven, *Sonata in C-sharp Minor*, op. 27, no. 2

Handel, *Fugue in E Minor*

[Mollenhauer], *Variations Brillantes: Duo for Two Violins*

Eduard and Friedrich Mollenhauer

[Antoine de?] Kontski, *Grand Caprice héroique*

Reviews/Announcements of no. **618**:

"William Mason's First Concert." *Boston Daily Journal*, 14 Sept 1854, p. [2], col. 2.

Announces Mason's recital.

> The desire to hear Mr. Mason increases daily, and the feeling extends to the suburbs. There will be large numbers present from out of town at the first concert.

"William Mason." *Daily Commonwealth* (Boston), 20 Sept 1854, p. 2, col. 4.

Announces Mason's recital.

> The young pianist . . . has, from his earliest youth, been surrounded by the genial atmosphere which should tend to develope [*sic*] any dawnings of genius that might be in him; has enjoyed all the advantages of education that this country could give; faithful to these, has followed up this training by a five years diligent study of his instrument and art in the cities of Europe, learning under the greatest living masters of the piano, in a time when its resources have been developed to a before unknown degree of perfection, enjoying the intimacy, instruction and friendship of such men as Liszt, and now has returned to give an account of his stewardship of the remarkable talents which he displayed before his departure.

"William Mason's Concert." *Boston Daily Evening Transcript*, 23 Sept 1854, p. [4], col. 2.

Announces Mason's concert.

"Musical." *Boston Daily Evening Transcript*, 27 Sept 1854, p. [2], col. 1.

Announces Mason's recital and the beginning of ticket sales.

> The price of tickets has been unalterably fixed at fifty cents, notwithstanding a strong effort on the part of many to have it placed at a dollar. The sale of tickets will commence tomorrow morning. . . . We understand that applications have already been made in advance for over five hundred tickets, and the probability is that they will go off with great rapidity. Most of the sofas in Tremont Temple hold ten persons each — just the number for a five dollar bill and a nice family party.

Within two days the tickets had "nearly all been disposed of" ("Musical," *Boston Daily Evening Transcript*, 29 Sept 1854, p. [2], col. 6).

"William Mason's Concert." *Dwight's Journal of Music* 5/26 (30 Sept 1854): 204-05.

Announces the recital. Mason's program (with explanatory notes) is included.

"Mr. Mason's Concert." *Boston Daily Evening Transcript*, 4 Oct 1854, p. [2], col. 3.

> It must have seemed to those who had not heard Mr. Mason before last evening, that the unanimous verdict of the press given as it were in advance, savored rather of puffery than criticism, but in truth we have never had any performer capable of suiting so many varying tastes and demands, or combining so much skill with so much tact and geniality. Most pianists have their specialties of playing some particular flourishes, which are resorted to again and again, till they become the principal part of the entertainment, and distinguish the performer from all others. Mr. Mason has none of these. . . . The advantage he has enjoyed of various teachers, each the best of their peculiar school, has given him a freedom from peculiarities, which while it may perhaps operate to diminish his individuality as a performer, will in the long run secure him a far more general and sure appreciation among the community.

"William Mason's Concert." *Boston Daily Journal*, 4 Oct 1854, p. 1, col. 5.

> The dampness in the atmosphere last evening was a severe trial to any instrument, and one of those used got so badly out of tune as to seriously mar the performance. But notwithstanding these drawbacks, it must be admitted that Mr. Mason won a triumph.

"Wm. Mason's Concert." *Boston Post*, 4 Oct 1854, p. [2], col. 3.

> His [Mason's] first night with his townspeople was a great triumph, and a prophet was, for once at least, honored in his own country. We congratulate him upon his complete success.

"William Mason's Debut." *Dwight's Journal of Music* 6/1 (7 Oct 1854): 5-6.

> . . . the characteristics of Mr. MASON'S playing seem to be these. First, a clear, crisp, vital touch. Secondly, the easy, quiet, graceful manner, with which he executes all the difficulties of modern pianism. . . . Thirdly, firmness, sonority. . . . Fourthly, great delicacy, purity, and evenness in his rapid scales and ornaments. . . . Fifthly, an expressive, truly singing *cantabile*. . . . Finally, an artistic, conscientious, sympathetic surrender of himself to the spirit of the author and the piece.

"Musical Intelligence, Boston, Oct. 9." *New York Musical Review and Choral Advocate* 5/21 (12 Oct 1854): 356.

> . . . I much doubt if there is another piano-forte player living who could, by any means whatever, draw out two so large and enthusiastic audiences at a mere piano-forte concert [refers to Mason's October 3d and 7th concerts].

For additional information related to this recital, see no. **1.**

619   New York, Niblo's Saloon, 5 Oct 1854

Matinée musicale for invited guests

Liszt, *Rhapsody on Hungarian Airs* (not further identified)

Rudolf Willmers, *Sehnsucht am Meere*

Alexander Dreyschock, *Saltarello*

Chopin, *Impromptu in A-flat Major*, op. 29

Handel, *Fugue in E Minor*

Alexander Dreyschock, *Rhapsodie zum Wintermärchen*, op. 40

[Antoine de?] Kontski, *Grand Caprice héroique*

Reviews/Announcements of no. **619:**

"A New Great American Pianist." *New York Daily Tribune*, 2 Oct 1854, p. 7, cols. 3-4.

Announces Mason's performance and tells of the excitement Mason was generating among the public.

Mr. William Mason of Boston, who has been six years studying in Germany . . . is now in Boston. . . . It excites — as an American event — there, in connection with music, more interest than any that has ever taken place, the best judges speaking of him as a first-class artist. . . .

"Mr. Mason, the Pianist." *New York Daily Tribune*, 6 Oct 1854, p. 7, col. 6.

It is almost superfluous to say that Mr. Mason has overcome the present difficulties, and, up to the time of Liszt; the impossibilities of the piano-forte. These melt under his fingers, so they cease to appear wonderful. . . . What may be mentioned as a peculiar thing in his playing is the sensitive delicacy of his touch in quiet passages. This we take to be his marked characteristic; not wishing to convey the idea that his handling is not abundantly strong. In a word, he is master of his instrument, in the wide signification now attached to the term.

"Mr. Mason's Musical Levee." *Evening Mirror* (New York), 6 Oct 1854, p. [3], col. 3.

A long, positive review.

"Musical and Dramatic." *New York Morning Express*, 6 Oct 1854, p. [2], col. 7.

Mr. MASON'S *debut* was perfectly successful, and the occasion passed off with so much *eclat* that we are confident he will meet with a brilliant reception, next week, at his first public concert in New York.

"Musical Intelligence, . . . New York." *New York Musical Review and Choral Advocate* 5/21 (12 Oct 1854): 355-56.

In his rendering, one is struck with the entirely different character which different compositions assume. This was very apparent at his *matinée*, when he played a fugue by Handel, immediately succeeding an impromptu by Chopin. The grace and chastened playfulness of the latter author stood out in marked contrast with the bold, vigorous, irresistible march of the fugue. The very touch of the performer was entirely changed, and it seemed like a different player and a different instrument.

"The World of Music, . . . New York." *Musical World* 10/7 (14 Oct 1854): 78-79.

A lukewarm review.

> Mr. Mason is a masterly pianist in every respect. By this we mean, that he is not only a finished player, but an intelligent player. . . . A thing or two to be gained, we think, in Mr. Mason's playing yet, is an adaptation of his *tempo* to the locality he is in.

620 Boston, Tremont Temple, 7 Oct 1854

Solo recital, assisted by Eduard and Friedrich Mollenhauer

Mollenhauer, *Concerto: Duo for Two Violins*

> Eduard and Friedrich Mollenhauer

Alexander Dreyschock, *Rhapsodie zum Wintermärchen*, op. 40

De Bériot, *Adagio and Rondo Russe: Violin*

> Friedrich Mollenhauer

Mason, *Amitié pour amitié: Morceau de salon*, op. 4

Mason, *Valse de bravoure*, op. 5

Rudolf Willmers, *Sehnsucht am Meere*

Alexander Dreyschock, *Saltarello*

[Mollenhauer], *Grand Variations: Two Violins*

> Eduard and Friedrich Mollenhauer

Liszt, *Illustrations du prophète,* no. 2

> Reviews/Announcements of no. **620**:

"Wm. Mason's Concerts." *Boston Daily Journal*, 3 Oct 1854, p. [3], col. 4.
  Announces Mason's recital.

> THE tickets to MR. MASON'S FIRST CONCERT having been sold four days in advance, and many hundred persons who wished to attend having been unable to secure seats, Mr. M. will give another (and his LAST) Concert. . . .

"Mr. Mason's Second Concert." *Boston Post*, 5 Oct 1854, p. 2, col. 2.
  Announces Mason's recital and reports on ticket sales.

> The tickets for next Saturday evening are selling very rapidly, and the indications are that a great house will confirm the verdict of Tuesday evening.

"Mr. Mason's Concert." *Boston Post*, 7 Oct 1854, p. [1], col. 4.
  Announces Mason's recital. It is evident that Mason had a very clever and thorough press agent.

> This evening we shall have another opportunity of listening to the performances of Mr. Mason. . . . We are requested to state that the concert will be over at 9 or 9 1/4 o'clock, so that persons residing out of town will be enabled to take the railroad trains or coaches which leave the city at half-past 9.

"William Mason's Concert." *Boston Daily Evening Transcript*, 7 Oct 1854, p. [2], col. 1.

Announces Mason's recital.

The programme offered by this distinguished pianist for his concert this evening, is varied and attractive, and we hope to see as full and fashionable an audience in attendance as greeted him upon his first appearance.

"Musical." *Boston Daily Evening Transcript*, 9 Oct 1854, p. [2], col. 3.

New beauties of execution, each tending to exhibit the thoroughness of his training, are continually developing themselves, while he plays, not at the expense of the unity and harmony of the composition, but apparently called up by some requirement of the score, and as quickly relinquished when the occasion for their need is past.

"Musical Intelligence, Boston, Oct. 9." *New York Musical Review and Choral Advocate* 5/21 (12 Oct 1854): 356.

A very favorable review.

"William Mason's Second Concert." *Boston Daily Journal*, 9 Oct 1854, p. [2], col. 3.

The enthusiasm was immense, nearly every piece in the programme being *encored.* Mr. Mason answered two or three of these pleasing demands upon his powers, and it really seemed as though the audience were not satisfied even then, for he was called out on one occasion after he had played an *encore.*

"William Mason's Second Concert." *Dwight's Journal of Music* 6/2 (14 Oct 1854): 13-14.

Mason's performance is reviewed favorably, but his program selection does not meet with Dwight's approval.

Having achieved two such successes in our city, to be repeated in New York and elsewhere, we trust that Mr. MASON will ere long return to the legitimate and high sphere of a piano-forte artist, and give some concerts in which the music interpreted shall be the thing *most* memorable.

621 New York, Niblo's Saloon, 12 Oct 1854

New York debut recital

Liszt, *Rhapsody on Hungarian Airs* (not further identified)

Beethoven, *Sonata in C-sharp Minor*, op. 27, no. 2

Handel, *Fugue in E Minor*

Rudolf Willmers, *Sehnsucht am Meere*

Alexander Dreyschock, *Rhapsodie zum Wintermärchen*, op. 40

[Antoine de?] Kontski, *Grand Caprice héroique*

Reviews/Announcements of no. **621**:

"Mr. Mason's Concert." *New York Times*, 10 Oct 1854, p. [1], col. 3.

Announces the recital.

> We hope a New-York audience will show the same quick consideration for a countryman as did the Boston musical community, who purchased every ticket for his [Mason's] Tuesday's concert on the Saturday previous.

"Mr. Mason's Concert." *Evening Mirror* (New York), 13 Oct 1854, p. 3, col. 5.

A very short, but laudatory review.

"Mr. Mason's Concert." *Evening Post* (New York), 13 Oct 1854, p. 2, cols. 2-3.

A long, highly favorable review.

> We have long ceased to wonder at the feats of execution of great pianists: but if any one could provoke amazement it would be Mr. Mason. He possesses wonderful strength of wrist and finger, and under his hands the piano thunders like a mimic orchestra—his runs possess brilliancy and finish, and when delicacy of touch is wanted he strikes the keys so lightly that it would ravish the ear of a listening fairy.

"Musical and Dramatic." *New York Morning Express*, 13 Oct 1854, p. [2], col. 4.

> Mr. WILLIAM MASON gave a highly pleasing and successful concert . . . last night. . . .

Anonymous review. *New York Times*, 14 Oct 1854, p. 4, col. 4.

> Mr. MASON has evidently been a diligent student in the Old Country, and returns a thorough master of the modern German school of piano-forte playing. His touch is wonderfully vigorous, all his harmonies massive, and his effects finely wrought. One of his greatest recommendations is that he does not follow the THALBERG school. Thoughtful completeness rather than flippant brilliancy is his characteristic.

"The Man in the Omnibus. Number VI. Mr. Wm. Mason's Piano Playing." *Musical World* 10/8 (21 Oct 1854): 89-90.

This review—unsigned, but probably written by Richard Storrs Willis—is decidedly negative in tone. It is one of the infrequent negative reviews which Mason received.

> . . . Mr. Mason . . . cannot yet play classic music. Not that he has not the technicality—the execution I mean, and all that: but he does not apparently know *how* to play such music.

FERN, Fanny. "A Letter. . . ." *New York Musical Review and Choral Advocate* 5/22 (26 Oct 1854): 369.

> Mr. Mason's talent as an artist is only equaled by his modesty. He does not avail himself of the *prestige* of his gifted father's name; he simply trusts to his own individual merits. . . . While Europe inundates us with her cast-off *passée* artists, (who are tolerated too often merely because they *are* foreign,) let it not be said that our own talented countrymen shall be driven to do us honor only on *foreign shores.*

"Musical Intelligence, . . . New York." *New York Musical Review and Choral Advocate* 5/22 (26 Oct 1854): 370-71.

Includes a brief, laudatory review followed by citations of reviews from the *Evening Post* (see above), the *Courier & Enquirer*, and the *Musical World* (see above). (Also includes a brief review of Mason's recital on 14 October 1854; see next item.)

622   New York, Niblo's Saloon, 14 Oct 1854

Mason's program for this recital has not been located. An advertisement in the *New York Times* (13 Oct 1854, p. 5, col. 6) notes that the recital will include performances of works by

. . . Willmers, Chopin, Liszt, Dreyschock, Heller, Handel, &c. . . ."

Reviews/Announcements of no. **622**:

"Mr. Wm. Mason's Concert Tonight." *New York Daily Tribune*, 14 Oct 1854, p. 7, col. 3.

Announces Mason's recital.

His [first] concert on Thursday was one of the most successful kind. The loss of the Arctic [steamship], striking widely in New-York society, kept a number of amateurs away, but yet the audience was large, and what was more, lyrically intelligent. . . . We feel it due to an American — the first in all the northern States who has placed himself on the same platform of excellence with European celebrities on the piano — that his countrymen should recognize his deserts.

Anonymous review. *New York Times*, 16 Oct 1854, p. 4, col. 4.

The entertainment was very fine, and merited not only the attendance but the applause bestowed by the attendants. It is a little difficult to popularize entertainments that depend mainly on the piano for their attractiveness, but Mr. MASON will, we think, undoubtedly do so.

"Musical Intelligence, . . . New York." *New York Musical Review and Choral Advocate* 5/22 (26 Oct 1854): 370-71.

Includes a brief, favorable review. (Also includes reviews of Mason's recital on 12 October 1854; see no. **621**.)

623   New England area tour

Immediately following his recitals in Boston and New York, Mason made a five-day tour of the New England area, giving recitals in New Haven, Connecticut; Hartford, Connecticut; Springfield, Massachusetts; Worcester, Massachusetts; and Providence, Rhode Island. Recital programs for this tour have not been located. An advertisement for the Worcester recital in the *Daily Transcript* [Worcester] (18 Oct 1854, p. [3], col. 2) reads, in part, as follows:

. . . including selections from the words [*sic*] of Handel, Beethoven, Mendelssohn, Chopin, Liszt, Stephen Heller, and others; also, Popular Arrangements of National Airs, and Improvisations on familiar melodies.

An advertisement for Mason's Springfield recital in the *Springfield Daily Republican* (17 Oct 1854, p. [3], col. 3) lists his program in detail:

[Antoine de?] Kontski, *Grand Caprice héroique*
Rudolf Willmers, *Sehnsucht am Meere*
Alexander Dreyschock, *Saltarello*
Mason, *Amitié pour amitié: Morceau de salon*, op. 4
Mason, *Grand Valse de bravoure*, (op. 5?)
Liszt, *Rhapsody on Hungarian Airs* (not further identified)
Handel, *Fugue in E Minor*
Mason, Improvisations on National Airs

In all likelihood the programs for the other recitals given on this brief tour were similar in composition. Mason's tour itinerary and selected reviews are given below.

New Haven, Conn., Brewster's Hall, 16 Oct 1854

Reviews/Announcements of Mason's recital in New Haven on 16 Oct 1854:

"Mason—the American Pianist." *New Haven Daily Register*, 14 Oct 1854, p. [2], col. 5.

   Announces the recital.

"Mr. Mason's Concert." *New Haven Daily Register*, 16 Oct 1854, p. [2], col. 6.

   Announces Mason's recital.

   Although Mr. Mason does not appeal to his countrymen for support, on the ground that he is an American; still we are permitted to take a patriotic pride in the reflection that a native born citizen is the acknowledged peer of the best European artists. . . .

"This Evening's Concert." *New Haven Daily Palladium*, 16 Oct 1854, p. [2], col. 4.

   Announces Mason's recital.

"Mason's Concert." *New Haven Daily Register*, 17 Oct 1854, p. [2], col. 2.

   A brief review.

   His performances were wonderful. Under his manipulations, the Piano was made to discourse more intelligibly and eloquently, than we have ever before heard; unless we except Maurice Strakosch.

"Mr. Mason's Concert." *New Haven Daily Palladium*, 17 Oct 1854, p. [2], col. 1.

   His execution is extremely neat, but last night he failed to carry the hearts of the audience until the closing piece, although he previously received two *encores*. It was a difficult thing to carry them at all, with an hour and a half of piano and nothing else.

Hartford, Conn., Melodeon, 17 Oct 1854

Reviews/Announcements of Mason's recital in Hartford on 17 Oct 1854:

"Mr. Mason's Concert." *Hartford Daily Courant*, 17 Oct 1854, p. [2], col. 3.
Announces Mason's recital.

It is seldom that we have seen any artist so highly spoken of by the
press, as is Mr. Mason. . . .

"Mr. Mason's Concert." *Hartford Daily Courant*, 18 Oct 1854, p. [2], col. 2.

Mr. Mason had a good house last night, and certainly was equal to
all that has been said about him.

"Musical Intelligence, Hartford, Ct." *New York Musical Review and Choral
Advocate* 5/22 (26 Oct 1854): 372.

His playing astonished and charmed his auditors, who encored nearly
every piece on the programme.

Springfield, Mass., Hampden Hall, 18 Oct 1854

For a list of the works performed, see the general description of Mason's
tour above.

Reviews/Announcements of Mason's recital in Springfield on 18 Oct 1854:

"William Mason's Concert To-Night." *Springfield Daily Republican*, 18 Oct
1854, p. [2], col. 6.
Announces Mason's recital.

What we have often spoken of as in the future, is now a present joy
to our citizens. The great American pianist, as it is only just to call
him, William Mason, . . . is to be with us to-night. . . .

Anonymous review. *Springfield Daily Republican*, 19 Oct 1854, p. [2],
col. 4.

Mr. Mason delighted a moderate audience at Hampden Hall, last
evening, with his exquisite piano concert. He fulfilled expectation to
the fullest, and the enthusiasm of his hearers occasionally ran over. It
was decidedly the best piano-playing ever heard in Springfield, and with
[Maurice] Strakosch for a predecessor, that is praise indeed.

Worcester, Mass., Brinley Hall, 19 Oct 1854

For a general description of the works performed, see the summary description
of Mason's tour above.

Review of Mason's recital in Worcester on 19 Oct 1854:

"William Mason's Concert." *Daily Transcript* (Worcester), 20 Oct 1854, p.
[2], col. 2.

To say that his masterly performance fully satisfied his auditors, would
be insufficient to convey an adequate idea of the apparent delight with
which his astonishing execution was greeted.

Providence, R.I., Westminster Hall, 20 Oct 1854

Announcement of Mason's recital in Providence on 20 Oct 1854:

"Concert." *Providence Daily Journal*, 20 Oct 1854, p. [2], col. 5.
Announces Mason's recital.

624   Western recital tour

Buoyed by the success of his brief tour of New England, Mason proceeded
with plans for an extended recital tour of the United States. According to
a prospectus issued by Mason for the tour (see no. **474**), he originally intended
to go as far west as Iowa and Missouri, followed by a swing south through
New Orleans, Mobile, Charleston, Richmond, and Washington, D.C. For
a variety of reasons, including very inclement winter weather, illness, and
depleted finances, Mason cut the tour short, going only as far west as Chicago
and deleting the southern segment of the itinerary. The final tally for his
tour was twenty recitals in twelve different cities (Albany, Troy, Utica,
Syracuse, Rochester, Buffalo, Cleveland, Cincinnati, Louisville, Dayton,
Chicago, and Lockport).

From information garnered from reviews of recitals, it seems likely that
Mason used printed programs. None, however, have been located. Local
advertisements for his recitals given in the newspapers of some of the cities
in which he performed provide some indication of his programming. One
such advertisement for his November 20th recital in Albany (*Albany Evening
Atlas*, 20 Nov 1854, p. [3], col. 4) states that the concert will include

> . . . selections from the works of Handel, Beethoven, Mendelssohn,
> Chopin, Liszt, Stephen Heller, and others. . . .

The wording of this section of the advertisement seems to come directly from
the prospectus issued by Mason (see no. **474**); therefore, Mason's actual
programming may have varied a bit from this announcement. Newspaper
items giving specific lists of works are available for several of Mason's
recitals. One such recital is that given by Mason on 26 December 1854 in
Dayton, Ohio. An advertisement in the *Daily Dayton Journal* (25 Dec 1854,
p. [2], col. 6) gives the following program:

[Antoine de?] Kontski, *Grand Caprice héroique*
Rudolf Willmers, *Sehnsucht am Meere*
Alexander Dreyschock, *Saltarello*
Mason, *Les Perles de rosée: Mélodie variée*, [op. 2]
Mason, *Grand Valse de bravoure*, (op. 5?)
Liszt, *Rhapsody on Hungarian Airs* (not further identified)
Alexander Dreyschock, *Rhapsodie zum Wintermärchen*, op. 40
Mason, Improvisations on National Airs and on Themes Handed in by
the Audience

For additional information regarding Mason's tour, see nos. **324, 325, 451**.

Mason's tour itinerary and selected reviews are given below.

Albany, N.Y., Association Hall, 20 Nov 1854

For a general description of the works performed, see introductory comments above.

Reviews/Announcements of Mason's recital in Albany on 20 Nov 1854:

"Piano Concert." *Albany Evening Journal*, 18 Nov 1854, p. [2], col. 5.
Announces Mason's recital.

> We have not had the pleasure of hearing, and cannot, therefore, express any opinion in regard to his merits. But, beside being highly spoken of by those who have heard him, nothing but a consciousness of extraordinary powers would induce any sane person to attempt to draw an audience with the Piano alone.

"Mr. Mason's Concert." *Albany Evening Journal*, 21 Nov 1854, p. [2], col. 3.

> He [Mason] deserves, what must be soon conceded to him, a place in the very first rank of Pianists. . . .

"Our Musical Correspondence, . . . Albany." *Musical Gazette* (New York) 3 (25 Nov 1854): 21.

> WM. MASON gave a concert . . . last evening, to a most cultivated and appreciative audience. His performance excited great enthusiasm; he may hereafter count on a crowded house.

Troy, N.Y., Harmony Hall, 22 Nov 1854

Reviews/Announcements of Mason's recital in Troy on 22 Nov 1854:

"Musical Entertainment Extraordinary." *Troy Daily Times*, 20 Nov 1854, p. [2], col. 3.
Announces the recital.

"The Concert This Evening." *Troy Daily Traveller*, 22 Nov 1854, p. [2], col. 5.
Announces the recital.

> A musical feast may be anticipated. . . .

"Mason's Concert." *Northern Budget* (Troy), 22 Nov 1854, p. [2], col. 3.
Announces the recital.

"Mr. Mason's Concert." *Troy Daily Times*, 22 Nov 1854, p. [2], col. 3.
Announces Mason's recital.

> As an artist he deservedly ranks at the head [of] all performers on the Piano, and enjoys a reputation not confined to one hemisphere.

"Mr. Mason's Concert." *Troy Daily Whig*, 22 Nov 1854, p. [3], col. 3.
Announces the recital.

Anonymous review. *Northern Budget* (Troy), 23 Nov 1854, p. [2], col. 3.

A brief report on the concert.

"Mr. Mason's Concert." *Troy Daily Times*, 23 Nov 1854, p. [2], col. 4.

The audience were remarkably well pleased with the entertainment, and did not evince any of that impatience often exhibited at Concerts, even where a more diversified programme and entertainment is given. Mr. MASON, unassisted by vocal or instrumental performers, rendered the Concert a highly entertaining and brilliant affair by his own individual efforts on the piano.

"Mr. Mason's Concert." *Troy Daily Traveller*, 23 Nov 1854, p. [2], col. 3.

We . . . will admit that Mr. Mason's ability is great, and has not been over estimated.

"William Mason's Concert." *Troy Daily Whig*, 23 Nov 1854, p. [3], col. 3.

Mr. Mason concluded with a medley, embracing striking combinations and variations on Old Hundred, Yankee Doodle, Oft in the Stilly Night, Schubert's Ave Maria, Hail Columbia and Jordan is a Hard Road.

"Musical Intelligence, Troy, N.Y., Dec. 1, 1854." *New York Musical Review and Choral Advocate* 5/25 (7 Dec 1854): 420.

A positive review (signed "E").

. . . WILLIAM MASON gave a rare, rich, and rapturous musical entertainment, which, sorry to say it, on account of the foulness of the weather, was but moderately attended.

"Our Musical Correspondence, . . . Troy." *Musical Gazette* (New York) 5 (9 Dec 1854): 37.

Mr. Mason experienced a most unpropitious combination of circumstances, namely, another concert, three lectures, and a stormy evening. However, he had a fine audience, and gave the utmost satisfaction.

Utica, N.Y., Concert Hall, 24 Nov 1854

Reviews/Announcements of Mason's recital in Utica on 24 Nov 1854:

"Mr. Mason's Concerts." *Utica Morning Herald*, 24 Nov 1854, p. [2], col. 4.

Announces the recital.

"William Mason, the Pianist." *Utica Daily Gazette*, 24 Nov 1854, p. [2], col. 3.

Announces the recital.

Anonymous review. *Utica Daily Gazette*, 25 Nov 1854, p. [2], col. 3.

A brief, favorable review.

Much was expected, but more was realized.

"Mr. Mason's Concert." *Utica Morning Herald*, 25 Nov 1854, p. [2], col. 4.

His execution was truly wonderful, and so far as we are able to judge, entirely satisfied the high expectations excited by the unbounded applause which his former efforts have called forth.

Syracuse, N.Y., Wieting Hall, 27 Nov 1854

Announcements of Mason's recital in Syracuse on 27 Nov 1854:

"Mr. Mason's Concert." *Syracuse Daily Standard*, 25 Nov 1854, p. [2], col. 7.

Announces Mason's recital.

The fame of his father as a Musician and Composer, and the reputation already gained by the young man in the eastern cities, lead our music lovers to expect a great musical treat.

"Mr. Mason's Concert." *Syracuse Daily Standard*, 26 Nov 1854, p. [2], col. 6.

Announces Mason's recital.

Rochester, N.Y., Corinthian Hall, 29 Nov 1854

Reviews/Announcements of Mason's recital in Rochester on 29 Nov 1854:

"William Mason's Concert." *Rochester Daily American*, 24 Nov 1854, p. [2], col. 5.

Announces Mason's recital.

Mr. M. is a Pianist of the first order. Some years ago, being then a very young man, he was regarded as a prodigy. He has since availed himself of the best European cultivation. There can be no doubt that his Concert will be a treat.

"Mr. Mason's Concert." *Rochester Daily Union*, 29 Nov 1854, p. [3], col. 2.

Announces the recital.

The fame of Mr. Mason has been heralded before him by the press. . . .

"William Mason's Concert." *Rochester Daily American*, 29 Nov 1854, p. [2], col. 6.

Announces Mason's recital.

Mr. Mason has many friends here, who will turn out to greet him after his return from his long stay in Europe.

"William Mason's Concert." *Rochester Daily American*, 2 Dec 1854, p. [2], col. 4.

A long, highly favorable review.

Mr. MASON'S position as a performer and composer is a proud one. He can do more for the musical art in this country than any man in that profession. He has a marked genius, decided talent, thorough scholarship, a most accomplished hand, a ready perception of what expression demands, a perfect ear, and a skill and dexterity in execution that seems almost a marvel. . . . He knows as much as the first of trans-atlantic artists, and he surpasses them all, and overreaches all their powers of adaptation, because he thoroughly understands the character of the people before whom he plays.

"Our Musical Correspondence, . . . Rochester." *New York Musical Review and Choral Advocate* 6/2 (18 Jan 1855): 30.

A short, favorable review.

Mr. Mason took us by storm.

Buffalo, N.Y., American Hall, 4 Dec 1854

Reviews/Announcements of Mason's recital in Buffalo on 4 Dec 1854:

"Concert on Monday Evening." *Buffalo Evening Post*, 2 Dec 1854, p. [2], col. 4.

Announces Mason's recital.

"William Mason's Concert." *Buffalo Daily Courier*, 2 Dec 1854, p. [2], col. 4.

Announces Mason's recital.

He is equally at home in the most sublime and difficult music, and in those delicate, touching airs which come home to the heart like "household words."

"Mr. Mason's Concert." *Buffalo Evening Post*, 4 Dec 1854, p. [2], col. 4.

Announces Mason's recital.

The recent Concert of Mr. M., in Rochester has elicited the warm commendation of the Press of that city. . . .

"Wm. Mason—His Concert To-Night." *Buffalo Morning Express*, 4 Dec 1854, p. [3], col. 1.

Announces Mason's recital.

"Mr. Mason's Concert." *Buffalo Commercial Advertiser*, 5 Dec 1854, p. [2], col. 3.

The immense reputation which had preceded Mr. MASON, procured for him a very handsome audience last evening, notwithstanding the terrible storm which prevailed. . . . His several performances were many of them warmly encored last evening and his improvisations were peculiarly happy—the characteristic of a "Snow Storm" was an admirable portrayal.

"Mr. Mason's Concert." *Buffalo Daily Republic*, 5 Dec 1854, p. [3], col. 1.

In spite of the storm of wind and snow that raged last night, American Hall contained some 300 or 400 individuals. . . . He is the Czar of the piano—ruling absolute—there is nothing that the piano is capable of, but what he goes beyond. . . .

The reviewer also includes a brief account of an "after-recital" performance.

After the concert, we were invited to SAGE & SONS' splendid music rooms, and listened to this marvellous pianist. He gave imitations of all the distinguished masters of this instrument, preserving their identity with that brilliance and effect that all recognized the styles.

"Mr. Mason's Concert." *Buffalo Evening Post*, 5 Dec 1854, p. [2], cols. 1-2.

A long, basically negative review.

Mr. Mason did *not* . . . in our opinion come up as a whole to the commendations which we had copied from the Boston *Post*, Rochester *Advertiser*, etc.

The reviewer was also annoyed at the unannounced appearance of Oliver Dyer (Mason's agent) during the recital to promote the sales of a book published by the Mason Brothers publishing firm.

We allude to the evidently prepared introduction by Mr. MASON'S Agent, of FANNY FERNS works to the consideration of the audience. As we understand it, the audience like ourselves attended American Hall for the purpose of hearing Mr. MASON PLAY. We confess therefore our surprise at the cool, and self-possessed manner in which the Agent on such an occasion expatiated on the merits of a very worthy and quite talented Authoress.

"Wm. Mason's Concert." *Buffalo Morning Express*, 6 Dec 1854, p. [3], col. 1.

A long, highly favorable review.

His power over the piano is analogous to that exerted by the Arab over his steed. It will do anything for him.

"William Mason's Concert." *Buffalo Daily Courier*, 7 Dec 1854, p. [3], col. 1.

A mixed review.

Mr. Mason has made himself highly versed in the science of music, and practiced it with a constancy, ardor and love. . . . There is, however, nothing classical in his playing.

"Musical Intelligence, Buffalo, Dec. 14, 1854." *New York Musical Review and Choral Advocate* 5/26 (21 Dec 1854): 439-40.

A positive review (signed "Bachelor").

I have been looking for him [Mason] with high expectations, and at last he has come, to satisfy and far exceed them. Seven years ago, I heard him in Boston, and *then* thought him a wonder. *Now*, when thorough training has developed those prodigious powers nature gave him, he is worthy, without question, to take that rank so universally . . . accorded to him. He won many friends here. . . .

"Our Musical Correspondence, . . . Buffalo." *Musical Gazette* (New York) 12 (27 Jan 1855): 93.

Merely reports that the recital was given; not a review as such.

Cleveland, Ohio, Concert Hall, 8 Dec 1854

Reviews/Announcements of Mason's recital in Cleveland on 8 Dec 1854:

"Mason's Concert." *Cleveland Daily Express*, 7 Dec 1854, p. [3], col. 2.

Announces Mason's recital.

> There is now a good opportunity offered our citizens to show their appreciation of *native* genius and we hope they will generally avail themselves of it. Give the *American* Pianist a full house.

"Mr. Mason." *Daily Cleveland Herald*, 7 Dec 1854, p. [3], col. 2.

Announces Mason's recital and gives an extensive quotation from the review in the *Buffalo Commercial Advertiser* of Mason's recital in Buffalo on 4 December (see "Mr. Mason's Concert" above).

"Wm. Mason's Concert." *Cleveland Daily Plain Dealer*, 7 Dec 1854, p. [3], col. 2.

Announces Mason's recital.

> In Boston, New York, and all the way from the latter city to Cleveland, Mr. MASON has attracted large audiences, who have received his performances with enthusiasm, and gone away hungering for more.

"Mr. Mason's Concert." *Cleveland Morning Leader*, 8 Dec 1854, p. [3], col. 3.

Announces Mason's recital.

> He is one of the masters. . . .

The article includes a citation from the review in the *Buffalo Morning Express* of Mason's recital in Buffalo on 4 December (see "Wm. Mason's Concert" above).

"Mason's Concert." *Cleveland Daily Plain Dealer*, 9 Dec 1854, p. [3], col. 2.

> Our ears never having been elongated so as to appreciate Piano music played in Greek, Etalyon [*sic*], and Hindoo; we pass over that part which most electrified the very fashionable audience present, but which only astonished us, and will mention such parts as found their way through the head into the heart [Mason's improvisations].

"Mr. Mason's Concert." *Daily Cleveland Herald*, 9 Dec 1854, p. [3], col. 2.

> A large number of persons listened to Mr. MASON'S piano playing last evening. . . . He combines power and smoothness of touch with unrivalled brilliancy of execution.

"Wm. Mason's Concert." *Cleveland Morning Leader*, 12 Dec 1854, p. [3], col. 2.

A long, favorable review (signed "Max").

> The second part [of the recital] was opened by a composition of the world renowned LISZT, the King of Piano Forte Players. The "Rhapsody on Hungarian Airs" is one of those immense pieces, full of rich, wild harmony, such as none but a LISZT can originate, and requiring the genius of a MASON to interpret. In this piece, the qualities of a great Pianist were exhibited; and again Mr. MASON retired amid the most hearty applause, to which he cheerfully responded.

During the recital Mason was requested by a member of the audience to improvise a fugue on "Blow Ye Winds of Morning." The reviewer reports that Mason

> . . . attacked it vigorously, leading off with the treble, then came the alto, shortly the tenor was heard, and anon the bass was heard to growl "Blow ye Winds of Morning," to the entire satisfaction of many professors and amateurs. . . .

BRADBURY, William Batchelder. "Notes by the Way." *New York Musical Review and Choral Advocate* 6/1 (4 Jan 1855): 14.

Bradbury writes from Cleveland, Ohio:

> Arrived just too late to hear WM. MASON'S Grand Concert, but not too late to hear the highest encomiums upon his performance, by the most competent critics and artists.

Cincinnati, Ohio, Melodeon, 14 Dec 1854

Reviews of Mason's recital in Cincinnati on 14 Dec 1854:

"Mason's Concert." *Cincinnati Daily Columbian*, 15 Dec 1854, p. [2], col. 3.

> A larger number of amateurs of music, than we remember to have seen together, for a long time, attended Masons' [*sic*] concert, at the Melodeon last night. The audience testified their appreciation of the performance, by repeated rounds of applause.

"Mr. Mason, the Pianist." *Cincinnati Daily Enquirer*, 16 Dec 1854, p. [3], col. 4.

> To those who were present at his concert on Thursday evening it is unnecessary, and would be an almost endless task, to point out the multitude of beauties with which his performances abounded.

"Mr. Mason's Concert." *Daily Cincinnati Gazette*, 16 Dec 1854, p. [2], col. 2.

> The audience on Thursday evening were delighted, as well as astonished, and testified their gratification by the most enthusiastic applause — every piece on the programme, with one exception, being *encored*.

"Wm. Mason's Concert." *Cincinnati Daily Columbian*, 16 Dec 1854, p. [2], col. 5.

> From the most thundering fortissimos and prodigious octave passages, to the lightest pianissimos and sweet, bird-like warblings; from the most rapid runs, flashing out dazzling ribbons of sound, to the softest singing tones, he displays consummate command of his instrument. . . . He has also a strong vein of musical humor, . . . and often sets the audience in a roar.

Cincinnati, Ohio, Melodeon, 16 Dec 1854

Louisville, Ky., Odd Fellows' Hall, 21 Dec 1854

Announcements of Mason's recital in Louisville on 21 Dec 1854:

"Mr. Mason's Concert." *Louisville Daily Courier*, 19 Dec 1854, p. [3], col. 1.

A lengthy article heralding Mason's upcoming recital.

> It may be stated with great propriety that Mr. Mason is *an American*, a matter of gratification to those who have so long believed that musical genius must necessarily be an exotic. We are not of that class who praise because *it is foreign*, as has been the fashion in the musical circles for the past few years. We hope that *American genius* will be appreciated in this country, and especially in music.

"Mr. Mason's Concert." *Louisville Daily Journal*, 20 Dec 1854, p. [3], col. 2.

Announces Mason's recital.

> It is announced that Mr. WM. MASON (son of LOWELL MASON, of Boston,) will give a concert . . . to-morrow . . . evening. Mr. Mason is said to possess very superior musical skill. . . .

"The Great Pianist." *Daily Louisville Times*, 21 Dec 1854, p. [3], col. 2.

Announces that Mason's recital is to be given that evening.

> This evening, at Odd Fellows' Hall, Mr. William Mason, who has been styled the "King of Pianists," will give his first and his only concert in Louisville.

"Mr. Mason's Concert." *Louisville Daily Courier*, 21 Dec 1854, p. [3], col. 1.

Following two introductory paragraphs, an annotated program for that evening's recital by Mason is given. Commenting on Liszt's *Rhapsody on Hungarian Airs*, the writer states:

> In the performance of this piece, Mr. Mason displays the qualities of a great pianist, in a most marked degree. He touches the instrument with a power and precision truly astonishing. The heavier tones ring out like trumpet blasts, and the softer passages are as clear and sweet and limpid as the songs of vernal birds.

"Mr. Mason's Concert This Evening." *Louisville Daily Journal*, 21 Dec 1854, p. [3], col. 4.

> Mason's recital is again announced. Much of the article consists of a quotation from the review in the *Boston Daily Evening Transcript* of Mason's October 3d recital in Boston (see no. **618**).

Dayton, Ohio, Clegg's Hall, 26 Dec 1854

For a list of the works performed, see the general description of Mason's tour above.

Review of Mason's recital in Dayton on 26 Dec 1854:

"Mr. Mason's Concert." *Daily Dayton Journal*, 28 Dec 1854, p. [2], col. 1.

Mason's choice of repertoire is criticized.

> But the truth is, that however grand may be the "compositions of the Grand Caprices Heroiques," the "Rhapsodies," the "Saltarellos," and the "Zum Wintermahrschens [*sic*]," they sound to most people like mere piano exercises, and however fine the execution or exquisite the touch, they pass

for mere "flourishes" and nothing more. Those who can appreciate and enjoy the execution of these pieces with big names are not sufficiently numerous to make up an audience respectable in numbers.

Chicago, Ill., Metropolitan Hall, 2 Jan 1855

Reviews/Announcements of Mason's recital in Chicago on 2 Jan 1855:

"Wm. Mason's Concert." *Daily Democratic Press* (Chicago), 29 Dec 1854, p. [3], col. 1.

A brief announcement of Mason's recital.

"Mr. Mason's Concert." *Daily Chicago Journal*, 30 Dec 1854, p. [2], col. 5.

Announces Mason's recital.

MR. MASON'S intended concert . . . is exciting an unusual degree of interest in our musical circles.

Anonymous review. *Daily Chicago Journal*, 3 Jan 1855, p. [3], col. 1.

MR. MASON'S CONCERT was given last evening, according to announcement, to an audience, numerically considered, unworthy the extraordinary merits of the Pianist. The character, however, of the listeners was such as especially delights men of genius, and their opinion will insure a Hall completely packed with humanity, on Friday evening next, when he gives a second Concert.

"Mason's Concert." *Daily Democratic Press* (Chicago), 3 Jan 1855, p. [3], col. 2.

The first concert of Mr. MASON, at Metropolitan Hall, last evening, was not as *numerously* attended as the high reputation of the artist would have led us to prophecy, but the audience was nevertheless large and of the *character* before which performers of the highest rank prefer to appear. . . . The improvisations by Mr. MASON upon themes handed him from the audience, whether original or selected, formed a very delightful portion of the concert, and reveal the fertile genius and surpassing skill of the pianist to a wonderful degree.

"Wm. Mason's Concert." *Daily Democratic Press* (Chicago), 4 Jan 1855, p. [3], col. 1.

Every performance was masterly, and before the concert was concluded the audience was worked up into a state of enthusiasm such as we never before witnessed at a concert, and the last piece called forth a perfect storm of applause.

Chicago, Ill., Metropolitan Hall, 5 Jan 1855

Announcements of Mason's recital in Chicago on 5 Jan 1855:

"The Concert To-Night." *Daily Democratic Press* (Chicago), 5 Jan 1855, p. [3], col. 2.

Announces Mason's recital.

Mr. MASON'S playing last Tuesday evening established him in the minds of his audience as a perfect master of his instrument, and demonstrated that the opinions concerning him which have appeared in the musical journals of the day were not extravagant expressions of praise. . . .

"Mr. Mason's Concert." *Daily Chicago Journal*, 5 Jan 1855, p. [3], col. 4.

Announces Mason's recital on 5 January 1855.

. . . Mr. Mason gives a second concert at Metropolitan Hall this evening. We speak "that we do know," when we say that his touch has magic in it. Either the instrument beneath his fingers is one of very extraordinary construction, gifted with genius and a living soul, or else there is something about the musician himself, not usually found among eminent performers, who touch the charmed string.

Cleveland, Ohio, Concert Hall, 9 Jan 1855

Reviews/Announcements of Mason's recital in Cleveland on 9 Jan 1855:

"Wm. Mason's Concert." *Cleveland Daily Plain Dealer*, 8 Jan 1855, p. [3], col. 2.

Announces Mason's recital.

Everybody probably remembers, or has been told, what a *furore* he created here a month ago. . . .

"Mason's Concert." *Daily Cleveland Herald*, 9 Jan 1855, p. [3], col. 2.

Announces Mason's recital.

Attend if you like superior piano playing.

A short announcement (no heading) of Mason's recital had also been given in the *Daily Cleveland Herald* on 8 January (p. [3], col. 2).

"Mr. Mason's Concert." *Cleveland Daily Plain Dealer*, 9 Jan 1855, p. [3], col. 3.

Announces Mason's recital.

MR. MASON is equally at home on a Fugue, by HANDEL, or "Susan Jane," and suits all tastes to a demisemiquaver. In short, he is a genius, and beats all creation on the pianoforte.

"Mr. Mason's Concert." *Cleveland Daily Plain Dealer*, 10 Jan 1855, p. [3], col. 2.

A positive review (signed "REFLECTOR").

The wonderful power of this extraordinary Pianist completely took away from us the usually calm and quiet control which upon all occasions — and especially public — we have studied to exercise. . . .

"Mr. Mason's Concert." *Daily Cleveland Herald*, 10 Jan 1855, p. [3], col. 2.

A positive review.

In these modern days of Concert-giving, when even OLE BULL and JENNY LIND have the aid of distinguished artistes [*sic*] to entertain for an evening, it was a bold stroke for a young Pianist, a modest American at that, almost unheralded to offer his rich musical gifts . . . in a series of Concerts in the principal cities, "solitary and alone." Mr. MASON has done so, and . . . he has met with marked success. . . . We may be over partial . . . , but we think Mr. MASON on the Piano justly ranks with OLE on the cremona and JENNY in song.

Buffalo, N.Y., American Hall, 12 Jan 1855

Reviews/Announcements of Mason's recital in Buffalo on 12 Jan 1855:

"Wm. Mason's Concert." *Buffalo Evening Post*, 11 Jan 1855, p. [2], col. 4. Announces Mason's recital.

"Wm. Mason." *Buffalo Morning Express*, 12 Jan 1855, p. [3], col. 1. Announces Mason's recital.

> It is hardly necessary . . . to say that we hope his eloquent claims will not be disregarded, and that his freedom from foreign pretensions and airs will be duly remembered.

"Mason's Concert." *Buffalo Morning Express*, 13 Jan 1855, p. [3], col. 2.

> MASON had a good house last evening, and played gloriously. The piano gave up its will to his, on the start, and he did with the instrument just as he pleased. A performance equal to this was never given in Buffalo—not even by MASON himself.

"Mr. Mason's Concert." *Buffalo Commercial Advertiser*, 13 Jan 1855, p. [2], col. 5.

> Mr. MASON may be said to have achieved a great triumph.

"Mr. Mason's Concert Last Evening." *Buffalo Evening Post*, 13 Jan 1855, p. [2], col. 3.

> We were much better pleased last evening, with Mr. MASON, than on the previous occasion when we heard him. We think he played with more true ease, elegance and power. When we consider that he alone entertained a quite numerous and very intelligent auditory and enlisted their earnest attention and approbation, we certainly feel disposed to award to him a very high degree of praise.

"William Mason's Concert." *Buffalo Daily Courier*, 15 Jan 1855, p. [3], col. 1.

> Mr. Mason's . . . playing afforded the appreciating audience a pleasure of the highest kind.

"Our Musical Correspondence, . . . Buffalo." *Musical Gazette* (New York) 12 (27 Jan 1855): 93.

> More of a report that the recital was given than a review.

> WM. MASON gave a concert here on the 4th of December last; on the 12th of January following he returned to give a second concert, and found that the pieces which he played at his first concert . . . had been bought by many teachers and scholars, and were being rigorously practiced.

Lockport, N.Y., 13 Jan 1855

Rochester, N.Y., Corinthian Hall, 16 Jan 1855

Reviews/Announcements of Mason's recital in Rochester on 16 Jan 1855:

"Wm. Mason's Concert." *Rochester Daily American*, 13 Jan 1855, p. [2], col. 4.
Announces the recital.
> Mr. MASON, it will be remembered appeared here in November and gave a musical entertainment of unrivaled brilliancy.

"William Mason's Concert." *Rochester Daily American*, 15 Jan 1855, p. [2], col. 4.
Announces the recital.
> With the memory of his "Old Hundred" yet lingering with us, we do not hesitate to rank Mr. Mason with Jenny Lind in song, and Ole Bull on the violin.

"The Concert." *Rochester Daily American*, 16 Jan 1855, p. [2], col. 4.
Announces the recital.
> All will be entirely satisfied that a concert made up solely of Piano performances, may be made in the highest degree interesting, when a master hand is at the keys.

"Concert." *Rochester Daily Democrat*, 16 Jan 1855, p. [3], col. 3.
Announces the recital.

Anonymous review. *Rochester Daily Democrat*, 18 Jan 1855, p. [2], col. 4.
> MR. MASON'S Concert . . . was given under the embarrassment of ill-health, but it was an artistic display rarely equalled, more rarely excelled.

"Wm. Mason's Concert." *Rochester Daily American*, 18 Jan 1855, p. [2], col. 6.
> Mr. Mason has been on a tour to the West, since he was here in November, which tour was cut short by an attack of sickness. He was laboring under the effects of this at his concert, and his playing was less marked by vigor and energy that is natural to him.

Syracuse, N.Y., Wieting Hall, 18 Jan 1855

Announcement of Mason's recital in Syracuse on 18 Jan 1855:

"The Concert." *Syracuse Daily Standard*, 17 Jan 1855, p. [2], col. 7.
Announces Mason's recital.

Utica, N.Y., Mechanics' Hall, 19 Jan 1855

Reviews/Announcements of Mason's recital in Utica on 19 Jan 1855:

"William Mason." *Utica Morning Herald*, 18 Jan 1855, p. [2], col. 5.
Announces the concert.

"The Concert This Evening." *Utica Morning Herald*, 19 Jan 1855, p. [2], col. 5.

Announces the recital.

"Mr. Mason's Concert." *Utica Morning Herald*, 20 Jan 1855, p. [2], col. 5.

In making of Old Hundred and our national airs such a musical chowder as he did, he evinced his facility and familiarity in the science of music; but his "Valsa [sic] de Bravoure" and "Sonata" with other pieces, were to us more convincing evidence of his excellence as a pianist.

Albany, N.Y., Association Hall, 22 Jan 1855

Reviews/Announcements of Mason's recital in Albany on 22 Jan 1855:

"Wm. Mason's Concert This Evening." *Albany Evening Journal*, 22 Jan 1855, p. [2], col. 7.

An announcement (signed "G. W. W.") of Mason's recital.

The glowing accounts given of his last concert have created a desire in all music-lovers to hear him, for he is the only pianist who has ever entertained an audience without other musical assistance.

"William Mason's Concert." *Albany Evening Journal*, 24 Jan 1855, p. [2], col. 4.

In rapidity of movement, delicacy of touch, and power of execution, he has no superior. But, as only the few (and we are not in the number) can appreciate the most masterly skill on this instrument, Mr. MASON can never attract the crowd. He must, so long as he attempts to conduct a concert alone, perform to thin houses. The piano, at best, is not an instrument to command attention through an entire evening.

625   New York, Dodworth's Hall, 27 Mar 1855

Theodor Eisfeld Soirée

Beethoven, *Trio in B-flat Major*, op. 97

Chopin, *Impromptu in A-flat Major*, op. 29

Handel, *Suite in F Minor*

Mason, "Pensée fugitive"

No copy of this work has been located; from descriptions given in reviews, it seems probable that it was later published by Mason as *Silver Spring*, op. 6. For the circumstances surrounding Mason's invitation to play at Eisfeld's soirée, see no. **326**.

Reviews of no. **625**:

"Eisfeld's Soiree." *New York Times*, 28 Mar 1855, p. 4, cols. 5-6.

A very positive review.

The prominent feature of the evening was undoubtedly Mr. WILLIAM MASON'S rendering of the trio as well as the solo pieces. This young artist has decidedly very happy dispositions for a first rate pianist. He commands a *pianissimo* which we think cannot be surpassed in delicacy, and on the other hand his *forte* is as vigorous and powerful as the resources of the instrument will permit.

"Musical Correspondence, . . . New York, March 28th." *Dwight's Journal of Music* 6/26 (31 Mar 1855): 207.

The review (signed "BORNONIS") finds fault with Mason's playing.

> . . . his articulation is often indistinct, and a strong tendency to a *tempo rubato*, and to too rapid playing is sometimes annoying. The latter was observable, more than I ever heard it before, in the triplet portion of the "Impromptu" of CHOPIN. It was rendered a mass of confused sounds.

"Theodore Eisfeld's Fifth Soiree." *Musical Gazette* (New York) 21 (31 Mar 1855): 162.

A favorable review. Also published—with minor revisions—as "Theodore Eisfeld's Fifth Soiree," *New York Musical Review and Choral Advocate* 6/8 (12 Apr 1855): 122.

"The Other Side." *Dwight's Journal of Music* 7/1 (7 Apr 1855): 7.

A letter to Dwight (signed "JUSTICE") which takes exception to the review by "BORNONIS" above (see "Musical Correspondence, . . . March 28th").

> The "confusion of sounds" must have been in your correspondent's own brain; for I am sure no one else felt it who was present, and I for one am confident I heard every note.

"Musical Correspondence, . . . New York, April 9." *Dwight's Journal of Music* 7/2 (14 Apr 1855): 11.

Mr. "BORNONIS" restates his case (see "Musical Correspondence, . . . March 28th" above).

> I . . . love that composition [Chopin's *Impromptu*] as well as any one can, and because I love it so, and know it so well, am very jealous of its rendering, and I still maintain that on that evening, the apple of discord between your unknown correspondent and myself, it was *not* played as well as it should have been.

626 Philadelphia, Musical Fund Hall, 18 Apr 1855

Soirée musicale

[Antoine de?] Kontski, *Grand Caprice héroique*

Rudolf Willmers, *Sehnsucht am Meere*

Mason, "Pensée fugitive" (see explanatory note under no. **625**)

Liszt, *Rhapsody on Hungarian Airs* (not further identified)

Handel, *Suite in F Minor*

Chopin, *Impromptu in A-flat Major*, op. 29

Alexander Dreyschock, *Rhapsodie zum Wintermärchen*, op. 40

Mason, Improvisations on Themes Handed in by the Audience

Reviews/Announcements of no. **626**:

"Musical Gossip." *Musical Gazette* (New York) 23 (14 Apr 1855): 177-78.

Includes a brief announcement of the upcoming recital in Philadelphia.

"Musical." *Cummings' Evening Bulletin* (Philadelphia), 19 Apr 1855, p. [2], col. 2.

Includes a favorable review of Mason's recital.

> Mr. Mason's programme contained such a variety of new and excellent compositions, and his playing was so superior, that everybody was delighted.

"Our Musical Correspondence, . . . Philadelphia." *Musical Gazette* (New York) 24 (21 Apr 1855): 190-91.

> The idea of any body's giving a piano concert unassisted, seemed a most hazardous undertaking, and no one expected the experiment would be successful. But we were all mistaken. A more spirited, interesting, *enjoyable*, and *satisfactory* concert I do not remember to have attended.

627 New York, Niblo's Theater, 21 Apr 1855

Philharmonic Society — Carl Bergmann

Weber, *Concertstück in F Minor*, op. 79

Reviews of no. **627**:

"The Philharmonic Concert." *New York Times*, 23 Apr 1855, p. 4, cols. 4-5.

> Mr. MASON possesses great facility of execution, and a firm, sonorous, manageable touch. The orchestral accompaniments to the "Concertstück" were of a very showy character, and interfered seriously with the excellence of Mr. MASON'S performance. He was heard to greater advantage in the second piece. . . .

"Musical Matters in New York." *New York Musical Review and Choral Advocate* 6/9 (26 Apr 1855): 140-41.

A very positive assessment.

> . . . Mr. Mason's performances were so satisfactory that he barely escaped a double *encore*.

DWIGHT, John Sullivan. ". . . Philharmonic Concert." *Dwight's Journal of Music* 7/4 (28 Apr 1855): 28-29.

> When we arrived, sometime before the hour appointed, not a seat remained unoccupied in the parquet or either circle; it was a most brilliant audience. . . . Mr. MASON'S playing of the *Concertstück* did not seem to us to do him so much justice, as his remarkably fluent, delicate and easy rendering of the florid and rather Willmers-like *Nocturne* with which he answered the *encore*. The Concerto was skilfully, and, in some parts, beautifully played, but hardly with such sustained power and firmness, and such masterly unity of style as one could wish.

"The Fourth and Last Philharmonic Concert at Niblo's." *Musical Gazette* (New York) 25 (28 Apr 1855): 194-95.

Mr. WILLIAM MASON played it [Weber's *Concertstück*] so well as to produce an encore, which he answered by an elegant and unapproachable rendering of his impromptu. . . .

"Philharmonic Concert." *Musical World* 11/17 (28 Apr 1855): 193-94.
A negative review.

He [Mason] is master of the resources of the instrument so far as technicalities go. But, *pectus est quod disertos facit*: and inasmuch as this soul of playing and the power of interpreting music beyond the mere notes are lacking, the player lacks, as yet, that which reaches the heart of the audience and controls their sensibilies.

628   Burlington, Vt., Concert Hall, 13 June 1855

Solo recital

[Antoine de?] Kontski, *Grand Caprice héroïque*

Rudolf Willmers, *Sehnsucht am Meere*

Alexander Dreyschock, *Saltarello*

Mason, "Pensée fugitive" (see explanatory note under no. **625**)

Mason, *Valse de bravoure*, op. 5

Liszt, *Rhapsody on Hungarian Airs* (not otherwise identified)

Alexander Dreyschock, *Rhapsodie zum Wintermärchen*, op. 40

Mason, Improvisations on National Airs and on Themes Handed in by the Audience

Review of no. **628**:

"Mr. Mason's Concert." *Daily Free Press* (Burlington), 14 June 1855, p. [2], col. 2.

Concert Hall was *filled* last evening with a select and appreciative audience, who came expecting much and went away lacking words with which to express their admiration and delight. Mr. Mason, though quite a young man, is a great pianist.

629   New York, Niblo's Saloon, 12 Sept 1855

Felicita Vestvali Farewell Concert

Mason, "Toujours Waltz" (later published as op. 7, no. 2?)

Mason, "Silver Spring" (later published as op. 6)

[Antoine de?] Kontski, *Grand Caprice héroïque*

Reviews/Announcements of no. **629**:

"Musical Gossip." *New York Musical Review and Gazette* 6/19 (8 Sept 1855): 301-02.

Announces Mason's participation in Vestvali's upcoming concert.

... Mr. WILLIAM MASON, who has not performed in the city since the last Philharmonic concert, is added to the attraction. . . .

"Farewell Concert of Mlle Vestvali." *New York Times*, 13 Sept 1855, p. 4, col. 4.

... Mr. WILLIAM MASON, the talented American pianist, played two pieces of his own and the "Caprice Heroique," by KONTSKI, with that brilliant touch and powerful execution for which he is justly famous.

630   Brooklyn, Polytechnic Hall, 25 Sept 1855

Felicita Vestvali Concert

Liszt, *Illustrations du prophète*, no. 1

Reviews of no. **630**:

"The Vestvali Concert." *Brooklyn Daily Eagle*, 26 Sept 1855, p. [3], col. 1. Mason's performance is not mentioned.

"Vestvali's Concert." *New York Times*, 26 Sept 1855, p. 4, col. 5.

Signorina VESTVALI was assisted by Mr. WILLIAM MASON, the eminent pianist, (a sufficient attraction in himself;). . . .

"Musical Gossip." *New York Musical Review and Gazette* 6/21 (6 Oct 1855): 333-34.

Signorina Vestvali gave a concert in Brooklyn last week, assisted as previously in New-York. The novelty in the programme was Mr. William Mason's performance of the first of Liszt's illustrations of Meyerbeer's *Prophète*. . . .

631   Brooklyn, Athenaeum, 4 Oct 1855

Eduard and Friedrich Mollenhauer Concert

Mason, "Silver Spring" (later published as op. 6)

Mason, "L'Opole—valse de salon" (later published as op. 7, no. 1 or 3?)

Liszt, *Illustrations du prophète*

Reviews/Announcements of no. **631**:

"Musical Gossip." *New York Musical Review and Gazette* 6/20 (22 Sept 1855): 317-18.

Announces the forthcoming concert and Mason's participation in it.

Anonymous review. *New York Times*, 5 Oct 1855, p. [1], col. 3.

There is a broad musical completeness in his [Mason's] style, at variance with and far superior to the trivial mimicry of most Concert players. . . . In the second part Mr. MASON performed LISZT'S grand Fantasia from the "Prophet," and did justice to it. . . . Mr. MASON, however, has enjoyed the advantage of LISZT'S instruction, and possesses, moreover, a natural instinct for the blinding combinations of that master.

632   New York, Dodworth's Hall, 27 Nov 1855

Mason and Bergmann Matinée

Schubert, *Quartet in D Minor*, D. 810

> Theodore Thomas and Joseph Mosenthal, violins; George Matzka, viola; Carl Bergmann, cello.

Wagner, "O, du mein holder Abendstern," from *Tannhäuser*

> Otto Feder, vocalist

Chopin, *Fantaisie-Impromptu in C-sharp Minor*, op. 66

Heller, *Preludes in D-flat and G*, op. 24 [*sic*]

Mendelssohn, *Variations concertantes*, op. 17

> Carl Bergmann, cello

O. Nicolai, "Feldwärts flog ein Vögelein"

> Otto Feder, vocalist

Brahms, *Trio in B Major*, op. 8

> Theodore Thomas, violin; Carl Bergmann, cello; this performance was the world premiere of this work.

> This concert on 27 November 1855 marked the beginning of a long and distinguished series of performances by the group of musicians who came to be known as the "Mason-Thomas Quartette." Organized by Mason (with the help of Carl Bergmann), the ensemble consisted of Theodore Thomas, first violinist; Joseph Mosenthal, second violinist; George Matzka, violist; and Bergmann, cellist. Bergmann was replaced by Frederic Bergner after the performance of the second concert of the sixth season on 27 November 1860.

> Eight concerts were given during the first (1855-56) season in New York. No performances were scheduled in 1856-57, but the series was resumed in 1858 and continued without interruption through 1868, for a combined total of thirteen seasons. The world premiere performance of Brahms's *Trio in B Major* proved to be a harbinger of things to come. The literature performed by this ensemble documents a record of serious musical intent quite remarkable for that time in the United States. The works for voice included in the debut concert were an obvious deference to public taste. But that practice was soon dropped, and, with rare exceptions, concerts were devoted solely to instrumental music. During the earlier years, solos (most frequently piano) and miscellaneous pieces for various combinations of instruments were mixed with the more central string quartets and works for piano and strings. In later seasons the number of solos slowly declined, often resulting in programs consisting entirely of major chamber music works.

> Original programs for the New York chamber music series are with the William Mason Papers (New York Public Library) and the Theodore Thomas Collection (Newberry Library). A complete listing of the programs is also given in appendix A of Graber's "The Life and Works of William Mason . . ." and the 1905 edition of Theodore Thomas's *A Musical Autobiography*, vol. 2, pp. 37-51 (see nos. **126, 440**).

Concerts by the Mason-Thomas Quartette were intermittently reviewed by a number of New York newspapers, including the *New York Times*. Several music periodicals reviewed the concerts on a regular, long-term basis; noteworthy in this respect were the following: *Dwight's Journal of Music*, *New York Musical Review and Gazette*, *Musical World*, and *Musical Review and Musical World*. Reviews of the debut concert of 27 November 1855 are given below.

Reviews/Announcements of no. **632:**

"Matinees Musicale." *New York Times*, 27 Nov 1855, p. 4, col. 4.

Announces the performance.

> Considered in any light, either with regard to the eminence of the principal artists or the excellence of the music performed, these concerts deserve and must be popular. We are happy to hear that the subscription list exceeds the most sanguine expectations of the managers.

"Musical Matinees." *Evening Post* (New York), 28 Nov 1855, p. [3], col. 7.

> . . . we listened with great satisfaction to an exquisite *Fantasie* of Chopin, and two simple but very suggestive *preludes* of Stephen Heller, artistically performed by Mr. Mason.

"Classical Matinee." *New York Times*, 29 Nov 1855, p. 4, cols. 3-4.

A long, seven-paragraph review.

> A soloist does not usually shine in concerted music, but Mr. MASON in this trio [Brahms's], and in MENDELSSOHNS *Variations Concertantes*, put forth fresh and legitimate claims to public distinction.

"Musical Matters." *New York Tribune*, 30 Nov 1855, p. 8, col. 2.

Includes brief mention of the concert.

"Musical Correspondence, New York, Nov. 27." *Dwight's Journal of Music* 8/9 (1 Dec 1855): 68.

A very favorable review (signed "MILAMO").

> . . . Mr. MASON played with a fire and vigor; a spirit, that left all thought of mere technicals far behind. . . .

"William Mason's and Carl Bergmann's Classical Matinees." *New York Musical Review and Gazette* 6/25 (1 Dec 1855): 400-01.

> We do not think there are altogether three public musical entertainments in the world, of the kind, which Messrs. William Mason and Carl Bergmann have started in this city. With exception of those which are held under the immediate influence of Liszt in Weimar, and some few in Berlin, the majority of them give only occasionally a modern work of this kind; and decidedly such programmes, the prominent features of which are able compositions of Schumann, Schubert, Brahms, Frank, Berwald, and Rubinstein, are a manifest progress in the history of *public* performances of classical chamber-music.

For other series of concerts begun by the Mason-Thomas Quartette, see nos. **636, 652, 653.**

633   Boston, Music Hall, 22 Dec 1855

Boston Philharmonic — Carl Zerrahn

Weber, *Concertstück in F Minor*, op. 79

Reviews/Announcements of no. **633**:

"Musical." *Boston Evening Transcript*, 22 Dec 1855, p. [2], col. 1.
Announces the concert.

"Orchestral Concerts." *Boston Daily Advertiser*, 22 Dec 1855, p. [1], col. 8.
Announces the concert.

"Orchestral Union." *Boston Daily Atlas*, 22 Dec 1855, p. [2], col. 2.
Announces the concert.
. . . Mr. William Mason, the eminent pianist, will also appear. We
hope to see the hall thronged.

"Music." *Boston Daily Atlas*, 24 Dec 1855, p. [2], col. 3.
A long, favorable review.

Mr. Mason has prodigious power over his instrument; the energy and
precision with which he gave the chords, fairly maintaining his ground
against the full orchestra, was truly wonderful. Still it was done without
any of the gesticulation which some pianists affect; it was a quiet
execution of will. . . .

"Musical." *Boston Evening Transcript*, 24 Dec 1855, p. [2], col. 1.

William Mason elicited great applause by his performances on the piano,
and was so heartily cheered that he was recalled and executed a solo piece.

"Our Musical Correspondence, . . . Boston." *New York Musical Review
and Gazette* 6/27 (29 Dec 1855): 434-35.

Mr. Mason played the Concert-stük [*sic*] in F, by C. M. Von Weber,
better than we ever recollect to have heard it in Boston.

"Third Orchestral Concert." *Dwight's Journal of Music* 8/13 (29 Dec 1855):
101-02.
A generally favorable review.

Mr. WILLIAM MASON'S pianism had never before exhibited itself to
so great advantage in his Boston home, as this night in the *Concertstück* of WEBER. His rendering of it we have not heard equalled, many
times as it has been played, by any except JAELL. Mr. MASON has
greatly gained in self-possession, as in strength and evenness of execution,
since we heard him last.

634   Boston, Chickering's Warerooms, 26 Dec 1855

Soirée musicale with the Mendelssohn Quintette Club

Chopin, *Fantaisie-Impromptu in C-sharp Minor*, op. 66

Heller, *Preludes*, op. 24 [*sic*]

Mason, "Toujours, valse de salon" (later published as op. 7, no. 2)

Mason, "Silver Spring" (later published as op. 6)

Brahms, *Trio in B Major*, op. 8

> August Fries, violin; Wulf Fries, cello

> Reviews/Announcements of no. **634**:

> "Musical." *Boston Evening Transcript*, 24 Dec 1855, p. [2], col. 1.
> Announces the concert.

>> . . . we shall have the pleasure of hearing for the first time a trio by Johannes Brahms, a young German composer of great promise, who has been styled, (somewhat irreverently, perhaps,) the "Messiah of the new dispensation in music."

> "Musical." *Boston Evening Transcript*, 27 Dec 1855, p. [2], col. 2.
> A three-paragraph review.

>> The two compositions of his own, . . . [which] evince great improvement in composition, and in originality and treatment, revealed that he has much of the true spirit, and needs but practice to attain rank as a composer. They were also exceedingly well-played.

> "Music." *Boston Daily Atlas*, 28 Dec 1855, p. [2], col. 2.
> Includes a review of Mason's concert.

>> Mr. Mason played with as much energy and spirit as at his previous appearance with the Orchestral Union [see no. **633**]. . . . In a composition of his own, Mr. Mason gave a specimen of the "prodigious" style of playing, which, before a larger audience, would have brought down thunders of applause.

> "William Mason's Soiree." *Dwight's Journal of Music* 8/13 (29 Dec 1855): 102.
> A positive assessment.

>> The Trio was wonderfully well played (and it abounds in difficulties) by Mr. MASON and the brothers FRIES, but we must confess that we received no clear impression of it as an artistic whole. That it has some strange and powerful effects, some ingenious combinations, remarkable for a mere boy, is undeniable. It seemed very enterprising, very adventurous, very self-confident, full of bold graspings after ideas, but we were never satisfied that the ideas really *were* ideas.

635   New York, Spingler Institute, 1 Feb 1856

Soirée musicale

Rudolf Willmers, *Sehnsucht am Meere*

Mason, "Valse de salon" (op. 7?)

Mason, *Silver Spring*, op. 6

636 Farmington, Conn., 26 June 1856

Soirée musicale

Mason, *Étude de concert*, op. 9

Mason, *Silver Spring*, op. 6

Anton Rubinstein, *Trio in G Minor*, op. 15, no. 2

Theodore Thomas, violin; Carl Bergmann, cello

This concert on June 26 was the first of a series of performances given by the Mason-Thomas Quartette in Farmington — a series similar to that which they offered in New York City. The concerts were given at Miss Porter's School for Young Ladies. Begun at the instigation of Karl Klauser, head of Miss Porter's music department, the series continued until 1870, with over forty performances given during this fourteen-year period. Programs for the concerts are with the William Mason Papers (New York Public Library); the last Farmington program with Mason's papers is dated 13 May 1868, thirty-fourth concert. Mason seems not to have participated in the Farmington concerts after this date. A nearly complete set of programs for the Farmington series is also with the Theodore Thomas Collection (Newberry Library); in addition, a number of programs from the series are contained in the archives of Miss Porter's School for Young Ladies. Unfortunately, the program for the thirty-fifth concert is missing in both locations, leaving the identity of the pianist for that performance unknown. From the thirty-sixth concert on 3 December 1868 to the forty-sixth (and last) concert on 7 June 1870, pianists other than Mason were used.

Reviews of no. **636** (26 June 1856 concert):

"Musical Chit-Chat." *Dwight's Journal of Music* 9/15 (12 July 1856): 119-20.

Includes an announcement/review of the Farmington concert.

"Our Musical Correspondence, Farmington, Conn." *New York Musical Review and Gazette* 7/14 (12 July 1856): 214-15.

A long, favorable review.

637 Newark, N.J., Library Hall, 19 Dec 1856

Solo recital, assisted by Henrietta Behrend, soprano; Mr. Eben, flute; Messrs. Feigel and [John Nelson?] Pattison, piano

No program has been located.

Reviews/Announcements of no. **637**:

"Local Intelligence." *Newark Daily Mercury*, 19 Dec 1856, p. [2], cols. 3-4.

Includes an announcement of Mason's recital.

As a pianist he possesses genuine execution, a brilliant touch, and the most poetic qualities; in contrast to his friend Gottschalk, he is much more German than French, and possesses the solid qualities and classical tastes of the former nation.

"Mr. Wm. Mason's Concert." *Newark Daily Advertiser*, 20 Dec 1856, p. [2], col. 4.

> Mr. Mason's performances on the grand piano were brilliant and masterly, evincing the feeling and superior training of a true artist, as he is, and he was constantly applauded to the encore.

"Our Musical Correspondence, . . . Newark, N.J." *New York Musical Review and Gazette* 7/26 (27 Dec 1856): 407.

> Mr. Mason's quiet, unobtrusive manner of execution conceals from the audience those mechanical difficulties by which most of the first-class pianists endeavor to astonish their hearers; and in his truly musician-like method he presents the musical idea through the ear alone.

638   Newark, N.J., Library Hall, 8 Jan 1857

Solo recital, assisted by Maria S. Brainerd, vocalist; John Nelson Pattison and T. M. Brown, pianists; Clare W. Beames, (conductor?)

No program has been located.

Reviews/Announcements of no. **638**:

"Local Matters." *Sentinel of Freedom* (Newark), 6 Jan 1857, p. [2], cols. 6-7.

Includes an announcement of Mason's recital.

"Local Intelligence." *Newark Daily Mercury*, 8 Jan 1857, p. [2], cols. 2-5.

Includes an announcement of Mason's recital.

> Mr. Mason has established a reputation as one of the first Pianists of our country. . . .

"Our Musical Correspondence, . . . Newark, N.J." *New York Musical Review and Gazette* 8/2 (24 Jan 1857): 23.

> Mr. WM. MASON'S second concert took place last night, when a large and appreciative audience greeted him. . . .

639   Boston, 13 Jan 1857

Sigismond Thalberg Matinée

Sigismond Thalberg, *Grand Fantasy and Variations on Bellini's "Norma,"* op. 12

Thalberg and Mason, pianists

Although the recital was scheduled for January 13, the actual performance was postponed to January 20.

Reviews of no. **639**:

"Musical." *Boston Evening Transcript*, 21 Jan 1857, p. [2], col. 1.

A favorable, three-paragraph review.

"Thalberg's Matinees." *Dwight's Journal of Music* 10/17 (24 Jan 1857): 134.

On Tuesday he played the "Huguenots" fantasia, with prodigious effect; also the fantasias on "Masaniello," "Sonnambula," and "Norma," (for two pianos,) with WILLIAM MASON. All these were astonishing.

640   Boston, Music Hall, 16 Jan 1857

Sigismond Thalberg's "Last Concert"

Sigismond Thalberg, *Grand Fantasy and Variations on Bellini's "Norma,"* op. 12

Thalberg and Mason, pianists

Reviews/Announcements of no. **640:**

"Thalberg's Last Concert." *Boston Daily Advertiser*, 16 Jan 1857, p. [1], col. 8.

Announces the concert.

"Musical Intelligence." *Boston Evening Transcript*, 17 Jan 1857, p. [2], col. 1.

Includes a review of Thalberg's concert.

Mr. William Mason, who whilom, so ably and artistically interpreted the master pieces of the great Thalberg to us, was in no ways abashed in the presence of the maestro himself, but contributed greatly with his unquestioned skill of execution and intelligent method to the success of the piece.

"Sigismond Thalberg." *Boston Daily Advertiser*, 17 Jan 1857, p. [1], col. 8.

A positive review.

"Thalberg's Fifth Concert." *Boston Post*, 17 Jan 1857, p. [2], col. 4.

The gem of the evening was the execution of a fantasia from *Norma*. . . . Although of great length, the artists courteously complied with the earnestly expressed desire for a repetition, and a greater portion was given for the second time.

"Thalberg's Last Concert." *Dwight's Journal of Music* 10/17 (24 Jan 1857): 132-33.

Wonderfully well was the whole thing executed. the younger pianist bearing his banner proudly side by side with the winner of a thousand battles. The difficulties were about equally shared between them, and the ensemble was quite perfect. Yet on Thalberg's side there was the still finer touch and what was clear before, stood out all the clearer and the bolder when his fingers took their turn.

641   Boston, Hallet, Davis & Co. Rooms, 21 Jan 1857

Gustav Satter Philharmonic Soirée

Liszt, *Les Préludes* (arranged for two pianos)

Satter and Mason, pianists

Reviews of no. **641**:

"Musical." *Boston Evening Transcript*, 22 Jan 1857, p. [2], col. 2.

> The closing piece was . . . by Liszt, played by Wm. Mason and Satter on two pianofortes, — a noisy, boisterous affair, little else than a grand study for hand and finger exercise that did not commend itself by any melodic beauty either to the mind or ear of the listener.

"Concerts of the Week." *Dwight's Journal of Music* 10/18 (31 Jan 1857): 142-43.

> What shall we say of "Les Preludes," a *Poesie Symphonique* by LISZT, for two pianos, performed by Messrs. WILLIAM MASON and SATTER? This also purports to have been reared on a poetic basis, to-wit, Lamartine's "Meditations Poetiques." The poetry we listened for in vain. It was lost as it were in the smoke and stunning tumult of a battle-field. There were here and there brief, flitting fragments of something delicate and sweet to ear and mind, but these were quickly swallowed up in one long, monotonous, fatiguing melée of convulsive, crashing, startling masses of tone, flung back and forth as if in rivalry from instrument to instrument. We must have been very stupid listeners; but we felt after it as if we had been stoned, and beaten, and trampled under foot, and in all ways evilly entreated. . . .

"Our Musical Correspondence, . . . Boston." *New York Musical Review and Gazette* 8/3 (7 Feb 1857): 37-39.

> Merely reports that the concert was given; not a review as such.

642　　Orange, N.J., Waverly Hall, 5 Feb 1857

Solo recital, assisted by Maria S. Brainerd, vocalist; Theodore Thomas, violin; Clare W. Beames, conductor

No program has been located.

Reviews of no. **642**:

"Mr. Mason's Concert." *Orange Journal*, 7 Feb 1857, p. [2], col. 1.

> The performances of Mr. Mason were masterly, and gave complete satisfaction; his own composition, "Silver Spring," is a gem of "the first water," and was rapturously encored.

"Musical Gossip." *New York Musical Review and Gazette* 8/3 (7 Feb 1857): 33-34.

> Merely reports that the recital was given; not a review as such.

643　　New York, 27 Feb 1857

Sigismond Thalberg Matinée

Sigismond Thalberg, *Grand Fantasy and Variations on Bellini's "Norma,"* op. 12

Thalberg and Mason, pianists

Review of no. **643:**

"Musical Correspondence, New York, March 2." *Dwight's Journal of Music,* 10/23 (7 Mar 1857): 179.

A positive review (signed "-t-").

644 Brooklyn, Plymouth Church, 28 Apr 1857

Brooklyn Young Men's Christian Association Benefit Concert

Weber, "March" and "Finale" from *Concertstück in F Minor,* op. 79

Performed with the New York Harmonic Society

Mason, *Grand Valse de bravura* (op. 5?)

Reviews of no. **644:**

Anonymous review. *Brooklyn Daily Eagle,* 29 Apr 1857, p. [3], col. 1.

A brief review. Mason's performance is not mentioned.

"Musical Correspondence, New York, April 29." *Dwight's Journal of Music* 11/5 (2 May 1857): 37.

The review (signed "-t-") mentions Mason's performance only in passing.

645 Boston, Music Hall, 22 May 1857

Boston Philharmonic — Carl Zerrahn

The performance was part of the Handel and Haydn Society's music festival.

Weber, *Concertstück in F Minor,* op. 79

Reviews of no. **645:**

"The Musical Festival — Second Day." *Boston Daily Advertiser,* 23 May 1857, p. [1], col. 6.

Mason's performance is not mentioned in the review.

"Second Day of the Musical Festival." *Boston Evening Transcript,* 23 May 1857, p. [2], col. 2.

. . . Mr. William Mason . . . played with marked ability. . . .

"The Great Musical Festival." *Dwight's Journal of Music* 11/9 (30 May 1857): 65-69.

WILLIAM MASON played the *Concert-stück* in a most artistic and finished style, and, on being *encored*, won new admiration by his own brilliant "Silver Spring."

"The Musical Festival at Boston." *New York Musical Review and Gazette* 8/11 (30 May 1857): 163-65.

> . . . Mr. William Mason performed in a most artistic manner, and received an encore.

646   Baltimore, Carroll Hall, 3 Dec 1857

Solo recital, assisted by Mme Gregoor, vocalist; T. Ahrend, cello; J. F. Petri, conductor; Messrs. Mahr, Scheidler, Schaeffer, and Thiede of the Germanians

[Antoine de?] Kontski, *Grand Caprice héroique*

Mason, *Silver Spring*, op. 6

Mason, *Étude de concert*, op. 9

Beethoven, *Sonata in C Minor* (not otherwise identified)

Adolph von Henselt, "*Si Oiseau j'étais*," *Étude in F-sharp Major*, op. 2, no. 6

Mason, "Paraphrase de concert—sur 'God Save the Queen'"

> Reviews/Announcements of no. **646**:

> "Grand Concert." *Daily Baltimore Republican*, 1 Dec 1857, p. [3], col. 3.
> Announces the recital.

> "Mr. Wm. Mason's Concert." *Baltimore American*, 3 Dec 1857, p. 2, cols. 2-3.
> Announces the recital.

> "Vocal and Instrumental Concert." *Sun* (Baltimore), 3 Dec 1857, p. [2], col. 3.
> Announces the recital.
>> This gentleman [Mason] enjoys an established reputation, and is esteemed by many as second only to Thalberg in this country.

> "Musical Gossip." *New York Musical Review and Gazette* 8/25 (12 Dec 1857): 385-87.
> Merely reports that the concert was given; not a review as such.

647   New York, Academy of Music, 6 Mar 1858

Philharmonic Society—Theodor Eisfeld

Adolph von Henselt, *Concerto in F Minor*, op. 16

> Second and third movements only

> Reviews of no. **647**:

> "Philharmonic Society." *New York Times*, 8 Mar 1858, p. 4, col. 6.

The mechanical difficulties of this piece are very great, and demand a pianist of good power. Mr. MASON played with ability and fully merited the warm appreciation of the audience—especially in the third movement; his performance of the *Larghetto*, however, was cold and unemotional.

"Musical Correspondence, New York, Mar. 9." *Dwight's Journal of Music* 12/24 (13 Mar 1858): 397.

A positive review (signed "t").

Mr. Mason rendered with his usual excellence, two movements from a Concerto . . . by Henselt. . . .

648 Brooklyn, Athenaeum, 11 Dec 1858

Brooklyn Philharmonic Society—Carl Bergmann

Adolph von Henselt, *Concerto in F Minor*, op. 16

Second and third movements only

Mason, "Grand Galop fantastique" (later published as *Pell-Mell Galop fantastique*, op. 29?)

Reviews of no. **648**:

Anonymous review. *Brooklyn Daily Eagle*, 13 Dec 1858, p. [3], col. 2.

Mason's performance is not mentioned.

"Musical Correspondence, Brooklyn, N.Y., Dec. 14." *Dwight's Journal of Music* 14/13 (25 Dec 1858): 308.

A favorable review (signed "BELLINI").

Mr. MASON played, as he always does, to the satisfaction of everybody. His second piece was honored with an encore, when he gave us his "*Silver Springs*" which appeared to me more worthy of a place in the programme than the "Grand Galope Fantastique," which seemed to contain more difficulties than beauties. But the audience seemed to relish it very much.

"Second Philharmonic Concert." *New York Musical Review and Gazette* 9/26 (25 Dec 1858): 403.

A positive review.

649 New York, Cooper Institute, 23 Dec 1858

Robert Goldbeck Concert

Liszt, *Les Préludes* (arranged for two pianos)

Robert Goldbeck, second pianist

Reviews of no. **649**:

"Cooper Institute." *New York Times*, 24 Dec 1858, p. 5, col. 1.

Mason's performance is not mentioned.

"Musical Correspondence, New York, Dec. 31, 1858." *Dwight's Journal of Music* 14/16 (15 Jan 1859): 332-33.

A favorable review (signed "t").

> Liszt's "Preludes" for two pianos, though excellently played by Messrs. GOLDBECK and MASON, was as uninteresting as are all the *compositions* of the great pianist.

650   New York, Academy of Music, 7 Mar 1859

George Frederick Bristow Complimentary Concert

Schumann, *Andante and Variations in B-flat Major for Two Pianos*, op. 46

Henry C. Timm, second pianist

Reviews of no. **650**:

"Academy of Music." *New York Times*, 9 Mar 1859, p. 4, col. 5.

Mason's performance is not mentioned.

"Musical Correspondence, New York, March 8." *Dwight's Journal of Music* 14/24 (12 Mar 1859): 397.

The review (signed "TROVATOR") mentions Mason only in passing.

"Musical Gossip." *New York Musical Review and Gazette* 10/6 (19 Mar 1859): 81-82.

> The testimonial concert for Mr. George Bristow, at the Academy of Music, was quite a success. The house was well filled. Messrs. Timm and Wm. Mason performed the Andante by Schumann for two piano-fortes.

651   New York, Chickering's Rooms, 4 Apr 1859

Lucy Escott Complimentary Concert

Mason, "Ballade" (later published as op. 12?)

Mason, "Grand Galop fantastique" (later published as *Pell-Mell Galop fantastique*, op. 29?)

Reviews of no. **651**:

"Mrs. Lucy Escott." *Musical World* 21/15 (9 Apr 1859): 226.

> Mr. William Mason fully sustained his great reputation, a well earned one, of the most solid description. . . . The performance . . . met with a rapturous encore; the composer then gave his ever fresh and beautiful "Silver Spring."

"Musical Correspondence, New York, April 5." *Dwight's Journal of Music* 15/3 (16 Apr 1859): 21-22.

A favorable review (signed "-t-").

"Musical Gossip." *New York Musical Review and Gazette* 10/8 (16 Apr 1859): 113-14.

Merely reports that the concert was given; not a review as such.

652   Brooklyn, Hall of the Polytechnic Institute, 14 Nov 1861

Classical Soirée [Mason-Thomas Quartette]

Handel, *Suite in F Minor*

Schubert, *Trio in E-flat Major*, op. 100

Theodore Thomas, violin; Frederic Bergner, cello

In 1861 the Mason-Thomas Quartette made arrangements to begin a series of soirées in Brooklyn similar to those already being given in Manhattan and Farmington. (A copy of the prospectus for the Brooklyn soirées is with the William Mason Papers, New York Public Library.) Although apparently well planned, this venture was unsuccessful. Only two (a second concert was given on 5 December 1861) of the four concerts scheduled for the 1861-62 season were played, and the series was dropped after the first year.

Reviews of no. **652**:

"Musical." *Brooklyn Daily Eagle*, 15 Nov 1861, p. [3], col. 1.

The programme was a choice and grateful feast of pure astheticism [*sic*] to all who love music. . . . The attendance was poor, but those who were present seemed to relish the performances very keenly.

"Musical Correspondence, Brooklyn, November 18, 1861." *Dwight's Journal of Music* 20/8 (23 Nov 1861): 271.

The correspondent (identified as "BAGGS") comments on the attendance at the opening concert.

The list of subscribers is very gratifying for a commencement and is another evidence of the growing taste for really good music here.

653   Orange, N.J., Library Hall, 12 Feb 1862

Classical Soirée [Mason-Thomas Quartette]

Handel, *Suite in F Minor*

Schubert, *Trio in E-flat Major*, op. 100

Theodore Thomas, violin; Frederic Bergner, cello

This was the first of three programs presented by the Mason-Thomas Quartette in Orange in 1862. (The dates of the other concerts were March 12 and April 16.) Another set of three programs was presented in Orange in 1866 (January 18, February 13, and June 20), but a continuing series of programs similar to those in New York and Farmington was never established.

654   Boston, Music Hall, 8 Mar 1862

Boston Philharmonic — Carl Zerrahn

Schubert-Liszt, *Fantasy in C Major*, op. 15

Mason, *Spring-Dawn: Mazurka-Caprice*, op. 20

Mason, *Silver Spring*, op. 6

> Reviews of no. **654**:

> "Dramatic and Musical." *Boston Daily Advertiser*, 10 Mar 1862, p. [4], cols. 1-2.

>> Mr. Mason's playing was all that could be desired; every new thought was expressed distinctly, every intricate phrase resolved, and every powerful or swift passage delivered accurately.

> "Mr. Zerrahn's Concert." *Boston Post*, 10 Mar 1862, p. [4], col. 2.

>> Mr. Wm. Mason played Schubert's Fantasia in C, smoothly and fluently, though without any special vigor or warmth. In fact, the orchestral portion was so prominent and attractive as to overshadow the piano. His own pieces in the second part, which were trickling arpeggi around a simple theme, were very gracefully rendered, and won him an encore.

> "The Philharmonic Concert." *Boston Evening Transcript*, 10 Mar 1862, p. [2], col. 3.

>> A brief, favorable review.

> "Concerts of the Week: Fourth Philharmonic." *Dwight's Journal of Music* 20/24 (15 Mar 1862): 398.

>> Mr. WILLIAM MASON was very warmly greeted, as he always is on his artistic visits to his native city. We heartily thank him for giving us a hearing, and so satisfactory a one, of a very interesting work. . . . The only difficulty was that, though the pianoforte part was admirably played, the ear did not get quite so much of it, or sieze [sic] it so distinctly and conspicuously among the brilliant mass of orchestration, as one could have desired. Evidently Liszt has rather overloaded it; there could be no doubt that the piano rendering was masterly.

655   Philadelphia, Academy of Music, 21 Apr 1862

Mark Hassler Testimonial Concert

Mason, *Spring-Dawn: Mazurka-Caprice*, op. 20

Mason, *Silver Spring*, op. 6

Schubert-Liszt, *Fantasy in C Major*, op. 15

> Theodore Thomas, conductor

> Reviews of no. **655**:

"Mr. Mark Hassler's Concert." *Daily Evening Bulletin* (Philadelphia), 22 Apr 1862, p. 4, cols. 2-3.

> Mr. Mason had the honor of introducing to our public Listz's [*sic*] arrangement of a grand fantasia by Schubert. The orchestra was led by Mr. Thomas, and admirably supported Mr. Mason. He afterwards played two solos, and notwithstanding the lateness of the hour, awakened a genuine enthusiasm.

"Musical Correspondence, Philadelphia, April 22." *Dwight's Journal of Music* 21/4 (26 Apr 1862): 31.

> A favorable review (signed "MERCUTIO").

> We were all greatly delighted to hear Mr. Mason, who has not performed here for over five years; his elegant performance . . . was the very perfection of piano playing.

656   New York, Irving Hall, 13 May 1862

Thomas Orchestra — Theodore Thomas

Schubert-Liszt, *Fantasy in C Major*, op. 15

Ignaz Moscheles, *Les Contrastes* (for piano quartet)

> Robert Goldbeck, Sebastian Bach Mills, and E. Hartman, second, third, and fourth pianists

Reviews of no. **656**:

"Mr. Theo. Thomas' Concert." *Musical Review and Musical World* 13/11 (24 May 1862): 122-23.

A positive review.

> Mr. Mason was warmly applauded. . . .

"Musical Correspondence, New York, May 19." *Dwight's Journal of Music* 21/8 (24 May 1862): 64.

> A positive review (signed "ALMA").

"Musical Correspondence, New York, May 20, 1862." *Dwight's Journal of Music* 21/9 (31 May 1862): 71.

> A positive review (signed "TROVATOR").

657   New York, Niblo's Saloon, 20 May 1862

Gottschalk's Concert

Sigismond Thalberg, *Grand Fantasy and Variations on Bellini's "Norma,"* op. 12

> Gottschalk and Mason, pianists

Review of no. **657**:

"Gottschalk's Last Concert." *New York Times*, 21 May 1862, p. 8, col. 4.

The "star" instrumental performance of the evening was the duett on the "Norma," arranged by THALBERG, which was played by GOTTSCHALK and MASON. Our opinion of the former instrumentalist has been so repeatedly expressed, that we feel no necessity for repeating it here. We may, however, say that MASON proved himself a thorough and finished artist, as he always does. We can pay him no higher compliment.

658   New York, Irving Hall, 18 Sept 1862

Theodore Thomas Vocal and Orchestral Concert

Meyerbeer-Liszt, *Festmarsch zu Schillers 100-Jährigen Geburtsfeier*

Mason, *Silver Spring*, op. 6

Mason, *Concert Galop*, op. 11

Reviews of no. **658**:

"Mr. Theodore Thomas' Grand Concert." *Musical Review and Musical World* 13/20 (27 Sept 1862): 230-31.

A favorable review.

"Music in New York." *Dwight's Journal of Music* 21/26 (27 Sept 1862): 205.

Mr. William Mason played in a masterly manner, a piano "transcription" of Meyerbeer's Schiller March—a massive and effective work; also, a new and brilliant Concert Gallop [*sic*] of his own.

"Musical Correspondence, New York, September 23." *Dwight's Journal of Music* 21/26 (27 Sept 1862): 204.

A positive review (signed "ZINCALO").

Of Mr. MASON'S selections, we much preferred his own compositions, "Silver Spring" and the "Concert Galop;" Liszt's transcription of the Schiller March is heavy, and the principal *motivo* of the march a trivial one.

659   New York, Irving Hall, 8 Nov 1862

Philharmonic Society—Theodor Eisfeld

Schubert-Liszt, *Fantasy in C Major*, op. 15

Chopin, *Ballade in A-flat Major*, op. 47

Reviews of no. **659**:

"Musical Correspondence, New York, Nov. 11." *Dwight's Journal of Music* 22/7 (15 Nov 1862): 262.

A favorable review (signed "T. W. M.").

"... First Philharmonic Concert." *Musical Review and Musical World* 13/24 (22 Nov 1862): 278.

> Schubert's Fantasia in C, with the additional orchestral accompaniment by Liszt, is one of the few pieces which improve by repeated hearing. . . . And this is entirely owing to the characteristically beautiful orchestration with which Liszt has clothed the work. . . . But let us also say that Mr. William Mason played it superbly, with exquisite taste, fine artistic feeling, and correctness. He gave evidently universal satisfaction. So did the fine Grand (one of Steinway's) which he used on this occasion.

660   Hartford, Conn., Allyn Hall, 27 Jan 1863

Mason-Thomas Quartette Chamber Music Concert

Mason, *Silver Spring*, op. 6

Mason, *Concert Galop*, op. 11

Schumann, *Quintet in E-flat Major*, op. 44

> Theodore Thomas and Joseph Mosenthal, violins; George Matzka, viola; Frederic Bergner, cello

> Reviews/Announcements of no. **660**:

> "The Concert To-Night." *Hartford Daily Courant*, 27 Jan 1863, p. [2], col. 4.

>> Announces Mason's recital.

>>> Those who appreciate the sweetest harmony with delightful instrumental and vocal performances, will not willingly be absent this evening.

> "The Classical Concert." *Hartford Daily Courant*, 28 Jan 1863, p. [2], col. 4.

>> Mason and Thomas each performed a solo, both of which were well received and a repetition demanded, which however, was not given.

> "Musical Gossip." *Musical Review and Musical World* 14/3 (31 Jan 1863): 28.

>> Merely reports that the concert was given and lists a program of the performance; not a review as such.

661   Brooklyn, Academy of Music, 7 Mar 1863

Brooklyn Philharmonic Society—Theodore Thomas

Schubert-Liszt, *Fantasy in C Major*, op. 15

> Reviews of no. **661**:

> Anonymous review. *New York Times*, 9 Mar 1863, p. 3, col. 5.

>> Mr. MASON gave only SCHUBERT'S Fantasia for the piano, and though vociferously called for a second rendition did not refavor the audience.

"Philharmonic Concert." *Brooklyn Daily Eagle*, 9 Mar 1863, p. [7], col. 1.

The Fantasia for Piano, by Schubert, [was] played very acceptably by Mr. Mason. . . .

662   New York, Irving Hall, 21 Mar 1863

Robert Goldbeck Grand Orchestral and Vocal Concert

Schumann, *Andante and Variations in B-flat Major for Two Pianos*, op. 46

Sebastian Bach Mills, second pianist

Reviews of no. 662:

"Goldbeck's Concert." *Musical Review and Musical World* 14/7 (28 Mar 1863): 75-76.

A positive review (signed "K. K.").

. . . Schumann's Variations for two Piano-fortes . . . played by Messrs. Mills and Mason brought out each of these gentlemen in his best light. The brilliant Variation belonged more especially to Mills, while the more delicate one with the syncopations was entirely Mason's own.

"Musical Correspondence, New York, March 23." *Dwight's Journal of Music* 22/26 (28 Mar 1863): 409-10.

A favorable review (signed F-sharp, E, D in musical notation).

663   New York, Irving Hall, 20 Apr 1864

Theodore Thomas Complimentary Concert

Beethoven, *Sonata in A Major*, op. 47

Second and third movements only

Theodore Thomas, violin

664   New York, Dodworth's Hall, 25 Apr 1864

Frederic Bergner Concert

Mason, *Ballade*, op. 12

Mason, *Silver Spring*, op. 6

Review of no. 664:

"Musical Gossip." *Musical Review and Musical World* 15/10 (10 May 1864): 153-54.

Mason's performance is not mentioned.

665   New York, Academy of Music, 28 Jan 1865

Philharmonic Society — Theodor Eisfeld

Schubert-Liszt, *Fantasy in C Major*, op. 15

Reviews of no. **665:**

Anonymous review. *New York Times*, 30 Jan 1865, p. 4, col. 5.

> One of the most agreeable features of the evening was SCHUBERT'S
> fantasia for piano, (orchestra part added by LISZT,) most deliciously
> performed by Mr. WM. MASON, whose rich and beautiful touch is
> heard to particular advantage in this charming but over-long work.

"Musical Correspondence, New York, Feb. 13." *Dwight's Journal of Music*
24/24 (18 Feb 1865): 399-400.

A favorable review (signed "LANCELOT").

> Mr. Mason has once before delighted us with his artistic interpretation
> of this work. If, on this occasion, he was scareely [*sic*] himself, yet
> we could not but wonder that he found it possible to play in the manner
> he did; for he was ill and lame, and only carried his task to an end
> by means of great mental exertion.

666 New York, Dodworth's Hall, 18 Apr 1865

Frederic Bergner Grand Annual Concert

Mason, *Monody*, op. 13

Mason, *"Ah! Vous dirais-je maman," caprice grotesque*, [op. 22]

Review of no. **666:**

"Musical Correspondence, New York, May 8." *Dwight's Journal of Music*
25/4 (13 May 1865): 29.

Signed "LANCELOT."

> Mr. W. Mason played two compositions of his own finely (this we
> always expect from such an artist), "Monody," and "Ah! vous dirais-
> je Maman." In both of these Mr. Mason displayed his skill as harmonist
> and pianist; they are full of fine pianoforte effects and will not fail
> to become very popular.

667 New York, Irving Hall, 11 Nov 1865

Thomas Symphony Soirée — Theodore Thomas

Chopin, *Allegro de concert*, op. 46

Review of no. **667:**

"Musical Correspondence, New York, Nov. 21." *Dwight's Journal of Music*
25/18 (25 Nov 1865): 140-41.

The review is signed "LANCELOT."

> Mr. MASON played a seldom heard work of Chopin, which deserves
> greater popularity in the concert room.

668   New York, Irving Hall, 10 Feb 1866

Thomas Symphony Soirée—Theodore Thomas

Mozart, *Concerto for Two Pianos in E-flat Major*, K. 316a

Sebastian Bach Mills, second pianist

Review of no. **668**:

Anonymous review. *New York Times*, 12 Feb 1866, p. 5, cols. 4-5.

> The technical difficulties of the concerto, apart from the cadenzas are not
> great. It is anything but easy, however, to preserve the exact coloring
> required. This Messrs. MILLS and MASON certainly did. We have
> never listened to a more enjoyable performance. Each gentleman's
> touch was perfect and well balanced, and the rest was of course facile
> with them. Nothing could have been better.

669   New York, Academy of Music, 21 Apr 1866

Philharmonic Society—Carl Bergmann

Norbert Burgmüller, *Concerto in F-sharp Minor*, op. 1

Reviews of no. **669**:

Anonymous review. *New York Times*, 23 Apr 1866, p. 5, col. 3.

> The soloist was Mr. WILLIAM MASON. When this gentleman plays
> in public, and he does so far too seldom, we are pretty sure to hear
> a piece of more than average interest. . . . The music [of Burgmüller's
> concerto] lies nicely beneath the hand, and was rendered faultlessly by
> Mr. MASON, whose beautiful touch imparted a degree of warmth and
> coloring to what might otherwise have seemed inanimate and artificial.

"Musical Correspondence, New York, April 23." *Dwight's Journal of Music*
26/3 (28 Apr 1866): 231-32.

> Dwight's correspondent (identified as "LANCELOT") writes:

> Mr. WILLIAM MASON introduced Norbert Burgmüller's piano-forte
> Concerto to us. We had expected more from a composer once held
> by Schumann in such high estimation. The composition offers very
> few new ideas, and is not interestingly instrumented. It was, however,
> played finely by Mr. Mason.

670   New York, Irving Hall, 20 Oct 1866

Thomas Symphony Soirée—Theodore Thomas

Beethoven, *Concerto in G Major*, op. 58

Review of no. **670**:

"New York—Season of 1866-7—." *New York Musical Gazette* 1/1 (Nov
1866): 5.

More of an announcement than a review.

> The first concert [of Thomas's Symphony Soirées] was given at Irving Hall, October 20th, when the orchestral pieces presented [included] . . . Beethoven's Concerto, opus 58, with Mr. WM. MASON at the pianoforte.

671 New York, Steinway Hall, 26 Jan 1867

Philharmonic Society — Carl Bergmann

Beethoven, *Concerto in G Major*, op. 58

Reviews of no. **671:**

Anonymous review. *New York Times*, 28 Jan 1867, p. 5, col. 4.

> BEETHOVEN'S *Concerto* in G is a great and beautiful work. . . . Mr. WM. MASON played it very finely; the beauty of his touch lending particular charm and brilliancy to the many scale passages. An effective *cadenza* was introduced in the first movement, written by the pianist. It possesses the merits of retaining preceding ideas and of being short.

"New York." *Dwight's Journal of Music* 26/23 (2 Feb 1867): 392.

> A favorable review.

"New York." *New York Musical Gazette* 1/5 (Mar 1867): 37.

> There is no player who more completely controls the sympathies of his listeners than Mr. Mason, and, to our taste, there is no one who gives a more satisfying interpretation to Beethoven's music.

672 New York, Steinway Hall, 4 May 1867

Philharmonic Society — Carl Bergmann

(Twenty-fifth anniversary celebration concert)

Mozart, *Concerto for Two Pianos in E-flat Major*, K. 316a

Emile Guyon, second pianist

Reviews of no. **672:**

"The Musical Season." *New York Times*, 6 May 1867, pp. 4 (col. 7) and 5 (col. 1).

> The *Concerto* on the programme was MOZART'S No. 17, in E flat, with Mr. WM. MASON and EMILE GUYON at the pianos — thinking less of self-display than of the sublime old Master — and the full Orchestra . . . in fastidious harmony. The result was one of the most faultless performances. . . .

"New York." *Dwight's Journal of Music* 27/4 (11 May 1867): 31-32.

> The programme still further included a Concerto for two pianos, by Mozart, delightfully played by Mr. William Mason and Mr. Emile Guyon. . . .

673 Orange, N.J., Library Hall, 22 Jan 1868

   Theron Baldwin, Jr., Complimentary Concert

   Liszt, *Réminiscences de "Lucia di Lammermoor"*

   Mason, *Silver Spring*, op. 6

> Reviews/Announcements of no. 673:

> "Grand Concert." *Orange Journal*, 18 Jan 1868, p. [2], col. 2.
> Announces the concert.

> Anonymous review. *Orange Journal*, 25 Jan 1868, p. [2], col. 3.
> > Of our own great favorite, Wm. Mason, pianist, little need be said.
> > His renderings . . . were as wonderful as they were thrilling and
> > delightful. . . .

674 Orange, N.J., Library Hall, 12 Mar 1868

   Soirée of classical music (benefit recital for the Orange Valley Church's organ
   fund)

> A concert by the Mason-Thomas Quartette; no program has been located.
> See also no. 54.

> Reviews/Announcements of no. 674:

> "Grand Benefit Concert." *Orange Journal*, 9 Mar 1868, extra, p. [1], col. 4.
> Announces the concert.

> "Musical Entertainments." *Orange Journal*, 14 Mar 1868, p. [2], col. 4.
> > One of the most delightful musical entertainments it has ever been our
> > pleasure to enjoy. . . . This grand musical soiree was given by Mr.
> > Mason, for the benefit of the organ fund of the new Valley Church,
> > and we are glad to announce that it was a complete success. In spite
> > of the stormy weather there was a full house of our most refined and
> > appreciative citizens, and over $500 were netted to the object.

675 Orange, N.J., First Presbyterian Church, 20 Apr 1870

   Organ and Vocal Concert

> Three organists participated in this concert: Mason, Charles Schuyler, and one
> Mr. Morgan. Mason's performances on the organ usually took the form of
> improvisations, as was the case in this concert. For additional commentary
> on Mason's improvisational style, see nos. 61, 62, 147, 213, 247, 329.

> Reviews/Announcements of no. 675:

> "Another Organ Concert." *Orange Chronicle*, 16 Apr 1870, p. [3], col. 4.
> Announces the concert.

"Organ Concert." *Orange Chronicle*, 23 Apr 1870, p. [3], col. 3.

> In striking contrast was the previous performance of Mr. Wm. Mason. His improvised effort was in his own peculiar, graceful, flowing, and power-acquiring method, embracing two or three familiar themes, and ending in a masterly fugue. It was to be regreted [*sic*] that another opportunity was not afforded this gentleman, whose appearance and performances are always gladly hailed by the admirers of the unostentatious and true in music, which by many are preferred to mere racket and expenditure of force.

"Popular Organ Concerts." *Orange Chronicle*, 30 Apr 1870, p. [2], col. 1.

> Announces the concert.

676 Orange, N.J., Valley Church, spring 1870

Series of six organ recitals

> In this series of six recitals (May 14, May 21, May 28, June 4, June 11, and June 18) Mason was joined by a second organist for each concert—Samuel Warren in the first, third, fifth, and sixth recitals; Charles B. Schuyler in the second recital; and John P. Morgan in the fourth recital. True to his usual procedure, Mason's contributions to the programs were in the form of improvisations. The program for the fourth recital on 4 June 1870 (given below) was typical for the series.

[Mason], Improvisation in Strict Style

> William Mason, organist

Bach, *Prelude and Fugue in E-flat Major*

Morgan, *Prelude and Choral on "Dundee"*

Ritter, *Prelude and Choral: "Jesus Meine Freunde"*

Fink, *Andante from Sonata in E-flat Major*

Ritter, *Sonata in D Minor*, op. 2

> John P. Morgan, organist

[Mason], Improvisation in Free Style: "Home, Sweet Home"

> William Mason, organist

> Reviews/Announcements of no. **676**:

"Organ Recitals." *Orange Chronicle*, 30 Apr 1870, p. [3], col. 2.

> Announces the series of six recitals.

>> We are authorized to mention the names of Mr. William Mason, and Mr. S. P. Warren of Grace Church, New York. . . .

"Popular Organ Concerts." *Orange Chronicle*, 30 Apr 1870, p. [2], col. 1.

> Announces the series of six recitals.

"Fourth Recital." *Orange Chronicle*, 11 June 1870, p. [3], col. 4.

> A brief review of the concert; Mason's performance is not mentioned.

677   South Bend, Ind., summer 1870

Normal Music School

> Mason played two recitals weekly for the duration of the normal school (programs not located). See George F. Root's *The Story of a Musical Life*, no. **404.**

678   New York, Steinway Hall, 30 Aug 1870

National Musical Congress Convention

Chopin, *Ballade in A-flat Major*, op. 47

Mason, *Silver Spring*, op. 6

> Review of no. **678:**
>
> > "National Musical Congress." *New York Tribune*, 2 Sept 1870, p. 8, cols. 2-3.
> > Reports that Mason performed.

679   Binghamton, N.Y., July-Aug 1871

Normal Music School

> Mason played at least five lecture-recitals. For programs of these performances, see nos. **71, 248, 253, 273.**

680   Binghamton, N.Y., summer 1872

Normal Music School

> Plans announced for the school indicated that Mason would play two recitals per week for the duration of the school term (see no. **250**). Mason played at least six lecture-recitals. For programs of recitals nos. 1-4 and 6, see nos. **277, 298, 299.**

681   New York, Steinway Hall, 25 Apr 1873

Music Festival—Theodore Thomas

Bach, *Triple Concerto in D Minor*, BWV 1063

> Anton Rubinstein and Sebastian Bach Mills, second and third pianists
>
> Reviews of no. **681:**
>
> "Festival Week at Steinway Hall." *New York Times*, 26 Apr 1873, p. 6, col. 7.
>
> > As promised, the three artists appeared, somewhat after the fashion of an enlarged edition of the Siamese twins, and delivered with unimpeachable precision the composition named. We are, however, by no means willing to accept the applause of the audience as the result of the

concerto's impression; . . . we incline to the belief that the spectators, in recalling the pianists cared more for the agreeable historical remembrance to grow out of the sight of the trio, than for the special merit of their united effort.

"Musical Correspondence, New York, April 28." *Dwight's Journal of Music* 33/2 (3 May 1873): 15-16.

Signed "A. A. C."

The most interesting feature of this concert was the performance of Bach's great triple Concerto by Messrs. Rubinstein, Mills and Mason.

See also no. **230.**

682 Binghamton, N.Y., summer 1873

Normal Music School

Mason played eight lecture-recitals. For programs of these performances, see nos. **22, 276.**

683 Watertown, N.Y., July-Aug 1875

Normal Music School

Mason played five recitals. See no. **8.**

684 Boston Music Hall, 16 Feb 1876

Thomas Orchestra — Theodore Thomas

Mozart, *Concerto in C Major*, K. 467

Reviews of no. **684:**

"Theodore Thomas's Fifth Symphony Concert." *Boston Post*, 17 Feb 1876, p. [3], col. 6.

Mr. William Mason was given perhaps the heartiest reception of the evening, and his performance of the piano-forte part in the Mozart concerto was thoroughly artistic, though he did not have as much of an opportunity as some other work might have given him.

"Music in Boston." *Dwight's Journal of Music* 35/24 (4 Mar 1876): 190-91.

Mr. MASON's nice manipulation, and very even, finished, quiet style of execution, after the old Hummel school, which might have made it all delightful in a small room, seemed to lack force and vital accent *there*; it was like remembering music in one's sleep.

685 New York, Steinway Hall, 26 Feb 1876

Thomas Symphony Concert — Theodore Thomas

Mozart, *Concerto in C Major*, K. 467

A matinée performance of this program was given on February 24. Reviews of the matinée can be found in the *Evening Post* (25 Feb 1876, p. [2], col. 4) and the *New York Daily Tribune* (25 Feb 1876, p. 4, col. 6).

Reviews of no. **685**:

"Theodore Thomas' Fourth Symphony Concert." *New York Herald*, 27 Feb 1876, p. 9, col. 5.

> The piano concerto . . . was played by William Mason with exceeding delicacy, grace and expression. It was one of the most attractive concerts of the season.

"Fourth Symphony Concert." *New York Daily Tribune*, 28 Feb 1876, p. 5, col. 1.

> Mr. Mason, who has long been a stranger to the concert-room, played with all his old beauty of touch and precise accuracy. . . .

"Mr. Thomas' Symphony Concerts." *New York Times*, 28 Feb 1876, p. 4, col. 7.

> Mr. Mason has . . . retained his even and delicate touch and his simple phrasing, and if the impression of his refined and scholarly style is not so deep as it would have been ten years since, there is no occasion for wonderment. Equally reverent and dainty interpretations of Mozart are seldom heard, but the modern school has given birth to other demands, and the *diletianti* [sic] of the period seek sentiment, passion, and contrast in everything. To the *laudatores temporis acti*, Mr. Mason's playing must have afforded genuine pleasure. . . .

"The Thomas Concert." *Evening Post* (New York), 28 Feb 1876, p. [2], col. 4.

> He [Mason] delivered the whole on this occasion with the firmness of grasp and vigor which distinguishes his tone. . . .

"Music in New York, March 27." *Dwight's Journal of Music* 35/26 (1 Apr 1876): 205-06.

Signed "A. A. C."

> Mr. Wm. Mason, whose reappearance in the concert hall we note with pleasure, gave an admirable rendering of Mozart's Concerto in C. . . . A better performance could hardly be imagined. Mr. Mason played with precision and good taste, which was supplemented by a faultless orchestral accompaniment.

686 Orange, N.J., High School Hall, 5 June 1876

New York Quartette Club Concert

Chopin, *Ballade in A-flat Major*, op. 47

Schumann, *Quintet in E-flat Major*, op. 44

> Eduard Mollenhauer and Max Schwarz, violins; George Matzka, viola; Frederic Bergner, cello

Reviews/Announcements of no. **686:**

"Concert of Chamber Music." *Orange Journal*, 3 June 1876, p. 5, col. 3.
  Announces the concert.

"The Quartette Club—Mason Concert." *Orange Chronicle*, 3 June 1876,
p. [3], col. 2.
  Mr. Mason's name alone would be sufficient to attract a large audience
  to hear his cultivated execution upon the pianoforte, and coupled with
  that of the New York Quartette Club, . . . it forms an attraction that
  cannot be resisted by the true lover of music.

"The Concert of Chamber Music." *Orange Chronicle*, 10 June 1876, p. [3],
col. 2.
  It is not often, now-a-days, that Dr. William Mason can be induced
  to favor the public with his pianoforte performances. Whenever he
  chooses to do so in New York city, he is welcomed as an infrequent
  and inaccessible artist, and draws about him a circle of musical spirits
  who enjoy their brief moment of his skill, and then go away to carry
  their recollection of him with them for another indefinite period.

"Concert of Chamber Music." *Orange Journal*, 10 June 1876, p. 5, col. 3.
  Dr. Mason's rendering of Chopin's Ballade in A Flat needs no praise
  to people of this town.

687   New York State, various places, summer 1876
  Recitals performed at musical conventions, festivals, etc. Specific dates and
  locations are unknown, but a brief account of Mason's recitals, including a
  repertoire list, is given in the review below.

Review of no. **687:**

"The Mason Recitals." *Dwight's Journal of Music* 36/13 (30 Sept 1876): 312.
  The following list of works performed in various cities in the interior
  of New York . . . by Mr. WILLIAM MASON, certainly shows a great
  improvement in the general taste, to which programmes of so high an
  order are acceptable. In one city Mr. Mason gave nine pianoforte
  recitals, playing at the ninth entirely from Schumann's composition.

688   Orange, N.J., First Presbyterian Church, 8 Mar 1877
  Solo recital sponsored by the New England Society of Orange
  Handel, *Suite in F Minor*
  J. S. Bach, *Gavotte et Musette in D Minor*
    Gavotte in D Major
  Gluck, *Gavotte from the Ballet of "Don Juan"*
  Beethoven, *Sonata in E-flat Major*, op. 7

Schubert, *Impromptu in G-flat Major*, op. 90, no. 3

Mendelssohn, *Rondo capriccioso*, op. 14
Songs without Words (selections)

Schumann, *Novellette in F Major*, op. 21, no. 1
Romance in F-sharp Major, op. 28, no. 2
Novellette in E Major, op. 21, no. 7
Phantasiestücke, op. 12, nos. 1 & 8

Chopin, *Waltz in E-flat Major*, op. 18
Polonaise in C-sharp Minor, op. 26, no. 1
Impromptu in A-flat Major, op. 29
Nocturne in G Major, op. 37, no. 2
Waltzes in D-flat Major and C-sharp Minor, op. 64, nos. 1 & 2

Liszt, *Hungarian Rhapsody No. 12 in C-sharp Minor*

Reviews/Announcements of no. **688**:

"Pianoforte Recital." *Orange Journal*, 3 Mar 1877, p. 5, col. 5.
Announces Mason's recital (program included).

"Pianoforte Recital and Lecture." *Orange Chronicle*, 3 Mar 1877, p. [3], col. 5.
Announces Mason's recital.

"Mr. Mason's Pianoforte Recital." *Orange Journal*, 10 Mar 1877, p. 5, col. 4.
A long, highly favorable review.

To compliment Mr. Mason would seem like an impertinence on our part, but we may congratulate him heartily on the success of his efforts. . . .

"Pianoforte Recital." *Orange Chronicle*, 10 Mar 1877, p. [3], col. 2.
A long, favorable review.

The programme ended with five brilliant selections from Chopin and Liszt's "Rhapsodie Hongroise," No. 12, all of which involved rare skill and rapidity of execution, and Mr. Mason rendered them in a manner above criticism. . . .

689   New York, Steinway Hall, 19 May 1877
Anna Essipoff Matinée
Bach, *Triple Concerto in D Minor*, BWV 1063
Anna Essipoff and F. Boscovitz, second and third pianists

Schumann, *Andante and Variations in B-flat Major for Two Pianos*, op. 46
Anna Essipoff, second pianist

Reviews of no. **689:**

Anonymous review. *New York Times*, 20 May 1877, p. 7, col. 2.

> The concerto is not a very interesting work, but the "Variations" afforded general delight.

"Music in New York, May 21." *Dwight's Journal of Music* 37/4 (26 May 1877): 29-30.

> Signed "A. A. C."

> At her farewell matinée at Steinway Hall on Saturday last, Bach's celebrated triple concerto was performed; in this Mme. Essipoff had the co-operation of Messrs. Wm. Mason and F. Boscovitz. The programme also included Schumann's variations for two pianos, performed by Mme. Essipoff and Mr. Mason.

690 New York, Steinway Hall, 5 Jan 1878

Thomas Symphony Concert — Theodore Thomas

Bach, *Triple Concerto in D Minor*, BWV 1063

> Richard Hoffman and Ferdinand Dulcken, second and third pianists

Review of no. **690:**

"Mr. Thomas' Concerts." *New York Times*, 6 Jan 1878, p. 7, col. 4.

> Bach's D minor concerto, for three pianos, did not move the assemblage to anything approaching enthusiasm, in spite of the precision and tastefulness of the mild performances supplied by Messrs. Hoffman, Mason, and Dulcken. As a rule, nothing can be less interesting in a large concert hall than Bach's piano music, and three pianists are just thrice as tedious as one, in handling most of the old musician's legacies to students of harmony and counterpoint.

691 Orange, N.J., First Presbyterian Church, 20 Mar 1878

Solo recital sponsored by the New England Society of Orange

Beethoven, *Sonata in C Minor*, op. 13
> *Sonata in A-flat Major*, op. 26
> *Sonata in C-sharp Minor*, op. 27, no. 2

Schumann, *Faschingsschwank aus Wien*, op. 26

Chopin, *Ballade in A-flat Major*, op. 47
> *Nocturne in D-flat Major*, op. 27, no. 2
> *Waltz in A-flat Major*, op. 34, no. 1

Mason, *Danse rustique à la gigue*, op. 16
> *Silver Spring*, op. 6
> *"Ah! Vous dirais-je maman," caprice grotesque*, [op. 22]

Reviews/Announcements of no. **691**:

"Mason's Pianoforte Recital." *Orange Journal*, 16 Mar 1878, p. 5, col. 3.
An announcement of the recital.

"Pianoforte Recital by Dr. Mason." *Orange Chronicle*, 16 Mar 1878, p. [3], col. 3.
Announces the recital.

"Dr. Mason's Recital." *Orange Journal*, 23 Mar 1878, p. 5, col. 4.

Dr. Mason introduced the performances [of the Beethoven sonatas] by a brief account of the Sonata as a distinct form of musical composition. . . . Having given three specimens of the style of this great master, Schumann was introduced. . . . Dr. Mason said that Schumann's compositions were a step below Beethoven's. His music belonged a little less to the intellectual and a little more to the romantic school; that the step was a short one, but it was distinctly marked.

"Pianoforte Recital." *Orange Chronicle*, 23 Mar 1878, p. [3], col. 2.

It is needless to speak in detail of the rendering of each selection. All were treated with the utmost skill and a degree of expression was given them that was remarkable even for so thorough an artist as Mr. Mason.

692   New Haven, Conn., Music Hall, 27 Mar 1878

Thomas Orchestra — Theodore Thomas

Mozart, *Concerto in E-flat Major for Two Pianos*, K. 316a
Samuel Simons Sanford, second pianist

Mason, *Silver Spring*, op. 6

Reviews/Announcements of no. **692**:

"Thomas Concert." *New Haven Evening Register*, 26 Mar 1878, p. [4], col. 1.
Announces the concert.

. . . [in] one of the principal attractions of the evening, namely, Mozart's grand concerto in E flat, the piano parts [will be] sustained by Dr. William Mason and Samuel E. Sanford, and accompanied by the orchestra.

"Thomas Concert." *New Haven Evening Register*, 27 Mar 1878, p. [4], col. 2.
Announces the concert.

"The Thomas Concert." *Morning Journal and Courier* (New Haven), 28 Mar 1878, p. [3], col. 8.

One of the best things of the evening was the pianoforte playing by Dr. Mason and Mr. Sanford, who interpreted the Mozart Concerto in a very effective manner, to the delight of all listeners. The solo by Dr. Mason was a delicious piece of work, and aroused much enthusiasm.

693   Orange, N.J., First Presbyterian Church, 26 Mar 1879

Solo recital sponsored by the New England Society of Orange

Scarlatti, *Sonatas in G Major, E Minor, and G Major*

J. S. Bach, *Prelude and Fugue in C-sharp Major*, WTC

Beethoven, *Sonata in E-flat Major*, op. 31, no. 3

Schubert, *Impromptu in A-flat Major*, op. 90, no. 4

Schumann, *Kreisleriana*, op. 16, nos. 2 & 8

Chopin, *Tarantella in A-flat Major*, op. 43
    Nocturne in F-sharp Major, op. 15, no. 2
    Nocturne in G Major, op. 37, no. 2
    Polonaise in A-flat Major, op. 53

Joseph Raff, *Étude mélodique in A Major*, op. 130, no. 2
    Minuetto in B-flat Major, op. 126, no. 1

Liszt, *Réminiscences de "Lucia di Lammermoor"*

Reviews/Announcements of no. **693**:

"New England Society's Entertainments." *Orange Journal*, 22 Mar 1879, p. 5, col. 3.

    Includes an announcement of Mason's recital.

        The demand for tickets will no doubt be unusually brisk, Dr. Mason's mastery of the piano being so well known, that the simple announcement of his appearance in public is sufficient to interest every lover of music in the city.

"Pianoforte Recital by Mr. Mason." *Orange Chronicle*, 22 Mar 1879, p. [3], col. 2.

    Announces Mason's recital.

"Dr. Mason's Pianoforte Recitals." *Orange Journal*, 29 Mar 1879, p. 4, col. 5.

    A long, favorable review.

"Mason Piano Recital." *Orange Chronicle*, 29 Mar 1879, p. [3], col. 2.

        These pianoforte recitals have given the people of Orange a rare opportunity to listen to a fine class of musical works played in a most thoroughly artistic and admirable style, and at the same time they have afforded them the chance of studying and comparing the various composers . . . from the earliest to the present day. Such an opportunity is rarely afforded any class of persons, and would be regarded by many artists and amateurs as one of the few choice opportunities of their lives.

694   Farmington, Conn., 6 Dec 1883

Pianoforte Conversazione

Handel, *Suite in F Minor*

Beethoven, *Sonata in D Major*, op. 28

Schubert, *Impromptu in G-flat Major*, op. 90, no. 3

Schumann, *Faschingsschwank aus Wien*, op. 26

Chopin, *Nocturne in G Major*, op. 37, no. 2
 Ballade in A-flat Major, op. 47

Anton Rubinstein, *Portrait from Kamennoi-Ostrow*, op. 10, no. 22

Mason, *Dance Caprice*, op. 36
 Serenata, op. 39
 Minuet, op. 43
 Melody, op. 40
 Berceuse, op. 34
 Romance-Idyl, op. 42
 Amité pour amitié: Morceau de salon, op. 4 (arr. for four hands by Karl Klauser)

695 Orange, N.J., 7 Dec 1883

Pianoforte Conversazione

J. S. Bach, selections from the Suites:
 Gavotte in G Major
 Menuett in G Minor
 Passepied in E Minor
 Sarabande in E Minor
 Gavotte in D Minor
 Bourrée in A Minor
 Gigue in B-flat Major
 Gavotte in G Minor
 Bourrée in G Major
 Gavotte in D Major

Gluck, *Gavotte from the Ballet of "Don Juan"*

Beethoven, *Sonata in E Minor*, op. 90

Schumann, *Intermezzo*, op. 4, no. 2
 Kreisleriana, op. 16, nos. 2, 4, 6, 8

Chopin, *Nocturne in F-sharp Major*, op. 15, no. 2
 Impromptu in A-flat Major, op. 29

Joseph Raff, *Minuetto in B-flat Major*, op. 126, no. 1
 Étude mélodique in A Major, op. 130, no. 2

Mason, *Monody*, op. 13
 Romance-Etude, op. 32

Dance Antique, op. 38

Scherzo, op. 41

"Ah! Vous dirais-je maman," caprice grotesque, [op. 22]

696   Freehold, N.J., Young Ladies' Seminary Hall, 13 May 1884

Caecilian Club Entertainment — Mason Piano Conversazione

J. S. Bach, selections from the Suites:

> *Gavotte in G Major*
> *Menuett in B-flat Major*
> *Passepied in E Minor*
> *Gavotte in D Minor*
> *Bourrée in A Minor*
> *Gavotte in G Minor*
> *Bourrée in G Major*

Beethoven, *Sonata in C-sharp Minor*, op. 27, no. 2

Schubert, *Impromptu in G-flat Major*, op. 90, no. 3

Schumann, *Faschingsschwank aus Wien*, op. 26

Chopin, *Nocturne in F-sharp Major*, op. 15, no. 2

> *Nocturne in G Major*, op. 37, no. 2
> *Ballade in A-flat Major*, op. 47

Mason, *Serenata*, op. 39

> *Spring-Dawn: Mazurka-Caprice*, op. 20
> *Romance-Idyl*, op. 42
> *Danse rustique à la gigue*, op. 16
> *Berceuse*, op. 34
> *Silver Spring*, op. 6
> *"Ah! Vous dirais-je maman," caprice grotesque*, [op. 22]

Review of no. **696**:

"From the County Seat." *Red Bank Register*, 14 May 1884, p. [1], col. 7.

> Includes a review (signed "TELEPHONE") of Mason's recital.

> > Dr. Mason and daughter, of New York city, gave a very select instrumental concert . . . on Tuesday evening. . . . After the concert he gave a short talk on the proper use of a piano or other musical instrument.

4

Catalog of Compositions and Editions

Instrumental Music

Keyboard Works with Opus Number

ALL WORKS ARE FOR SOLO PIANO UNLESS OTHERWISE INDICATED.

TITLES OF PUBLISHED WORKS ARE ITALICIZED;
TITLES OF MANUSCRIPT WORKS ARE IN ROMAN TYPE.

697-98   *Deux Romances sans paroles*, op. 1, nos. 1 & 2

697   No. 1 of *Deux Romances sans paroles*, op. 1

A review by Dwight of this work (see citation below) indicates that it was published (probably in 1845) by G. P. Reed of Boston; no copy located. Also published (n.d.) by S. Brainard's Sons, Cleveland; PP.

In ABA form with coda. Lyrical conjunct melodies set against light, transparent accompaniments. Irregular phrase lengths in B section. Occasional mild chromaticism. Delicate close. Moderately difficult. Duration: ca. 2 minutes.

Review of no. **697**:

DWIGHT, John Sullivan. "Musical Review." *Harbinger* 2/19 (18 Apr 1846): 298-99.

> Amongst the swarm of songs, waltzes, marches, rondos, *rifaciamentos* of opera airs, and all manner of cunningly contrived and cheap effects, now put forth as original music, it is refreshing to meet something that may be called a *composition*, — something which has in it a touch of artistic feeling and refinement, something which, while it is simple in

its means and modest in its pretensions, yet bears the marks of study, and testifies to acquaintance with deep styles, and with masters of whom the frivolous are afraid.

698   No. 2 of *Deux Romances sans paroles*, op. 1

Presto.
Con Spirito.

Published in 1845 by G. P. Reed, Boston; MH-Mu, PP.

In ABA form with 16-measure introduction. Generally conjunct, single-note melodic lines with broken-chord accompaniments. Section B offers only slight melodic contrast. Simple rhythmic structures with consistent use of ♩♪♩ or ♩.♩. in melody and ♩♪♩ in bass line. Modulations limited to plus one or minus two flats. Moderately difficult. Duration: ca. 2 minutes.

Review of no. **698**:

DWIGHT, John Sullivan. "Musical Review." *Harbinger* 2/21 (2 May 1846): 333-34.

> Mr. Mason in this second of his "Romances without Words" has kept the promise of the first. It is a Presto movement, full of life and grace, and not without a certain quaintness in its harmony, (as for instance, the alternating between the chords of E flat major and of C flat major) which seems dictated more by feeling than by any whim of trying experiments.

699   *Les Perles de rosée: Mélodie variée,* [op. 2]

Published in 1849 by Schuberth & Co., Hamburg and New York; CtY. New edition, rev., cor., and fingered by Karl Klauser, published as op. 5 in 1868 by J. Schuberth & Co., Leipzig and New York; MH-Mu. Holograph score not located, but evidence suggests that the preliminary MS was entitled "La Goutte de rosée: Mélodie variée," a work performed by Mason on 10 February 1849 at a concert of the Musical Fund Society in Boston (see no. **605**). Dedication: Franz Liszt.

Theme with two variations. Basic melodic and harmonic structure of theme maintained throughout except for 4-measure extension at end of each variation; variable elements consist of figural accompaniment patterns. Chromatic scales in first variation; sweeping arpeggiated figuration in second variation; quiet close. Difficult. Duration: ca. 7 minutes.

Review of no. **699**:

"New Musical Publications." *Saroni's Musical Times* 1/36 (1 June 1850): 421.

> WE have before us a very beautiful composition. . . . It is . . . dedicated to the great Liszt. The theme is distinguished by a graceful flow of melody, and by plain and simple harmonies. The variations are extremely brilliant, and will pay well for practising them.

The review continues with an account of Mason's efforts to make certain that Liszt would approve the dedication of this work to him by sending him a copy of the manuscript through an intermediary—Julius Schuberth.

> . . . [Liszt] took the manuscript, and after looking it through, played it upon his Piano Forte; he then . . . wrote his name on the bottom of the first page, and handed the sheet back to Mr. Schuberth, . . . giving his consent to the dedication. He then . . . set [*sic*] down and again played the piece through from memory; saying, as he closed, "Tell Mr. Mason I shall remember his piece and will play it to him when I see him in Hamburgh [*sic*]."

This anecdote about Liszt is also published as "Liszt," *Choral Advocate and Singing-Class Journal* 1/2 (July 1850): 23. Mason's account of this incident is given on pp. 31-32 of his *Memories of a Musical Life* (see no. **557**).

700   *Impromptu*, op. 3

Published (n.d.) by Frederic Hofmeister, Leipzig; MH-Mu. Lists of Mason's works published in the *Etude* (see no. **498**) and the *Cyclopedia of Music and Musicians* (see no. **74**) both give an 1851 publication date. Dedication: Alexander Dreyschock.

A brilliant display piece in ABA form with introduction and coda. Rhythmic relationships more complex than in opuses 1 and 2. Reprise of section A uses finger crossings reminiscent of Chopin's *Étude* op. 10, no. 2. Sweeping fortissimo arpeggios in coda. Difficult. Duration: ca. 5 minutes.

Review of no. **700**:

"Musical Review." *Dwight's Journal of Music* 1/12 (26 June 1852): 92-93.

Reviewed jointly with Mason's *Amitié pour amitié*, op. 4.

These are graceful little compositions, with themes agreeable and characteristic, although not strikingly original, and wrought out to considerable elaborateness after the modern fantasia style. They evince true study of harmony and of the art of carrying along and interweaving individual parts.

701 *Amitié pour amitié: Morceau de salon,* op. 4

First edition not located; available evidence suggests that it was published in about 1851 by Frederic Hofmeister, Leipzig. (See *Hofmeister's Handbuch der Musikliteratur*, vol. 4, p. 135 [no. **145**], and p. 88 of Mason's *Memories of a Musical Life* [no. **557**].) Second edition, rev., cor., and fingered by the composer, published in 1854 by Nathan Richardson, Boston; DLC, NN, RPB. The second edition also published in 1883 by S. Brainard's Sons, Cleveland; DLC, MH-Mu. The second edition, arr. for four hands by Karl Klauser, published in 1883 by S. Brainard's Sons, Chicago; MH-Mu. Revised second edition published in 1892 by S. Brainard's Sons, Chicago (reprinted in *Brainard's Musical World* 29/347 [Nov 1892]: 349-55); PP. Also published in 1936 in an arrangement for violin and piano as *Lyric Poem (Amitié pour amitié)* by Harcourt, Brace & Co., New York (see Albert Wier, no. **455**). Dedication: Charles Wehle (in second edition).

Lyrical work in ABA form. Section A and abbreviated reprise focus melodic attention on duet between soprano and tenor voices. Moderately difficult. Duration: ca. 4 minutes.

Reviews of no. **701**:

See "Musical Review," cited in no. **700**.

"New Music Reviews." *New York Musical Review and Choral Advocate* 6/1 (4 Jan 1855): 16.

> This composition consists of two themes excessively lovely and melodious. The first in A flat major, the more extensively developed one, begins with a quiet and dignified movement. . . . The second, in D flat major, is imbued with pensiveness and *reverie*, and not less tasteful than the first. Both form a beautiful *ensemble* and a true gem.

702   *Valse de bravoure,* op. 5

Published as op. 15 in 1854 by Nathan Richardson, Boston; CtY, DLC, NRU-Mus, PP. Early date of publication makes it highly probable that Richardson's opus number was a printing error; both the *Etude* (see no. **498**) and *A Handbook of American Music* (see no. **137**) list the work as opus 5. Composer's preliminary MS entitled "Le Rossignal. Capriccio en forme de valse pour le pianoforte" (dated Saturday, 27 May 1848); DLC. Dedication: Mary Isabella Webb.

Brilliant work in ABA form with introduction and coda. Wide variety of melodic material set against traditional waltz bass accompaniment. Staccato chords, octaves, broken-chord figuration, trills, cadenzas. Climactic coda in vivace tempo. Difficult. Duration: ca. 8 minutes.

Reviews of no. **702**:

"Musical Intelligence, Boston, Sept. 25." *New York Musical Review and Choral Advocate* 5/20 (28 Sept 1854): 338-39.

> It is written in brilliant waltz style, and yet it is kept somewhat strict with regard to form.

"New Sheet Music." *Boston Daily Evening Transcript*, 27 Sept 1854, p. [2], col. 3.

> A favorable review.

703 *Silver Spring*, op. 6

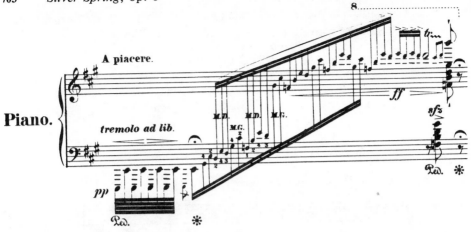

Published in 1856 by Firth, Pond & Co., New York; CtY, DLC, RPB. Reprint of above edition, published (n.d.) by Wm. A. Pond & Co., New York; MB, NN, NRU-Mus, PP, RPB; copyright renewal edition, published in 1884 by Wm. A. Pond & Co., New York; DLC, MH-Mu. New edition, rev. by the composer, published in 1885 by Wm. A. Pond & Co., New York; CtY, DLC, IU, NN, RPB. New edition, ed. and fingered by Louis Oesterle, published in 1906 by G. Schirmer, New York; DLC. New edition, rev. and fingered by Thos. à Becket, published in 1907 by Hatch Music Co., Philadelphia; DLC. New edition, ed. Robert Goldbeck, published in 1907 by Theodore Presser, Philadelphia; DLC. New edition, ed. and fingered by M. Greenwald, published in 1907 by Century Music Publishing Co., New York; DLC, PP. New edition, ed. John Orth, published in 1907 by Oliver Ditson Co., Boston; DLC. Facsimiles of Wm. A. Pond reprint of 1856 Firth, Pond & Co. edition published in *Nineteenth-Century American Piano Music*, 239-51 (see no. **119**) and *Democratic Souvenirs*, 65-77 (see no. **167**). Holograph score of 1856 edition; DLC. (Mason may already have performed an early version of this work in New York in 1855 under the title "Pensée fugitive"; see no. **625**.) Dedication: Wm. V. Wallace.

In ABA form with introduction and coda. Web of rapid arpeggio figuration using interlocking hand technique woven around a slow-moving cantabile melody. Exploitation of extreme registers of keyboard; wide variety of pedal effects. Difficult. Duration: ca. 6 minutes.

704-06   *Trois Valses de salon*, op. 7, nos. 1-3

Published in 1856 by Firth, Pond & Co., New York; DLC, PP (no. 3 only). Reprint of above edition, published (n.d.) by Wm. A. Pond & Co., New York; CtY, MH-Mu (no. 2 only), RPB (nos. 1 and 3 only); copyright renewal edition, published in 1884 by Wm. A. Pond & Co., New York; DLC. No. 2 also published (n.d.) as *Fleurs d'été: Valse brillante* by Hopwood & Crew, London; British Library. Dedications (American editions only): F. G. Hill (no. 1), Gustav Satter (no. 2), Josephine Hutèt (no. 3).

704   *Rien que la valse*, no. 1 of *Trois Valses de salon*, op. 7

In ABACDA form with introduction and coda. Single- and double-note melody with waltz bass accompaniment in A sections; bass countermelodies in section B. Scalar melodic material in sections C and D. Moderately difficult. Duration: ca. 3 minutes.

705   *Toujours*, no. 2 of *Trois Valses de salon*, op. 7

In loose ABA form with brief introduction and coda. More lyrical than op. 7, no. 1 above. Single-line melody with staccato chord afterbeats set against broken-chord bass line in middle section. Interlocking arpeggio passages in coda. Moderately difficult. Duration: ca. 4 minutes.

706   *Pour la dernière fois*, no. 3 of *Trois Valses de salon*, op. 7

In ABACA form with coda. Wide range of melodic styles effectively contrasting legato and staccato articulations. Sweeping arpeggios and octaves in brilliant coda. Difficult. Duration: ca. 5 minutes.

707-09   *Trois Préludes*, op. 8, nos. 1-3

Published in 1856 by Firth, Pond & Co., New York; DLC, PP. Reprint of above edition, published (n.d.) by Wm. A. Pond & Co., New York; MH-Mu; copyright renewal edition, published in 1884 by Wm. A. Pond & Co., New York; DLC. Holograph scores of no. 1 (entitled "Sportiveness," the second of two "Little Pieces"; dated 21 August 1855), no. 2 (entitled "Andante Cantabile"; dated Silver Spring Villa, Orange, N.J., Sunday afternoon, 19 August 1855), and no. 3 (entitled "Impatience," the first of two "Little Pieces"; dated 8 July 1855); DLC. Dedication: Carl Bergmann.

707   No. 1 of *Trois Préludes*, op. 8

A short, monothematic work in AA′ form with coda. Instrumentally conceived melodic material consists mainly of arpeggio and broken-chord figurations. Nearly perpetual sixteenth-note motion. Moderately difficult. Duration: ca. 1 minute.

Review of no. **707**:

LISZT, Franz. Letter to William Mason, Rome, 26 May 1869. Published in Liszt's *Letters* . . . , collected and ed. Ida Maria Lipsius [La Mara], trans. Constance Bach, vol. 2, pp. 177-78. New York: Charles Scribner's Sons, 1894.

> Liszt evaluates the opus 8 *Préludes* as well as several other of Mason's compositions.

> > The Etude de Concert (Op. 9) and the Valse Caprice (Op. 17) are of a distinguished style and make a good effect. I shall also sincerely praise the 3 Préludes (Op. 8) and the two Ballades, but with some reservation. The first Ballade appears to me somewhat cut short; it wants I know not what at the beginning and towards the middle . . . of something needed to make the melody stand out; and the pastorale of the 2nd Ballade . . . figures like a too-cheap piece of "padding." . . . And, since I am in the vein for criticising [*sic*], let me ask why you call your "Ah! vous dirai-je, Maman" — "Caprice grotesque?" Apart from the fact that the grotesque style should not intrude into music, that title is unjust to the clever imitations and harmonies of the piece, very charming by the way, and which it would be more suitable to entitle "Divertissement" or "Variazione scherzose."

> Also published in Mason's *Memories of a Musical Life*, 294-96 (see no. **557**). Holograph letter is with the William Mason Collection of Autographs of Musicians, NNC (see no. **1016**).

708   No. 2 of *Trois Préludes*, op. 8

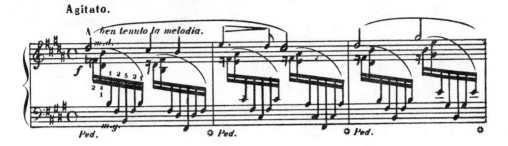

Brief work in through-composed form. Lyrical melody with broken-chord accompaniment. Abrupt phrase endings. Modulations to distant keys. Moderately difficult. Duration: ca. 1 minute.

Review of no. **708:**

See letter by Franz Liszt, cited in no. **707.**

709   No. 3 of *Trois Préludes*, op. 8

Very short (twenty-six measures), rapid work in loose AA′ form with coda. All melodic material derived from first four measures. Transparent two-voice contrapuntal texture with imitation, sequences, and invertible counterpoint. Moderately difficult. Duration: ca. one-half minute.

Review of no. **709:**

See letter by Franz Liszt, cited in no. **707.**

710   *Étude de concert*, op. 9

Published in 1856 by William Hall & Son, New York; DLC, MH-Mu.
Dedication: Louis Moreau Gottschalk.

A brilliant work in loose ABA form requiring both power and delicacy.
Theme in thumb of left hand against perpetual double-note accompaniment
(at intervals of fifths and sixths) in the right hand. Thunderous martellato
conclusion. Difficult. Duration: ca. 4 minutes.

Review of no. **710:**

See letter by Franz Liszt, cited in no. **707.**

711   *Lullaby*, op. 10

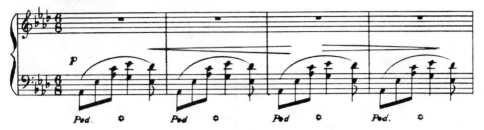

Subtitled *Cradle Song for the Piano*. Published in 1857 by Firth, Pond & Co., New York; CtY, DLC, MB, NN. Copyright renewal edition, published in 1885 by Oliver Ditson & Co., Boston; DLC, MH-Mu. Also published in *Music in America*, 334-36 (see no. **214)** and *The America Book for Piano*, 19-21 (see no. **75)**. Poem at head of composition:

> Like a gentle Zephyr,
> Floating, floating by,
> Ev'ry sorrow healing,
> Hushing ev'ry cry;

> Full of love and kindness,
> Stopping ev'ry sigh,
> Comes a mother [*sic*] soothing
> Lullaby.

Dedication: Geo. L. Babcock.

A gentle, lyrical work in ABCABC form with introduction and coda. Cantabile melody set against continuous 1-measure accompaniment pattern of alternating tonic and dominant harmonies. Modulations restricted to plus or minus one flat and relative minors. Reminiscent of Chopin's *Berceuse*, op. 57. Easy. Duration: ca. 2 minutes.

Review of no. **711**:

"New Publications." *Dwight's Journal of Music* 11/12 (20 June 1857): 94.

> This is by no means so very difficult as earlier publications of the young pianist. . . . The tune is singing and graceful, the treatment clear and artistic, and the piece quite a little gem.

712   *Concert Galop*, op. 11

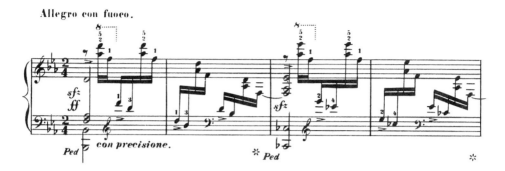

Published in 1862 by Firth, Pond & Co., New York; DLC, NRU-Mus, RPB. Reprint of above edition, published (n.d.) by Wm. A. Pond & Co., New York; PP, RPB; copyright renewal edition, published in 1890 by Wm. A. Pond & Co., New York; DLC, MH-Mu. Dedication: Sebastian Bach Mills.

Spirited display piece in large ABACA form with introduction and coda. Traditional galop dotted rhythms especially prominent in A sections. Wide variety of pianistic effects, including octaves, scales, broken chords, and arpeggios. Stunning coda in tremolo chords and interlocking octaves. Difficult. Duration: ca. 5 minutes.

713 *Ballade*, op. 12

Published in 1863 by Wm. A. Pond & Co., New York; DLC; copyright renewal editions, published in 1885 and 1891 by Wm. A. Pond & Co., New York; DLC (1885 ed.), MH-Mu (1891 ed.). Holograph score of an arrangement by Mason for piano (dated Orange, Friday, 30 January 1885) and organ (dated 29 January 1885); DLC. Although no copy has been located, the arrangement for piano and organ was apparently published by Wm. A. Pond & Co., for it is listed on the collective title page of the 1885 and 1891 copyright renewal editions of the solo piano version of opus 12. Dedication: Robert Goldbeck.

In ABA form. Opening and closing sections in tranquil, cantabile style; middle section more energetic with sudden opposition of contrasting styles and use of imitative techniques. Entire work permeated by ♩. ♪ ♪ ♪ rhythmic pattern. Chromatic harmonies, especially in B section. Moderately difficult. Duration: ca. 5 minutes.

Review of no. **713**:

See letter by Franz Liszt, cited in no. **707**.

714   *Monody,* op. 13

Published in 1865 by Wm. A. Pond & Co., New York; DLC, MH-Mu, NN, PP; copyright renewal edition, published in 1892 by Wm. A. Pond & Co., New York; CtY. Published in fingered edition in 1907 by Wm. A. Pond & Co., New York; DLC. Also published in 1907 by Theodore Presser, Philadelphia; DLC. Dedication: Wm. Scharfenberg.

Languid work in **ABA** form with coda. Begins with cantabile melody supported by broken-chord figurations. Material in section B closely derived from opening. Varied reprise, including brief, stormy cadenza with interlocking hand technique. Moderately difficult. Duration: ca. 3 minutes.

715   *Polka gracieuse,* op. 14

Published in 1861 by Root & Cady, Chicago; DLC, NN, RPB. Reprint of above edition, published (n.d.) by S. Brainard's Sons, Cleveland; MH-Mu, PP.

In ABA form with coda. Light, festive mood. Staccato articulations; short, disjunct melodic motives; dazzling coda. Moderately difficult. Duration: ca. 4 minutes.

716   *Ballade et barcarole*, op. 15

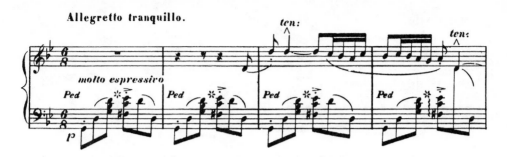

Published in 1864 by Wm. A. Pond & Co., New York; DLC, MH-Mu, NN, PP. Holograph score (dated 18 September 1859, Orange, N.J.); DLC. The work is titled *Ballade et barcarole* on title page; title is reordered to *Barcarole et ballade* at the head of the first page of music in the published score; MS is without title or opus number. Dedication: Theodore Thomas.

In large three-part (barcarole, ballade, barcarole) form. Single-line melody in barcarole accompanied by traditional rocking bass pattern. Homophonic texture (almost hymnlike) in ballade. Relatively conservative harmonic vocabulary. Moderately difficult. Duration: ca. 7 minutes.

Review of no. **716:**

See letter by Franz Liszt, cited in no. **707.**

717 *Danse rustique à la gigue,* op. 16

Published in 1860 by Firth, Pond & Co., New York; DLC, NN, NRU-Mus, PP, RPB. Reprint of above edition, published (n.d.) by Wm. A. Pond & Co., New York; CtY, MH-Mu, NN, PP, RPB; copyright renewal edition, published in 1888 by Wm. A. Pond & Co., New York; DLC. New edition, rev. by the composer, published in 1888 by Wm. A. Pond & Co., New York; CtY, DLC, RPB; also published in 1908 by Theodore Presser, Philadelphia (reprinted in *Etude* 27/6 [June 1909]: 394-96); DLC; also published in 1910 by G. Schirmer, New York; DLC, PP. New edition, arr. for four hands by P. W. Oren, published in 1909 by Theodore Presser, Philadelphia (reprinted in *Etude* 27/2 [Feb 1909]: 102-05); DLC. New edition, arr. for four hands by Wm. Dressler, published in 1910 by Wm. A. Pond & Co., New York; DLC, NN. Holograph score of first edition (dated 21 September 1859, South Orange, N.J.); DLC. Dedication: Theodore Hagen.

Light, rollicking, perpetual-motion piece in ABA form. Melodic material made up of short, 2-measure motives set against staccato-chord accompaniments. Sudden dynamic contrasts. Moderately difficult. Duration: ca. 3 minutes.

718   *Valse-Caprice*, op. 17

Published in 1865 by Wm. A. Pond & Co., New York; DLC, MH-Mu, NN, PP; copyright renewal edition, published in 1893 by Wm. A. Pond & Co., New York; DLC. Dedication: Henry C. Timm.

In large ABA form with coda. Pensive, cantabile melody shifts back and forth between soprano and bass voices. Opening and closing sections firmly grounded in G-sharp minor; extensive modulations in middle section. Waltz characteristics highly stylized. Moderately difficult. Duration: ca. 7 minutes.

Review of no. **718**:

See letter by Franz Liszt, cited in no. **707**.

719   *Bittle-It Polka*, op. 18

Published in 1860 by Firth, Pond & Co., New York; DLC. Reprint of above edition, published (n.d.) by Firth, Son & Co., New York; PP. Copyright renewal edition, published in 1888 by Oliver Ditson & Co., Boston; DLC, MH-Mu. Also published in 1883 as *La Ravissante: Polka de salon* by Les Fils de B. Schott, Mainz; DLC. Dedication: Georgie (probably Mason's son George).

In ABA form. Stereotyped polka rhythmic patterns. Modulations restricted to plus or minus one flat and relative minors. Predominantly staccato or nonlegato articulations occasionally relieved with pedal effects. Moderately difficult. Duration: ca. 4 minutes.

720-21 *Deux Rêveries*, op. 19, nos. 1 & 2

> Published in 1860 by Firth, Pond & Co., New York; CtY (no. 1 only), DLC (no. 2 only), NN (no. 1 only), NRU-Mus (no. 1 only). Reprint of above edition, published in 1889 by Oliver Ditson & Co., Boston; DLC, MH-Mu. Also reprinted (n.d.) by Firth, Son & Co., New York; PP (no. 1 only). Dedication: Mary Isabel (Mason's wife, Mary Isabella?).

720 *Au Matin*, no. 1 of *Deux Rêveries*, op. 19

> In ABA form. Musical interest in A sections sustained mainly by rhythmic interplay of triplets and eighth notes. Contrasting scherzo-like middle section. Moderately difficult. Duration: ca. 3 minutes.

721 *Au Soir*, no. 2 of *Deux Rêveries*, op. 19

> Tender, lyrical work in ABA form. Simple homophonic texture; principal melodic lines in the soprano voice with delicate countermelodies in inner voices. Lightly syncopated in A sections. Moderately difficult. Duration: ca. 2 minutes.

722 *Spring-Dawn: Mazurka-Caprice*, op. 20

Published in 1861 by C. Breusing, New York; DLC, NN, NNC. Reprint of above edition, published (n.d.) by G. Schirmer, New York; CtY, NNC, PP. Also reprinted (n.d.) by Beer & Schirmer, New York; MB, NRU-Mus. Also published (n.d.) as *Aurore de printemps: Caprice-Mazurka* by Schott Frères, Brussels; DLC. New edition, rev. and fingered by the composer, published in 1889 by G. Schirmer, New York; MH-Mu, NN, NRU-Mus, PP; also published in 1908 by Theodore Presser, Philadelphia; DLC. New edition, ed. and fingered by M. Greenwald, published in 1908 by Century Music Publishing Co., New York; DLC. Holograph score of first edition (dated 9 April 1861, 10:30 P.M.); DLC. Dedication: Carrie Webb.

Graceful work in ABA form. Figurative melodic material idiomatic to the keyboard. Lydian mode scale passages in middle section. Characteristic mazurka rhythms. Moderately difficult. Duration: ca. 4 minutes.

Review of no. **722**:

SCHWEIKHER, Frederick. "Spring-Dawn, Thoughts on a Composition by William Mason." *Musician* 4/6 (June 1899): 219.

Not a review as such. Schweikher's article is little more than a highly romanticized extramusical program he devised for Mason's piece.

723   *Spring Flower Impromptu*, op. 21

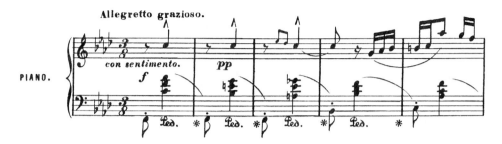

Published in 1862 by Theodore Hagen, New York; DLC. New edition, rev. by the composer, published in 1885 by G. Schirmer, New York; DLC, MH-Mu. Dedication: J. S. Jameson.

In ABA form with coda. Haunting melody with displaced accent on second beat in A sections. Use of so-called gypsy scale in section B. Subtle countermelodies and imitative effects. Moderately difficult. Duration: ca. 5 minutes.

724   *"Ah! Vous dirais-je maman," caprice grotesque,* [op. 22]

Published in 1864 by Wm. A. Pond & Co., New York; CtY, DLC, MH-Mu, PP, RPB.

Theme with three variations. Chromatic harmonies, abrupt modulations, humorous use of nonchord tones. Broken-chord accompaniment in first and third variations, sweeping scales in second variation. Cadenza with interlocking hand technique leads to pompous close in full chords. Difficult. Duration: ca. 3 minutes.

Review of no. **724**:

See letter by Franz Liszt, cited in no. **707**.

725-26 *Deux Humoresques de bal*, op. 23, nos. 1 & 2

> Published in 1866 by J. Schuberth & Co., Leipzig and New York; DLC, MH-Mu, NRU-Mus (no. 2 only), RPB (no. 2 only). Reprint of above edition, published (n.d.) by G. Schirmer, New York; PP. New and rev. edition (no. 1 rev. and fingered by Wm. Scharfenberg), published in 1885 by G. Schirmer, New York; DLC (no. 1 only; no. 2 not located). No. 1 also published (n.d.) as *L'Espiègle: Polka-Caprice* by Edwin Ashdown, London; British Library. Dedication: J. H. Leconey (Schuberth and Schirmer editions only).

725 *Polka-Caprice*, no. 1 of *Deux Humoresques de bal*, op. 23

> In ABA form with coda. Melody in dotted rhythms over chordal accompaniment alternates with two-voice canon in opening and closing sections; middle section predominantly homophonic. Abrupt modulations; short articulative units. Easy. Duration: ca. 3 minutes.

726 *Mazurka-Caprice*, no. 2 of *Deux Humoresques de bal*, op. 23

> In ABA form with coda. Heavy accents on third beat in opening and closing sections. Arpeggio and broken-chord figuration in B section revolving around the remote key of E major (and its relative minor). Use of Lydian mode. Much more energetic than op. 20 mazurka (see no. **722**). Moderately difficult. Duration: ca. 2 minutes.

727   *Rêverie poétique*, op. 24

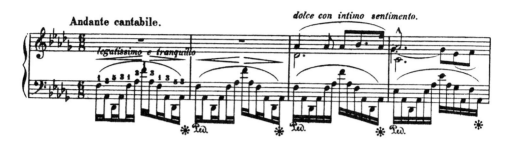

Published in 1868 by J. Schuberth & Co., Leipzig and New York; DLC, MH-Mu. Cor., rev., and fingered edition, published in 1885 by G. Schirmer, New York; CtY, DLC, PP. Quotation from Victor Hugo at head of composition:

> J'etais seul près des flots, par une nuit d'étoiles,
> Pas un nuage aux cieux, sur les mers pas de voiles,
> Mes yeux plongeaient plus loin que le monde réel,
> Et les bois, et les monts, et toute la nature
> Semblaient interroger dans un confus murmure
> Les flots des mers, les feux du ciel.

Dedication: Leonie Coudert.

In AA′ form with coda. Tranquil cantabile melody over gently undulating broken-chord pattern. Right hand double-note passages with shifting interval relationships. Effective use of extreme upper range of keyboard. Difficult. Duration: ca. 5 minutes.

728   *So-So Polka*, op. 25

Published in 1868 by Wm. A. Pond & Co., New York; DLC, MH-Mu, NN, PP; copyright renewal edition, published in 1896 by Wm. A. Pond & Co., New York; DLC. Holograph score (dated 25 September 1868); DLC. Dedication: Marion (probably Mason's son).

In ABA form with coda. Slightly more stylized than the op. 14 and 18 polkas (see nos. **715, 719**), but short articulative groupings and characteristic rhythms still prominent. Moderately difficult. Duration: ca. 3 minutes.

729-36 *Teacher and Pupil: Eight Duos for Instruction and Recreation*, op. 26, nos. 1-8

Published in 1869 by Wm. A. Pond & Co., New York; DLC, MB, MH-Mu, NN (no. 1 only), RPB (nos. 1 and 8 only). The first and fifth duos are published in *The America Book for Piano*, 26-29 (see no. **75**). The first and seventh duos are published in *Duets of Early American Music*, 20-27 (see no. **208**). Dedication: Minna (Mason's daughter).

Eight duets for student (primo) and teacher (secondo) on well-known tunes: no. 1, "Malbrook"; no. 2, "Charming Little Valley"; no. 3, "Mary Had a Little Lamb"; no. 4, "Life Let Us Cherish"; no. 5, "Sleep, Baby Sleep"; no. 6, "Baby Bye, Here's a Fly"; no. 7, "The Honest Old Miller"; no. 8, potpourri on "Buy a Broom," "Waltz" from *Der Freischütz*, "Air" from *William Tell*, and "Pretty Polly Hopkins." Each is a little gem. Primary tune in primo; harmonizations, countermelodies, etc., in secondo. Primo parts in nos. 1-7 consist of single notes in octave unison; no. 8 only slightly more complex. Primo: very easy; secondo: easy. Duration: ca. 9 minutes.

729 "Malbrook," no. 1 of *Teacher and Pupil*, op. 26

737   *Badinage*, op. 27

Published in 1870 by Koppitz, Prüfer & Co., Boston; DLC, NN. Reprint of above edition (cites the Koppitz, Prüfer & Co. copyright date as being 1869), published (n.d.) by Wm. A. Pond & Co., New York; MH-Mu, NN. Holograph score (dated 1 July 1869); DLC. Dedication: Jeanie K. Fraser.

Piano duet in ABA form with coda. Somewhat mundane melodic material; effectiveness of the work dependent upon rhythmic drive and canonic interplay between primo and secondo. Diatonic harmonies, dry sonorities, repeated note patterns. Moderately difficult. Duration: ca. 3 minutes.

738   *Valse-Impromptu*, op. 28

Published in 1869 by Koppitz, Prüfer & Co., Boston; CtY, PP, RPB. Reprint of above edition, published (n.d.) by Wm. A. Pond & Co., New York; MH-Mu, PP. Dedication: Richard Hoffman.

In large ABA form. Contrasting articulations ranging from legatissimo broken-chord melodies to marcato staccato passages. Frequent modulations. Use of upper range of keyboard. Moderately difficult. Duration: ca. 4 minutes.

739   *Pell-Mell Galop fantastique*, op. 29

Published in 1870 by Chas. Bunce, Brooklyn; CtY, MH-Mu, PP. Composer's preliminary MS entitled "Grand Galop fantastique pour le piano" (dated 25 August 1858) and pencil sketches (under the heading "'Pell-Mell' Galop fantastique") of the introduction (three separate versions) and a cadenza (not included in published work); DLC. Dedication: Carl Frommel.

In large ABA form with introduction and coda. Diatonic harmonies with a minimum of modulation; chord progressions frequently limited to alternation of tonic and dominant. Detached, crystalline sonorities, abrupt dynamic contrasts; use of extended keyboard range within short time span; interlocking tremolo chords, brilliant octaves in coda. Difficult. Duration: ca. 4 minutes.

740   *Prelude (A Minor) in Scherzo Form*, op. 30

Published in 1870 by Koppitz, Prüfer & Co., Boston: CtY, DLC, NN, NRU-Mus, PP. Reprint of above edition (cites the Koppitz, Prüfer & Co. copyright date as being 1869), published (n.d.) by Wm. A. Pond & Co., New York; MH-Mu. Holograph scores entitled "Scherzo-Prelude for Pianoforte, Op. 29" (dated Orange, 13 November 1869) and "Prelude in A minor (in Scherzo-form) for the Pianoforte, Op. 30" (dated 13 November 1869); DLC. Dedication: Lillie Merrick.

In ABA form with coda. Perpetual broken-chord eighth-note motion in opening and closing sections. Middle section more scherzo-like with scalar patterns interrupted by staccato chords. Flowing finger legato with occasional extended hand positions. Difficult. Duration: ca. 5 minutes.

741-42 *Two Caprices*, op. 31, nos. 1 & 2

Published in 1870 by Koppitz, Prüfer & Co., Boston; DLC, MH-Mu (no. 1 only), PP (no. 2 only). Reprint of above edition (cites the Koppitz, Prüfer & Co. copyright date as being 1869), published (n.d.) by Wm. A. Pond & Co., New York; MH-Mu (no. 2 only). Facsimile of 1870 Koppitz, Prüfer & Co. edition of no. 2 published in *Nineteenth-Century American Piano Music*, 233-39 (see no. **119**). Dedication: Anna Mehlig.

741 *Scherzo*, no. 1 of *Two Caprices*, op. 31

In large ABA form with coda. Short three-note melodic motives thrown back and forth between the hands. Minimum of passage work; rapid changes in hand position. Light, clean sound; no pedaling marked until last chord. Moderately difficult. Duration: ca. 4 minutes.

742 *Novelette*, no. 2 of *Two Caprices*, op. 31

In ABA form with coda. Cantabile melody moving in stepwise motion in A sections. Generally more agitated writing in middle section with chromatic harmonies and melodic fragmentation. Short, quick scale and arpeggio passages. Moderately difficult. Duration: ca. 4 minutes.

743 *Romance-Etude*, op. 32

Published in 1871 by Wm. A. Pond & Co., New York; CtY, DLC, MH-Mu, NRU-Mus, PP; copyright renewal edition, published in 1899 by Wm. A. Pond & Co., New York; DLC, NN, PP. Holograph score; DLC. Dedication: Charles W. Force.

In ABABA form with introduction and coda. Melody in thirds accompanied by sweeping four-octave scales in section A and by arpeggiated broken chords in section B. Use of so-called gypsy scale. Canonic writing in introduction and coda. Difficult. Duration: ca. 3 minutes.

744 *La Sabotière: Danse aux sabots*, op. 33

Published in 1871 by Oliver Ditson & Co., Boston; DLC, MH-Mu, PP. Dedication: Leila L. Morse.

In large ABA form with coda. Lilting melody in opening and closing sections with chordal accompaniment figure. Section B dominated by rhythmic (♫♫ ♩) accompaniment pattern. Moderately difficult. Duration: ca. 5 minutes.

745   *Berceuse*, op. 34

Published in 1871 by Wm. A. Pond & Co., New York; DLC, MH-Mu, NRU-Mus; copyright renewal edition, published in 1899 by Wm. A. Pond & Co., New York; DLC. New edition, rev. by the composer, published in 1896 by Wm. A. Pond & Co., New York; CtY, DLC, PP. Dedication: Frederick Wrisley.

In ABAB form with the A sections functioning as an introduction and interlude. Material of B section is basically monothematic, a single motive being subjected to various modifications as the music modulates from key to key. Accompanying chord patterns alternate tonic and dominant harmonies. Moderately difficult. Duration: ca. 3 minutes.

Review of no. **745**:

MATHEWS, William Smythe Babcock. "William Mason's Berceuse." *Musical Independent* 3/35 (Sept 1871): 136.

> Includes musical examples. A favorable review.

> > The bass figure is adhered to throughout the piece, except on page 9, where it is relieved by the recurrence of the introduction. But all danger of monotony is obviated by the unexpected yet agreeable modulations which everywhere meet us, and in the management of these, no man is more skillful than Mr. Mason.

746-48   *Three Characteristic Sketches*, op. 35, nos. 1-3

> Published in 1876 by Edward Schuberth & Co., New York; CtY (no. 1 only), DLC, MH-Mu. Holograph score (entitled "Characteristic Pieces for Pianoforte"); DLC. Dedication: Henry Mason.

746   *Fantasy*, no. 1 of *Three Characteristic Sketches*, op. 35

In ABA form. Primary melody contained in upper notes of chords played with alternating hand technique. Four-note rhythmic ostinato used throughout the piece. Easy. Duration: ca. 1 minute.

747   *Contentment*, no. 2 of *Three Characteristic Sketches*, op. 35

In ABA form. Homophonic texture with lyric melodic material in opening and closing sections. Rapid modulations and imitative writing in middle section. Steady eighth-note motion throughout the piece. Easy. Duration: ca. 3 minutes.

748   *Whims*, no. 3 of *Three Characteristic Sketches*, op. 35

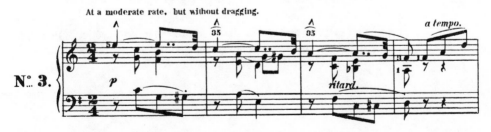

Entitled "Irresolutions" in the MS. In ABA form. Conjunct melodic material, often moving by whole or half steps. Chromatic harmonies. Frequent ritards. Easy. Duration: ca. 3 minutes.

749   *Dance Caprice*, op. 36

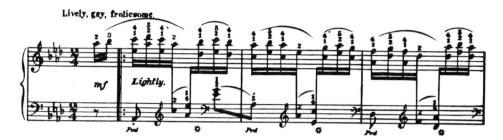

Published in 1882 by Edward Schuberth & Co., New York; CtY, DLC, IU, MB, MH-Mu, NNC, PP. Dedication: Jessie Pinney.

In ABA form with coda. Continuous sixteenth-note motion with subtle modifications in length of phrase groupings. Limited contrast between sections. Interlocking double-note passages. Buildup of sonorous sound masses; includes Mason's first use of the sostenuto pedal. Moderately difficult. Duration: ca. 4 minutes.

750   *Toccata*, op. 37

Published in 1882 by Edward Schuberth & Co., New York; CtY, DLC, IU, MB, MH-Mu, NNC, PP. Dedication: Agnes Morgan.

In ABA form with coda. A study in octaves for the right hand in the opening and closing sections and for the left hand in the middle section. Principal melodic material in upper notes of accompanying chords. Brilliant perpetual-motion effect. Difficult. Duration: ca. 3 minutes.

751 *Dance Antique*, op. 38

Published in 1882 by Edward Schuberth & Co., New York; CtY, DLC, IU, MB, MH-Mu, PP. Also published in *Piano Music in Nineteenth Century America*, vol. 1, pp. 25-29 (see no. **142**). Also published (n.d.) as *Danse antique* by Edwin Ashdown, London; British Library. Also published (n.d.) as *Danse antique* by Patey & Willis, London; British Library. Also published (n.d.) as *Danse antique* by Robert Cocks & Co., London; British Library. Composer's pencil sketch of measures 1-4, preliminary MS (dated 27 February 1882), and completed MS (dated 28 February 1882); DLC. Dedication: Mary Wilhelmine Mason (in Schuberth edition only; in preliminary MS: Alice W. Heald).

In ABA form. Marchlike theme set in simple, transparent texture. Extensive use of imitative writing. Diatonic harmonies; modulations restricted to relative and parallel minors. Easy. Duration: ca. 3 minutes.

752 *Melody*, op. 40

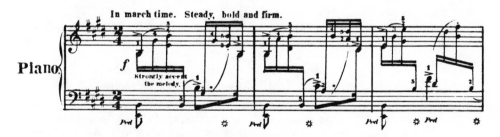

Published in 1882 by Edward Schuberth & Co., New York; CtY, DLC, IU, MB, MH-Mu, NNC, NRU-Mus, PP. Dedication: Alice W. Heald.

Constructed in loose AA' form. Limited melodic and textural contrast. Warm, lyrical melody played by thumbs of both hands in alternation. Frequent use of Neapolitan relationship. Moderately difficult. Duration: ca. 2 minutes.

753   *Scherzo*, op. 41

Published in 1882 by Edward Schuberth & Co., New York; CtY, DLC, IU, MB, MH-Mu, PP. Dedication: Wm. H. Sherwood.

In large ABA form with coda. Biting staccato in opening themes. Section B more lyrical but still scherzando in character, building up to an imposing climax in heavy chords. Double-note and octave passages; wide variety of articulations; profuse performance directions. Difficult. Duration: ca. 5 minutes.

754   *Romance-Idyl*, op. 42

Published in 1882 by Edward Schuberth & Co., New York; CtY, DLC, IU, MB, MH-Mu, NNC, PP. Holograph score; DLC. Dedication: Imogene Eidlitz.

In large ABA form with coda. Study in voicing; the melody in the opening section and reprise is played by the fifth finger of the right hand followed by the thumbs of both hands in alternation. Use of low register in middle section. Extensive use of sostenuto pedal. Moderately difficult. Duration: ca. 4 minutes.

755   *Minuet*, op. 43

Published in 1882 by Edward Schuberth & Co., New York; CtY, DLC, MH-Mu, PP. Composer's preliminary pencil sketch of measures 73-84 and completed MS (dated Saturday, 30 September 1882); DLC. Dedication: Samuel S. Sanford.

In ABA form with coda. Majestic opening theme set in homophonic texture gives way to two-voice canon over a free bass. Section B has extensive canonic writing at the octave. Moderately difficult. Duration: ca. 5 minutes.

Review of no. **755**:

"Review of New Music." *Musical Courier* 6/1 (3 Jan 1883): 4.

> . . . a somewhat complicated and labored species of "Minuet," but it is a sterling composition, and can be recommended to persons in search of a novelty.

756-57   *Two Album Leaves*, op. 45, nos. 1 & 2

Published in 1895 by G. Schirmer, New York; DLC, IU, NN, PP. Holograph score of no. 1; DLC. Facsimile MS of no. 1 published in *Music* 3 (Mar 1893): 580-81. Dedications: Marie (no. 1), Martha (no. 2); probably Marie and Martha Walther, two of Mason's students.

756   No. 1 of *Two Album Leaves*, op. 45

In AA' form with coda. A delicate miniature in generally homophonic texture with scattered imitative sections. Irregular phrase lengths; abrupt modulations. Easy. Duration: ca. 1 minute.

757   No. 2 of *Two Album Leaves*, op. 45

Short, lyrical work in ABA form. Bell-like sonorities set against legato, conjunct lines. Chromatic harmonies in middle section. Easy. Duration: ca. 1½ minutes.

758-59   *Two Pianoforte Pieces*, op. 46, nos. 1 & 2

Published in 1895 by Theodore Presser, Philadelphia; CtY (no. 2 only), DLC, IU, NN (no. 2 only), PP. Also published in 1895 by Weekes & Co., London; British Library. Excerpt from no. 1 published in *Etude* 13/3 (Mar 1895): 16. Holograph score of no. 2 (dated 17 December 1894); CtY. Dedication: Madeline Buck (in Presser edition only).

758   *Toccatina*, no. 1 of *Two Pianoforte Pieces*, op. 46

In ABA form. Perpetual-motion chord study with melody voiced by thumbs in alternation. Mason's instructions to play the thumbs as legato as possible and the accompanying harmonies somewhat staccato seem impractical at the required tempo. Difficult. Duration: ca. 2 minutes.

Review of no. **758**:

"Reviews and Notices." *Music* 8 (June 1895): 222-24.

> Includes a review of Mason's op. 46.

>> The first of these is a bravura study in which the melody occurs as a tremolo between the two thumbs in a manner essentially new.

> The reviewer continues:

>> The Prelude in F [op. 46, no. 2] is a short piece, an octave study, splendidly done and capable of great effect.

759   *Prelude in F*, no. 2 of *Two Pianoforte Pieces*, op. 46

A short, fiery octave study in through-composed form. Most of the octave motion is limited to diatonic or chromatic scale patterns. Use of extreme registers of the keyboard. Difficult. Duration: ca. 1 minute.

Review of no. **759**:

See "Reviews and Notices," cited in no. **758**.

760   *Prélude mélodique,* op. 47

Published in 1895 by G. Schirmer, New York; NN, PP. Also published in 1895 by Weekes & Co., London; British Library. Dedication: Martha Walther.

In ABA form with coda. Figurative melody in 12-measure phrases in opening and closing sections. Long-lined cantabile melody with broken-chord accompaniment in section B. Abrupt shifts in register. Brilliant broken chords in coda. Moderately difficult. Duration: ca. 2½ minutes.

761   *Amourette,* op. 48

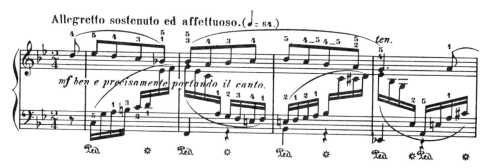

Published in 1896 by G. Schirmer, New York; DLC, NN. Holograph score; DLC. Composer's MS of first three measures (dated 2 February 1895); NN (cataloged as "Album leaf"). Dedication: A. Hermione Biggs.

In large ABA form. Cantabile melody accompanied by broken chords and scales in opening and closing sections. Variety of textures in section B, including choralelike four-part harmonization. Some tonal instability due to frequent modulations and chromaticism. Improvisatory in character. Numerous tempo changes. Moderately difficult. Duration: ca. 4 minutes.

Review of no. **761**:

"Reviews and Notices: Amourette, op. 48. . . ." *Music* 13 (Jan 1898): 401.

> . . . a strange and interesting composition in which a few leading ideas appear and disappear in all kinds of unexpected places; and yet, on the whole, when well played, it has a certain kind of poetry in it.

762 *Mazurka brillante,* op. 49

Published in 1897 by G. Schirmer, New York; DLC, NN, PP. Dedication: Mme Szumowska-Adamowska.

In ABCABC form. Themes derived from broken-chord figures and scale patterns. Wide range of dynamics; frequent tempo fluctuations; long pedal points. Most performance directions given in English rather than Italian (a practice continued in subsequent works). Moderately difficult. Duration: ca. 4 minutes.

Review of no. **762**:

"Reviews and Notices: 'Mazurka brillante,' op. 49 . . . [and] 'Capriccio fantastico,' op. 50. . . ." *Music* 13 (Dec 1897): 263-64.

> The Mazurka is built almost entirely upon two or three motives which are turned over in a great variety of ways and in this instance takes an unusually large range of modulation.

The reviewer continues:

> The "Capriccio" . . . has a very pleasing subject indeed. . . .

763 *Capriccio fantastico,* op. 50

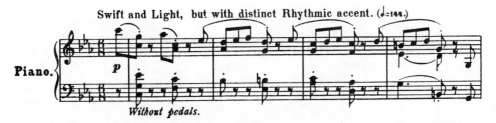

Published in 1897 by G. Schirmer, New York; CtY, DLC, NN, PP. Dedication: Edward Morris Bowman.

In ABCABC form. Capricious, instrumentally conceived themes in A and B sections; quiet cantabile melody in section C. Wide separation of hands. Broken-chord figurations. Difficult. Duration: ca. 4 minutes.

Review of no. **763**:

See "Reviews and Notices," cited in no. **762**.

764   *Improvisation*, op. 51

Published in 1900 by G. Schirmer, New York; DLC, IU, MH-Mu, NN, PP. Proof copy of 1900 G. Schirmer edition; CtY. Dedication: Edward MacDowell.

Fantasylike form in which two thematic groups are alternated in an ABABAB sequence with a brief codetta. Triplet accompaniment figure against eighth-note melody. Uses technique of silently depressing the keys of a chord while a heavy second chord is being sustained by the pedal; the pedal is then released and the pitches of the depressed keys continue to sound alone. Difficult. Duration: ca. 3 minutes.

Review of no. **764**:

"Reviews and Notices: Improvisation. . . ." *Music* 18 (June 1900): 205-06.

> It is a brilliant . . . [work], in the key of F sharp major, in style not unlike various studies of Liszt, well conceived for piano and musical.

765   *Scherzo-Caprice*, op. 52

Published in 1905 by G. Schirmer, New York; DLC, IU. Composer's preliminary MS entitled "Caprice for Pianoforte" (dated Saturday, 26 October 1901) and final MS (dated Friday, 16 September 1904); DLC. Dedication: Katharine C. Linn.

In large ABA form. Entire work based on two motives: the first a two-note slur figure moving mainly by stepwise motion and the second a descending broken-chord figure. Frequent modulations but generally diatonic harmony. Light, transparent texture. Moderately difficult. Duration: ca. 3 minutes.

Keyboard Works without Opus Number

766   *La Belle Lucie Waltz*

Published in 1846 by G. P. Reed, Boston; NN, RPB.   Dedication: Lucy M. Howard.

A set of three 16-measure waltz movements of contrasting character arranged in an ABACA sequence.   Prevailing mood is coquettish rather than sentimental.   Modulations restricted to relative minor and dominant. Easy.   Duration: ca. 1½ minutes.

Review of no. **766**:

DWIGHT, John Sullivan.   "New Publications."   *Harbinger* 3/14 (12 Sept 1846): 219.

> [It is] . . . a quite original and pleasing Waltz. . . .   The last strain has a style and an expression not unlike those of the running passage in Weber's inimitable "Invitation to the Waltz."

767 *La Capricieuse: Grande Valse pour le pianoforte*

Published (ca. 1847) by Oliver Ditson, Boston; PP, RPB. Dedication: B. Headden.

In ABA form with coda. Light, rollicking themes in predominantly staccato articulations. Modest harmonic vocabulary. Dashing coda. Moderately difficult. Duration: ca. 4 minutes.

Review of no. **767**:

DWIGHT, John Sullivan. "Musical Review." *Harbinger* 4/22 (8 May 1847): 346-47.

> We have examined this graceful and rather original little production with much pleasure. It is composed in good taste, with more than the ordinary knowledge and command of harmony, and by its freedom from mere commonplaces proves its author's familiarity with and preference for the higher styles of music. It seems to us to lack warmth, and has the appearance of being somewhat studied, — which last, however, is a good quality in a young composer who has talent. Not steeped in any deep sentiment, and having hardly the irresistible fervor of a waltz, yet it has vigor, brightness, beauty and variety.

768   *Ecossaise (Old Style)*

M.M. ♩ = 112. Not too fast. With expression.

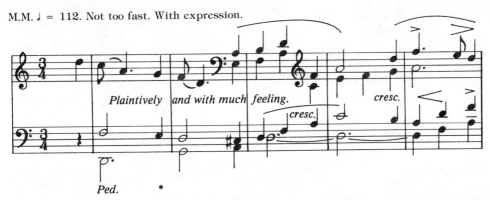

Written for souvenir magazines sold at a benefit fair for the Orange Memorial Hospital in New Jersey; no copy located. Holograph score (dated 8 June 1903, New York, N.Y.); DLC.

In through-composed form. A very short work (twenty-one measures) in highly lyrical style using characteristic three-beat rhythmic pattern of ♪♩.♩. Easy. Duration: ca. 1 minute.

769   *Home Sweet Home: A One-Finger Pedal Study*

Published in 1904 by Theodore Presser, Philadelphia; CtY, NN. Also published in 1904 by Weekes & Co., London; British Library. Reprinted in the *Etude* 22/10 (Oct 1904): 21. Also published in *The America Book for Piano*, 67 (see no. **75**).

A short study (based on Henry Bishop's well-known tune) in which one finger is used to play both the melody and accompaniment, requiring the use of the damper pedal to maintain a legato effect. Pedal markings are purposely omitted to encourage the use of the ear to determine the correct pedaling. Includes 1½ pages of written explanations and suggestions for practice. Easy. Duration: ca. 1½ minutes.

770   *March for the Pianoforte for Four Hands: For Teacher and Pupil*

Published in 1870 by Oliver Ditson & Co., Boston; DLC. Dedication: To his nephews Eddie, Alan, and Henry [Mason].

The primo consists of single notes in octave unison limited to a compass of five tones. The more difficult secondo contains harmonizations and countermelodies. Easy. Duration: ca. 3½ minutes.

771   *A Pastoral Novellette*

Published in 1895 by J. B. Millet & Co. in *Half Hours with the Best Composers*, pt. 25, pp. 1253-58 (see nos. **134, 458**); DLC, NN. Holograph score (dated New York, 2 December 1894); MB.

A graceful work in ABA form. Delicate legato effects in A section contrast with heavier texture and dynamics in section B. Moderately difficult. Duration: ca. 4 minutes.

772   *Redowa for the Pianoforte for Four Hands: For Teacher and Pupil*

Published in 1870 by Oliver Ditson & Co., Boston; DLC, RPB. Dedication: To his nephew Johnnie.

Spirited work in ABA form. Staccato articulations in opening and reprise; lyrical melody in middle section. Easy. Duration: ca. 2½ minutes.

773   *Valse*

Published in 1846 by A. A. Van Gelder, New York; NN. Holograph score; NN. Dedication: Mlle P. P. Flint.

A short work in ABA form. The early publication date is reflected in the use of unsophisticated compositional techniques. Staccato repeated notes and two-note slur groups dominate the work. Easy. Duration: ca. 1½ minutes.

774 *The Zephyr Waltz*

Published in 1887 by the John Church Co., Cincinnati; DLC.

A work of questionable authenticity. The very simple melodic and harmonic structure, in light of the 1887 publication date, would indicate that this work was written by a Mason namesake. Easy. Duration: ca. 1½ minutes.

Keyboard Works in Manuscript

775 "Barcarolle"

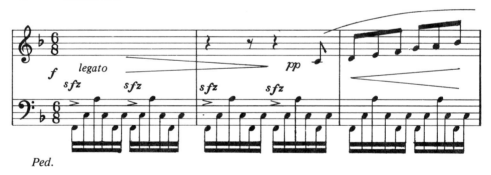

Two holograph scores in DLC. The first copy designates this work as opus 11, but in the second copy the opus number is omitted.

In loose ABA form with shortened reprise. Rocking bass pattern in accompaniment. Moderately difficult. Duration: ca. 4 minutes.

776 Fragment no. 1

Holograph score (not cataloged) in DLC.

An unnamed and unsigned 6-measure musical sketch (triple meter) in the handwriting of William Mason.

777   Fragment no. 2

Holograph score in DLC.

An unnamed and unsigned 59-measure musical sketch (G-sharp minor, 4/8 meter) in the handwriting of William Mason.

778   Fragment no. 3

Holograph score in DLC.

An unnamed and unsigned 30-measure three-voice fugue (F major, 4/4 meter) in the handwriting of William Mason.

779   Fragment no. 4

Holograph score (not cataloged) in DLC.

An unnamed and unsigned 4-measure musical sketch (A-flat major, quadruple meter) in the handwriting of William Mason.

780   Fragment no. 5

Holograph score (not cataloged) in DLC.

An unnamed and unsigned 4½-measure musical sketch (B major, 4/4 meter) in the handwriting of William Mason.

781   Fragment no. 6

Holograph score (not cataloged) in DLC.

An unnamed and unsigned 4-measure musical sketch (F minor, 3/4 meter) in the handwriting of William Mason.

782   Fragment no. 7

Holograph score (not cataloged) in DLC.

An unnamed and unsigned 4-measure musical sketch (E major, 3/4 meter) in the handwriting of William Mason.

783   Fragment no. 8

Holograph score (not cataloged) in DLC.

An unnamed and unsigned 1½-measure musical sketch (G major, 6/8 meter) in the handwriting of William Mason.

784   Fragment no. 9

Holograph score (not cataloged) in DLC.

An unsigned 7½-measure musical sketch identified only as "2nd Part" (2/4 meter) in the handwriting of William Mason.

785   Fragment no. 10

Holograph score (not cataloged) in DLC.

An unsigned 9-measure musical sketch entitled "Polka" (A major, 2/4 meter) in the handwriting of William Mason.

786   Fragment no. 11

Holograph score in the Denver Public Library.

A 4-measure musical sketch (E-flat major, 4/4 meter) in the handwriting of William Mason. The fragment is captioned "The opening four measures of a little Pedal Study for one finger alone. The melody must be played legato and with Expression."

787   "March"

Holograph scores in DLC.

Two separate, incomplete musical sketches (G minor/G major, common time) of sixteen (dated 20 July 1868) and twenty-five measures in the handwriting of William Mason.

788   "Marie Valse"[1]

Holograph score in MB. Dedication: Marie.

In ABCA form with 8-measure introduction. Sweeping arpeggiated figures and driving rhythms in the "valse brillante" tradition. Moderately difficult. Duration: ca. 2 minutes.

---

[1] Courtesy of the Trustees of the Boston Public Library.

789   Unnamed composition

Moderately fast—but with quiet and repose.   ♩ = 126.

Holograph score (cataloged as Fragment no. 4) in DLC. Unsigned, but in the handwriting of William Mason; dated 1 January 1897.

A short (thirty-two measures) piece in through-composed form. Frequent tempo changes. Quotations from the song "I Wish You a Happy New Year." Moderately difficult. Duration: ca. 1½ minutes.

790   "Valse joyeuse"

Fragments from two holograph scores in DLC.

An incomplete musical sketch (D-flat major, 3/4 meter).

Keyboard Works Edited or Arranged by Mason

ENTRIES IN WHICH THE NAME OF THE PUBLISHER IS FOLLOWED
BY THE LETTERS CTP ARE TAKEN FROM LISTINGS FOUND ON
COLLECTIVE TITLE PAGES; NO COPIES OF THESE WORKS
HAVE BEEN LOCATED FOR VERIFICATION.

---

791   BACH, Johann Sebastian. *Fugue in A Minor.* Rev. and fingered by William Mason. New York: Edward Schuberth & Co. (CTP).

792   BACH, Johann Sebastian. *Gavotte from the Second Violin Sonata.* Arranged by Camille Saint-Saëns, rev. and fingered by William Mason. New York: Edward Schuberth & Co., 1884.

793   BACH, Johann Sebastian. *Gavotte in D Major from the Sixth Sonata for Violoncello.* Transcribed by William Mason. New York: Carl Heuser, 1874; reprint, New York: G. Schirmer, n.d.

794   BACH, Johann Sebastian. *Short Preludes and Fugues for the Pianoforte* (1895). Ed. and fingered by William Mason. New York: G. Schirmer, 1923.

795   BACH, Johann Sebastian. *Two- and Three-Part Inventions for the Piano.* Ed. and fingered by William Mason. New York: G. Schirmer, 1894.

       Review of no. **795:**

       MATHEWS, William Smythe Babcock. "Reviews and Notices: The Two- and Three-Part Inventions of Bach. . . ." *Music* 7 (Jan 1895): 311-14.

       A twofold review of Mason's edition of the inventions and sinfonias and Busoni's edition of the inventions (Breitkopf & Härtel).

       This one of Dr. Mason has the merit of careful fingering, complete writing out of the embellishments, and generally judicious phrasing, which however, is not always consistent with itself.

796   BACH, Carl Philipp Emanuel. *Rondo andantino.* Rev. and fingered by William Mason. New York: Edward Schuberth & Co. (CTP).

797   BARGIEL, Woldemar. *Marcia fantastica*, op. 31. Rev. and fingered by William Mason. New York: Edward Schuberth & Co., 1883.

798   BERLIOZ, Hector. "Serenade of Mephistopheles," from the *Damnation of Faust.* Rev. and fingered by William Mason. New York: Edward Schuberth & Co. (CTP).

799   BIZET, Georges. *Menuet de l'arlésienne.* Fingered by William Mason. New York: Edward Schuberth & Co., 1882.

800   BRAHMS, Johannes. "Andante," from the *Sonata in F Minor*, op. 5. Rev. and fingered by William Mason. New York: Edward Schuberth & Co. (CTP).

801   CHAMINADE, Cécile. *Zingara*, op. 27, no. 2. Rev. and fingered by William Mason. New York: Edward Schuberth & Co. (CTP).

802   CHOPIN, Frédéric. "Funeral March," from the *Sonata in B-flat Minor*, op. 35. Rev. and fingered by William Mason. New York: Edward Schuberth & Co. (CTP).

803   FRANCK, César. *Symphony in D Minor.* Transcribed by William Mason. New York: G. Schirmer.

804   FRANZ, Robert. *Der Schalk.* Transcribed by Franz Liszt, rev. and fingered by William Mason. New York: Edward Schuberth & Co., 1886.

805   GLUCK, Christoph Willibald. "Gavotte," from *Don Juan.* Rev. and fingered by William Mason. New York: Edward Schuberth & Co., 1875.

806   GODARD, Benjamin. *Renouveau*, op. 82. Rev. and fingered by William Mason. New York: Edward Schuberth & Co., 1888.

807   HANDEL, George Frideric. *Air à la bourrée in G Major.* Transcribed by William Mason. New York: Wm. A. Pond & Co., 1874.

808   HANDEL, George Frideric. *Bourrée.* Transcribed by William Mason. New York: Edward Schuberth & Co., 1888.

809   HANDEL, George Frideric. *Largo* [from *Xerxes*] *as Played by Theodore Thomas' Orchestra.* Arranged for piano by William Mason. New York: Edward Schuberth & Co., 1877.

       Also published (n.d.) as *G. F. Händel's Celebrated Largo* . . . by J. McDowell & Co., London.

       Holograph score (dated Friday evening, 6 April 1877); DLC.

       See also Mason's arrangement for voice and piano, no. **910**.

810   HENSELT, Adolph von. *Morning Serenade*, op. 39. Rev. and fingered by William Mason. New York: Edward Schuberth & Co., 1881.

811   HENSELT, Adolph von. *Si Oiseau j'étais*, op. 2, no. 6. Rev. (third revision) and fingered by William Mason. New York: Edward Schuberth & Co., 1881.

812   HENSELT, Adolph von. *Spring Song*, op. 15. Rev. and fingered by William Mason. New York: Edward Schuberth & Co. (CTP).

813 HOFMANN, Heinrich. *Polonaise*, op. 55, no. 3. Rev. and fingered by William Mason. New York: Edward Schuberth & Co. (CTP).

814 HOLTEN, Carl von. *Melody.* Rev. and fingered by William Mason. New York: Edward Schuberth & Co., 1884.

815 HUMMEL, Johann Nepomuk. *Rondeau favori*, op. 11. Rev. and fingered by William Mason. New York: Edward Schuberth & Co. (CTP).

816 JADASSOHN, Salomon. *Albumleaf.* Fingered by William Mason. New York: Edward Schuberth & Co., 1883.

817 JENSEN, Adolf. "Bridal Song," from *Wedding Music for Four Hands*, op. 45, no. 2. Arranged for solo piano by William Mason. New York: Edward Schuberth & Co., 1877.

818 JENSEN-NIEMANN. *Murmuring Breezes.* Transcribed, rev., and fingered by William Mason. New York: Edward Schuberth & Co. (CTP).

819 JENSEN-NIEMANN. *On the Banks of the Manzanares.* Transcribed, rev., and fingered by William Mason. New York: Edward Schuberth & Co. (CTP).

820 KULLAK, Theodor. *La Gazelle*, op. 22. Rev. and fingered by William Mason. New York: Edward Schuberth & Co. (CTP).

821 LISZT, Franz. *Dreams of Love: Three Nocturnes.* Rev. and fingered by William Mason. New York: Edward Schuberth & Co., 1886.

822 LISZT, Franz. *Étude de concert in D-flat Major.* Rev. and fingered by William Mason. New York: Edward Schuberth & Co., 1886.

823 LISZT, Franz. *Polonaise in E Major.* Rev. and fingered by William Mason. New York: Edward Schuberth & Co., 1888.

824 LISZT, Franz. *Rhapsodie hongroise no. 11.* Rev. and fingered by William Mason. New York: Edward Schuberth & Co. (CTP).

825   LISZT, Franz. *Rigoletto: Concert Paraphrase.* Rev. and fingered by William Mason. New York: Edward Schuberth & Co. (CTP).

826   LOEWE, Carl. *An Indian Tale*, op. 107, no. 2. Rev. and fingered by William Mason. New York: Edward Schuberth & Co. (CTP).

827   LÜBECK, Ernst. *Berceuse*, op. 13. Rev. and fingered by William Mason. New York: Edward Schuberth & Co. (CTP).

828   LYSBERG, Charles-Samuel. *La Fontaine*, op. 34. Rev. and fingered by William Mason. New York: Edward Schuberth & Co. (CTP).

829   MOSZKOWSKI, Moritz. *Albumblatt*, op. 2. Rev. and fingered by William Mason. New York: Edward Schuberth & Co., 1885.

830   MOSZKOWSKI, Moritz. *Berceuse*, op. 38, no. 2. Rev. and fingered by William Mason. New York: Edward Schuberth & Co., 1887.

831   MOSZKOWSKI, Moritz. *Intermezzo*, op. 39. Rev. and fingered by William Mason. New York: Edward Schuberth & Co. (CTP).

832   MOSZKOWSKI, Moritz. *Moment musical*, op. 35, no. 2. An edition by Mason in MS, apparently intended for publication, is in the Library of Congress.

833   MOSZKOWSKI, Moritz. *Scherzino*, op. 18, no. 2. Rev. and fingered by William Mason. New York: Edward Schuberth & Co. (CTP).

834   MOSZKOWSKI, Moritz. *Skizzen*, op. 10, no. 2. An edition by Mason in MS, apparently intended for publication, is in the Library of Congress.

835   MOSZKOWSKI, Moritz. *Valse brillante in A-flat Major.* Rev. and fingered by William Mason. New York: Edward Schuberth & Co. (CTP).

836   MOSZKOWSKI, Moritz. *Waltz*, op. 17, no. 3. Rev. and fingered by William Mason. New York: Edward Schuberth & Co. (CTP).

837   MOZART, Wolfgang Amadeus. *The Violet*, K. 476. Transcribed by Theodor Kullak (op. 111, no. 3), rev. and fingered by William Mason. New York: Edward Schuberth & Co., 1888.

838   NICODÉ, Jean-Louis. *Minuet*, op. 19. Rev. and fingered by William Mason. New York: Edward Schuberth & Co. (CTP).

839   NICODÉ, Jean-Louis. *Tarantelle*, op. 13, no. 1. Rev. and fingered by William Mason. New York: Edward Schuberth & Co. (CTP).

840   PADEREWSKI, Ignacy Jan. *Menuet célèbre*, op. 14, no. 1. Rev. and fingered by William Mason. Philadelphia: Theodore Presser, 1896.

841   PIRANI, Eugenio. *Gavotte*, op. 25, no. 1. Rev. and fingered by William Mason. New York: Edward Schuberth & Co., 1888.

842   RAFF, Joseph Joachim. *Am Loreley Fels*, op. 134, no. 3. Rev. and fingered by William Mason. New York: Edward Schuberth & Co., 1885.

843   RAFF, Joseph Joachim. *Eglogue*, op. 105, no. 3. Rev. and fingered by William Mason. New York: Edward Schuberth & Co. (CTP).

844   RAFF, Joseph Joachim. *La Fileuse*, op. 157, no. 2. Ed. and fingered by William Mason. New York: G. Schirmer, 1896.

845   RAFF, Joseph Joachim. *Larghetto*, op. 55, no. 12. Rev. and fingered by William Mason. New York: Edward Schuberth & Co. (CTP).

846   RAFF, Joseph Joachim. *Märchen*, op. 162, no. 4. Rev. and fingered by William Mason. New York: Edward Schuberth & Co. (CTP).

847   RAFF, Joseph Joachim. *Menuet*, op. 163, no. 4. Rev. and fingered by William Mason. New York: Edward Schuberth & Co. (CTP).

848   RAFF, Joseph Joachim. *Valse*, op. 111, no. 2. Rev. and fingered by William Mason. New York: Edward Schuberth & Co. (CTP).

849   RAFF, Joseph Joachim. *Valse-Impromptu à la tyrolienne.* Fingered by William Mason. New York: Edward Schuberth & Co., 1883.

850   REINECKE, Carl. *Ballade*, op. 20. Rev. and fingered by William Mason. New York: Edward Schuberth & Co., 1886.

851   RHEINBERGER, Joseph. *The Chase: Impromptu*, op. 5, no. 1. Rev. and fingered by William Mason. New York: Edward Schuberth & Co., 1883.

852   RHEINBERGER, Joseph. *Menuetto for the Left Hand Alone*, op. 113, no. 2. Rev. and fingered by William Mason. New York: Edward Schuberth & Co., 1883.

853   RHEINBERGER, Joseph. *Serenata*, op. 29, no. 3. Rev. and fingered by William Mason. New York: Edward Schuberth & Co. (CTP).

854   RHEINBERGER, Joseph. *Toccatina*, op. 5, no. 2. Rev. and fingered by William Mason. New York: Edward Schuberth & Co. (CTP).

855   RUBINSTEIN, Anton. *Kamennoi-Ostrow: Album de portraits*, op. 10, no. 22. Rev. and fingered by William Mason. New York: Edward Schuberth & Co., 1883.

       Also published by the same company in an arrangement by Mason for piano and organ (1883).

856   SAINT-SAËNS, Camille. *Alceste de Gluck: Excerpt from the Caprice on the Airs de ballet.* Fingered by William Mason. New York: Edward Schuberth & Co., 1888.

857   SAINT-SAËNS, Camille. *Première Mazurka*, op. 2. Rev. and fingered by William Mason. New York: Edward Schuberth & Co., 1888.

858   SCHARWENKA, Philipp. *Moment musical.* Fingered by William Mason. New York: Edward Schuberth & Co., 1883.

859   SCHARWENKA, Xaver. *Polish National Dances*, op. 3, no. 1. Rev. and fingered by William Mason. New York: Edward Schuberth & Co., 1885.

860   SCHOLTZ, Herrmann. *Concert Polonaise*, op. 6. Rev. and fingered by William Mason. New York: Edward Schuberth & Co. (CTP).

861 SCHUMANN, Robert. "Polonaise," from *Papillons*, op. 2. Rev. and fingered by William Mason. New York: Edward Schuberth & Co. (CTP).

862 SCHYTTE, Ludvig. *At Night*. Rev. and fingered by William Mason. New York: Edward Schuberth & Co., 1885.

863 SILAS, Eduard. *Second Bourrée*, op. 88. Rev. and fingered by William Mason. New York: Edward Schuberth & Co. (CTP).

864 SITT, Hans. *Gavotte*, op. 15. Rev. and fingered by William Mason. New York: Edward Schuberth & Co., 1884.

865 SMETANA, Bedřich. *Bohemian Dance*. Rev. and fingered by William Mason. New York: Edward Schuberth & Co., 1888.

866 TCHAIKOVSKY, Piotr Ilyich. *Chant sans paroles*, op. 2, no. 3. Rev. and fingered by William Mason. New York: Edward Schuberth & Co. (CTP).

867 VOLKMANN, Robert. *Walzer, Serenade*, op. 63. Rev. and fingered by William Mason. New York: Edward Schuberth & Co. (CTP).

868 WAGNER, Richard. "Oh Thou Sublime Evening Star," from *Tannhäuser*. Transcribed by Franz Liszt, fingered by William Mason. New York: Edward Schuberth & Co., 1884.

869 WAGNER, Richard. "Walter's Prize Song," from *Die Meistersinger*. Transcribed by F. Bendel, rev. and fingered by William Mason. New York: Edward Schuberth & Co. (CTP).

870 WEBER, Carl Maria von. *Aufforderung zum Tanze*, op. 65. Rev. and fingered by William Mason. New York: G. Schirmer, 1893.

871 WEBER, Carl Maria von. *Concertstück*, op. 79. Rev. and fingered by William Mason. New York: G. Schirmer, 1893.

872   WEBER, Carl Maria von. *Concertstück, Pieces, and Variations.* Ed., rev., and fingered by William Mason, with a biographical sketch by Philip Hale. New York: G. Schirmer, 1893.

> Contents: *Momento capriccioso*, op. 12; *Grande Polonaise*, op. 21; *Rondo brillante (La Gaieté)*, op. 62; *Invitation to the Dance*, op. 65; *Polacca brillante*, op. 72; *Concertstück*, op. 79; *Les Adieux*, op. 81; *Seven Variations on the Air "Vien quà, Dorina bella,"* op. 7; *Variations on the Russian Air "Schöne Minka,"* op. 37 [*sic*].

> All of the works in this collection were apparently also published individually. This collection was reissued, minus the *Concertstück*, in 1943 by G. Schirmer under the title *Miscellaneous Compositions for the Piano.*

> Review of no. **872**:

> "Reviews and Notices: Dr. Mason's Edition of Weber's Works." *Music* 5 (Feb 1894): 494-95.

>> A review of Mason's edition of Weber's opuses 7, 12, 21, 37 [*sic*], 62, and 79.

>> The editing . . . is of the most conscientious and painstaking description. The text is scrupulously revised, the notation improved wherever possible; the extended chords supplied with alternate passages for small hands, and above all the fingering carefully indicated by a pianist who was educated in the school which these works represent, and has played them in public many and many times. . . .

873   WEBER, Carl Maria von. *Perpetuum-Mobile*, op. 24. Rev. and fingered by William Mason. New York: Edward Schuberth & Co., 1884.

> Consists of the fourth movement of his *Sonata no. 1 in C Major.*

874   *The William Mason Collection of Select Pianoforte Compositions: Carefully Revised and Fingered for Instructive Purposes.* New York: Edward Schuberth & Co., 1900.

> Contents: J. S. Bach, *Gavotte from the Second Violin Sonata*; Woldemar Bargiel, *Marcia fantastica*, op. 31; Georges Bizet, *Menuet de l'arlésienne*; Benjamin Godard, *Renouveau*, op. 82; Adolph von Henselt, *Morning Serenade*, op. 39, and *Si Oiseau j'étais*, op. 2, no. 6; Salomon Jadassohn, *Albumleaf*; Adolf Jensen, "Bridal Song," from *Wedding Music*, op. 45, no. 2; Franz Liszt, *Liebesträume*, no. 3; Moritz Moszkowski, *Albumblatt*, op. 2, and *Berceuse*, op. 38, no. 2; W. A. Mozart, *The Violet*, K. 476; Joseph Joachim Raff, *Am Loreley Fels*, op. 134, no. 3, and *Valse-Impromptu à la tyrolienne*; Joseph Rheinberger, *The Chase: Impromptu*, op. 5, no. 1, and *Menuetto for the Left Hand Alone*, op. 113, no. 2; Anton Rubinstein, *Kamennoi-Ostrow: Album de portraits*, op. 10, no. 22; Camille Saint-Saëns, *Première Mazurka*, op. 21; Philipp Scharwenka, *Moment musical*; Xaver Scharwenka, *Polish National Dances*, op. 3, no. 1; Ludvig Schytte, *At Night*; Richard Wagner, "Oh Thou Sublime Evening Star," from *Tannhäuser*; Carl Maria von Weber, *Perpetuum-Mobile*, op. 24.

> All of the works in this collection were also published separately.

Chamber Music

875   *Serenata*, op. 39

For cello and piano, published in 1882 by Edward Schuberth & Co., New York; DLC. Transcription by the composer for piano solo, published in 1882 by Edward Schuberth & Co., New York; CtY, DLC, IU, MH-Mu, NN, NRU-Mus. New edition, rev. by the composer, published in 1882 by Edward Schuberth & Co., New York; PP. Composer's 37-measure sketch (partially corresponding to measures 1-25, 42-46, and 49-53 of published score) and completed MS of arrangement for piano (dated 1 March 1882); DLC. Signed MS of the first five measures of the arrangement for piano (dated 25 March 1904); Broadcast Music Inc. Archives (part of the Carl Haverlin Collection). Dedication: Frederic Bergner.

Loosely constructed ABA form with coda. Lyric melody grouped in irregular phrase lengths. Numerous sudden changes of tempo, many of them indicated in English rather than Italian terms. Juxtaposition of major and minor modes in coda. Easy. Duration: ca. 3 minutes.

Vocal Music

Secular Solo Songs

876   *The Cot with Sanded Floor*

Advertisement in the *Musical World* 10/7 (14 Oct 1854): 86 indicates that this work was published in Boston by Nathan Richardson; no copy located. Also cited in the Pazdírek *Universal-Handbuch der Musikliteratur* (see no. **443)** as being published in Cleveland by Brainard; no copy located. Holograph score (dated Frankfurt, Monday evening, 10:45 o'clock, 13 September 1852); DLC.

In strophic form. Lyric, generally conjunct melodic line supported by a simple, but expressive, accompaniment. Compass: *c'-g''*. Duration: ca. 2 minutes.

877   *Fading Flowers*

Published in 1852 by Firth, Pond & Co., New York; DLC. Holograph score (dated Berlin, Monday, 24 November 1851); DLC. Text by Clarence May. Dedication: to Mason's mother [Abigail].

In strophic form with literal repetition of the music for each stanza. Warm, idyllic melody in the direct, expressive style of a folksong. Diatonic harmonies with occasional chromatic coloring. Piano part generally restricted to the role of a simple accompaniment. Compass: $e^{b'}$-g''. Duration: ca. 4 minutes.

Reviews of no. **877**:

"Musical Review." *Dwight's Journal of Music* 1/12 (26 June 1852): 92-93.

> A very simple, but by no means commonplace melody, in the minor mood. . . . The accompaniment, too, while very simple, is unique in form and quite expressive.

"New Music." *Musical Review and Choral Advocate* 3/5 (1 May 1852): 73.

> This is a beautiful minor melody with a unique and pleasing accompaniment.

878   "Happy New Year to You My Friend"

Holograph score (uncataloged) in DLC.

An incomplete, unsigned 7-measure sketch (B major, 3/4 meter) in the handwriting of William Mason.

879   "Hush a Bye Baby"

Unsigned holograph score; DLC.

An 8-measure ditty set to a nursery rhyme. Very simple accompaniment.
Compass: *c'-e''*.

880   "Once as Little Isabella Ventured"

Unsigned holograph score; DLC.

Brief, 12-measure tune set to a nursery rhyme. Playful pictorial accompaniment. Compass: *d'-d''*.

881   "See-Saw Sacra-Down, Which Is the Way to Boston Town"

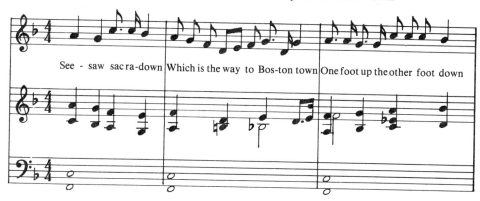

See - saw sac ra-down |Which is the way to Bos-ton town|One foot up the other foot down

Unsigned holograph score; DLC.

A 4-measure ditty. Simple chordal accompaniment. Compass: *d'-c''*.

882   "Sing to Me, Love"

Holograph score (dated Berlin, Saturday, 23 August 1851); DLC. MS copy of this work (with minor revisions) apparently made by Mason at some later date; DLC. Text by J. A. C.

In strophic form with minor changes in both the vocal line and accompaniment in the second stanza. Introspective, elegiac mood. Compass: *d#'-f''*. Duration: ca. 2 minutes.

883   *The Tree of Odenwald: A Ballad*

Published in the *New York Musical Review and Gazette* 9/18 (4 Sept 1858): 283.

Short, simple, strophic song. Tune taken from Lowell Mason's *Normal School Singer.* William Mason's accompaniment is supportive, but clearly subordinate to the solo line. Diatonic harmonies. Subdued, melancholy mood. Compass: $e^{b\prime}$-$e^{b\prime\prime}$. Duration: ca. 3½ minutes.

Secular Works for Mixed Voices

ALL WORKS FOR SATB (UNACCOMPANIED),
UNLESS OTHERWISE INDICATED.

---

884   *Broken Threads*

Text by Dexter Smith. Published in the *New York Musical Gazette* 4/7 (May 1870): 26 (of music section). Also published in SEWARD/Glee, 8.

885 *Cheerfulness*

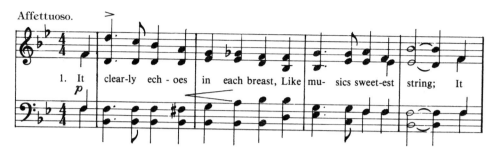

Published in MASON-BANCROFT/Glee, 30-31.

886 *The Complaint*

Published in MASON-BANCROFT/Glee, 56.

887 *The Farewell*

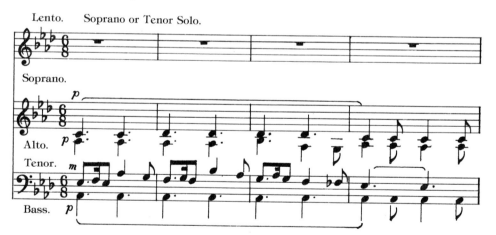

SATB with soprano or tenor solo. Published in MASON/Fireside, 92-95.

888 *Glad Notes of Joy*

SAB with tenor or soprano solo. Published in ROOT/Vocalist, 178-79. Music is an abridged and slightly varied version of the *Gondolier's Serenade* (see next item).

889 *Gondolier's Serenade*

Published in MASON-WEBB/Glee Hive, 51-56; MASON-WEBB/Glee Hive (rev.), 65-70; MASON-BANCROFT/Glee, 44-49; SEWARD/Glee, 180-85; SEWARD-ALLEN/Coronation, 86-88. Also published (with a piano accompaniment) on pp. 1-6 in *The Choral Handbook, no. 377* (London: J. Curwen & Sons). Also cited in the Pazdírek *Universal Handbuch der Musikliteratur* (see no. **443**) as being published by Echo Music (Chicago).

See also *Glad Notes of Joy*, no. **888**.

890   *The Hunter*

Published in MASON/Fireside, 30-31.

891   *The Light at Home*

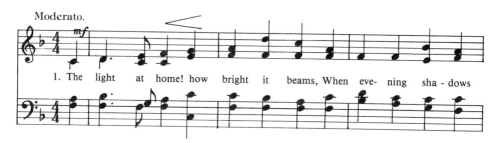

Published in ROOT/Glee, 118; SEWARD/Glee, 115.

892   *Near the Lake Where Drooped the Willow*

Published in the *New York Musical Review and Gazette* 6/20 (22 Sept 1855): 327. Also published in MASON/Singer, 150; WEBB-MASON/Odeon, 106.

893   *Ocean Lullaby*

Published in MASON/American, 66; MASON/Carmina Enlarged, 66; MASON/Song-Garden (3), 164-65; MASON-MASON/Asaph, 114.

894   *O, Eolus Singeth*

Text by J. Johnson, Jr. Published in the *Musical Gazette* (Boston) 1/10 (8 June 1846): 79.

895   *O Fleecy Snow*

1. Float - ing, glid-ing, gent-ly down, You soft-   ly go, ...   Hith-er, thith-er,

Published in MASON-MASON/Asaph, 118.

896   *Oh! Come to Me*

Oh!   come   to   me   when   day - light   sets,   Sweet! then come to

Oh!   come   to   me   when   day - light   sets,   Sweet!   then come to

Oh!   come   to   me   when   day - light   sets,   Sweet!   then come to

Published in MASON-BANCROFT/Glee, 60-65.

897   *The Painter's Wandering Song*

1. Who would be mer-ry in the world, A paint-er let him be, When

Published in MASON/Fireside, 122-25.

898   *Serenade*

Slum - - - - ber sweet-ly, dear-est, Close . . . thy wear-ry eyes,

Slum - - - - - ber sweet-ly, dear-est, Close . . . thy wear-ry eyes,

Slum - - - - - ber sweet-ly, dear-est, Close . . . thy wear-ry eyes,

Slum - - - - - ber sweet-ly, Close thy eyes,

Published in MASON-BANCROFT/Glee, 94-95. Performed at the New York Philharmonic Society's concert on 5 March 1853 by George F. Root's Quartette Party. Also published under the title *Slumber Sweetly, Dearest* (see no. **901**).

899   "Shuttle Song"

> Performed at the 1871 normal school in Binghamton, New York (see no. **248**). No copy located.

900   *Sleighing Song*

> Published in the *New York Musical Gazette* 1/1 (Nov 1866): 3 (of musical supplement). Also published in SEWARD/Temple Choir, 73.

901   *Slumber Sweetly, Dearest*

> Published in ROOT/Glee, 119; SEWARD/Glee, 34-35; also in Root's *The Story of a Musical Life*, 228-29 (see no. **404**). Also published under the title *Serenade* (see no. **898**).

902   *Spring*

> Published in MASON/Hallelujah, 277; MASON-WEBB/Psalmist, 235; MASON-MASON/Asaph, 263.

903   *Spring*

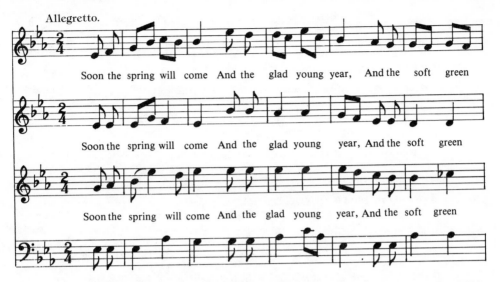

Published in the *Choral Advocate and Singing-Class Journal* 1/4 (Sept 1850):
61-63. Also published in MASON-WEBB/Glee Hive (rev.), 110-12; WEBB-
MASON/Melodist, 132-34.

904   *The Wanderer's Farewell*

Published in MASON/Fireside, 46-47.

905   *Welcome Gentle Friends*

1. Wel-come gen- tle friends of song, Wel-come, hap - py, peace-ful

Published in MASON-MASON/Asaph, 106.

906   *Welcome in the Glad New Year*

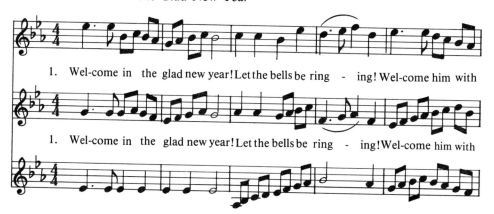

1. Wel-come in the glad new year! Let the bells be ring - ing! Wel-come him with

1. Wel-come in the glad new year! Let the bells be ring - ing! Wel-come him with

Three-part SSA. Text by Marie Mason. Published in MASON/Song-Garden (3), 86-87.

907   *When Spring Is Calling*

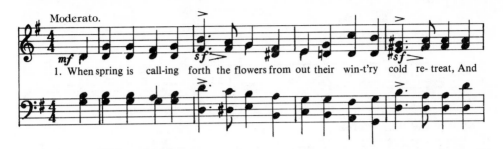

Beneath title: "Words by ENGLISH. Composed for this work, by WILLIAM MASON, of Berlin, Prussia, June 19, 1851." Published in the *Musical World* 2/25 (1 Aug 1851): 182. Also published in MASON-WEBB/Glee Hive, 88; MASON-WEBB/Glee Hive (rev.), 98.

908   *When Twilight Dews Are Falling Soft*

Published in WEBB-MASON/Melodist, 137. Also published in the *Choral Advocate and Singing-Class Journal* 1/5 (Oct 1850): 76; MASON-WEBB/ Glee Hive (rev.), 93.

909   *Youth's Brightest Day*

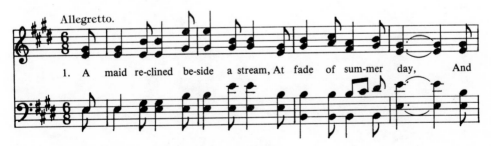

Published in SEWARD/Glee, 138-39.

Sacred Solo Songs

910   *Hope in the Lord*

Adapted to Handel's "Largo" from *Xerxes*, for soprano, or alto, or tenor, or baritone by William Mason. Published in 1877 by Edward Schuberth & Co., New York; NN, RPB. Dedication: L. L. Danforth.

See also Mason's arrangement of this work for piano solo, no. **809**.

Sacred Works for Mixed Voices

ALL WORKS FOR SATB (UNACCOMPANIED).

---

911   *Blessed Is He Whose Transgression*

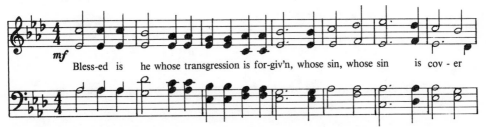

Bless-ed is   he whose transgression is for-giv'n, whose sin, whose sin   is cov - er

Published in MASON-MASON/Asaph, 312-14.

912   "Give Thanks to God, He Reigns on High"

Give thanks to God, He reigns   on high; Kind are His thoughts, His name is

Composer's holograph score; DLC.

913 *Hosanna*

Ho - san-na, Ho-san- na, Ho-san - na. Blessed is he that cometh in the name of the

Published in the *Musical Gazette* (Boston) 2/5 (29 Mar 1847): 40.

914 *How Lovely Are Thy Dwellings*

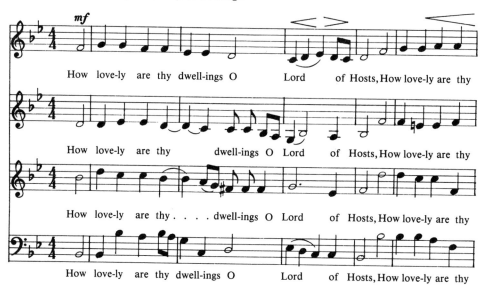

How love-ly are thy dwell-ings O Lord of Hosts, How love-ly are thy

How love-ly are thy dwell-ings O Lord of Hosts, How love-ly are thy

How love-ly are thy . . . . dwell-ings O Lord of Hosts, How love-ly are thy

How love-ly are thy dwell-ings O Lord of Hosts, How love-ly are thy

Published in MASON-MASON/Asaph, 298-99.

915 *The Lord Is My Shepherd*

The Lord is my Shep-herd, I shall not want. He mak-eth me to

Published in ROOT/Choir, 204-05; ROOT/New Choir, 194.

916 *Seek Ye the Lord*

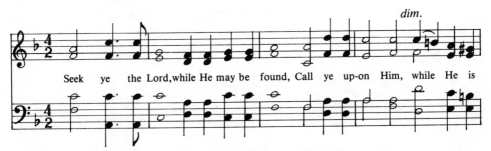

Seek ye the Lord, while He may be found, Call ye up-on Him, while He is

Published in the *Musical Review and Musical World* 11/19 (15 Sept 1860): 13.

Hymn-Tune Harmonizations

917 *Alet*

Published in MASON-MASON/Asaph, 178.

918   *Aral*

Published in MASON/American, 86; MASON/Carmina Enlarged, 86;
MASON-MASON/Asaph, 142.

919   *Avison*

Published in the *Musical Gazette* (Boston) 1/5 (30 Mar 1846): 40.

920   *Axel*

Published in MASON/American, 150; MASON/Carmina Enlarged, 150;
MASON-MASON/Asaph, 165.

921   *Bach*

Published in the *Musical Gazette* (Boston) 1/24 (21 Dec 1846): 192.

922   *Beckford*

Published in MASON/Tune Book, 141; MASON-PARK-PHELPS/ Sabbath Hymn, 330; MASON-PARK-PHELPS/Sabbath Tune, 177; PARK-PHELPS-WAYLAND-MASON/Sabbath School, 16, 40, 55.

923   *Beryl*

Published in SEWARD/Temple Choir, 200.

924   *Blois*

Published in MASON/Tune Book, 131; MASON-PARK-PHELPS/Sabbath Hymn, 130; MASON-PARK-PHELPS/Sabbath Tune, 178.

925   *Bridges*

Published in the *Musical Gazette* (Boston) 3/10 (5 June 1848): 80.

926   *Calabria*

Published in SEWARD/Temple Choir, 163.

927 *Cane*

Published in SEWARD-ALLEN/Coronation, 160.

928 *Chapin*

Published in MASON-WEBB/Psalmist, 171.

929 *Chenago*

Published in SEWARD-ALLEN/Coronation, 166.

930 *Choral*

Published in MASON-WEBB/Psalmist, 57.

931 *Collard*

Published in MASON-MASON/Asaph, 200.

932 *Conant*

Published in SEWARD/Temple Choir, 161.

933 *Corbet*

Published in MASON/American, 164; MASON/Carmina Enlarged, 164;
MASON/Song-Garden (2), 195; MASON-MASON/Asaph, 167.

934 *Cuvier*

Published in MASON-MASON/Asaph, 227.

935 *Dolland*

Published in MASON-MASON/Asaph, 198.

936 *Dufray*

Published in MASON-MASON/Asaph, 172.

937   *Eckley*

Dated Frankfurt, 1852. Published in MASON/Hallelujah, 185.

938   *Elben*

Published in MASON-MASON/Asaph, 221.

939   *Enna*

Published in BRADBURY/Key-Note, 271.

940   *Erk*

Published in MASON/American, 271; MASON/Carmina Enlarged, 271;
MASON-MASON/Asaph, 214.

941   *Ewer*

Dated Leipzig, March 1850. (In an entry in his Anniversary Book [see no. **1017**], Mason states that he composed this work on 26 February 1850.) Published in BRADBURY-ROOT/Shawm, 184; MASON/American, 239; MASON/Carmina Enlarged, 239; MASON/Hallelujah, 208; MASON-WEBB/Cantica, 177; ROOT/Diapason, 200; SEWARD/Temple Choir, 207.

942   *Fenner*

Published in SEWARD/Temple Choir, 236.

943   *Galand*

Published in MASON/American, 285; MASON/Carmina Enlarged, 285; MASON-MASON/Asaph, 220.

944   *Gilbert*

Published in SEWARD-ALLEN/Coronation, 152.

945   *Gilman*

Published in MASON/American, 104; MASON/Carmina Enlarged, 104.

946   *Greenfield*

Published in ROOT-SWEETSER/Collection, 77.

947   *Helmer*

Published in SEWARD/Temple Choir, 169.

948   *Hobart*

Dated 1848. Published in MASON/Hallelujah, 216; MASON/Tune Book, 129; MASON-MASON/Asaph, 193; MASON-PARK-PHELPS/Sabbath Hymn, 287; MASON-PARK-PHELPS/Sabbath Tune, 197; MASON-WEBB/Cantica, 329; MASON-WEBB/Psalmist, 148; ROOT/Singing Book, 208.

949   *Holbein*

Published in BRADBURY/Eclectic, 108; MASON/Tune Book, 115;
MASON-MASON/Asaph, 186; MASON-PARK-PHELPS/Sabbath Hymn,
68; MASON-PARK-PHELPS/Sabbath Tune, 124.

950   *Holman*

Published in SEWARD-ALLEN/Coronation, 134.

951   *Homerton*

Allegretto.

Dated London, 12 March 1853. Published in MASON/Hallelujah, 126.

952   *Hutton*

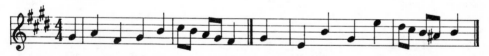

Published in SEWARD-ALLEN/Coronation, 113.

953   *Ilber*

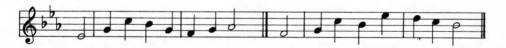

Published in MASON-MASON/Asaph, 139.

954   *Inigo*

Published in AIKEN-MAIN-ALLEN/Imperial, 49; ALLEN-SEWARD/ Vineyard, 160; SEWARD/Temple Choir, 139; SEWARD-ALLEN/ Coronation, 125.

955   *Kidron*

Dated 1845. Published in MASON-WEBB/Cantica, 338; MASON-WEBB/ Psalmist, 202; MASON-WEBB/Psaltery, 207.

956   *Kingdom*

Published in SEWARD-ALLEN/Coronation, 206.

957   *Lafner*

Published in MASON-WEBB/Cantica, 55.

958   *Leith*

Published in MASON-MASON/Asaph, 202.

959   *Locke*

Published in MASON-MASON/Asaph, 142.

960   *Loda*

Published in MASON-MASON/Asaph, 175.

961   *Manly*

Published in BRADBURY/Eclectic, 169.

962   *Mayence*

Published in MASON-WEBB/Psalmist, 47.

963   *Merton*

Published in MASON/American, 289; MASON/Carmina Enlarged, 289;
MASON-MASON/Asaph, 216.

964   *Messer*

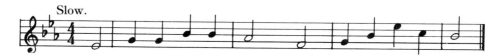

Dated Frankfurt, 21 October 1852. Published in MASON/Hallelujah, 206.

965   *Midas*

Dated Leipzig, December 1849. Published in MASON-WEBB/Cantica, 137.

966   *Morin*

Published in MASON-MASON/Asaph, 226.

967   *Naples*

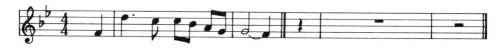

Published in the *New York Musical Gazette* 1/11 (Sept 1867): 42. Also published in SEWARD/Temple Choir, 217.

968   *Newton Vill*

Published in MASON-WEBB/Psalmist, 232.

969   *No. 14 . . . Canon: Two in One, Tenor and Treble*

Published in MASON-MASON/Hymnist, vol. 2, p. 15.

970   *Numa*

Published in MASON-MASON/Asaph, 194.

971   *Ola*

Published in MASON/American, 123; MASON/Carmina Enlarged, 123;
MASON-MASON/Asaph, 140; SEWARD/Temple Choir, 143.

972   *Onel*

Published in BRADBURY/Key-Note, 252.

973   *Ooral*

Published in MASON/American, 204; MASON/Carmina Enlarged, 204;
MASON-MASON/Asaph, 153; SEWARD/Temple Choir, 180.

974   *Oporto*

Dated 1848. Published in MASON/American, 292; MASON/Carmina, 196; MASON/Carmina Enlarged, 292; MASON/Hallelujah, 230; MASON-MASON/Asaph, 221; MASON-WEBB/Cantica, 193; MASON-WEBB/Psalmist, 201; ROOT/Bell, 206; ROOT/Singing Book, 160. Also published in *The Book of Worship: Prepared for the Use of the New Church . . .* , New York (3d) ed. (New York: New Church Board of Publications, 1877), 221.

975   *Orial*

Published in MASON/American, 122; MASON/Carmina Enlarged, 122; MASON-MASON/Asaph, 144.

976   *Ostend*

Published in SEWARD/Temple Choir, 218.

977   *Pearl*

Published in SEWARD-ALLEN/Coronation, 134.

978   *Pekin*

Published in MASON/American, 254; MASON/Carmina Enlarged, 254; MASON/Tune Book, 140; MASON-MASON/Asaph, 202; MASON-PARK-PHELPS/New Sabbath, 252; MASON-PARK-PHELPS/Sabbath Hymn, 252; MASON-PARK-PHELPS/Sabbath Tune, 206; PARK-PHELPS-WAYLAND-MASON/Sabbath School, 42.

979   *Pineland*

Published in ROOT/Bell, 159.

980   *Portsmouth*

Published in SEWARD-ALLEN/Coronation, 116.

981   *Potosi*

Published in MASON-WEBB/Psalmist, 189.

982   *Rhone*

Published in MASON-MASON/Asaph, 171.

983   *Roome*

Published in BRADBURY/Key-Note, 250.

984   *Rubini*

Published in MASON-WEBB/Cantica, 144.

985   *Sanctus*

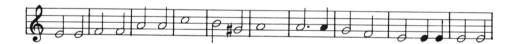

Published in MASON-MASON/Asaph, 345.

986   *Sarol*

Dated Prague, Bohemia, September 1850. Published in the *Choral Advocate and Singing-Class Journal* 1/6 (Nov 1850): 95.

987   *Soran*

Published in MASON-MASON/Asaph, 161.

988   *Sorata*

Published in MASON-WEBB/Tune Book, 43; MASON-WEBB/Psalmist, 111.

See also *Soroto* (next item).

989   *Soroto*

Published in MASON/Hallelujah, 179. Same as *Sorata* (see previous item) except for slight changes in measure 11 and the use of 2/4 rather than 3/2 meter.

990   *Southington*

Published in SEWARD/Temple Choir, 145.

991   *Spring*

Published in BRADBURY/Jubilee, 225.

992   *Stolberg*

Published in SEWARD/Temple Choir, 146.

993   *Strand*

Dated London, 17 February 1853. Published in MASON/American, 259; MASON/Carmina Enlarged, 259; MASON/Hallelujah, 205; MASON/Tune Book, 138; MASON-MASON/Asaph, 199; MASON-PARK-PHELPS/ Sabbath Hymn, 98; MASON-PARK-PHELPS/Sabbath Tune, 212; PARK-PHELPS-WAYLAND-MASON/Sabbath School, 25; SEWARD/Temple Choir, 220.

994   *Talbot*

Published in MASON-MASON/Asaph, 138.

995   *Thema*

Published in BRADBURY-ROOT/Shawm, 215.

996   *Thorpe*

Published in SEWARD/Temple Choir, 147.

997   *Tunbridge*

Published in SEWARD/Temple Choir, 187.

998   *Tunis*

Published in MASON-MASON/Asaph, 141.

999   *Verd*

Published in MASON-MASON/Asaph, 130.

1000   *Wilkes*

Published in MASON-MASON/Asaph, 173.

1001 *Wirt*

Published in MASON-MASON/Asaph, 181.

1002 *Wren*

Published in MASON-MASON/Asaph, 133.

1003 *Wylde*

Published in MASON-MASON/Asaph, 196.

1004 *Zoo*

Published in BRADBURY/Key-Note, 257.

Collections

LISTED IN CHRONOLOGICAL ORDER

1005 MASON, William, and Silas A. BANCROFT, comps. *The Social Glee Book: Being a Selection of Glees and Part Songs by Distinguished German*

Composers Never Before Published in This Country, Together with Original Pieces. Boston: Wilkens, Carter & Co., 1847.

Reviews of no. **1005**:

Anonymous review. Unidentified clipping in MASON/Scrapbook.

A brief, primarily descriptive review.

DWIGHT, John Sullivan. "Art Review: New Chorus and Glee Books." *Harbinger* 6/6 (11 Dec 1847): 46-47.

Includes a generally favorable review of Mason and Bancroft's book.

It contains thirty-six pieces. Of these, ten are by MENDELSSOHN; twelve by Weber, Kreutzer, Kalliuada [*sic*], and other Germans; five by each of the editors; the rest English. . . . Mr. Bancroft's pieces are simple melodies, plainly harmonized, mostly of a sweet and gentle character. . . . Mr. Mason has assayed bolder flights, composing in the interwoven, learned style somewhat; with original and delicately fanciful melodies, sometimes betraying the good influence of Mendelssohn. They are hopeful products, certainly, for Yankee land.

"New Works." *Musical Gazette* (Boston) 2/21 (8 Nov 1847): 164.

A very short, positive review.

The glees in this book are from the best sources, and they form a collection of a higher order than is usually found in glee books.

1006 MASON, William, ed. *Fireside Harmony: A New Collection of Glees and Part Songs Arranged for Soprano, Alto, Tenor, and Base [sic] Voices.* Boston: Tappan, Whittemore & Mason, 1848.

Reviews of no. **1006**:

Anonymous review. Unidentified clipping in MASON/Scrapbook.

. . . contains some fifty pretty melodies, arranged so as to be sung as solos, duetts, trios, or quartetts. The greater part of the music is taken from the works of German composers. . . .

"Literary Notices." *Saroni's Musical Times* 1/37 (8 June 1850): 436-37.

We should be glad to find this little selection at every fireside in the land. It is the only publication of the kind we have yet noticed that is not prefaced with a long and tedious discussion on the theory or science of music.

1007 MASON, Lowell, and William MASON, eds. *The Hymnist: A Collection of Sacred Music, Original and Selected.* 2 vols. Boston: Tappan, Whittemore & Mason, 1849.

1008   WEBB, George James, and William MASON, eds. *The Melodist: A Collection of Popular and Social Songs, Original or Selected, Harmonized and Arranged for Soprano, Alto, Tenor, and Base [sic] Voices.* New York: Mason & Law, 1850.

      Reviews of no. **1008:**

      "Musical Publications." *Choral Advocate and Singing-Class Journal* 1/6 (Nov 1850): 91.

        A very favorable review.

      "New Publications." *Saroni's Musical Times* 2/19 (1 Feb 1851): 194.

        A positive review.

          . . . the excellent judgment displayed in the selections well warrants us to place this volume, as far as practical utility is concerned, at the head of everything thus far published of this class.

1009   MASON, Lowell, and William MASON, eds. *Asaph; or, the Choir Book: A Collection of Vocal Music, Sacred and Secular, for Choirs, Singing Schools, Musical Societies and Conventions, and Social and Religious Assemblies.* New York: Mason Brothers, 1861.

5

Sources

1010 Boston, Massachusetts. Boston Public Library.

In addition to copies of a variety of Mason's published works, holdings include autograph manuscripts of *A Pastoral Novellette* and "Marie Valse" (see nos. **771, 788**).

1011 Chicago, Illinois. Newberry Library.

Holdings include the Hubert P. Main Collection, the William Smythe Babcock Mathews Music Scrapbooks, and the Theodore Thomas Collection. The Hubert P. Main Collection is a valuable reference source for Mason's published hymn tunes. The Mathews Scrapbooks (four volumes) contain chiefly programs and clippings related to music in and around Chicago from about 1872 to 1908; several items concern normal music schools in which Mason and Mathews collaborated (see no. **359**). Two parts of the Thomas Collection are of particular interest: the Programs of Chamber Music Concerts (two volumes) and the Thomas Papers (six volumes containing 631 items). The Programs of Chamber Music Concerts provide a nearly complete record of the performances by the Mason-Thomas Quartette in New York City and Farmington, Connecticut (see nos. **632, 636**). One volume of the Thomas Papers consists of photographs; the remaining five volumes contain primarily letters, including eight from Mason to Thomas (Orange, New Jersey, 25 June 1889; Isles of Shoals, 6 August 1889; New York, 17 November 1891; New York, n.d. [ca. 1900]; New York, 7 October 1900; New York, 14 September 1901; New York, 27 September 1901; and New York, 19 October 1901).

1012 College Park, Maryland. University of Maryland Libraries, Hornbake Library.

Holdings include a manuscript by Lowell Mason and William Mason on harmony. The manuscript is titled "Harmony: or Chord formation, relation and progression, being introductory to the art of Musical Composition, To which is prefixed a brief view of Musical Notation." Two drafts of the title page exist: one lists Lowell Mason and William Mason as coauthors; the second (and later?) draft reduces William Mason's role to that of editing and revising the text. The latter draft seems to be an accurate description of the contents of the manuscript. The major portion of the text was clearly written by Lowell Mason, with only occasional emendations made by his son William.

1013   Denver, Colorado. Denver Public Library, Western History Department.

Holdings include the Musicians Society of Denver Collection, which contains four separate items from two (?) autograph letters from Mason to William Smythe Babcock Mathews: a clipping from the *New York Review* (labeled in Mason's handwriting) containing a report on Mason's concerts with Felicita Vestvali in New York and Brooklyn in 1855 (see nos. **629, 630**), the "opening four measures of a little Pedal Study for one finger alone" (see no. **786**), the closing lines of a letter dated 22 December 1902, and a four-sentence paragraph (undated) containing Mason's comments about Liszt's attitude toward piano technique.

1014   New Haven, Connecticut. Yale University, John Herrick Jackson Music Library.

Holdings include a fairly large collection of William Mason's music: over twenty-five published works for piano; the holograph score of the *Prelude in F*, op. 46, no. 2; and the proof copy (G. Schirmer) of *Improvisation*, op. 51. Childe Hassam's pen drawing of Mason seated at the piano with the inscription "To William Mason[,] Isles of Shoals[,] Aug. '91[,] Childe Hassam[,] 1891" is also part of the library's collection. Yale University also houses the Lowell Mason Library, together with his diaries, correspondence, and other papers (entire collection: ca. 10,200 items with some 700 manuscripts). Included with the papers are the following autograph letters: 1) William Mason to George B. Bacon, Orange, New Jersey, 16 October 1867; 2) William Mason to "Nellie" [T. Russell?], Orange, New Jersey, 9 December 1883; 3) Abigail Mason (wife of Lowell) to Nellie T. Russell, Orange, New Jersey, 4 December 1888 (contains information about various members of the Mason family, including William); and 4) William Mason to Henry L. Mason, Orange, New Jersey, 17 April 1890. Two other items in the Lowell Mason collection are of special interest:

1. Abigail Mason Journal, 1 January 1852 to 28 December 1852. Kept by Abigail Mason when she accompanied her husband Lowell on his visit to Europe in 1851-53. William Mason was also in Europe at this time, and he spent many hours with his parents, particularly in the period from January 17 through June 23, when he accompanied them on their tour of the continent, principally to serve as their interpreter. Mrs. Mason's journal contains numerous references to William, some of a personal nature, others relating to William's professional activities as a musician.

2. Lowell Mason, Journals nos. 4-6, 20 December 1851 to 25 April 1853. Kept by Lowell Mason during his second trip to Europe. (For a discussion of Mason's journals, see Michael Broyles's "Lowell Mason on European Church Music and Transatlantic Cultural Identification: A Reconsideration," *Journal of the American Musicological Society* 38/2 [Summer 1985]: 316-48.) Lowell Mason's comments in his journals provide good supplementary reading to his *Musical Letters from Abroad* (see no. **224**), which covers approximately the same time period. References to William Mason are scattered throughout the journals. Among other things, the journals (no. 6, entry for 6 January 1853) reveal that Lowell Mason may have been at least indirectly responsible for the invitation William received to play in London on 20 January 1853 (see no. **613**).

1015 New York City. Carl Haverlin Collection/BMI Archives.

Holdings include an autograph manuscript fragment of Mason's *Serenata*, op. 39, dated 1904.

1016 New York City. Columbia University, Butler Library.

Holdings include three collections which contain important material relating to William Mason: 1) the William Mason Collection of Autographs of Musicians, 2) the MacDowell Collection, and 3) the Daniel Gregory Mason Collection.

The William Mason Collection of Autographs of Musicians contains autographs of more than eighty prominent nineteenth-century musicians and several literary authors. Most of the autographs consist of a few measures of music, date, location, closing, and signature. Other items include letters (among them are seven from Liszt to Mason), photographs, brief notes, slips of paper bearing only a date and signature, and a telegram.

The MacDowell Collection includes eight autograph letters from MacDowell to Mason, one manuscript letter from MacDowell to Mason (in Marian MacDowell's hand), and a manuscript letter (copy) from William Mason to Edward MacDowell, New York, 19 January 1894.

The Daniel Gregory Mason Collection contains a variety of items; among them:

1. Autograph letters: William Mason to Daniel Gregory Mason; two letters; New York, 1 January 1902 and Portsmouth, New Hampshire, 7 June 1902.
2. Music: copies of vols. 1-4 of William Mason's *Touch and Technic*, op. 44, and scores previously owned by William Mason, including vols. 1-2 and 5-8 of the Steingräber edition of the complete works of Chopin (ed. Mertke) and vols. 1-2 of the Steingräber edition of Schumann's piano works (ed. Hans Bischoff). The Chopin and Schumann scores have the name "William Mason" embossed in gold on the covers; annotations in William Mason's handwriting are contained in the scores of both composers.
3. Daniel Gregory Mason Journals (14 journals plus indices). Includes scattered references to William Mason, particularly in the period from around 1895 to 1904.

1017 New York City. New York Public Library, Performing Arts Research Center, Lincoln Center.

A large collection. Holdings include an anniversary book, a manuscript catalog of Mason's music library, a scrapbook of recital programs and clippings, the William Mason Collection of Autograph Letters, the William Mason Papers, an iconography file, a clipping file, and an extensive collection of published music and books. Descriptions follow:

1. Anniversary Book. Holograph, in ink. Entries are made in John Keble's *The Christian Year Birthday Book* (New York: A. D. F. Randolph, n.d.). The arrangement of the book is by day of the month rather than by year. Thus events from several different years frequently appear under the heading of a single day. Mason apparently began keeping the anniversary book sometime in the late 1880s, but made many retrospective entries dating back as far as 1829. A wide variety of information is recorded; it is nearly evenly divided between that of personal and that of professional interest. Entries describing three trips Mason made to Europe (in 1849-54, 1879-80, and 1890) are particularly vivid.

2. Catalog of Music. Holograph, in ink. On the cover: "Boston, Jan. 25, 1847." A catalog of Mason's music library. Includes titles of piano, organ, and chamber music works.

3. Scrapbook Containing Programs and Clippings. Written on the cover: "Programmes of all concerts I have played in from Nov. 3rd, 1846." The items in the collection date through about 1878. The clippings are of Mason's published letters and periodical articles, reviews of concerts, and reviews of Mason's works.

4. William Mason Collection of Autograph Letters. A set of forty-five letters from famous musicians to William Mason. Not all of the items are letters *per se*; a number of them are merely calling cards or slips of paper (in one case a ticket stub) bearing a musician's signature. Index cards for the letters are filed under the heading "William Mason Collection" in the library's "letter file." (The letter index is not duplicated in the main catalog of the library.)

5. William Mason Papers. This collection of papers contains programs of Mason's concerts (including a nearly complete set of the Mason-Thomas chamber music series in New York and Farmington, Connecticut), programs of concerts which Mason merely attended, and clippings of reviews and musical news items of the day from American and European newspapers.

6. Other items: 1) a holograph score of Mason's *Valse* (see no. **773**); 2) a manifesto (holograph, in ink) dated 10 September 1856, signed by Mason, Gottschalk, and several other notable musicians, announcing the formation and purpose of the New York American Music Association; 3) a holograph letter from William Mason to F. H. Bigelow, 13 February 1885; 4) three holograph letters from William Mason to Henry Holden Huss: Orange, New Jersey, 8 March 1888; New York, 21 December 1894; New York, 20 December 1900; and 5) a holograph letter from William Mason to Clara Gottschalk Peterson (Louis Moreau Gottschalk's sister), October 1900.

1018 Washington, D.C. Library of Congress, Music Division.

A major collection of Mason's published music (many duplicate titles), books, and periodical articles. Other holdings include: 1) over forty-five holograph music manuscripts, completed scores as well as fragments; 2) Mason iconography (indexed); 3) two autograph letters from William Mason to John Paul Morgan (1841-79): Orange, [N.J.], 16 April 1871; Orange, [N.J.], 23 April 1871 (both with the John Paul Morgan Family Papers); 4) two items of correspondence from William Mason to Mrs. John Paul Morgan: an autograph letter dated Orange, N.J., 16 September 1876, and a brief note on a piece of wrapping paper, n.p., n.d. (both with the John Paul Morgan Family Papers); 5) four autograph letters from William Mason to one Miss Bailie: New York, 3 November 1890; New York, 26 April 1891; New York, 30 April 1900; and New York, 22 March 1905; 6) an autograph letter from William Mason to Rafael Joseffy, New York, 24 March 1893; 7) an autograph letter (with a calling card) from William Mason to Madeline Buck, New York, 5 June 1894 (with the Dudley Buck Papers); and 8) an autograph letter (facsimile) from William Mason to August W. Hoffman, New York, 27 September 1902.

Index

Item numbers are in **boldface**; page numbers are in roman. The index includes the names of persons, places, organizations, and institutions. Secondary references to titles of Mason's works and primary catalog entries for his keyboard works with opus numbers are also listed (by title). Since the primary entries of all other original compositions by Mason are arranged in the catalog by alphabetical order, they are not included in this index (please refer to the table of contents for performing medium classifications). Editions and arrangements made by Mason are indexed by the names of the original composers. All works listed by title in the index are by Mason unless otherwise indicated. Titles of published works are in *italics*; titles of manuscript works are in roman type, with quotation marks.

Ablamowicz, Madame **599**
Adams, Oscar Fay **4**
"Ah! Vous dirais-je maman," caprice grotesque **666, 691, 695-96, 724**
Ahrend, T. **646**
Aikin, Jesse B. xxv
Aldrich, Richard **6**
Alexander, James Waddel **184, 312, 319**
Allen, Chester G. xxv, xxx, **7-8**
American College of Musicians: Board of Examiners xxii, **10-13, 189, 435**
  Board of Trustees xxiv, **3, 14, 241**
  congress of (1893) **39**
  formation of **435**
  paper on function of, by Edward Morris Bowman **41**
American Institute of Applied Music **16**
American Institute of Normal Methods **16**
American Music Association: demise of **314**
  formation and purpose of **317, 350, 401**
  holograph manifesto of **1017**
American Vocal Music Association xxii, **19**
Amitié pour amitié **145, 224, 455, 509, 610, 612, 620, 623, 694, 700-01**

Amourette **761**
"Andante Cantabile" **707-09**
Angell, Richard S. **20**
Antrim, Doron K. **29-31**
Appledore House (Isles of Shoals) xxi, **414**
Apthorp, William Foster **74, 557**
Asaph; or, the Choir Book xxvii, **1009**
Ashton, Leonora Sill **32**
Aurore de printemps: Caprice-Mazurka **722**

Babcock, Geo. L. **711**
Bach, C. P. E. **175, 230, 796**
Bach, Constance **201**
Bach, Johann Sebastian: memorization by Mason of Fugue in F-sharp Major by **171**
  performance of works by xvii, **502-03, 615-16, 676, 681, 688-90, 693, 695-96**
  realization of ornaments of **49, 230**
  use of music by, in teaching **523, 540**
  works by, edited by Mason **791-95, 874**
  mentioned **555, 587**

About the Author

KENNETH GRABER, pianist, holds a B.A. degree from Bethel College (Kansas), a M.M. degree from Wichita State University, and a Ph.D. from the University of Iowa. His teachers have included John Simms and Robert Steinbauer. He has performed and given master classes both in this country and in East Asia. Currently he is a member of the piano faculty and chair of the music department at St. Olaf College in Northfield, Minnesota.